"Get Out of the Building!"

THE STARTUP OWNER'S MANUAL™

The Step-by-Step Guide for Building a Great Company

Steve Blank and Bob Dorf

The Startup Owner's Manual Vol. 1™
The Step-by-Step Guide for Building a Great Company
by Steve Blank and Bob Dorf

Published by:

K&S Ranch, Inc.
Publishers

K&S Ranch Press, div. K&S Ranch, Inc.
4100 Cabrillo Highway, Pescadero, California 94060
Visit our website at www.steveblank.com.
to contact K&S Ranch, email info@kandsranch.com

Library of Congress Cataloging-in-Publication Data

ISBN-10: 0984999302
ISBN-13: 978-0-9849993-0-9

Printed in the United States of America

Book design by Karrie Ross, www.KarrieRoss.com

First Edition: March 2012
Fourth Printing

Table of Contents

How to Read This Book

CLEARLY, *THE STARTUP OWNER'S MANUAL* IS not a novel. This book is a step-by-step how-to guide that details a process for building a successful, profitable, scalable startup. It has more in common with a car repair manual than it does with your favorite page-turner. Don't attempt to read this book in a single sitting or long weekend. It will be your companion—and, we hope, your very best friend—for the six to 30 months or more that it often takes to begin building a successful, scalable startup business.

Organization

This book is organized in four distinct sections. The first, Getting Started, describes the Customer Development methodology and ends with the "Customer Development Manifesto," a series of 14 guiding principles for startups deploying the Customer Development process.

Don't read too much at a time.

The next section, Step One, *"Customer Discovery,"* turns the founders' vision into a business model canvas and then into a series of hypotheses. Those hypotheses are turned into experiments, and tested with customers to see if your understanding of the customer problem and proposed solution mesh.

Step Two, *"Customer Validation,"* expands the scope of the business model testing to see if you can get enough orders or users to prove that you have a repeatable and scalable business model.

The fourth key section, found in Appendix A, is a series of Checklists that help you track your progress at every stage of the Customer Development process. Use the checklists at the end of each step (yes, there's one for each) to make sure you have completed all the key tasks outlined in that step. Photocopy them, scan them, and circulate them to team members. But most important, use them to be sure you have completed each step—before you move on to the next.

Web/Mobile vs. Physical Channels

This book recognizes that Customer Development operates at different speeds for web/mobile startups versus products sold through physical distribution channels. The process to "Get/Keep/Grow" customers—the core job of *any* business—is different, and web products are built and obtain feedback faster. Recognizing this, we offer parallel tracks through the book: one focused on physical goods and channels, and one focused on web/mobile products and channels. Often, the book addresses them separately. When it does, we begin with the physical channel, then follow with web/mobile.

In each phase of customer discovery and validation, you'll see diagrams like this to help you understand where you are in the process:

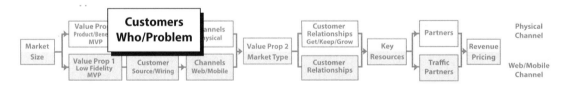

The upper row indicates the recommended steps for physical channel startups. The lower row depicts steps for web/mobile startups. When the steps are nearly identical, the boxes merge.

⇨ When we're discussing web and mobile channels, products, strategies or tactics, you'll see the ⇨ at the start of those discussions, always in this typeface, alongside the text that shows you've "changed channels."

It's worth reading both versions of a step before turning to the one explaining "your" business type. When information in one channel is essential for startups in the other, we'll tell you so—and tell you what to read. Web/mobile startup founders should skim the physical section before they read and begin implementing the web/mobile processes in each section.

Paths Through This Book

- *Read the glossary in the back of the book first.* Customer Development has a language all its own.

- Before you dive into the details, *read the Customer Development Manifesto* on page 31-49.

- *If you are familiar with Customer Development*, skim Chapters 1-3, then start with Chapter 4, "the business model hypotheses."

- If you want to *align co-founders, initial employees, investors and advisors around the Customer Development philosophy,* have them read Chapters 1 and 2.

- *If you want a high-speed overview and little more*, there are two approaches:
    (a) skim the checklists at the back of the book, which will give you a sense of all the tasks you must complete to implement Customer Development; or

    (b) flip through the book, looking for "jumbo quotes" like this:

This book is not a novel…
It's a reference manual.

These quotes highlight the 100 or so "big ideas" found throughout the book and offer a "CliffsNotes" or "Twitter" sense of the nearly 600 pages of text.

- *If you want a detailed checklist of the things founders need to get right,* start with Chapter 4, "the business model hypothesis," and use the checklists in Appendix A page 469.

- *If your startup is well under way*, you might want to start at Chapter 7, "Pivot or Proceed," to gauge your progress. Then you can jump to Chapter 12, "Metrics that Matter," to see if you're ready to scale.

- To *develop and test a web/mobile minimum viable product* (MVP), read: Design Tests (page 191), Build Your Low Fidelity MVP (page 200), Low Fidelity MVP Problem Test (page 211), and Optimize Getting More Customers (page 380).

- To *develop and test a physical minimum viable product* (MVP), read: Customer Contacts (page 195), Problem Understanding (page 203), Customer Understanding (page 218), and The Sales Roadmap (page 344).

- To focus on *web/mobile marketing* (how to "get," "keep" and "grow" customers), read:
  - Hypotheses: Customer Source/Wiring (page 93), Channels (page 104), and Customer Relationships (page 144).
  - Build Your Low Fidelity MVP (page 200), Low Fidelity MVP Problem Test (page 211), Traffic/Competitive Analysis (page 225), High Fidelity MVP Test (page 237), and Measure Customer Behavior (page 245).
  - Get Ready to Sell: Craft Positioning Statement (page 293), Acquire/Activate Customers Plan (page 304), Create a High Fidelity MVP (page 330), Build a Metrics Tool Set (page 338), and Hire a Data Analytics Chief (page 350).
  - Get Out of the Building: Prepare Optimization Plans/Tools (page 362), Optimize Getting More Customers (page 380), Optimize "Keep" and "Grow" (page 396), Test Sell Traffic Partners (page 409).

- To focus on *physical channel sales and marketing* (how to "get", "keep" and "grow" customers), read:
    - Hypotheses: Customer Segments Who/Problem (page 85), Channels (page 98), Customer Relationships (page 144), and Revenue Stream Pricing (page 180).
    - Prepare for Customer Contacts (page 195), Problem Understanding (page 203), Market Knowledge (page 222), Create Product Presentation (page 235), and Test Solution with Customer (page 239).
    - Get Out of the Building: Create Sales and Collateral Materials (page 296), Hire Sales Closer (page 329), Sales Channel Roadmap (page 332), and Develop the Sales Roadmap (page 344).

- Educators who want to *teach Customer Development* or the experiential *Lean LaunchPad* class should read:
    - Our website, www.steveblank.com, with links to our syllabi used at Stanford, Berkeley and the National Science Foundation.
    - Before the class meets, have the students read:
        - *The Customer Development Manifesto* in Chapter 2
        - *An Introduction to Customer Development* in Chapter 2
    - Each week's lectures are organized around each of the individual hypotheses in Phase 1, pages 69-188.
    - For the *Lean LaunchPad* class, have students read:
        - Get Out of the Building and Test the Problem in Chapter 5, pages 189-226.
        - Get Out of the Building and Test the Product Solution in Chapter 6, pages 227-256.
    - All classes should read:
        - Pivot or Proceed, in Chapter 7, pages 270-273.
        - Metrics that Matter, in Chapter 12, pages 438-459.

A Few Helpful Tips

We see a direct correlation between the entrepreneurs' success and the degree to which their copy is dog-eared, beat up and tattered. USE the book, don't just read it!

We see a direct correlation between the entrepreneurs' success and the degree to which their copy is dog-eared, beat up and tattered.

Use the checklists. There are more than 40 at the back of the book—one for every step.

Don't read too much at a time. This is a reference manual. It's exhausting when read as a book. Take "small bites" of a few sections at a time, at most. Dog-ear it and use Post-it notes to mark your place, and keep the book close at hand so you can refer to it often.

Scan ahead. It gives you context for what you are currently doing. If you're starting work on Chapter 4, for example, quickly scan Chapter 5 first so you understand how what you're doing now supports what comes next.

Look out for warning signs *like this one*:

> **PROCEED WITH CAUTION:** Remember, this is an overview/tutorial. There's no way you can implement all this or even process this in one sitting.

Entrepreneurship is not a cookbook or a checklist. At the end of the day, founders are artists. Don't expect everything to work like the book. It's impossible for this book to address every entrepreneurial decision and every type of startup. You're outside the building not only looking for facts, but for insight and inspiration. Not every piece of advice fits every situation you'll encounter. And not every piece of advice will always work. That's what entrepreneurs are for.

Preface

In 1602, the Dutch East India Company, generally regarded as the first "modern company," issued the first stock certificates. In the intervening 300 years, companies managed to start, build and grow without formally trained executives. By the 20th century, the complexity of modern corporations demanded a cadre of executives trained to administer large companies. In 1908, Harvard awarded the first master of business administration (MBA) degree to fill the need to bring professional education standards to big business. The MBA curriculum standardized and codified the essential elements an operating executive in a modern company needed to know: cost accounting, strategy, finance, product management, engineering, personnel management and operations.

Formal management tools are about 100 years old.

Fast-forward to the mid-20th century. The pairing of venture capital and startup entrepreneurship emerged in its modern form, and the startup industry they fostered has been exploding ever since. Yet for the past 50 years, finding the successful formula for repeatable startup success has remained a black art. Founders have continually struggled with and adapted the "big business" tools, rules and processes taught in business schools and suggested by their investors. Investors have been shocked when startups failed to execute "the plan," never admitting to the entrepreneurs that *no startup executes to its business plan*. Today, after half a century of practice, we know unequivocally that the traditional MBA curriculum for running large companies like IBM, GM and Boeing *does not* work in startups. In fact, it's toxic.

With the benefit of hindsight, entrepreneurs now understand the problem, namely that *startups are not simply smaller versions of large companies.* Companies execute business models where customers, their problems, and necessary product features are all "knowns." In sharp contrast, startups operate in "search" mode, seeking a repeatable and profitable business model. The search for a business model requires dramatically different rules, roadmaps, skill sets, and tools in order to minimize risk and optimize chances for success.

By the beginning of the 21st century, entrepreneurs, led by web and mobile startups, began to seek and develop their own management tools. Now, a decade later, a radically different set of startup tools has emerged, distinct from those used in large companies but as comprehensive as the traditional "MBA Handbook." The result is the emerging "science of entrepreneurial management." My first book, *The Four Steps to the Epiphany,* was one of its first texts. It recognized that the classic books about large-company management were ill-suited for early-stage ventures. It offered a reexamination of the existing product-introduction process and delineated a radically different method that brings customers and their needs headfirst into the process long before the launch.

We are building the first management tools specifically for startups.

At the time I wrote it, the book was my proposed methodology for getting startups right. But just as it was published, agile engineering became the preferred product-development method. This iterative and incremental method created a need and a demand for a parallel process to provide rapid and continual customer feedback. The Customer Development process I articulated in *The Four Steps* fit that need perfectly.

Over the past decade, thousands of scientists, engineers and MBAs in my classes at Stanford's engineering school and U.C. Berkeley's Haas School of Business—plus those sponsored by the National Science Foundation—have discussed, deployed, assessed and enhanced the Customer Development process. It has since been implemented by tens of thousands of entrepreneurs, engineers, and investors worldwide.

While the fundamental, powerful "Four Steps" remain at its core, this book is far more than a second edition. Nearly every step in the process, and in fact the entire approach, have been enhanced and refined based on a decade of Customer Development experience.

Customer development is paired with agile product development.

Even more gratifying: now, a decade later, multiple books and authors, are filling shelves in the newly created section for the strategy and science of entrepreneurship. Some of the other areas in this emerging field of entrepreneurial management are:

- agile development, an incremental and interactive approach to engineering that enables product or service development to iterate and pivot to customer and market feedback
- business model design, which replaces static business plans with a nine-box map of the key elements that make up a company
- creativity and innovation tools for creating and fostering winning ideas
- the Lean Startup, an intersection of customer and agile development
- lean user interface design to improve web/mobile interfaces and conversion rates
- venture and entrepreneurial finance, to attract and manage funds that fuel the innovation

No one book, including this one, offers a complete roadmap or all the answers for entrepreneurs. Yet together, the texts in the entrepreneurial management science library offer entrepreneurs guidance where none existed before. Startups, driven by potential markets measured in billions of people, will use this body of knowledge to test, refine and scale their ideas far faster and more affordably than ever.

No one book, including this one, offers a complete roadmap…

My co-author Bob and I hope books like this one help speed the startup revolution and enhance its success—and yours.

Steve Blank
Pescadero, Calif., March 2012

Who Is This Book For?

THIS BOOK IS FOR ALL ENTREPRENEURS and uses the term *startup* literally hundreds of times. But what exactly is a startup? *A startup is not a smaller version of a large company.* A startup is a temporary organization in search of a scalable, repeatable, profitable business model. At the outset, the startup business model is a canvas covered with ideas and guesses, but it has no customers and minimal customer knowledge.

But we've only defined the words *startup, entrepreneur*, and *innovation* halfway. These words mean different things in Silicon Valley, on Main Street, and in Corporate America. While each type of startup is distinct, this book offers guidance for each one.

A startup is a temporary organization in search of a scalable, repeatable, profitable business model.

Small Business Entrepreneurship: In the United States, the majority of entrepreneurs and startups are found among 5.9 million small businesses that make up 99.7 percent of all U.S. companies and employ 50 percent of all nongovernment workers. These are often service-oriented businesses like drycleaners, gas stations and convenience stores, where entrepreneurs define success as paying the owners well and making a profit, and they seldom aspire to take over an industry or build a $100 million business.

Scalable startups are the work of traditional technology entrepreneurs. These entrepreneurs start a company believing their vision will change the world and result in a company with hundreds of millions if not billions of dollars in sales. The early days of a scalable startup are about the search for a repeatable and scalable business model. Scale requires external venture-capital investment in the tens of millions to fuel rapid expansion. Scalable startups tend to cluster in technology centers such as Silicon Valley, Shanghai, New York, Bangalore, and Israel and make up a small percentage of entrepreneurs, but their outsize return potential attracts almost all the risk capital (and press).

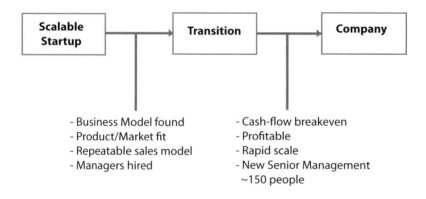

Scalable Startup *(Figure i.0)*

"Buyable" startups are a new phenomenon. With the extremely low cost of developing web/mobile apps, startups can literally fund themselves on founders' credit cards and raise small amounts of risk capital, usually less than $1 million. These startups (and their investors) are happy to be acquired for $5 million to $50 million, purchased by larger companies often to acquire the talent as much as the business itself.

Large Company Entrepreneurship: Large companies have finite life cycles. Most grow by offering new products that are variants of their core products (an approach known as *sustaining innovation*). They may also turn to *disruptive innovation,* attempting to introduce new products into new markets with new customers. Ironically, large companies' size and culture make disruptive innovation (really an effort to launch a scalable startup inside a big company) extremely difficult to execute.

...large companies' size and culture make disruptive innovation extremely difficult.

Social entrepreneurs build innovative nonprofits to change the world. Customer Development provides them a scorecard for assessing scalability, asset leverage, return on investment and growth metrics. These entrepreneurial ventures seek solutions rather than profits and happen on every continent in areas as diverse as water, agriculture, health, and microfinance.

While the Customer Development process helps scalable startups the most, each of these five startup types has entrepreneurship and innovation at its heart. And each improves its chances for finding the right path to success through the use of Customer Development.

Who Is This Book *Not* For?

There are cases where using the Customer Development methodology and this book is inappropriate.

Early-stage ventures fall into two types: those *with customer/market risk* and those with *invention risk*.

- Markets with invention risk are those where it's questionable whether the technology can ever be made to work, but if it does, customers will beat a path to the company's door. (Think lifesciences and cure for cancer.)

- Markets with customer/market risk are those where the unknown is whether customers will adopt the product.

For companies building web-based products, *product* development may be difficult, but with enough time and iteration, Engineering will eventually converge on a solution and ship a functional product—*it's engineering, not invention.* The real risk is in whether there is a customer and a market for the product as spec'ed. In these markets *it's all about customer/market risk.*

There's a whole other set of markets where the risk is truly *invention.* These are markets where it may take five or even 10 years to get a product out of the lab and into production (e.g., biotech). Whether it will eventually work, no one knows, but the payoff can be so large that investors will take the risk. In these markets *it's all about invention risk.*

Startups solve customer and market risk by reading this book.

A third type of market has *both invention and market risk.* For example, complex new semiconductor architectures mean you may not know if the chip performs as well as you thought until you get first silicon. But then, because there might be entrenched competitors and your concept is radically new, you still need to invest in the Customer Development process to learn how to get design wins from companies that may be happy with their existing vendors.

Startups solve invention risk by using simulation tools (computational fluid dynamics, finite element analysis, etc.). Startups solve customer and market risk by reading this book. When the issues are customer acceptance and market adoption, this book shows the path.

Introduction

*A legendary hero is usually the founder of something—the founder
of a new age, the founder of a new religion, the founder of a new city,
the founder of a new way of life. In order to found something new,
one has to leave the old and go on a quest of the seed idea, a germinal
idea that will have the potential of bringing forth that new thing.*

— Joseph Campbell, *The Hero with a Thousand Faces*

JOSEPH CAMPBELL POPULARIZED THE NOTION of an archetypal "hero's journey,"
a pattern that recurs in the mythologies and religions of cultures around the world.
From Moses and the burning bush to Luke Skywalker's meeting Obi-wan Kenobi,
the journey always begins with a hero who hears a calling to a quest. At the outset
of the voyage, the path is unclear and no end is in sight. Each hero meets a unique
set of obstacles, but Campbell's keen insight was that the outline of these stories
is always the same. There are not a thousand different heroes but *one hero with
a thousand faces*.

The hero's journey is an apt way to think of startups. All new companies and
new products begin with a vision—a hope for what could be and a goal few others
can see. It's this bright and burning founder's vision that differentiates an entrepreneur from a big-company CEO and separates startups from existing businesses.

Founding entrepreneurs are out to make their vision and business real.
To succeed, they must abandon the status quo, recruit a team that shares their

vision, and strike out together on what appears to be a new path, often shrouded in uncertainty, fear and doubt. Obstacles, hardships and potential disaster lie ahead, and their journey to success tests more than financial resources—it tests their stamina, agility, and courage.

Take a new path, often shrouded in uncertainty, fear, and doubt.

Every entrepreneur is certain his or her journey is unique. Each travels down the startup path without a roadmap and believes that no model or template could possibly apply. What makes some startups successful while others sell off the furniture often seems like luck. But it isn't. As Campbell suggests, *the outline is always the same*. The path to startup success is well-traveled and well-understood. There is a true and repeatable path to success. This book charts that path.

A Repeatable Path

In the last quarter of the 20th century, startups thought they knew the correct path for the startup journey. They adopted a methodology for product development, launch, and life-cycle management almost identical to the processes taught in business schools for use in large companies. These processes provide detailed business plans, checkpoints and goals for every step toward getting a product out the door—sizing markets, estimating sales, developing marketing-requirements documents, prioritizing product features. Yet at the end of the day, even with all these processes, the embarrassing fact is that in companies large and small, established corporate giants as well as new startups, more than nine of 10 new products fail. It's true in every product category—high-tech or low, online or off, consumer or business—well-funded or not.

Even after decades of similar failures, investors are always surprised when a new venture fails to execute its business "plan." *And still they continue to rely on the same product-introduction processes.*

We now know what the problem is. Startups have been using tools appropriate for executing a known business. But startups are all about *unknowns*. To find the path to build a winning startup, entrepreneurs must try a new way:

Winners throw out the traditional product management and introduction processes they learned at existing companies. Instead, they combine agile engineering and Customer Development to iteratively build, test and search for a business model, turning unknowns into knowns.

Winners also recognize their startup "vision" as a series of untested hypotheses in need of "customer proof." They relentlessly test for insights, and they course-correct in days or weeks, not months or years, to preserve cash and eliminate time wasted on building features and products that customers don't want.

Winners recognize their startup is a series of untested hypotheses.

Losers blindly execute a rigid product management and introduction methodology. They assume that the founder's vision drives the business strategy and product development plans and that all they need to do is to raise funds for execution.

Founders, not employees, must search for a business model. The best way to search is for the *founders themselves* to *get out of the building* to gain a deep, personal, firsthand understanding of their potential customers' needs *before* locking into a specific path and precise product specs. That's the difference between winners and losers. It's also the Customer Development process detailed in this book.

Why a Second Decade?

Startups have now been using Customer Development for a decade, since the initial publication of *The Four Steps to the Epiphany*. If this is your first contact with the *Four Steps*, welcome aboard. For the tens of thousands who've embraced that first version, *The Startup Owner's Manual* offers a great deal more. The first version assumed startups were high-tech ventures in Silicon Valley selling products through a physical sales channel and aiming to be billion-dollar businesses. A lot has happened in 10 years, and this version embraces those changes. For example:

Bits: The Second Industrial Revolution

For thousands of years after the invention of the wheel, a *product* was a physical object one could touch, such as food, cars, planes, books, and household goods. These physical products reached customers via a physical sales *channel:* salespeople visiting customers, or customers visiting stores. Figure i.1 shows this intersection of *physical products sold through a physical channel.*

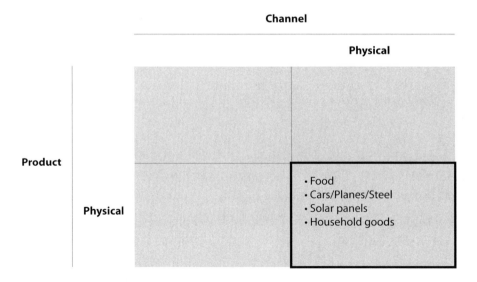

Channel

Physical

Product

Physical

- Food
- Cars/Planes/Steel
- Solar panels
- Household goods

Physical Products Sold Through a Physical Channel *(Figure i.1)*

One of the breakthroughs in commerce was the invention of products that were *ideas or promises that didn't exist in physical form*, such as life and health insurance, stocks and bonds, and commodity futures.

In the 1970s, software began to be sold as a product unbundled from any particular computer. The ability to purchase *bits* was a new concept. By themselves the bits were useless, but when combined with a computer in the form of software applications, bits solved problems or amused people (word processing, balancing checkbooks, game play). These software applications and entertainment, all in the form of bits, were sold to consumers through specialized retail computer stores, a physical channel.

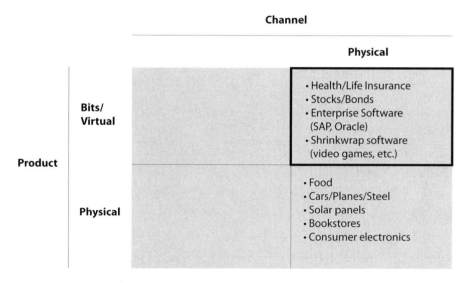

Software Products Sold Through Physical Channels *(Figure i.2)*

Still other software applications were designed to solve problems companies had (database access, manufacturing automation, sales automation), and added the upper right box to Figure i.2, Software Products Sold Through Physical Channels.

As the Internet created a new form of sales channel, a new class of company emerged with the value proposition to sell physical products over the Internet. Amazon, Zappos, Dell, and a whole raft of other e-commerce companies filled a new niche: *physical products sold via a web channel*. This new sales channel created massive disruption in the existing world of physical distribution, as book and music retailers perhaps know best of all.

Channel

	Web	**Physical**
Bits/ Virtual		• Health/Life Insurance • Stocks/Bonds • Enterprise Software (SAP, Oracle) • Shrinkwrap software (video games, etc.)
Physical	• Shoes/Zappos • Books/Amazon • Movies/Netflix • Consumer electronics	• Food • Cars/Planes/Steel • Solar panels • Bookstores • Consumer electronics

Product (row label)

Physical Products in Web/Mobile Channels (Figure i.3)

Over the past decade a new class of product has emerged, where *BOTH the product and the channel are bits* (see Figure i.4). Startups can now be built for thousands rather than millions of dollars and in weeks rather than years. As a result, the number of startups founded each year has exploded. New applications such as social networks that duplicate the socialization we once had face-to-face are being mediated via machine. Search engines that scour the web, such as Google and Bing, exist only in bits, in a web/mobile channel.

More important, entire industries that started by selling physical products in physical locations have begun their migration to bits sold over the Internet. Originally, people sold books, music, videos, movies, travel, and stocks and bonds either face-to-face or in storefronts. Those channels are either radically transformed or disappearing as physical products turn into bits.

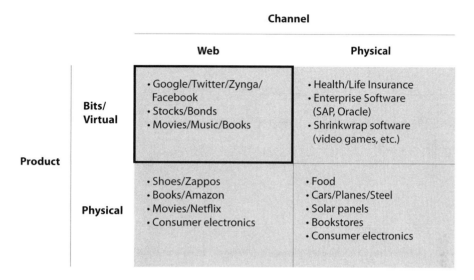

Channel

	Web	**Physical**

**Bits/
Virtual**
	• Google/Twitter/Zynga/
	  Facebook
	• Stocks/Bonds
	• Movies/Music/Books
		• Health/Life Insurance
		• Enterprise Software
		  (SAP, Oracle)
		• Shrinkwrap software
		  (video games, etc.)

Physical	• Shoes/Zappos • Books/Amazon • Movies/Netflix • Consumer electronics	• Food • Cars/Planes/Steel • Solar panels • Bookstores • Consumer electronics

Product (row label)

Software Products In Web/Mobile Channels *(Figure i.4)*

Speed, Time and Iterations: the "Second Industrial Revolution"

Regardless of the business, any enterprise focused on the bottom righthand box in figure i.1—Physical Goods Sold through a Physical Channel—has discovered over the past decade that the old rules and tools for physical businesses and channels no longer apply. They've learned that the closer a company gets to a web/mobile channel and a web/mobile product, the faster it can change, test and optimize both *product and offer*. They need a new process to quickly adapt to the new freedoms a web/mobile channel and product allow, and they've found it in Customer Development.

The Customer Development process gathers customer feedback about product, channel, price, and positioning, all of which can be modified and tested in near-real time, and uses it as immediate feedback to iterate and optimize. As a result, web/mobile channel startups can move forward at "Internet speed," an impossibility with physical distribution channels and products.

A mere decade ago, getting feedback on the features of a video game required recruiting focus groups to come in and play the game while being observed through one-way mirrors. Today, companies like Zynga test and tune the features of their online games in days. Are sales slow because the game is too hard? You can adjust the scoring or other game variables and change the product itself quicker than you can say touchdown.

Customer Development is the process to organize the search for the business model.

Theoretically, when startups' products and channels are bits, they can gather and act on information 100 times faster than companies delivering physical goods via physical sales channels (10 times the number of iterative learning cycles, each using only 10 percent of the cash.) In fact, companies like Facebook, Google, Groupon, and Zynga grew faster in a decade than most industrial corporations grew in the 20th century. That's why we call it the Second Industrial Revolution.

The Four Steps: A New Path

The core of Customer Development is blissfully simple: Products developed by founders who get out in front of customers early and often, win. Products handed off to sales and marketing organizations that are only tangentially involved in the new-product development process will lose. There are no facts inside your building, *so get the heck outside*. Getting out of the building means acquiring a deep understanding of customer needs and combining that knowledge with incremental and iterative product development. The mix of Customer Development and Agile engineering dramatically increases the odds of new product and company success, while reducing the need for upfront cash and eliminating wasted time, energy, money and effort.

There are no facts inside your building, *so get the heck outside.*

Customer Development recognizes the startup's mission as a relentless search to refine its vision and idea, and to make changes in every aspect of the business invalidated during the search process. An entrepreneur seeks to test a series of unproven hypotheses (guesses) about a startup's business model: who the customers are, what the product features should be, and how this scales into a hugely successful company. Customer Development recognizes a startup is *a temporary organization* built to search for the answers to what makes a repeatable and scalable business model. Customer Development is *the process to organize that search*.

THE STARTUP
OWNER'S MANUAL

I

Getting Started

Chapter 1:
The Path to Disaster:
A Startup Is Not a Small Version of a Big Company

Chapter 2:
The Path to the Epiphany:
The Customer Development Model

The Customer Development Manifesto

CHAPTER 1

The Path to Disaster:
A Startup Is Not a Small Version of
a Big Company

*The definition of insanity is doing the same thing over and over
and expecting different results.*

—Albert Einstein

WHILE THIS STORY IS OLD, ITS LESSONS are timeless. In the heyday of the dot-com bubble at the end of the 20th century, Webvan stood out as one of the most electrifying new startups, with an idea that would potentially touch every household in America. Raising one of the largest financial war chests ever seen (more than $800 million), the company aimed to revolutionize the $450 billion retail grocery business with online ordering and same-day door-to-door grocery delivery. Webvan believed this was one of the first "killer applications" for the Internet. Customers could just point, click, and order. Webvan's CEO told *Forbes* magazine that Webvan would "set the rules for the largest consumer sector in the economy."

Beyond amassing megabucks, the Webvan entrepreneurs seemed to do everything right. Backed by experienced venture-capital investors, the company raced to build vast automated warehouses and bought fleets of delivery trucks while building an easy-to-use website. Webvan hired a seasoned CEO from the consulting industry. What's more, most initial customers actually liked the service. But barely 24 months after the initial public offering, Webvan was bankrupt and out of business. What happened?

…barely 24 months after the initial public offering, Webvan was bankrupt.

This was not a failure of execution. Webvan did everything its board and investors asked. In particular, the company fervently followed the traditional new-product introduction model commonly used by most new ventures and embraced the mantras of the time: "first mover advantage" and "get big fast." Webvan's failure to ask "where are the customers?" illuminates how this tried-and-true model led one of the best-funded startups of all time down the path to disaster.

The Traditional New-Product Introduction Model

In the 20th century, every company bringing a new product to market used some form of product management model (Figure 1.1). Emerging early in the century, this product-centric model described a process that evolved in manufacturing industries. The consumer packaged-goods industry adopted it in the 1950s, and it spread to the technology business in the last quarter of the century. There it became an integral part of the startup culture.

At first glance, the new-product introduction model outlined in the diagram at right appears to be helpful and benign. It illustrates the process of getting a new product into the hands of waiting customers. A new product moves from development to customer testing (alpha/beta test), and using feedback from this initial testing, the product engineers fix technical errors in the product until the product launch date and first customer ship.

The new-product introduction model is a good fit for an existing company where the customers are known, the product features can be spec'ed upfront, the market is well-defined, and the basis of competition is understood.

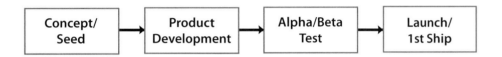

New Product Introduction Diagram (Figure. 1.1)

As for startups, a scant few fit these criteria. Few even know who their customers are. Yet many persist in using the new-product introduction model not only to manage product development but as a roadmap for finding customers and setting the timing for the startup's sales, launch and revenue plans. Investors use the new-product introduction diagram to set and plan funding. All parties involved in the startup use a roadmap leading toward a very different location, yet they're surprised to end up lost.

What's wrong with the old model, and how did it contribute to the billion-dollar Webvan implosion?

Concept and Seed Stage

At the concept and seed stage, founders capture their passion and vision for the company, sometimes on the back of a napkin, and turn them into a set of key ideas, which becomes the outline for the *business plan*.

Next, issues surrounding the product are defined. What is the product or service concept? What are the product features and benefits? Can it be built? Is further technical research needed? Who will the customers be, and where will they be found? Statistical and market research and a few customer interviews fuel the evaluation and business plan.

This step also brings forth a first guess at how the product will ultimately reach the customer, including discussions of competitive differences, distribution channels, and costs. An initial positioning chart explains the company and its benefits to venture capitalists or corporate higher-ups. The business plan now gets market-size, competitive and financial sections, with an appendix containing Excel spreadsheets forecasting revenue and expenses. Creative writing, passion and shoe leather combine in the concept and seed phase in hopes of convincing an investor to fund the company or the new division.

Once a waterfall process starts, the proverbial train has left the station…

Webvan did all of this extremely well. Founded in December 1996, with a compelling story and a founder with a track record, Webvan raised $10 million from leading Silicon Valley venture capitalists in 1997. In the next two years, additional private rounds totaling an unbelievable $393 million followed before the company's IPO.

Product Development

In stage two, product development, everyone stops talking and starts working. The respective departments go to their figurative corners as the company begins to specialize by function. Marketing refines the size of the market defined in the business plan and begins to target the first customers. In a well-organized startup (one with a fondness for process), the marketing folk might even run a focus group or two on the market they think they're in and work with Product Management on a market requirements document (MRD) for engineering to specify the product's final features and functions. Marketing starts to build a sales demo, writes sales materials (websites, presentations, data sheets), and hires a pr agency. In this stage, or by alpha test, the company traditionally hires a VP of Sales.

Meanwhile, Engineering focuses on specifying and then building the product. The simple box labeled "Product Development" typically expands into a "waterfall" or "spiral" or incremental process of interlacing steps, all focused on minimizing development risk of a defined feature set (Figure 1.2). This process starts with the founder's vision, which may be expanded into an MRD (and a product requirements document), and expands further into detailed engineering specifications. With those in hand, Engineering begins implementation fueled by cold pizza and long nights and weekends. Once a waterfall process starts, the proverbial train has left the station and the product is nearly impossible to revise. As a rule, the "train" can run almost nonstop for 18 or perhaps 24 months or more, uninterrupted by changes or new ideas no matter how good they might be for the business.

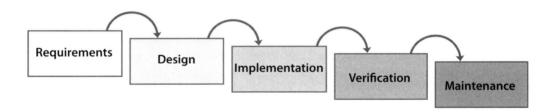

The Product Development "Waterfall" Model (Figure 1.2)

In Webvan's case, Engineering moved along two fronts: building the automated warehouses and designing the website. The automated warehouses were a technological marvel, with automated conveyors and carousels transporting food items off the shelves to workers who packed them for delivery. Webvan also designed its own inventory, warehouse, and route management systems and software to manage the entire customer order and delivery process. This software communicated with the Webvan website and issued order-fulfillment instructions to the distribution center. Once a delivery was scheduled, the system's custom route-planning feature determined the most efficient route for delivering the goods to customers' homes.

At the same time, planning began for a marketing and promotion program designed to strengthen the Webvan brand name, get customers to try the service in the first target market, build strong customer loyalty, and maximize repeat usage and purchases. The plan was to build Webvan's brand name (down to stickering every cup holder in San Francisco's AT&T Park) and customer loyalty through public relations programs, advertising campaigns and promotional activities. Spending for all these activities was part of the business plan.

Alpha/Beta Test

In stage three, the alpha/beta test, Engineering continues building along the classic waterfall development model, working toward the first customer ship date. And, by beta test time, working with a small group of outside users to test the product and ensure that it works as specified. Marketing develops a complete marketing communications plan, sets up the corporate website, provides Sales with a full complement of support materials, and starts the public relations bandwagon rolling. The pr agency polishes the positioning and starts contacting the long-lead-time press and blogs, while Marketing starts the branding activities.

Sales signs up the first beta customers (who may volunteer to pay for the privilege of testing a new product), begins to build the selected distribution channel, and staffs and scales the sales organization outside headquarters. The sales VP works toward achieving the revenue plan as specified in the business plan. Investors and board members start measuring progress by the number of orders in place by first customer ship. The CEO hits the streets and the phone or the parent-company headquarters, searching for additional capital.

Webvan began to beta-test its grocery delivery service in May 1999 with about 1,100 customers. At the same time, the marketing buzz started with a pr blitz with hundreds of articles touting the newest entrant in the online grocery business. Private investors poured hundreds of millions of dollars into the company.

Product Launch and First Customer Ship

With the product working (sort of), the company goes into "big-bang" spending mode. The product and the company are launched. The company has a large press event, and Marketing launches a series of programs to create end-user demand. In anticipation of sales, the company hires a national sales organization; the sales channel has quotas and sales goals. The board begins measuring company performance based on sales execution against its business plan, albeit one typically written at least a year earlier, when the company first sought investment.

Building a sales channel and supporting marketing burn a lot of cash. Assuming no early liquidity event for the company, more fund-raising is often required. The CEO looks at the product-launch activities and the scale-up of the sales and marketing team and goes out yet again, palm up, to the investor community. (In the dot-com bubble economy, investors used an IPO at product launch to take the money and run, before there was a track record of success or failure.) This operational model no doubt sounds familiar to many: a product- and process-centric model used by countless startups to take their first products to market.

Webvan launched its first regional web store in June 1999 (just a month after starting beta test) and filed for its public offering 60 days later. The company raised $400 million and had a market capitalization of $8.5 billion the day of its IPO—larger than the market cap of the top three grocery chains combined. The elation was short-lived.

The 9 Deadly Sins
of the New Product Introduction Model

For new products like Webvan, the business plan fails as a roadmap because both the product and the customer are unknown. For most startups, these nine flawed assumptions are the most toxic of all:

1. Assuming "I Know What the Customer Wants"

First is the founder's unwavering belief that he or she understands who the customers will be, what they need, and how to sell it to them. Any dispassionate observer would recognize that on Day One, a startup has no customers, and unless the founder is a true domain expert, he or she can only guess about the customer, problem, and business model. On Day One, a startup is a *faith-based* initiative built on guesses. Yet the traditional product introduction methodology has founders take these many business model guesses as facts and go design a product and start spending money to build it on a race to "first customer ship"—all before talking to a single customer.

On Day One, a startup is a *faith-based* initiative...

To succeed, founders need to turn hypotheses or guesses into facts as soon as possible by getting out of the building, asking customers if the hypotheses were correct, and quickly changing those that were wrong.

2. The "I Know What Features to Build" Flaw

The second flawed assumption is implicitly driven by the first. Founders, presuming they know their customers, assume they know all the features customers need. These founders specify, design, and build a fully featured product using classic product development methods without ever leaving their building. But wait—isn't that what startups *should* do? No—that's what companies with existing customers do.

...it's unknown whether the features appeal to customers.

The waterfall development process (see Figure 1.2) proceeds sequentially and without interruption for as long as a year or two. Progress is measured by each new line of code written or new piece of hardware built throughout the process until the product is released. Yet without direct and continuous customer contact, *it's unknown whether the features appeal to customers.* Fixing the inevitable product mistakes after building and shipping the entire product is costly and time-consuming, if not deadly. It can render the product obsolete by launch. Worse, it often causes huge engineering waste, with hundreds of hours of work tossed aside, or tons of code cut and dropped to the floor, when customers say the new features aren't ones they care about. Ironically, startups were often crippled by the very methodology they traditionally used to build new products.

3. Focus on Launch Date

The traditional product introduction model focuses engineering, sales and marketing on the all-important, immovable launch date. Marketing tries to pick an "event" (trade show, conference, blog, etc.) where they can "launch" the product. Executives look at that date and the calendar, working backward to ignite fireworks on the day the product is launched. Neither management nor investors tolerate "wrong turns" that result in delays. In fact, traditional engineering schedules have test cycles with the names *alpha, beta,* and *release* but rarely allow time to improve the product. They're still geared to putting out the original product with minimal bugs, though.

The product launch and first customer ship dates are merely the dates when a product development team thinks the product's first release is "finished." It doesn't mean the company understands its customers or how to market or sell to them, yet in almost every startup, ready or not, departmental clocks are set irrevocably to "first customer ship." Even worse, a startup's investors are managing their financial expectations by this date as well.

The chorus of investor voices says, "Why, of course that's what you do. Getting the product to market is what sales and marketing people do in startups. That's how a startup makes money." This is deadly advice. Ignore it. Focusing only on launch results in a "fire, ready, aim" strategy that ignores the customer discovery process—a fundamental and generally fatal error. Obviously, every startup or company wants to get a product to market and sell it, but that can't be done until the company understands *who* it's selling to and *why* they'll buy. The forced march ignores the iterative loop that says, "If our assumptions are wrong, maybe we need to try something different." It shuts off the "build, test and learn" flow and assumes that customers will come based merely on good engineering execution.

Time after time, only after launch does a startup discover that not enough customers visit its website, play the game, bring their friends, or convert to orders. Or it discovers that early customers don't scale into a mainstream market, or the product doesn't solve a high-value problem, or the cost of distribution is too high. While those discoveries are bad enough, the startup is now burdened with an expensive, scaled-up sales and marketing organization—effective only at burning mountains of cash—that's now trying to figure out what went wrong and how to fix it.

At Webvan, the dot-com mania may have intensified the company's drive to launch, but its single-minded focus was typical of most startups. At first customer ship, Webvan had close to 400 employees. It hired more than 500 more during the next six months. By May 1999, the company had opened its first $40 million distribution center, built and scaled for a customer base it could only guess at, and it had committed to 15 other distribution centers of the same size. Why? Because the Webvan business plan said to do so, regardless of whether the customers agreed.

4. Emphasis on Execution Instead of Hypotheses, Testing, Learning, and Iteration

Startup cultures emphasize "get it done, and get it done fast." So it's natural that heads of engineering, sales and marketing all believe they are hired for *what they know how to do, not what they can learn.* They assume that their experience is relevant to this new venture and that all they need do is put that knowledge to work managing the execution that's worked for them before.

While established companies *execute* business models where customers, problems, and necessary product features are all knowns, startups need to operate in a "*search*" mode as they test and prove every one of their initial hypotheses. They learn from the results of each test, refine the hypothesis and test again, all in search of a repeatable, scalable and profitable business model.

Relentless execution without knowing what to execute is a crime.

In practice, startups begin with a set of initial hypotheses (guesses), most of which will end up being wrong. Therefore, focusing on execution and delivering a product or service based on those initial, untested hypotheses is a going-out-of-business strategy.

In contrast, the traditional product introduction model assumes that building a startup is a step-by-step, sequential, execution-oriented process. Each step unfolds in a logical progression that can be captured in a PERT chart (a project management technique that maps the steps and time required for project completion), with milestones and resources assigned for the completion of each step. But anyone who has ever taken a new product out to a set of potential customers knows that a good day in front of customers is two steps forward and one step back. The ability to learn from these missteps distinguishes a successful startup from those that have vanished.

Like all startups focused on executing to a sequential product introduction plan, Webvan hired vice presidents of merchandising, marketing and product management—all oriented around executing a given sales and marketing strategy instead of listening to customers and discovering customer needs. Sixty days after first customer ship, those three VPs employed more than 50 people.

The ability to learn from missteps distinguishes a successful startup.

---

5. Traditional Business Plans Presume No Trial and No Errors

The one great advantage of the traditional product development model: it provides boards and founders an unambiguous path with clearly defined milestones the board *presumes* will be achieved. Most engineers know what *alpha test, beta test,* and *first customer ship* mean. If the product fails to work, everyone stops to fix it. In stark contrast, before first customer ship, sales and marketing activities are ad hoc and fuzzy, and seldom have measurable, concrete objectives. They lack any way to stop and fix what's broken (and don't even know *if* it's broken or *how* to stop).

Financial progress is tracked using metrics like income statement, balance sheet and cash flow even when there's no revenue to measure. In reality, none of these are useful for startups. Board directors have simply adopted the traditional metrics used in large companies with existing customers and known business models. In a startup, these metrics don't track progress against the startup's only goal: *to find a repeatable and scalable business model.* Instead, traditional metrics get in the way.

Instead of asking, "How many days to the beta test?" or, "What's in our sales pipeline?" a startup's board and management team need to ask specific questions about results of its long list of tests and experiments to validate all components of its business model.

If a startup's board of directors isn't asking these kinds of questions, it's wasting time without adding value. No matter what, directors and founders must stay focused on one financial metric that always matters: cash burn rate and number of months' worth of cash left in the bank.

If a startup's board of directors isn't asking these kinds of questions, it's wasting time...

Webvan had no milestones saying, "Stop and evaluate the launch results." Otherwise, it might have noticed the stark contrast between the 2,000 daily orders it was getting and the 8,000 in the business-plan forecast. Before any meaningful customer feedback was in hand and only a month after shipping began, Webvan signed a $1 billion deal (yes, $1,000,000,000) with Bechtel to build 26 additional distribution centers over the next three years.

6. Confusing Traditional Job Titles with What a Startup Needs to Accomplish

Most startups have simply borrowed job titles from established companies. But remember, these are jobs in an organization that's executing a *known* business model. The title *Sales* in an existing company reflects a team repeatedly selling a known product to a well-understood group of customers with standard presentations, prices, terms, and conditions. Startups by definition have few if any of these known elements. In fact, they're out searching for them!

Because target customers, product specs and product presentations may change daily, early-stage startup executives need dramatically different skills from executives who are working in an established company selling established products or line extensions. The demands of customer discovery require people who are comfortable with change, chaos, and learning from failure and are at ease working in risky, unstable situations without a roadmap. In short, startups should welcome the rare breed generally known as entrepreneurs. They're open to learning and discovery—highly curious, inquisitive, and creative. They must be eager to *search* for a repeatable and scalable business model. Agile enough to deal with daily change and operating "without a map." Readily able to wear multiple hats, often on the same day, and comfortable celebrating failure when it leads to learning and iteration.

Webvan's CEO and VPs all came from large-company backgrounds and experience. They were surprised and uncomfortable with the chaos of a startup and tried to solve the problem by scaling the company rapidly.

...measuring progress against a product launch or revenue plan is simply false progress.

---

7. Sales and Marketing Execute to a Plan

Hiring VPs and execs with the right titles but the wrong skills leads to further startup trouble as high-powered sales and marketing people arrive on the payroll to execute the "plan." Here's how it typically unfolds:

Following the business plan and the traditional product introduction model, the board and founders agree to a launch date, a burn rate, a revenue plan and a set of milestones. The sales VP begins to hire the core sales team, design sales pitches, and make appointments and attempts to acquire early "lighthouse" customers (prominent customers who will attract others). At the same time, the sales team uses revenue goals specified in the business plan to track its progress in understanding customers. Meanwhile, the marketing VP is busy designing websites, logos, presentations, data sheets and collateral, and hiring pr agencies to create buzz. These tactics become marketing objectives, *even though they're merely tactics*. Marketing discovers whether its positioning, messaging, pricing and demand-creation activities will work *only after first customer ship*.

Executives and board members accustomed to measurable signs of progress against "the plan" will focus on these execution activities because this is what they know how to do (and what they believe they were hired to do). Of course, in established companies with known customers and markets, this focus makes sense. And even in some startups in "existing markets," where customers and markets are known, it might work. But in a majority of startups, measuring progress against a product launch or revenue plan is simply false progress, since it transpires in a vacuum absent real customer feedback, instead of searching for an understanding of customers and their problems and replacing assumptions with facts.

Webvan set off on this kind of plan-driven "marketing death march." In its first six months, it acquired an impressive 47,000 new customers, but 71 percent of its 2,000 daily orders were repeat orders, which meant Webvan needed to quickly secure many more new customers and reduce its high customer attrition rate. Making matters worse, Webvan had scaled its spending based on unverified and, it turned out, highly optimistic marketing guesses.

8. Presumption of Success Leads to Premature Scaling

The business plan, its revenue forecast, and the product introduction model assume that every step a startup takes proceeds flawlessly and smoothly to the next. The model leaves little room for error, learning, iteration or customer feedback. Nothing says, "Stop or slow down hiring until you understand customers," or, "pause to process customer feedback." Even the most experienced executives are pressured to hire and staff per the plan regardless of progress. This leads to the next startup disaster: *premature scaling*.

In large companies, the mistakes just have additional zeros in them.

Hiring and spending should accelerate only after sales and marketing have become predictable, repeatable, scalable processes—not when the plan *says* they're scheduled to begin (or when the "lighthouse" account is signed or a few sales are made).

In large companies, the mistakes just have additional zeros in them. Microsoft and Google, powerhouses though may they be, launch product after product—Google's Orkut and Wave, Deskbar, Dodgeball, Talk and Finance; Microsoft's "Kin," Vista, Zune, "Bob," WebTV, MSNTV, PocketPC—on rigid schedules driven by "the model" and the presumption of success. Shortly thereafter, a lack of customer response delivers a fast, quiet funeral for product and management alike.

At Webvan, premature scaling permeated a company culture dominated by the prevailing venture-capital mantra of the time, "get big fast." It spent $18 million to develop proprietary software and $40 million to set up its first automated warehouse before it had shipped a single item. Premature scaling had dire consequences, assuring that the Webvan case will be taught in business schools for decades to come. As customer demand failed to live up to Webvan's business plan, the company slowly realized it had overbuilt and overdesigned. While Webvan had executed to its plan, it had also failed to pay attention to its customers.

…no business plan survives first contact with customers.

9. Management by Crisis Leads to a Death Spiral

At Webvan, the consequences of all the mistakes began to show by the time of first customer ship. The story usually unfolds like this:

Sales starts to miss its numbers and the board becomes concerned. The sales VP arrives at a board meeting, still optimistic, and provides a set of reasonable explanations. The board raises a collective eyebrow. The VP returns to the field to exhort the troops to work harder. Sales asks Engineering to build custom versions of the product for special customers, since this is the only way that the increasingly desperate sales force can close the sale. Board meetings become increasingly tense. Shortly thereafter, the sales VP is probably terminated as part of the "solution."

A new sales VP hired and quickly concludes that the company just didn't understand its customers or how to sell them. She decides that the company's positioning and marketing strategy were incorrect and that the product was missing critical features. Since the new sales VP was hired to "fix" sales, the marketing department must now respond to a sales manager who believes that whatever was created earlier in the company was wrong. (After all, it got the old VP fired, right?) A new sales plan buys the new sales VP a few months' honeymoon.

Sometimes all it takes is one or two iterations to find the right sales roadmap and positioning to attract exuberant customers. In tougher times, when dollars are tighter, the next round of funding may never come.

But the problem at Webvan was not an incorrect sales strategy or positioning statement. The problem is that *no business plan survives first contact with customers.* The assumptions in the Webvan business plan were simply a series of untested hypotheses. When real results came in, they learned that the guesses in their revenue plan were wrong. Focusing on executing their business plans, Webvan iterated their strategy and their search for a business model by firing executives.

Failure is an integral part of the search for a business model.

Webvan went public in 1999, and its sea of red ink was reported quarterly for all to see. Rather than acknowledge its unrealistic plan and scale back or retrench, the company kept spending against its flailing strategy, accumulating a $612 million deficit in the process. Seven months after its IPO, Webvan filed for Chapter 11 bankruptcy.

The ironic Webvan postscript: two other companies on two continents saw the same opportunity at the same time but developed their businesses by following Customer Development precepts even though they hadn't been published at the time. Peapod and Tesco are both successful, growing, and profitable today.

They started smaller, without carving hypothetical assumptions and plans in stone, and learned what customers wanted as they developed business and financial models that worked. Tesco, a UK company that used retail stores as its launch pad and "warehouse," today delivers more than 85,000 orders a week and earns more than $559 million in sales. Peapod, an American company, has delivered more than 10 million grocery orders to more than 330,000 customers. Explicitly or implicitly, both understood the test-and-iterate process of Customer Development.

The Path to the Epiphany:
The Customer Development Model

How narrow the gate and constricted the road that leads to life.
And those who find it are few.

—Matthew 7:14

WHEN WILL HARVEY APPROACHED STEVE BLANK with a new business idea in June 2004, Steve uncharacteristically almost took out his checkbook before hearing Will's pitch. Steve had invested in Will's previous company, There.com, and sat on its board. Before that, Will had been Steve's engineering VP at Rocket Science, a video-game company with Steve as founding CEO. Rocket Science is infamous for appearing on the cover of *Wired* magazine while blowing through $35 million in venture capital in less than three years, leaving a crater so deep it has its own iridium layer.

Sitting in Steve's living room, Will explained his vision for IMVU, a "virtual world" company with 3D avatar-based instant messaging and social networking. Will had a world-class reputation. He developed Music Construction Set, a worldwide best-selling video game, at the age of 15. He earned his bachelor's, master's and Ph.D. in computer science at Stanford while running a video-game company that developed hits like *Zany Golf, Immortal*, and *Marble Madness*.

Will's co-founder, Eric Ries, had started an online recruiting company while earning his computer science degree at Yale. Eric had joined Will's last startup as a senior software engineer. That company built a "virtual world" on the web using a multiyear waterfall development model. After three years, the product was ready to launch with a big-bang product introduction guided by a hired big gun, a CEO with large company experience. Only then did they discover that customers didn't want or care about most of the features they had so painstakingly built.

Steve told the IMVU founders that in exchange for his check to help fund their seed round, they were required to audit his Customer Development class at U.C. Berkeley's Haas Business School. As the semester unfolded, Will and Eric realized that the Customer Development principles they were learning would save them from repeating the same errors they made in their previous startup. Thus IMVU's co-founders became the first Customer Development pioneers.

...in exchange for his check to help fund IMVU's seed round, they were required to audit Steve's Customer Development class.

Steve sat on IMVU's board and watched, coached and cheered as Will and Eric paired the Customer Development process with agile software development. They built a process that used customer feedback and testing to help them determine the minimum product features customers most valued. Based on its initial set of hypotheses about its customer, IMVU set out to create a 3D chat add-on where users could create customizable avatars and talk to all their friends on the leading instant messenger of the day, America Online. After a year, IMVU could see that all its customer hypotheses were wrong. While customers liked the 3D avatars, they wanted to create their own separate buddy lists instead of using the one they already had on AOL. IMVU learned that customers didn't want to talk to their existing friends but wanted to meet new people and make *new* friends. Quarter after quarter, this kind of customer feedback created a "two steps forward, one step back" learning process that supplied the Customer Development principles they learned in class.

Most startups lack a structured process for testing their business model hypotheses.

IMVU tested, pivoted and tested again until it had the product right. Instead of creating a crisis, this learning process was an integral part of the company. IMVU had integrated Customer Development and agile engineering and had become the first Lean Startup.

The result was a profitable, growing company. Why was IMVU on the road to success while scores of other virtual world and avatar companies have long since folded? What was it about Customer Development that gave Will and Eric a clearer roadmap at IMVU than they had at their previous company?

An Introduction to Customer Development

Most startups lack a structured process for testing their business models' hypotheses—markets, customers, channels, pricing—and for turning those guesses into facts. The traditional new-product introduction model offers no customer feedback until beta, when it's too late. What separates a successful startup like IMVU from the rest of the pack is this: from Day One, IMVU embraced the Customer Development process and used it to rapidly test assumptions and make corrections in near real time.

The Customer Development model depicted in Figure 2.1 is designed to solve the nine problems of the product development model outlined in Chapter 1. The model breaks out all the customer-related activities of an early-stage company into their own processes, designed as four easy-to-understand steps. The first two steps of the process outline the "search" for the business model. Steps three and four "execute" the business model that's been developed, tested, and proven in steps one and two. The steps:

- *Customer discovery* first captures the founders' vision and turns it into a series of business model hypotheses. Then it develops a plan to test customer reactions to those hypotheses and turn them into facts

- *Customer validation* tests whether the resulting business model is repeatable and scalable. If not, you return to customer discovery

- *Customer creation* is the start of execution. It builds end-user demand and drives it into the sales channel to scale the business

- *Company-building* transitions the organization from a startup to a company focused on executing a validated model

Meshing seamlessly, these four steps support all elements of the startup's business activities. The specific processes associated with the first two, most powerful "search" steps are described in subsequent chapters.

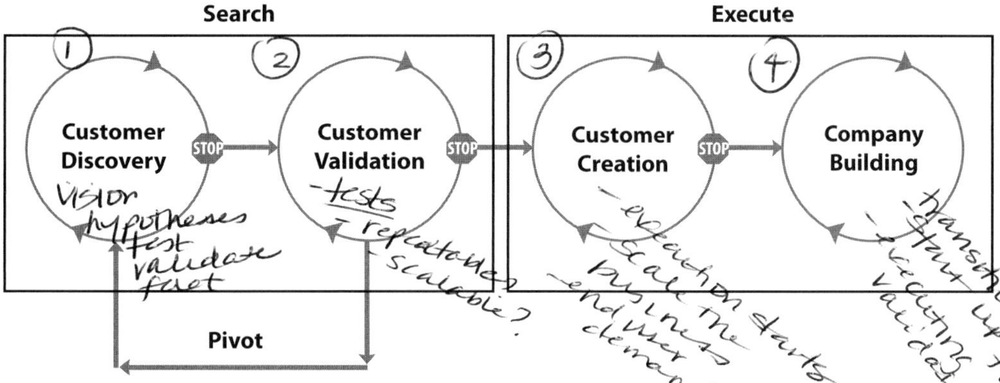

Search **Execute**

Customer Development Process *(Figure 2.1)*

(figure contains handwritten annotations: "vision", "hypotheses", "test / validate / first", "tests", "repeatable / scalable?", "execution starts / scale the / business / end user demand", "transitions / start up to a / well-defined / executing full validated / validated model company", "Don't want dynamic", and ";)")

"The Search for a Business Model:"
Steps, Iteration and Pivots

In the Customer Development model, each step is represented as a circular track with recursive arrows in order to highlight that each step is iterative. It's a polite way of saying, "Startups are unpredictable. We will have failures and we will screw it up several times before we get it right."

In contrast, a traditional product introduction plan makes no provision for moving backward. To do so would be considered a failure. No wonder most startup founders are embarrassed when they're out in the field learning, failing, and learning some more. The diagram their boards of directors have beaten into them says, "Move from left to right and you're a success. Go right to left and you'll get fired." This is why startup sales and marketing efforts tend to move forward even when it's patently obvious that they haven't nailed the market. Experience with scores of startups shows that only in business-school case studies does progress addressing customers' key needs happen in a smooth, linear fashion.

Meanwhile, the Customer Development model *embraces the way startups actually work,* with moving backward playing a natural and valuable role in learning and discovery. Startups will cycle through each step of the Customer Development process until they achieve "escape velocity"—enough measurable progress in finding the business model as defined by board and team—to propel forward to the next step.

...what could customers tell us except that we were right?

Eric Ries recalls his pre-IMVU days at There.com: "The company sort of wanted customer feedback but not really. From our perspective, what could customers tell us except that we were right? The marketing team held focus groups, but looking back, they were orchestrated to get the answers we wanted to hear." The Customer Development model assumes it will take several iterations of each of the four steps to get it right. The philosophy of "It's not only OK to screw it up—plan to learn from it" is the core of the process.

Note that each of the four steps has a stop sign at its exit. That's simply a reminder to think through whether enough has been learned to charge ahead to the next step. It's a place to stop and summarize all the learning and, of course, to candidly assess whether the company has reached "escape velocity."

Let's take a closer look at each of the four steps of the Customer Development model.

Step 1: Customer Discovery

Customer discovery translates a founder's vision for the company into hypotheses about each component of the business model and creates a set of experiments to test each hypothesis. To do this, founders leave guesswork behind and get out of the building to test customer reaction to each hypothesis, gain insights from their feedback, and adjust the business model. Of all the lessons of Customer Development, the importance of getting out of the building and into conversations with your customers is the most critical. Only by moving away from the comforts of your conference room to truly engage with and listen to your customers can you learn in depth about their problems, product features they believe will solve those problems, and the process in their company for recommending, approving and purchasing products. You'll need these details to build a successful product, articulate your product's unique differences and propose a compelling reason why your customers should buy it.

Customer discovery is not about collecting feature lists from prospective customers or running lots of focus groups. In a startup, the founders define the product vision and then use customer discovery to find customers and a market for that vision. (Read that last sentence again. The initial product specification comes from the founders' vision, not the sum of a set of focus groups.)

In a startup, the founders define the product vision and then use customer discovery to find customers and a market for that vision.

Customer discovery includes two outside-the-building phases. The first tests customer perception of the problem and the customer's need to solve it. Is it important enough that the right product will drive significant numbers of customers to buy or engage with the product? The second phase shows customers the product for the first time, assuring that the product (usually a minimum viable product at this point) elegantly solves the problem or fills the need well enough to persuade lots of customers to buy. When customers enthusiastically confirm the importance of both the problem and the solution, customer discovery is complete.

Pivots may happen in the customer discovery phase. Failure will happen. It is a normal part of the startup process. Misunderstanding or just getting wrong key assumptions about your business model happen often: who your customers are, what problems they needed to solve, what features would solve them, how much customers would pay to solve them, etc. Pivots are a response to these mistakes. A pivot is a major change to one of the nine business model hypotheses based on learning from customer feedback. Pivots happen often in the Customer Development process. A pivot is not a failure. In fact, embracing the fact that startups regularly fail and pivot along the way is perhaps one of the greatest insights in this book.

⇨ For web/mobile apps, or products, customer discovery begins when the first "low-fidelity" version of the website or app is up and running. The website is used to test the business model hypotheses against customers or users. When the product is bits, a rough minimum viable product can often be assembled in days if not hours, and entrepreneurs can start the search for customers almost at once, refining their product and customer-acquisition strategies on the fly. This approach served many recent startup stars quite well, including Facebook and Groupon, which began the quest for customers with rough-hewn products almost the day they opened their doors.

A pivot is not a failure.

Another key element of customer discovery is that the founder is free to ignore all of it. At times (particularly in a new market) a founder's vision of what can be is clearer than the vision of potential customers. But this corner case requires the founder to be able to articulate the "why," not just ignore it.

The IMVU team shipped a buggy, minimalist product quickly and deployed a whopping marketing budget of $5 a day, using Google AdWords to attract roughly 100 new daily users to the site. They vigilantly observed, monitored and assessed every user's on-site behavior. Heavy (paying) users were then assaulted with questions in online chats, surveys, phone calls from founders and more. Perhaps the ugliest (or most flattering) comment: "It seems to crash my computer every time I use it," said one user who *kept coming back for more!* But four months after funding, a (clearly minimal) new product was born, using feedback reflecting the power of customer discovery.

Step 2: Customer Validation

Customer validation proves that the business tested and iterated in customer discovery has a repeatable, scalable business model that can deliver the volume of customers required to build a profitable company. During validation, the company tests its ability to scale (i.e., product, customer acquisition, pricing and channel activities) against a larger number of customers with another round of tests, that are larger in scale and more rigorous and quantitative. During this step, a startup also develops a sales roadmap for the sales and marketing teams (to be hired later) or validates the online demand creation plan. Simply put, does adding $1 in sales and marketing resources generate $2+ of revenue (or users, views, clicks, or whatever the metric may be)? The resulting roadmap will be field-tested here by selling the product to early customers.

⇨ **In web/mobile apps, customer validation calls for the deployment of a "hi-fidelity" version of the MVP to test key features in front of customers. Customer validation proves the existence of a set of customers, confirms that customers will accept the MVP, and validates serious, measurable purchase intent among customers.**

How? Depending on the business model, validation is measured by "test sales" that get customers to hand over their money (or become actively engaged with the product). In a single-sided market (one where the user is the payer), a steady stream of customer purchases validates the concept far more solidly than lots of polite words. There's no surrogate for people paying for a product. In a "two-sided" or ad-supported business model, a customer base of hundreds of thousands that's growing exponentially usually implies that the company can find a set of advertisers willing to pay to reach those users.

In essence, the first two steps in the Customer Development model—customer discovery and customer validation—refine, corroborate, and test a startup's business model. Completing these first two steps verifies the product's core features, the market's existence, locates customers, tests the product's perceived value and demand, identifies the economic buyer (the person who writes the check to buy the product), establishes pricing and channel strategies, and checks out the proposed sales cycle and process. Only when an adequately sized group of customers and a repeatable sales process that yields a profitable business model are clearly identified and validated is "escape velocity" achieved. At that point, it's time to move on to the next step: scaling up, also known as customer creation.

Learning that a hypothesis is wrong is not a crisis.

In Will's and Eric's pre-IMVU startup, their CEO and board forced them to wait three years and spend $30 million to perfect the product with minimal customer feedback. By contrast, IMVU launched a buggy early product roughly 120 days after it was founded. Amazingly, some customers loved the buggy product enough not only to pay for it, but also to give the founders what they wanted: feedback (and money).

The IMVU team used customer feedback relentlessly to drive the enhancement, addition and deletion of features that "heavy users" liked or didn't. One critical pricing discovery led to a 30 percent increase in revenue. When teenagers bemoaned their lack of access to credit cards, IMVU reacted quickly by allowing users to pay IMVU via gift cards distributed through 7-Eleven and Walmart, online, and via other major retail channels.

A Customer Development Bonus: Minimum Waste of Cash and Time

The first two Customer Development steps limit the amount of money a startup spends until it has tested and validated a business model and is ready to scale. Instead of hiring sales and marketing staff, leasing new buildings or buying ads, startup founders get out of the building to test the business model hypotheses, and that costs very little in cash.

When paired with agile engineering, Customer Development reduces the amount of wasted code, features or hardware. Agile development builds the product in small increments, allowing the company to test and measure customer reactions to each new iteration of the product. It won't take three years to find out that customers don't want or need or can't use the features the team labored lovingly over.

Since the Customer Development model assumes that most startups cycle through discovery and validation multiple times, it allows a well-managed company to carefully estimate and frugally husband its cash. It also helps "husband" founders' equity, since the closer a company is to a predictable, scalable business model, the higher its likely valuation—preserving more stock for the founders at fundraising time. The IMVU founders, for example, only hired product development teams (not sales, marketing, or business development) until they had proof in hand of a business worth building. With that proof, the company can move through the third and fourth steps, customer creation and company-building, to capitalize on the opportunity.

Step 3: Customer Creation

Customer creation builds on the company's initial sales success. It's where the company steps on the gas, spending large sums to scale by creating end-user demand and driving it into the sales channel. This step follows customer validation, moving heavy marketing spending after a startup has learned how to acquire customers, thus controlling the cash burn rate to protect a most precious "green" asset, cash.

Customer creation varies by startup type. Some startups enter existing markets well-defined by their competitors, others create new markets where no product or company exists, and still others attempt a hybrid by re-segmenting an existing market as a low-cost entrant or by creating a niche. Each market-type strategy demands different customer creation activities and costs. (Market type is addressed in depth in Chapter 3.)

Initially, IMVU ran a wide range of low-cost customer segmentation experiments. Soon they identified two distinct customer segments—teens and moms—and spending ramped up to underwrite two entirely different customer creation efforts.

Step 4: Company-Building

"Graduation day" arrives when the startup finds a scalable, repeatable business model. At this point it's fundamentally no longer the temporary search-oriented organization known as a startup—it's a company! In a sometimes-bittersweet transition out of startup mode, company-building refocuses the team's energy away from "search" mode and to a focus on execution, swapping its informal learning- and discovery-oriented Customer Development team for formal, structured departments such as Sales, Marketing and Business Development, among others, complete with VPs. These executives now focus on building their departments to scale the company.

This is where the entrepreneurs' version of a Shakespearean tragedy often takes center stage, as VCs realize they have a "hit" with potential for a large return on their investment. All of a sudden, the passionate visionary entrepreneur is no longer deemed the right person to lead the now-successful company he or she has nurtured from cocktail napkin to high-trajectory. The board—graciously or not—ousts the founder and all his or her innate customer understanding, trading him or her in for a "suit," an experienced operating executive. There goes the neighborhood, as the company declares success, the entrepreneurial spark often sputters, and process often drowns energy.

At IMVU, the founders saw the company rapidly scaling beyond their skill set. But instead of being fired, they recognized the need for a seasoned operating executive, recruited a skilled CEO, and named themselves chairmen of the board and active board members. Their new CEO was skilled at managing the transition from searching for a business to execution and grew the company steadily.

The Customer Development Manifesto

BEFORE DIVING HEADFIRST INTO THE DETAILS of the Customer Development process, it's crucial to review the 14 rules that make up *The Customer Development Manifesto*. Embrace them. Review them regularly with the team and (maybe after the IPO) consider perhaps even etching them in marble at world headquarters.

Rule No. 1:
There Are No Facts Inside Your Building, So Get Outside.

On Day One, the startup is a faith-based enterprise built on its founders' vision and a notable absence of facts. The founders' job is to translate this vision and these hypotheses into facts. Facts live outside the building, where future customers (prospects, really) live and work, so that's where you need to go. Nothing is more fundamental to Customer Development, and nothing is harder to do. It's much easier to write code, build hardware, have meetings and write reports than it is to find and listen to potential customers. But that's what separates the winners from the losers.

Facts live outside the building, where future customers live and work…

In Customer Development, the *founders gather firsthand experience about every component of the business model. The team can support the founders, but firsthand experience by definition cannot be delegated.* This customer research must be done by founders because:

- Key customer feedback points are random, unpredictable, and often painful to hear. Employees hate to deliver bad news to higher-ups
- Employees have far less at stake and seldom listen as acutely, and they don't get heard adequately when they report back. It's too easy to dismiss their findings as "hearsay" or to ignore critical points of feedback
- Consultants have even less at stake than employees and often color their commentary to either tell the client what he wants to hear or deliver messages that can lead to extended consulting relationships. This is also second- or third-hand feedback and too diluted or diffused to provide value

Only a founder can embrace the feedback, react to it, and adeptly make the decisions necessary to change or pivot key business model components.

Rule No. 2:
Pair Customer Development with Agile Development

Customer Development is useless unless the product development organization can iterate the product with speed and agility.

Customer Development is useless unless the product development organization can iterate the product with speed and agility. If Engineering builds the product using waterfall development, it will be deaf, dumb and blind to customer input except during a short period when it's specifying the product. The rest of the time, engineers are locked into an implementation cycle, unable to change the product features without intolerable delay. By contrast, a startup engineering organization using an agile methodology is designed to continually take customer input and deliver a product that iterates readily around an MVP or its minimum feature set.

In this book, *agile engineering/development* refers to the rapid deployment, iterative development and continuous discovery processes that hardware or software companies can use. We don't advocate any particular flavor, just its necessity. The Customer Development process provides the continuous customer input to make agile work.

Before the company even starts, the founders need to reach a deep and inexorable commitment to the customer/agile development partnership.

Rule No. 3:
Failure is an Integral Part of the Search

One of the key differences between a startup and an existing company is the one that's never explicitly stated: "startups go from failure to failure."

In contrast, existing companies have learned what works and doesn't. Failures in an existing company are an exception. They happen when someone screws up. In a startup, you're *searching*, not *executing*, and the only way to find the right path is to try lots of experiments and take a lot of wrong turns. Failure is part of the process.

If you're afraid to fail in a startup, you're destined to do so.

Failures are not truly failures, per se but an integral part of the startup learning process. You'll be running dozens if not hundreds of pass/fail tests—on your pitch, your features, your pricing, and on and on—so get ready to accept failure and move on. When something isn't working, successful founders orient themselves to the new facts, decide what needs fixing, and act decisively.

The Customer Development process demands frequent, agile iteration, followed, of course, by testing of the iteration that often leads to another iteration or pivot, which leads to more testing and...

If you're afraid to fail in a startup, you're destined to do so.

Rule No. 4:
Make Continuous Iterations and Pivots

The strategy of embracing failure in Customer Development demands frequent, agile iteration and pivots. A pivot is a substantive change in one or more of the nine boxes of the business model canvas. (For example, a pricing change from freemium to subscription model or a customer segment shift from boys 12-15 years old to women 45-60.) Or it can be more complex, such as a change of target customer or user. Iterations, meanwhile, are minor changes to business model components (e.g., changing pricing from $99 to $79).

Groupon's legendary $12 billion pivot is a perfect example.

When a company is limping along, only a dramatic change to one or more business model components can get it back on the road to success. Groupon's legendary $12 billion pivot (their IPO valuation) is a perfect example. Groupon was started from a company called the Point. It was struggling, at best, as a social media platform working to get people together to solve problems, but was about to run out of money.

The most effective campaigns on The Point were those that saved people money by grouping or bundling their purchases. The founders started blogging various deals from different businesses each day. They called this, "Get Your Groupon.com." Groupon's first offer hit in October of 2008: buy two pizzas for the price of one in the shop on the first floor of its Chicago headquarters. Twenty people bought the deal and the company was well on its way to its $12-billion pivot.

Pivots are driven by the learnings and insight from a continuous stream of "pass/fail" tests you run throughout discovery and validation.

The best startup founders don't hesitate to make the change. They admit when hypotheses are wrong and adapt.

Rule No. 5:
No Business Plan Survives First Contact with Customers So Use a Business Model Canvas

There's only one reason for a business plan: some investor who went to business school doesn't know any better and wants to see one. But once it has delivered financing, the business plan is fundamentally useless. Entrepreneurs often mistake their business plan as a cookbook for execution, failing to recognize that it is only a collection of unproven assumptions. At its back, a revenue plan blessed by an investor, and composed overwhelmingly of guesses, suddenly becomes an operating plan driving hiring, firing, and spending. Insanity.

The difference between a static business plan and a dynamic model could well be the difference between flameout and success.

The difference between a static business plan and a dynamic business model could well be the difference between a flameout and success. Startups should dump the business *plan* and adopt the flexible business *model*.

A business model describes the flow between key components of the company:

- *value proposition,* which the company offers (product/service, benefits)
- *customer segments,* such as users, and payers, or moms or teens

- *distribution channels* to reach customers and offer them the value proposition
- *customer relationships* to create demand
- *revenue streams* generated by the value proposition(s)
- *resources* needed to make the business model possible
- *activities* necessary to implement the business model
- *partners* who participate in the business and their motivations for doing so
- *cost structure* resulting from the business model

The business model *canvas* (see Figure 2.2) presents a visual overview of the nine components of a business on one page. In this book, Alexander Osterwalder's business model canvas serves as the scorecard for the customer discovery process described in Step One. Osterwalder's book *Business Model Generation* (Wiley, 2010) provides the structure for the canvas.

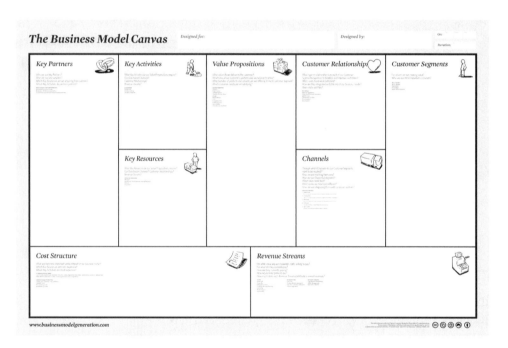

Business Model Canvas (Figure 2.2)

As a startup moves through the Customer Development process, it will use the business model canvas as a scorecard, by posting the hypotheses about each component of the model and then revising the hypotheses as the founders gather facts. Think of your first version of the business model canvas as the starting point showing the hypotheses that must be confirmed in face-to-face or online interaction with customers. More often than not, the customers will reject components of the business model, saying, "I'd rather buy that from a retailer," or, "The product needs to have these features to be important to me." As customers approve or dispute the business model hypotheses, the company either accepts the customers' approval or pivots to change its business model to better target the opportunity.

Using the business model canvas as a guide makes it easier to figure out where and how to pivot, since the team can visually diagram its alternatives and see what it needs to change. Each time the founders iterate or pivot (see Rule No. 4) in response to customer feedback, they draw a new canvas showing the changes. Over time, these multiple canvases form a "flip book" that shows the evolution of the business model. Agile startups can end up with a six-inch-thick stack of business model diagrams they can burn at the IPO-celebration bonfire.

Much more about how to use business model diagrams to "keep score" throughout the customer discovery process can be found in Chapter 3.

...hypothesis is just a fancy word for "guess."

Rule No. 6:
Design Experiments and Test to Validate Your Hypotheses

Initially, hypothesis is just a fancy word for "guess." To turn hypotheses into facts, founders need to get out of the building and *test* them in front of customers. But how do you test? And what do you want to learn from the tests? Testing and learning require you to be thoughtful on constructing and designing your tests. We call this "designing the experiments."

Customer Development experiments are short, simple, objective pass/fail tests. You're looking for a strong signal in the signal/noise noise ratio, something like five of the first 12 customers you call on saying "I need this right now, even if it's still buggy." Early tests aren't necessarily precise, but should give you a "good enough" signal to proceed.

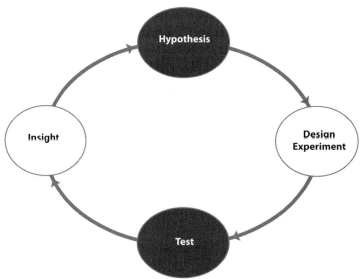

The Customer Development Insight Cycle *(Figure 2.3)*

Start by asking yourself, "What insight do I need to move forward?" Then ask, "What's the simplest test I can run to get it?" Finally, think about, "How do I design an experiment to run this simple test?"

One of the things that trips up engineering founders is thinking that these tests have to be actual code, hardware or the real product. Most of the time you can mock-up the web page or create a demo or physical prototype to elicit valuable learning.

Rule No. 7:
Agree on Market Type. It Changes Everything

One of the radical insights guiding this book is that *not all startups are alike*. One of the key ways in which they are different is in the relationship between a startup's new product and its market. These product/market relationships generally fit one of these descriptions:

- bringing a *new product* into an *existing market*
- bringing a new product into a *new market*
- bringing a new product into an existing market and trying to:
- re-segment that market as a low-cost entrant or
- re-segment that market *as a niche entrant*
- *cloning* a business model that's successful in another country

What confused entrepreneurs for decades is that the traditional product introduction model works when introducing a product into an existing market with a known business model (i.e., known customers, channels and markets). However, since the majority of startups are not pursuing known markets (those in new or re-segmented categories), they don't really know who their customers will be. These types of startups are searching for a repeatable and scalable business model.

 ## Market type influences everything a company does.

Market type influences everything a company does. Strategy and tactics that work for one market type seldom work for another. Market type determines the startup's customer feedback and acquisition activities and spending. It changes customer needs, adoption rates, product features and positioning as well as its launch strategies, channels and activities. In sum, *different market types require dramatically different discovery, MVPs, and sales and marketing strategies.*

In existing markets, where customers exist, marketing is relatively easy: users can describe the market and the attributes that matter the most to them. The new product or service typically runs faster, does something better or cheaper, or otherwise improves on a customer-defined attribute. Users, the market, and competitors are known, and competition involves comparing the product and its features with others.

In a new market, a company lets customers do something they couldn't do before by creating something that never existed before. Or it dramatically lowers costs to create a new class of users. By definition, new markets have no customers yet, so there's nobody to know what the product can do or why they should buy. This makes getting feedback and creating demand particularly challenging, since the product is unknown to users and the market is undefined and unknown, and costly to develop.

The key isn't competing, but instead understanding whether a large customer base exists and whether customers can be persuaded to buy. A classic founder error in a new market is the "fast-burn" spending of sales and marketing funds, a practice that may be appropriate when selling to existing customers in a known market, but makes no sense in a new market. The new-vs.-existing axis is at the core of the market-type definition.

Re-segmenting an existing market is useful when the incumbent is too difficult to attack head-on (like Amazon, Facebook, or Microsoft). A re-segmentation strategy is based on the startup's market and customer knowledge, ideally identifying a market opportunity that incumbents are missing, which usually takes one of two forms: a low-cost strategy or a niche strategy. (Unlike differentiation, segmentation forges a distinct spot in customers' minds that is unique, valuable, and in demand.)

Low-cost re-segmentation is just what it sounds like. Are there customers at the low end of an existing market who will buy "good enough" performance at a substantially lower price?

Niche re-segmentation looks at an existing market and asks whether some segment of this market would buy a new product designed to address more specific needs. Can some sizable portion of the market be convinced that a characteristic of the new product is radical enough to change the rules and shape of an existing market. See Chan Kim and Renee Mauborgne's work on "Blue Ocean Strategy" for another way to think of re-segmenting a market.

Cloning an existing business model is a powerful technique when an existing business has been proven in one country but has not yet been introduced in another. Startups in Russia, India, Indonesia, Brazil, Japan and China (each with its own large local market and language and cultural barriers) can adopt, borrow, or copy a successful American business model and customize it for local language and buying preferences. (Soon ideas from those countries will be cloned in the U.S.)

For example, Baidu in China and Yandex in Russia are the equivalent of Google in their respective markets. And Qzone, RenRen, PengYou and Kaixin are the Facebooks of China, while Vkontakte and Odnoklassniki play the same role in Russia.

Startup companies generally enter one of these four market types and ultimately must commit to one. The consequences of a wrong market-type choice will prove to be severe in the customer creation stage. While market type is ultimately a "late-binding decision," a working hypothesis helps frame early customer discovery issues. Market-type decision-making is explored in greater detail in Chapter 3.

…the few financial metrics to track: cash-burn rate, number of months' worth of cash left…

Rule No. 8:
Startup Metrics Differ from Those in Existing Companies

We now have several centuries' worth of performance metrics for existing businesses —P&Ls balance sheets, cash-flow forecasts and line-of-business analyses, plus scores of others. Here's hoping your startup becomes big enough to need them someday. In the past (not so long ago), we used these tools with startups because we didn't know what else to measure. We now know that startup metrics should focus on tracking the startup's progress converting guesses and hypotheses into incontrovertible facts rather than measuring the execution of a static plan. It's critical that board and management continuously test and measure each hypothesis until the entire business model is worth scaling into a company.

If the company is venture-backed, management and investors must agree on a set of metrics that truly matter and work toward a report or "dashboard" that essentially replaces the P&L, cash flow, and balance sheet as centerpieces of early board meetings.

Startup metrics track the results of pass/fail tests and the iterations they lead to:

- Have the customer problem and product features been validated?

- Does the minimum feature set resonate with customers?

- Who in fact is the customer, and have initial customer-related hypotheses on the likes of value proposition, customer segments, and channels been validated through face-to-face customer interaction?

- Customer-validation questions might include: average order size, customer lifetime value, average time to first order, rate of sales pipeline growth, improvement in close rate, and revenue per salesperson.

In addition to the startup metrics above, the relatively few financial metrics that a startup board should be tracking are cash-burn rate, number of months' worth of cash left, short-term hiring plans, and amount of time until the company reaches cash-flow break-even.

Make sure decisions are fact-based, not faith-based.

Rule No. 9:

Fast Decision-Making, Cycle Time, Speed and Tempo

Speed matters at startups where the only absolute certainty is that the bank balance declines every day. While Rule No. 4 addresses iterations and pivots, it doesn't specify how long they should take. Unequivocally, the faster the better, since the faster these "learn, build, pivot" or "iterate, build" cycles happen, the greater the odds of finding a scalable business model with the cash on hand. If cycles happen too slowly, the startup runs out of cash and dies. The biggest impediment to cycle time is psychological: it requires the admission of being wrong or even of suffering a short-term tactical defeat.

While pivots and iterations are about speed outside the building, speed also matters inside the company. Most startup decisions are made in the face of uncertainty. There's seldom a clear-cut, perfect solution to any engineering, customer or competitor problem, and founders shouldn't agonize over trying to find one. This doesn't mean gambling with the company's fortunes on a whim. It means adopting plans with an acceptable degree of risk and doing so quickly. (Make sure these decisions are fact-based, not faith-based.) In general, the company that consistently makes and implements decisions rapidly gains a tremendous, often-decisive competitive advantage.

...startups should make reversible decisions before anyone leaves the CEO's office.

Startup decisions have two states: *reversible and irreversible*. A reversible decision could be adding or dropping a product feature or a new algorithm in the code or targeting a specific set of customers. If the decision proves a bad one, it can be unwound in a reasonable period of time. An irreversible decision such as firing an employee, launching a product, or signing a long lease on expensive office space is usually difficult or impossible to reverse.

Startups should as policy, *make reversible decisions before anyone leaves the CEO's office* or before a meeting ends. Perfect decision-making is both unimportant and impossible, and what matters more is forward momentum and a tight, fact-based feedback loop to quickly recognize and reverse bad decisions. By the time a big company gets the committee to get the subcommittee to pick a meeting date, most startups have made 20 decisions, reversed five, and implemented the other 15.

Learning to make decisions quickly is just part of the equation. Agile startups have mastered another trick: tempo—the ability to make quick decisions consistently and at all levels in the company. Speed and tempo are integral parts of startup DNA, and a great startup's tempo is often 10 times that of a large company.

Rule No. 10:
It's All About Passion

A startup without driven, passionate people is dead the day it opens its doors. "Startup people" are different. They think different. In contrast, most people are great at execution. They work to live, do their jobs well, and enjoy their family, their lives, their hobbies and often even enjoy mowing the lawn. They're terrific at executing fixed tasks, and it's a wonderful life for almost everyone.

The people leading almost every successful startup in history are just different. They're a very tiny percentage of the world population, and their brains are wired for chaos, uncertainty, and blinding speed. They're irrationally focused on customer needs and delivering great products. Their job is their life. It's not 9-to-5, it's 24/7. These are the people who found high-growth, highly-successful scalable startups.

Startups demand execs who are comfortable with uncertainty, chaos and change.

Rule No. 11:
Startup Job Titles Are Very Different from a Large Company's

In an existing company, job titles reflect the way tasks are organized to execute a known business model. For example, the "Sales" title in an existing company means there's a sales team repeatedly selling a known product to a well-understood group of customers, using a standard corporate presentation with an existing price list and standard terms, conditions and contract. The "Sales" title in an existing company is all about execution around a series of knowns.

Compared with big companies, startups need executives whose skills are 180 degrees different. *Startups demand execs who are comfortable with uncertainty, chaos and change*—with presentations and offers changing daily, with the product changing often, with probing and gaining insights from failure rather than high-fiving a success. In short, they need the rare breed:

- open to learning and discovery—highly curious, inquisitive, and creative
- eager to search for a repeatable and scalable business model
- agile enough to deal with daily change and operating "without a map"
- readily able to wear multiple hats, often on the same day
- comfortable celebrating failure when it leads to learning and iteration

We suggest replacing traditional execution-oriented sales, marketing and business development titles with a single title: the Customer Development team. At first, this "team" will consist of the company's founder(s), who talks with customers to gain enough insights to develop the minimum viable product. Later, as the startup moves into customer validation, the team may grow to include a dedicated "sales closer" responsible for the logistics of getting early orders signed. The closer shouldn't be confused with a traditional sales VP. To succeed in this process, the team must have:

- the ability to listen to customer objections and understand whether they are issues about the product, the presentation, the pricing or something else (or the wrong type of customer)
- experience in talking to and moving between customers and engineers
- confidence amid a state of constant change, often operating "without a map"
- the ability to walk in their customers' shoes, understanding how they work and the problems they face

Some would say this checklist isn't bad for identifying great entrepreneurs.

Rule No. 12:

Preserve All Cash Until Needed. Then Spend.

The goal of Customer Development is not to avoid spending money but to *preserve cash while searching for the repeatable and scalable business model. Once found, then spend like there's no tomorrow.* This paragraph is worth deconstructing:

Preserve cash: When a startup has unlimited cash (Internet bubbles, frothy venture climate), it can iterate on its mistakes by burning more dollars. When money is tight, without dollars to redo mistakes, it's crucial to minimize waste. The Customer Development process preserves cash by not hiring any sales and marketing staff until the founders turn hypotheses into facts and discover a viable product/market fit.

While searching: Customer Development observes that at the start, the company and its business model are based solely on hypotheses, not facts, and that the founders need to get out of the building to turn these hypotheses into customer data. This "get out of the building" approach, combined with rapid iteration and pivots, is central to the model's customer discovery and validation steps.

**...preserve cash while searching for the repeatable
and scalable business model...**

Repeatable: Startups may get orders that stem from board members' customer relationships, engineering one-offs, or heroic single-shot efforts by the CEO. These are great, but they aren't repeatable by a sales organization. Search not for the one-off revenue hits but rather for a pattern that can be replicated by a sales organization selling off a price list or by customers regularly visiting the website.

Scalable: The goal is not to get one customer but many—and for each additional customer to add incremental revenue *and* profit. The test is: Does the addition of one more salesperson or more marketing dollars bring in more gross profit (or users or clicks) than you invested? Who influences a sale? Who recommends a sale?

Who is the decision-maker? Who is the economic buyer? Where's the budget for purchasing this type of product? What's the customer acquisition cost? Affirming the ~~repeatable, scalable sales model~~ is the customer validation step of Customer Development, its most important phase. Has the team learned how to sell a target customer? Can this happen before the startup runs out of money?

Search not for the one-off revenue hits but rather for a pattern...

Business model: A business model answers the basic questions of how the company makes money. Is this a revenue play, or is it a freemium model seeking users? Something else? Who's the customer?

Spend like there's no tomorrow: The goal of an investor-backed startup is not to build a lifestyle business. The goal is to reach venture scale (10 times the return on investment or more). When management and board agree that they've found a repeatable and scalable sales model (i.e., have a product/market fit), *then invest the dollars to create end-user demand and drive those customers into the sales channel.*

Rule No. 13:
Communicate and Share Learning

An integral part of Customer Development's "learning and discovery" philosophy is sharing everything that's learned outside the building with employees, co-founders and even investors.

The traditional way to do this is via weekly company meetings to keep employees informed and board meetings to let the investors understand the progress made in the search for the business model. But technology in the 21st-century has taken us to places we never could get to before. We can now communicate all we're learning in near-real time to everyone who needs to know.

We strongly recommend that the founders keep and share all their activities in the customer discovery step covered in Chapter 3 via a blog, CRM or product management tool. Think of it as a narrative of the customer discovery process. It records hypotheses the startup started with, who the team has talked to, the questions asked, the tests conducted, what's been learned, and questions for advisors or investors. While this may seem burdensome, it takes less time than having a weekly coffee with an advisory board member. What results is a communications tool allowing outsiders to view the company's progress up close and to offer suggestions and course corrections.

Rule No. 14:
Customer Development Success Begins With Buy-In

Customer Development's "learning and discovery" philosophy can be immensely disorienting to a founder, engineer or investor who has spent his or her career *executing a plan.* For Customer Development to succeed, everyone on the team—from investor or parent company to engineers, marketeers and founders—needs to understand and agree that the Customer Development process is different to its core. If the engineering VP is talking waterfall development or the board demands a rigid timetable, Customer Development is destined for disaster. Everyone must accept the process, recognizing that this is a fluid, nonlinear *search for a business model* that can sometimes last for years.

The Customer Development process is different to its core.

Customer Development changes almost every aspect of startup behavior, performance, metrics, and, as often as not, success potential. It's not just a "nice to do" while executing the revenue model in the back of the business plan. Customer Development *reinvents the business model on the fly,* iterating often and pivoting whenever indicated. Founders need to have the commitment of the team *and board* before embarking on Customer Development. Ensure that all understand and agree that it's iterative, necessary, and worthwhile and that it changes the benchmarks and metrics along the way.

Comments such as "The product is already spec'ed, and we can't change the features since development is already underway," or "We already have the factory (or sales team or marketing materials) built," or "We have to launch to make the numbers in the plan," are all red flags. To succeed at Customer Development, the company must abandon the old model's emphasis on execution of a fantasy business plan. Instead it must commit to a Customer Development process stressing learning, discovery, failure, and iteration in the search for a successful business model. If you're ready for this process, this book will tell you how to do it.

Summary: The Customer Development Process

The Customer Development process reflects the best practices of winning startups. It is the only approach for web-based businesses where failure is certain without constant customer feedback and product iteration as they search for their audiences. Customer Development's fast cycle times and inherent cash conservation gives all entrepreneurs more chances to pivot, iterate, and succeed before the bank account runs dry. Describe this model to entrepreneurs who have taken companies all the way to a lucrative exit and beyond, and heads nod in recognition.

While each step has its own specific objectives, the process as a whole has one overarching goal: discovering the repeatable, scalable, and ultimately profitable business before running out of cash. This transforms the company from a set of founding hypotheses into a moneymaking endeavor.

Customer Development is damn hard work. You can't fake it.

Customer Development is damn hard work. You can't fake it. You can't just do the slides or "do" the process in a weekend. It's a full-time, full-body-contact sport. It's a long-term commitment to changing the way a startup is built. But it's also proven to increase the chances of startup success.

II

Step One:
Customer Discovery

Overview of the Customer Discovery Process

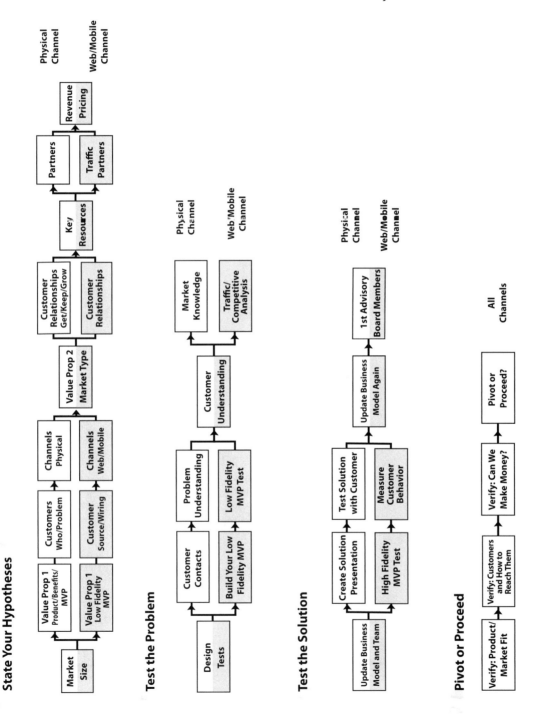

State Your Hypotheses

Test the Problem

Test the Solution

Pivot or Proceed

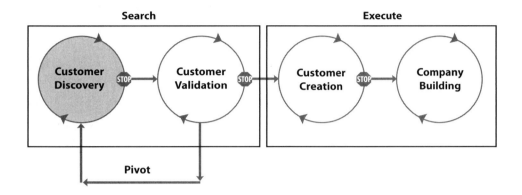

CHAPTER 3

An Introduction to Customer Discovery

No startup business plan survives first contact with customers.
—Steve Blank

A journey of a thousand miles begins with a single step.
—Lao Tzu

IRIDIUM WAS ONE OF THE BIGGEST STARTUP gambles ever made—a bold and audacious $5.2 billion bet. Founded by Motorola and a global partnership of 18 companies in 1991, Iridium planned to build a mobile telephone system that would work "anywhere on Earth," from ships in the middle of the ocean to the jungles of Africa to remote mountain peaks where no cell towers existed.

How? With an out-of-this-world business plan. First, the company bought a fleet of 15 rockets from Russia, the U.S. and China. Next, it launched an armada of 72 private satellites into orbit, where they acted like 500-mile-high cell towers providing phone coverage to any spot on Earth. Seven years after Iridium's founding, its satellites were in place. But nine months after the first call was made in 1998, the company was in Chapter 11 bankruptcy. When Iridium crashed back to Earth, it ranked as one of the largest startup failures on record. What went wrong?

When Iridium was founded in 1991, worldwide cell-phone coverage was sparse, unreliable and expensive. Cell-phone handsets were the size of lunch boxes. Iridium put together a business plan that made assumptions about customers, their problems and the product needed to solve those problems. Other assumptions about sales channel, partnerships, and revenue model all added up to a set of financial forecasts that Iridium would soon be printing money.

One of the largest startup failures on record as they executed their business plan.

But in the seven-plus years it took Iridium to go from concept to launch, innovation in mobile- and cell-phone networks moved at blinding speed. By the time Iridium launched, there were far fewer places on the planet where cell-phone service was unavailable. Traditional cell-phone companies provided coverage in the most valuable parts of the world. Prices for cell service shrunk as fast as phone handsets did. In contrast, Iridium's satellite phone was bigger than a brick and weighed about as much. Worse, Iridium's cell phone couldn't make calls from cars or buildings, since it required line-of-sight "connection" to the satellites. Instead of 50 cents per minute for a regular cell call, Iridium's calls cost $7 a minute, plus $3,000 for the handset itself.

Iridium's potential market shrunk nearly every day. Instead of a massive worldwide market of potential users, it had drawn only a small group willing to pay

its prices and put ~~~~~~~~~~~~~~~~ uct's many limitations. But Iridium's business
model assumptior ~~~~~~~~~~~~~ firmly fixed as if it was still 1991. The company
spent $5 billion bun. ~~~~~~~ s over eight years without ever focusing on four
key questions:

- Have we identified a problem a customer wants to see solved?
- Does our product solve this customer problem or need?
- If so, do we have a viable and profitable business model?
- Have we learned enough to go out and sell?

Answering these questions is the purpose of the first step in the customer
discovery process. This chapter explains how to go about it.

(Twenty years later, Iridium emerged from bankruptcy. In 2000, an investor
group bought $6 billion worth of its assets for $25 million. After a long climb back,
the company celebrated its 500,000th customer in September 2011.)

Customers don't behave like your business plan.

The Customer Discovery Philosophy

A startup begins with the vision of its founders: a vision of a new product or service
that solves a customer's problems or needs and of how it will reach its many
customers. Customer discovery lowers the odds of spending zillions and getting
zeros in return as the Iridium team did. So the No. 1 goal of customer discovery
amounts to this: turning the founders' initial hypotheses about their market and
customers into facts.

Get Out of the Building

Facts exist only outside the building, where customers live, so the most important aspect of customer discovery is getting out of the building, in front of customers. And not for a few days or a week, but repeatedly, over weeks if not months. This critical task can't be assigned to junior staffers and must be driven by founders. Only after the founders have performed this step will they know whether they have a valid vision or just a hallucination.

Sounds simple, doesn't it? But for anyone who has worked in established companies, the customer discovery process is disorienting. All the rules about new-product management in large companies are turned upside down. It's instructive to enumerate all things you are *not* going to do:

- understand the needs and wants of *all* customers
- make a list of *all* the features customers want before they buy your product
- hand Product Development a features list of the sum of *all* customer requests
- hand Product Development a detailed marketing-requirements document
- run focus groups and test customers' reactions to your product to see if they will buy

What you *are* going to do is develop your product for the few, not the many. Moreover, you're going to start building your product even before you know whether you have any customers for it.

On a startup's first day, there's limited—if any— customer input.

For an experienced marketing or product management executive, these ideas are not only disorienting and counterintuitive but heretical. Why aren't the needs of *all* potential customers important? What is it about a first product from a new company that's different from follow-on products in a large company? What is it about a startup's first customers that make the rules so different?

Search for the Problem/Solution Fit

The customer discovery process searches for problem/solution fit: "have we found a problem lots of people want us to solve (or a need they want us to fill)" and "does our solution (a product, a website, or an app) solve the problem in a compelling way?" At its core, the essence of customer discovery is to determine whether your startup's value proposition matches the customer segment it plans to target.

Problem/solution fit is virtually identical to what's sometimes called "product/ market fit," as the previous paragraph indicates. As a result, *we use the terms somewhat interchangeably* throughout the book. Do realize, however, that in multi-sided markets, there may be multiple value propositions and multiple customer segments. But problem/solution fit is only achieved when the revenue model, pricing, and customer acquisition efforts all match up with the customers' needs.

Develop the Product for the Few, Not the Many

In existing companies, the goal of traditional product management and marketing is to develop a market-requirements document (MRD) for engineering that contains the sum of *all* possible customer feature requests, prioritized in a collaborative effort among Product Management, Marketing, Sales, and Engineering. Marketing or Product Management hosts focus groups, analyzes sales data from the field, and looks at customer feature requests and complaints. This information leads to the adding of requested features to the product specification, and the engineering team builds them into the next product release.

While this process is rational for an established company entering an existing market, it's folly for startups. Why? Startups aren't small versions of large, existing companies where there's plenty of customer knowledge and input. In established companies, the MRD process ensures that engineering will build a product that appeals to existing customers in a known market, where customers and their needs are known. On a startup's first day, there's limited—if any— customer input for creating a formal product specification.

In a startup, the first product is not designed to satisfy a mainstream customer. No startup can afford to build a product with every feature a mainstream customer needs all at once. The product would take years to get to market and be obsolete by the time it arrived. Instead, successful startups solve this conundrum by focusing development and early selling efforts on a very small group of early customers who have bought into the startup's vision. These visionary customers will give the company the feedback necessary to add features to the product over time.

Earlyvangelists are willing to make a leap of faith and buy an early product.

Earlyvangelists: The Most Important Customers of All

Enthusiasts who spread the good news about your product to friends, family or co-workers are often called evangelists. But a new word is needed to describe the early adopters—the visionary customers—who buy unfinished and untested products, because they want to "first," whether it's for the sake of gaining a competitive edge or winning bragging rights. We call these early adopters *earlyvangelists*. Unlike "mainstream" business or consumer-product customers who want to buy a finished, completed, tested product, earlyvangelists are willing to make a leap of faith and buy an early product from a startup. Every industry has a small subset of visionaries willing to take a leap of faith on an early product.

One of the mistakes that startup founders make is to give away or heavily discount early alpha/beta products to blue-chip customers. In single-sided markets (where the user is the payer) earlyvangelists will be happy to *pay for early access to the product*. If they won't, they aren't earlyvangelists. Their willingness to pay is a critical part of the customer discovery process. You'll use it to test the entire buying process.

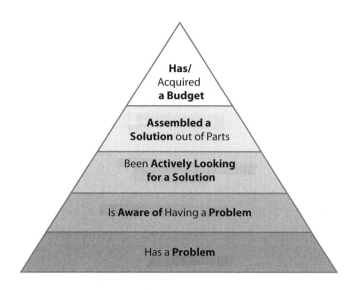

Earlyvangelist Characteristics *(Figure 3.1)*

⇨ In web/mobile apps, where multi-sided markets (separate users and payers) are often found, earlyvangelists can be users or payers. But even as nonpaying users, *these earlyvangelists are willing or eager accelerators of your viral growth.*

Earlyvangelists are willing or eager accelerators of your viral growth.

In both physical and web/mobile channels, earlyvangelists display these common characteristics (see Figure 3.1):

- They have a problem or need.
- They understand they have a problem.
- They're actively searching for a solution and have a timetable for finding it.

- The problem is so painful that they've cobbled together an interim solution.
- They've committed, or can quickly acquire, budget dollars to purchase.

Think of earlyvangelists' characteristics along a scale of customer pain. Earlyvangelist customers will be found only at the top of the scale—those who have already been looking for a solution, built a home-grown solution (whether in a company by building a software solution or at home by taping together a fork, a light bulb and a vacuum cleaner) and have or can acquire a budget. These people are perfect earlyvangelist candidates. They can be relied on for feedback and initial sales; they'll tell others about the product and spread the word that the vision is real. Moreover, they can be potential advisory board candidates (more about advisory boards in Chapter 6).

Build a Minimum Viable Product (MVP) First

The idea that a startup builds its product for a small group of initial customers rather than devising a generic mainstream spec is radical. What follows is equally revolutionary.

The goal of the MVP is to build the smallest possible feature set.

On the day the company starts, there is very limited customer input. All the startup has is a vision of what the problem, product and solution seem to be. Unfortunately, it's either a vision or a hallucination. The company doesn't know who its initial customers are or what features they'll want. One option is to start developing an entire full-featured first release of the product, with every feature the founders can think of. We now know this results in wasted engineering effort, time and cash, as customers don't use, want or need most of the features developed without their input.

Another path is to put Product Development on hold until the Customer Development team can find customers who can provide adequate feedback. The risk here is lost time and no product for customers to provide feedback against. A third, more productive approach is to develop the core features of the product (incrementally and iteratively with agile engineering methods), with the feature list driven by the vision and experience of the company's founders. *This is a minimum viable product.*

The goal of customer discovery is to test your understanding of the customer's problem and see if your proposed solution will prompt him to use or buy the product based on its most important features alone. Most users want finished products, but earlyvangelists are the perfect target for the MVP. Tailor the initial product release to satisfy their needs. If no one thinks your MVP solution is interesting or sufficient, iterate or pivot until an adequate number say "yes."

The shift in thinking to an incremental and iterative MVP as opposed to a fully featured first product release is important. Engineers tend to make a product bigger and more perfect. The MVP helps them focus the most important and indispensable features. Your goal in having an MVP is not to gather feature requests to change the product or to make the feature set larger. Instead, the goal is to put the MVP in front of customers to find out whether you understood the customer problem well enough to define key elements of the solution. Then you iteratively refine the solution. If, and only if, no customers can be found for the most important features of the MVP, bring customers' additional feature requests to the product development team. In the Customer Development model, feature requests to an MVP are by exception and iteration rather than by rule. This eliminates the endless list of feature requests that often delay first customer ship and drive product development teams crazy.

⇨ MVPs for Web/Mobile Are Different

Web/mobile businesses conduct customer discovery differently from those in the physical channel. They can reach hundreds or thousands more customers by combining online and face-to-face interactions. They place a greater emphasis on customer acquisition, activation, and referrals. Web/mobile minimum viable products can be developed faster and delivered earlier, accelerating the discovery process. When delivered, they can conduct more tests with customers, with more granular customer-response data. This results in a faster iteration of the problem statement, the proposed solution, and the MVP itself.

For web/mobile startups, here's how the MVP is used in the discovery process:

Phase	Page	Action	Goal
Prepare for Customer Engagement	200	-Build Lo-Fi MVP -Engage customers by driving a little traffic to the MVP.	See if the vision of the need/problem matches customers and how important this problem is to them.
Low Fidelity MVP Problem Test	211	-Gradually increase the number of invitations to the MVP. Closely study their behaviors on arrival and assess activities. -Keep meeting customers face to face. -Consider if it can scale.	-Understand the problem/need you are solving and how to explain it. -Does the customer care?
High Fidelity MVP Test	237	-Open the door and invite more customers in. -Watch for the velocity of customer activation.	-Determine whether customers will engage with or buy the product or use the site or app. (solution test) -Discover enough passionate, enthusiastic Earlyvangelists who clearly believe the product solves their problem.
Optimize getting more customers	380	Hang the "open" sign and the race to get customers begins.	-Optimize get customers strategy.

Developing the Minimum Viable Product for a Web/Mobile Product *(Figure 3.2)*

Use the Business Model Canvas as The Customer Discovery Scorecard

Often there's a lack of a shared and clear understanding of the business model throughout the company. This customer discovery step uses Alexander Osterwalder's business model canvas to diagrammatically illustrate how a company intends to make money. As shown in Figure 3.3 the canvas represents any company in nine boxes, depicting the details of a company's product, customers, channels, demand creation, revenue models, partners, resources, activities and cost structure. (We described the business model canvas in detail in the Customer Development Manifesto.)

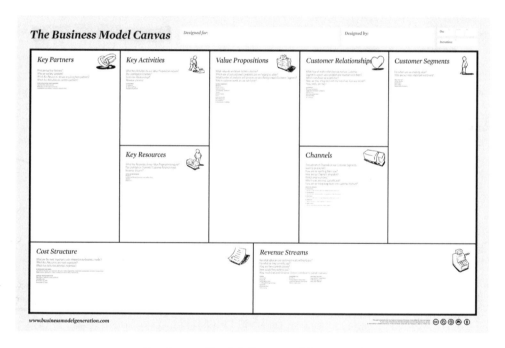

Business Model Canvas (Figure 3.3)

In this phase you'll develop a one- or two-page brief about each of the following boxes in the business model canvas:

- Market Size: how big the opportunity is
- Value Proposition, Part 1: the product/service, its benefits and minimum viable product

- Customer Segments: who the customer is and what problems the product solves
- Channels: how the product will be distributed and sold
- Customer Relationships: how demand will be created
- Value Proposition, Part 2: market-type hypothesis and competitive set/differentiation
- Key Resources: suppliers, commodities, or other essential elements of the business
- Key Partners: other enterprises essential to success of the business
- Revenue Streams: revenue and profit sources and size

When you first draft your initial hypotheses your canvas begins to fill up, looking like Figure 3.4.

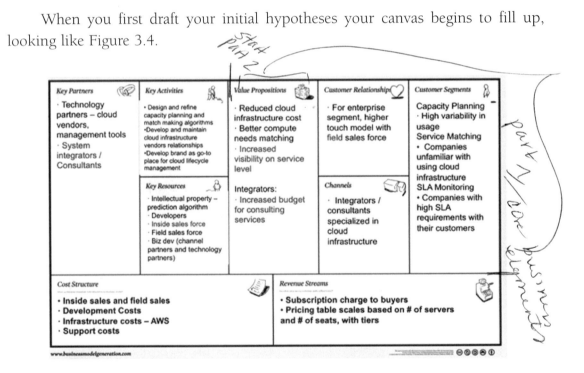

Sample Business Model Canvas—Initial Hypotheses (Figure 3.4)

But in addition to using the business model canvas as a static snapshot of the business at a single moment, frozen in time, Customer Development uses the canvas as a "scorecard" to track progress in searching for a business model.

Once a week update the canvas to reflect any pivots or iterations, highlighting in red the changes from the last week.

Then after you and your team agree on the changes to your business model, integrate them into what becomes your new canvas for the week (the accepted changes in red are then shown in black). During the next week any new changes are again shown in red. Then the process repeats each week – new changes showing up in red. Then a new canvas used for the week.

This method highlights the changes over time for your and the team's reference. Figure 3.5 shows how the canvases will look over time.

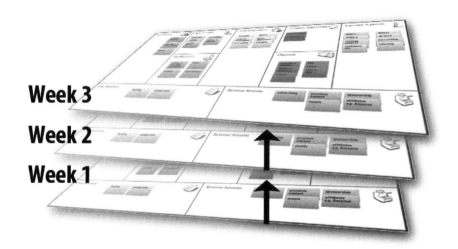

Using the Business Model Canvas as a Weekly Scorecard *(Figure 3.5)*

Had they read this book, and gotten out of the building, the folks at Iridium might have saved billions by learning just how small the market for their business had become. It would have allowed them to search for alternatives and survival.

To sum up the customer discovery philosophy: whether there's product/market fit by finding earlyvangelists, understanding their needs, and verifying that the initial minimum viable product solves a problem they'll eagerly pay to have solved. And if not, use near-continuous customer feedback to drive agile, frequent changes in product and business model alike.

As you complete the hypothesis development, your business model canvas quickly becomes multi-dimensional. You are really developing three initial canvases:

- Core elements of the business model itself (value proposition, channel, etc.)
- Hypotheses you have for each element of the business model (such as "people will want these features, "or "customers will buy our product because…")
- And a layer outlining the key pass/fail tests you will use to get face-to-face with customers and use their feedback to convert your hypotheses into facts.

Overview of Customer Discovery

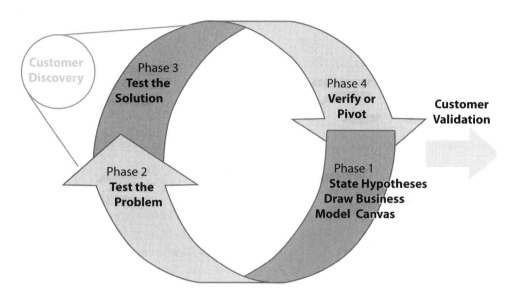

Customer Discovery: Overview of the Process (Figure 3.6)

Customer Discovery has Four Phases

Phase 1 deconstructs the founders' vision into the nine parts of the business model canvas (product, customers, channels, demand creation, revenue models, partners, resources, activities and cost structure). Then your team writes one-page briefs about each of the hypotheses, including the list of experiments or tests you'll need to conduct to prove or disprove each one.

In Phase 2 you conduct experiments to test your "problem" hypotheses. This helps you understand how important the problem is and how big it can become. You do so by testing most elements of the business model, including the value proposition, pricing, channel strategy, and sales process. Your goal is to turn hypotheses into facts or discard them if they're wrong, and replace them with new hypotheses. In the process, you'll gain a deep understanding of customers' business, workflow, organization, and product needs. When all the facts are in, update your results on the canvas.

⇨ Web-based products and channels often implement much of Phase 2 online in near-real time.

In Phase 3, you test your "solution," presenting your value proposition (product, pricing, features, and other business model components) and the minimum viable product to customers and compare their responses to the "pass/fail" goals you developed earlier. ⇨ For a web-based product, the MVP is a live site, a live demo, or a feature or piece of functionality or content. The goal is not to sell the product, but to validate how well you understood the problem in Phase 2 when you heard customers say, "Even these minimum features solve our problems," or, "I need this product." Ideally, customers ask, "When can I get it?"

⇨ Online, customers should engage and interact, spend time on it or with it, appear in droves, come back again and again, and bring their friends.

In Phase 4 you stop and assess the results of the experiments you've conducted and verify that you have:

- a full understanding of customers' problems, passions, or needs
- confirmed the value proposition solves problems, passions or needs
- determined that a sizable volume of customers exists for the product
- learned what customers will pay for the product
- made certain the resulting revenue should deliver a profitable business

With your product features and business model validated, decide whether you have learned enough to go out and try to sell a select your product to a few visionary customers, or whether you need to go back to customers to learn some more. If, and only if, you are successful in this step do you proceed to customer validation.

That's customer discovery in a nutshell. The remainder of this section details each of the phases just described. (The checklists in Appendix A summarize.)

Now let's get started.

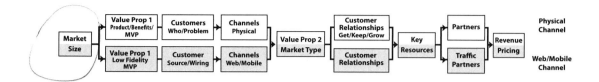

CHAPTER 4

Customer Discovery, Phase One:
State Your Business Model Hypotheses

THE DIAGRAM ABOVE IS AN OVERVIEW OF PHASE 1 of customer discovery. Note that hypotheses for physical products often differ from web/mobile products. Where the hypothesis issues differ, each is described separately, physical startups in the upper, lighter-tinted row and web/mobile startup considerations in the lower, darker row. Since physical startups are presented first, readers of the web/mobile process will be referred back to start with the physical-channel section when it's appropriate.

This phase starts by developing a rough market size estimate to size the opportunity for your new venture. Next, the rest of customer discovery uses the business model canvas to record short summaries (*hypothesis briefs*) of initial hypotheses about your business. The canvas provides a picture of the business model on a single page, serving as a reference for team members and a scorecard keeping track of pivots and iterations as the company's business model changes.

The hypothesis briefs provide the detail, but remain short and to the point, with enough clarity to ensure that all team members understand their meaning. No hypothesis brief should be more than two pages, and as a rule, bullet points are far more helpful than paragraphs or even sentences. Almost every hypothesis concludes with the experiments you'll use in phases 2 and 3, when you're out of the building talking to customers to prove or disprove the hypothesis. Sometimes you'll even need to get out of the building to do some research just to figure out what tests to conduct and the kinds of results to shoot for.

Initially, some briefs may seem shockingly empty. Not to worry—these briefs serve as an outline. The team will return to them often, filling in the blanks and modifying original hypotheses with new facts learned along the way.

Market Size Hypothesis (Physical and Web/Mobile)

This brief is an outlier—it doesn't directly map onto the business model canvas. But because there's nothing worse than spending years in a startup only to discover that it can never grow to more than a few million dollars in revenue, the market size hypotheses help you size the opportunity of your startup market. Estimating market size helps determine whether the payoff from your new venture is worth the toil, sweat and tears, or whether you're about to do your first pivot.

Aligning investor and founder objectives clearly at the outset is good "life insurance" for founders, since few disconnects cost founders their jobs more quickly than disputes over goals and gold.

...few disconnects cost founders their jobs more quickly than disputes over goals and gold.

The thinking applies regardless of whether it's in the physical or web/mobile channel. With one exception: buyable startups (see page xviii) founded for a fast sale to a larger-platform player like Facebook or Google. Buyable startups should consider the size of what is often a microsegment of a large market.

Market opportunities are fueled by three ingredients: a large number of potential active users or customers, clear future-user growth in a market with rapid and predictable growth, and the opportunity to attract active customers or users.

TAM, SAM and Target Market

Marketers and their investors typically think of market size as three numbers; TAM (total addressable market), SAM (served available market) and target market. The TAM for makers of a new smartphone app might be the 1 billion total smartphone owners worldwide, but if the application is available only in English or works only on an iPhone, the SAM or potential market served is far smaller. And the target market might be Apple App Store customers, so your next step would be to estimate what percentage of those shoppers might actually buy. Each estimate further narrows the target market.

TAM = how big is the universe
SAM = how many can I reach with my sales channel
Target Market *(for a startup)* = who will be the most likely buyers

TAM, SAM and Target Market *(Figure 4.1)*

Estimating TAM and SAM and target market is a good starting point for the market size hypothesis. Customers will help turn these hypotheses into facts.

A top-down estimate is a first step. Use industry-analyst reports, market-research reports, competitors' press releases, university libraries—and discussions with investors and customers to "size" the overall market. Use whatever metric is most appropriate—units, dollars, page views, eyeballs, whatever.

A note of caution: First-time entrepreneurs are seduced by market size data from research firms. They should keep in mind that market research firms are excellent at predicting the past. (If they were geniuses at predicting the future, they'd be running hedge funds.)

Therefore, a bottom-up estimate is usually more realistic for startups. Toy makers, for example do this quite easily: there are roughly 2 million girls born in the U.S. each year, and half can't afford a $90 doll, so the U.S. target market for a new doll for girls age 6 to 8 is at most 3 million.

Market research firms are great at predicting the past.

In assessing an *existing* or *re-segmented market*, be sure to consider the adjacent markets that customers might switch from. Millions of BlackBerry users traded in their RIM devices when Apple's iPhone arrived, for example. Will the startup's new product have the competitive power to encourage switching? Count only the switchable subset and beware of long-term contracts, service contracts, and "sunk costs" like training or installation, all of which are often hidden barriers to switching.

Of course, nobody can compute a *new market's* size today, since it doesn't exist yet. What to do? Estimate the opportunity based on proxies and adjacent markets. See if there are any comparable companies. Have others grown as fast as the estimate? Why will this startup perform similarly?

⇨ Sizing the web/mobile market

While some like to quote web/mobile market sizes in terms of eyeballs, page views, downloads, referrals, or hours, at the end of the day it's still about revenue. What confuses new entrepreneurs is that web/mobile markets may be multi-sided—the users (who may not pay) may be measured in eyeballs, page views, downloads, referrals, or hours, but there had better be payers who offer dollars for access to those users.

For example, market size could be calculated by multiplying the number of eyeballs by the dollars that each eyeball is worth to a payer.

Gathering a massive, growing audience efficiently and cost-effectively is job No. 1 for most web/mobile products (e-commerce is often an exception, as are niche vertical sites). This is the time to develop an initial hypothesis about where that audience might come from and how big it can become. At this stage, most web/mobile startups follow the Google/Facebook/YouTube strategy: gather a (hopefully massive) audience first and be sure it "sticks." Monetize it later.

Gathering a massive, growing audience efficiently and cost-effectively is job No. 1.

Calculating the audience without understanding who will pay money to access that audience is a mistake. In a multi-sided market, you need to estimate all sides of the market, particularly the side that will pay.

An easy way to gauge the "size" of a web market involves the free use of Google tools. Brainstorm all the keywords that prospective customers might use to find your product or site—"multiplayer monster games," "computer games with monsters," "creatures and online games" and on and on. The Google keyword tool summarizes how many people are searching for each keyword. Make some allowances for overlap or duplication in a month and this is yet another way to develop an estimate of market size. It's especially effective at identifying whether you're in a market that's too small to pursue—one where the total number of searches is measured in thousands, for example.

Another way to approach the market-sizing question is the "30/10/10" law of web/mobile "physics," first posited by leading venture capitalist Fred Wilson. Wilson observed that, across his entire portfolio of mobile apps, games, social and music services, this law applies consistently:

- Thirty percent of registered users and those downloading mobile apps will use the service each month.
- Ten percent of registered users and those downloading mobile apps will use the service each day.
- Concurrent users of a real-time service will seldom exceed 10 percent of the number of daily users.

Industry research will also help immensely in the market-sizing exercise. Learn how to research your market in Phase 2, Customer Understanding (page 218), which describes web-specific research tools and tactics.

Value Proposition Hypothesis (Part 1/Physical)

Start this step by filling out your canvas with the value proposition hypothesis: the product or service being offered to customers. You'll include details about the product, its features and benefits, as well as the company's long-term product vision and its initial minimum viable product. Think of the value proposition as a contract between the customer and your company where the customer "hires" your startup to solve a problem.

Write a series of briefs that capture the founders' hours of thinking, talking, and brainstorming about the product in three separate, specific areas:

- Product Vision
- Product Features & Benefits
- Minimum Viable Product (MVP)

The product development team produces much of the product brief, one of the few times it's asked to engage in a paper exercise. They put key value proposition hypotheses down on paper and turn them into briefs agreed to by all executives..

Product Vision

This portion of the value proposition brief captures your vision for what you want your successful company to become.

Over time, successful companies are usually more than a single product. What's your long-term vision for your company? What do you want to ultimately change? Are you going to do it with a series of products? How do you expand into adjacent markets? How do you get people to change behavior? What's the world look like three years after you arrive on the scene? Five years after?

Shape a long-term vision with a short narrative told in bullet points. For example in the 1990s, a financial software company might have described its user story this way:

- Consumers hate to reconcile their checkbooks
- We think we can develop a computer program that emulates a checkbook.
- It will automate all the hard and tedious parts of home banking
- Consumers can use it to pay bills by connecting to the Internet
- Millions of people will start using home computers to do something they never did before
- Today small businesses use bookkeepers to keep their books
- After we succeed in automating consumers we will expand into financial software for small businesses
- Millions of small businesses will start using computers to do something they never did before

Suddenly, the company vision is clear with a few simple bullet points. The vision is critical because the Customer Development team has to paint a picture for early-vangelists of what the product will look like a year or two into the future.

Only because earlyvangelists are buying into your total vision will they spend money for an incomplete, buggy, barely functional first product.

In the long-term vision, the product team specifies the delivery date for the MVP and for follow-on products or enhancements to the product as far out as the team can see (18 months to three years). In startups, this request usually elicits a response like, "How can I come up with future dates when we barely know the first MVP delivery date?" Reassure your anxious product development team that this first pass at a schedule isn't set in stone.

Only because earlyvangelists are buying into your total vision will they spend money for an incomplete, buggy, barely functional first product. The vision should convince everyone involved that this is an opportunity worth the investment of millions of dollars and years of work. Ironically, few startups end up with products that look like their initial vision.

Finally, it's never too early to think about strategic issues:

- Will it create network effects? A single fax machine was useless but became more valuable as more people acquired them
- Can you price it with a predictable pricing model—i.e., subscriptions versus one-time sales?
- Can you create customer lock in/high switching costs? Think of trying to get your data from Facebook or from your doctor's office
- Can you have high gross margins?
- Does it have organic demand versus marketing spend? Companies with organic demand have business models that don't require expensive marketing. Think Google, eBay, Baidu, Skype, etc.

Product Features and Benefits

This portion of the value proposition brief captures what the product is and why people will use or buy it.

While many engineers think new products are all about product features, the product is just one of many elements of a successful startup. The *product features list* is a one-page document consisting of one- or two-sentence summaries of the top 10 (or fewer) features of the complete product vision. (If there's some ambiguity in describing a particular feature, include a reference to a more detailed engineering document.)

Essentially, the feature list is Product Development's contract with the rest of the company. The biggest challenge will be deciding what features will ship in what order. Developing the MVP will start the prioritization process. Once you get out of the building, customers will guide the process as they begin interacting with the earliest version of the MVP.

Think of features as the things engineering is building, and think of benefits as the problem you're solving for the customer.

Think of benefits as the problem you're solving for the customer.

Once you have the feature list, you shape a product *benefits* list by describing the specific product benefits *as seen through customers' eyes*. (Something new? Something better? Faster? Cheaper?) Then develop a "user story." This short narrative explains *what job the product will do*. How will it solve a problem that customers are eager to fix, or fulfill a need they have? Ideally, the product solves a mission-critical problem, delivers a compelling, exciting consumer benefit, or addresses an unspoken need. (Saves money or time? Relieves a symptom? Fun, relaxing, faster? Better? Cheaper?) A bank-software company might describe its user story this way:

- Customers always face long lines at our bank on Fridays and on the first and last days of the month when they come in to cash or deposit checks; they get frustrated and often angry
- We think we lose 5 percent to 8 percent of our customers as a result of frustration
- We can measure lost profits of about $500,000 a year, significant because it's 7 percent of the total
- This $150,000 software package halves the time it takes to make a deposit and will be even faster in later versions

When thinking about product features, remember that a value proposition can take the form of a higher-performance product or a less expensive or more convenient product. It can address a market niche or segment or solve problems in a new or different, faster or cheaper way. Sometimes the product's physical or visual design or even the brand itself may be different enough to command attention. Products don't always solve problems, either. While most business products do, consumer goods more often serve *needs* in areas as diverse as online gaming, social networks, fashion, and cars.

It's normal for marketers to want to describe the product benefits, but it's likely that marketing doesn't have facts about customers yet, just opinions. In a start-up, the founders and Product Development are likely to be the ones with the facts. So at this point, the marketing people would be wise to bite their tongues and listen to the product development group's assumptions about the features and exactly how they'll benefit customers. These engineering-driven benefits represent hypotheses you'll test against real customer facts. In Phase 2, you'll get out of the building to collect this feedback directly from customers.

Minimum Viable Product (MVP)

The MVP is the final portion of this first value proposition brief. It's a concise summary of the smallest possible group of features that will work as a stand-alone product while still solving at least the "core" problem and demonstrating the product's value.

The MVP is:

- a tactic for cutting back on wasted engineering hours
- a strategy to get the product into earlyvangelists hands as soon as possible
- a tool for generating maximum customer learning in the shortest possible time

Start the MVP brief by defining what needs to be learned—and from whom. Customer Development efforts will engage a very small group of early visionary and passionate customers to guide product-feature development until a profitable business model emerges. The sooner the MVP is in their hands, the sooner feedback can arrive. Rather than asking customers explicitly about feature X, Y or Z, one approach to defining the MVP is to ask, "What is the smallest or least complicated problem that the customer will pay us to solve?"

This approach runs counter to the typical cry for more features, which is often based on what the competitors have or what the last customer visited had to say.

The MVP is the inverse of what most sales and marketing groups ask of their development teams.

A goal of Customer Development is to *understand what not to ship.*

Startups tend to collect a list of features that, if added to the product, would get just that one additional customer to buy. Soon a 10-page feature list evolves just to sell to 10 customers. That's a plan for failure. The goal of Customer Development is *not* to collect features from customers. *It's to understand what not to ship.* The perfect feature list is just one paragraph long and can be sold to thousands or millions of customers. A core tenet of the Customer Development Manifesto is "less is more." Minimize the number of features *not used* by getting a MVP into customers' hands as quickly as possible. An easy guideline: "no new features until you've exhausted the search for a business model."

Value Proposition 1: "Low Fidelity" MVP Hypothesis (Web/Mobile)

⇨ The MVP brief is a concise summary of the low fidelity web/mobile features that will work as a stand-alone product.

The first two MVP steps—crafting the company's long-term vision and listing the product's features and benefits—are virtually identical to those outlined in the preceding physical MVP section, so they aren't repeated here (refer to pages 76-81). Review those steps and develop those hypothesis statements before starting here.

The low fidelity MVP tests whether you've accurately identified a problem that customers care about.

In web/mobile channels, the MVP plays an even more important role than it does in the physical channel. It exposes the product to prospects as early as possible, even as continuous deployment adds new features, functionality or graphics. A low fidelity MVP can be as simple as a single web page used to gather customer feedback about the problem the product will solve. For web-based startups using agile development and continuous deployment, the delivery date for the low fidelity MVP is basically Day One. Ideally, though, it's a snapshot of the product as it exists on that day in the agile development process, in its "quick and dirty" form, even though that form will evolve almost every day.

Even the earliest MVP versions should include some way for interested users to register or self-identify, typically by leaving their e-mail addresses to receive updates. These early users will be helpful throughout the customer discovery process and beyond.

Web/Mobile channels will test both a low fidelity and a hi-fidelity MVP. The low- and hi-fidelity MVPs are used very differently: the low fidelity MVP tests whether you've accurately *identified a problem that customers care about* (based on user visits to your site, e-mail received, demos played, etc.), while the hi-fidelity MVP, detailed in Phase 3, will later test whether the product is on the right path to solving that problem (based on orders received, users' stays on the site, users' recommendations to others, etc.). Later, during customer validation, when the hi-fidelity MVP is exposed to many more customers, it should look and operate much more like a finished product. Taken together, the low and high fidelity MVP tests help establish product/market fit.

Write a User Story instead of a Feature List

A "user story" is important in web/mobile channels, where intense competition and millions of online products and properties often make product differentiation harder to "nail." For example: There are thousands of websites for nurses, and a user story can help explain the need for a new one. Here's one: Until now, operating-room nurses had trouble talking to one another about their stresses and "doctor problems" for fear of spawning gossip or incurring the wrath of HR. Now "ORNurse," "Nurseconfidential.net" allows these specialized nurses to:

- interact and chat anonymously with their peers nationwide and beyond
- pose questions to fellow nurses in similar situations and collect a variety of advice
- obtain advice anonymously from legal, HR, and clinical professionals
- send private messages to people they'd like to talk with personally

- post anonymous comments about specific doctors, problems, or patient situations
- get a daily e-mail summary of what's going on at the site

While this isn't exactly a "feature list," it provides a good sense of the product vision, its features and benefits, and why the site will attract a hard-to-reach audience.

Customer Segments: Who/Problem Hypothesis (Physical)

This brief describes who the customers are (the customer types) and what problems, needs or passions they have. It includes five components:

- customer problems, needs or passions
- customer types
- customer archetypes
- a day in the life of customer
- organizational map and customer influence map

The Customer Problem, Need or Passion

Products are sold because they solve a problem or fill a need. (See the bank teller story in Value Proposition, page 79.) Understanding problems and needs involves understanding their sources. Get out of the building to discover how customers experience the problem and why (and how much) it matters to them. Understand the organizational impact problem, and the intensity of pain it causes the company/family/consumer. Use a simple "problem recognition scale" for each important type of customer (Figure 4.2). Customers will express:

- a *latent problem*: they have a problem but don't know it
- a *passive problem*: they know of the problem but aren't motivated or aware of the opportunity to change
- an *active (or urgent) problem*: they recognize a problem or passion and are searching for a solution but haven't done any serious work to solve the problem
- a *vision*: they have an idea for solving the problem and even have cobbled together a home-grown solution, but are prepared to pay for a better one

Study the problem. Is your product solving a mission-critical company problem or satisfying a must-have consumer need? Is your product a must-have or a nice-to-have? When your product solves a problem that costs customers sleep, revenue, or profits, things are definitely looking up. When it's the hottest "new new thing" in town, whether that town is physical or virtual, capitalize on the opportunity. The best startups discover a situation where customers have tried to build a solution themselves—they simultaneously discover both a mission-critical problem and a customer-visualized solution. Wow. Now simply convince the customer that if they build it themselves, they're detouring into a different, usually non-core business—*your* new business!

The best startups discover a situation where customers have tried to build a solution themselves.

Then again, not every product solves problems. Some provide fun or information, others glamour or romance. Social networks don't solve problems but sure have millions of visitors—they fill consumer *needs and desires*. Even if it's fun or pure luxury, recognize that consumers require justification for a purchase.

After identifying the customer types, craft a hypothesis about their emotional wants and desires. Describe how to convince these customers that the product can deliver an emotional payoff: glamour, beauty, wealth, prestige, a hot date or lost pounds.

Customer Types

Whether a customer is spending time on a social network, buying a stick of gum, or purchasing a million-dollar telecom system, every sale involves a set of decision-makers. Thus customer analysis starts with an understanding of what types of customers to approach. Chances are several people in a number of categories have problems that your product can solve or needs or ambitions that it can satisfy. Customer discovery identifies and probes these different needs. Customer types include:

End Users: The day-to-day users of a product push the buttons, touch the product, use it, love it, and hate it. A deep understanding of their needs and motivations is vital, recognizing that the end user may often have the least influence in the sales or adoption process. This is typically true in complex corporate sales.

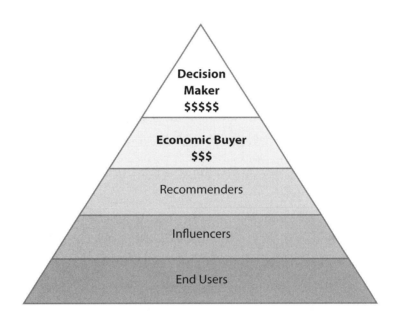

Customer Types (Figure 4.2)

Influencers: At times, the most powerful pressure on a customer's buying decisions may not be something the startup did directly but something done or said by someone who's uninvolved. In every market or industry, online and off, a select group of individuals pioneers the trends, styles and opinions. Ask a famous dress designer when a movie star wears her dress to the Oscars. Or consider the effect of thousands of people clicking their Facebook "like" button or Tweeting about a product, ad or service. Sometimes the influencers are paid bloggers or pundits in market-research firms. They may be kids or celebrities who wear the latest fashions.

Include the target list of outside influencers and address how they'll be reached. Free product, payments, celebrity events, free computers and online memberships are among the many options.

Recommenders: They influence purchase decisions but differ from influencers because their opinions can make or break a sale. A recommender could be a widely read blogger raving about a new online game, a department head saying any new PCs should come from Dell, a hospital committee approving a new medical device, or a spouse with a particularly strong brand preference. It can also be an external force like Gartner Group, Forrester Research, Martha Stewart or Consumer Reports.

Economic buyers: They sit further up the decision chain and often control or approve the purchase or budget. (Important people to know!) They can be corporate VPs, office managers, insurance companies with issuing reimbursement codes, teens with allowances, or spouses with vacation budgets.

Decision-makers: They may be the economic buyers or reside even higher up in the decision-making hierarchy. Decision-makers wield the ultimate purchase authority and are sometimes called UDMs (ultimate decision-makers) or VITOs (very important top officers) or perhaps "Mom," "Dad" or "honey." Be sure to understand their motivations.

Saboteurs: They can lurk anywhere (as saboteurs do) and hold titles including CFO, CIO, child, spouse, or purchasing agent with "friends." They can be found in strategic planning departments or in your own home, where their veto can slow things dramatically. Find them. Identify patterns that reveal where they're hiding in the decision process.

Later, during customer validation, knowing all the players in detail will be essential. For now, simply recognize that the customer is more complicated than a single individual.

Customer Archetypes

Remember the axiom "A picture is worth a thousand words"? There's no better way for the startup team to visualize its customer targets than to take the time to depict each of the key customer types—the end user and the decision-maker at a minimum (at least make a few sketches or doodles). Customer archetypes help the team visualize who will buy or use the product and helps crystallize product strategy, customer acquisition, and more.

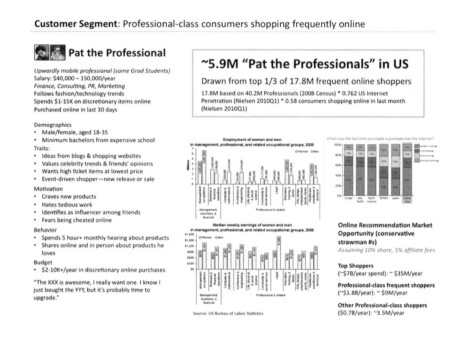

Customer Archetype *(Figure 4.3)*

In a business-to-business sale, does the end user work in an office, a cubicle or a boiler room? Is he or she a business traveler, a presenter, or a heads-down number cruncher? Is the decision-maker in a corner office, is she a scientist in a research lab with a wall lined with prestigious degrees and awards, or is she on the factory floor?

To understand more about customer archetypes and how they're used, review a detailed discussion in the next section, "Customers/Source—Web/Mobile." Once you've read that, create a comprehensive view of each key customer archetype, using the data you collected.

Consumer archetypes are generally easier to create than business-to-business, where relationships are far more complex. Identify as many hypotheses about the buyer's demographic and psychographic profile as possible. Is the buyer affluent, fashion-conscious, healthy and active? Married with pets and toddlers or teens? In a house, an apartment, or a trailer park? These characteristics will influence many aspects of the business model, including customer relationships, channel, and revenue model.

A Day in the Life of a Customer

One of the most powerful ways to understand your customers, whether they're consumer or business customers, is to discover how they "work" and write it down, delineating a day in their life.

…discover how customers "work" and write it down, delineating a day in their life.

In the case of businesses, this step requires a deep understanding of a target company on many levels. Let's use selling software to a bank as an example. How a bank works isn't something you'll discover by cashing a check. You want to know how the world looks from a banker's perspective. To begin with, how do the potential end users of the product (the tellers) spend their days? What products do they use? How much time do they spend using them? How would life change for these users after they have your product? Unless you've been a bank teller, these questions should leave you feeling somewhat at a loss, but how are you going to sell a product to a bank to solve tellers' problems if you don't understand how they work?

(If you're not an experienced salesperson, this whole notion of getting out of the building can sound intimidating. The "Get Out of the Building" section of customer discovery, Chapter 5, describes how to set up your first meetings.)

Now run this exercise from the perspective of branch managers. How do they spend their day? How would your new product affect them? Run it again, this time thinking about bank presidents. What on earth do they do? What do they read? Who influences their decisions? How will your product affect her? And if you're installing a product that connects to other software the bank has, you're going to have deal with the IT organization. How do the IT people spend their day? What other software do they run? How are their existing systems configured? Who are their preferred vendors? Are they standing at the door with confetti and Champagne waiting to welcome yet another new company with yet another product?

The answers are easy. Asking the right questions is hard.

Business products are generally purchased because they solve problems, so a deep understanding of the buyer is required. If you're selling a retailer point-of-sale tools, for example, can someone on your team work behind a busy counter for a few days? There's no better way to understand than to dive in. Learn how prospective users currently solve their problems, online or off, and how they'd do it differently using the new product. What will motivate these customers to buy? Draw a vivid and specific picture of a day in the life of the customer, and do the research in the same place where they do their work or have their fun, not in the company conference room or alone at a local Starbucks.

Finally, back to our banking example, do you know about trends in the banking industry? Is there a banking-industry software consortium? Are there bank software trade shows? Industry analysts? Unless you've come from your target industry, this part of your customer-problem brief may include little more than lots of question marks. That's OK. In customer development, the answers turn out to be easy; it's asking the right questions that's difficult. You'll be going out and talking to customers with the goal of filling in all the blank spots on the customer-problem brief.

For a consumer product, the same exercise is applicable. How do consumers solve their problems today? How would they solve their problems with your product? Would they be happier? Smarter? Feel better? Do you understand what will motivate these customers to buy?

Your final exam doesn't happen until you come back to the company and, in meetings with the product development team and your peers, draw a vivid and specific picture of a day in the life of your customer.

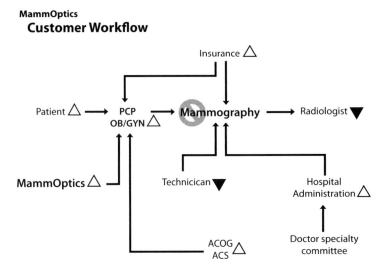

MammOptics
Customer Workflow

A Sample Organizational/Influence Map (Figure 4.4)

Organizational/Influence Maps

Now having a deeper understanding of a customer's typical day, you realize that except in rare cases, most customers don't work by themselves. Consumers interact with friends and family, while businesspeople interact with their colleagues. List the people who could influence a customer's buying decisions and draw a tentative diagram of the prospective customer and all the influences surrounding him or her. Also depict the product's impact on their day-to-day work or personal life. Then build a map showing potentially influential people who surround the user. At a large company, the diagram will be complex, with lots of initial unknowns.

Customer Segments: Source/Wiring Hypothesis (Web/Mobile)

⇨ When you're done with this brief, you'll have developed a customer archetype and be able to say things like, "We believe most of our customers are age-18-to-25 tech-savvy young urban professionals who use Macs and spend two hours a day on Facebook" or "Twenty-five percent of my customers read *Science* and *Nature* magazine religiously and want a better way to order chemical reagents and lab supplies." And you'll be able to understand and draw a day in the life of a customer and draw a consumer web influence map.

Start by reviewing the previous "customer segments/physical" hypotheses.

The Customer Archetype: a Guide to Who Your Customers Are

A customer archetype combines everything you know about your "most typical" customers or users into one or more complete profiles. (Obviously not every customer will look like this homogenized "average." In fact, you more than likely will have several archetypes.)

Compile the picture by gathering statistics about customers' demographics and behavior. (For help, see Customer Understanding in Phase 3, page 218.) Use Google Trends, Google Insights, and Facebook ads to look at web/mobile customer demographics. Use Crunchbase to look at who competitors are selling to. Interview people you think look most like your potential customers and understand who they are, what they do, and how they behave. Search online for studies, news articles, and reports about your target consumers. Study competitors' media choices, press coverage and annual reports. Most important, continue to update the archetype as you learn more about customers over time.

Archetype Highlights	Customer Acquisition Guidance
Age 40-55, high income	Use for targeting mass banner ad, textlink campaigns
Two working professionals	Don't advertise or promote during the workday; inefficient
Buy fresh gourmet produce	Reach these bloggers, co-promote with gourmet food sites
Drive luxury cars	Consider co-promotion offers from high-end auto Websites
Frequent business travelers	Send press releases to travel Web sites, bloggers
Cooks only on weekends	Don't run AdWords during the week to save dollars send e-mail blasts, Tweets, texts Thursday/Friday
Entertain friends at home often	Co-promote with home, entertainment sites, blogs

A Guide to Using Customer/Archetypes to Drive Strategy (Figure 4.5)

Are your target customers or users big executives, networking nannies, or teen gamers? Suburbanites or city dwellers? Single or married? Gather as much detail as possible. How old are they? How much do they earn? How much leisure time do they typically have and how much spending money? Focus on their web/mobile-device ownership or access: desktop, laptop, iPad, or smartphone—or all four? Are they loners or social-network heavyweights, and do they share sites and information generously with others? When they're online, are they alone at home or in a crowd at school? Use the detailed example in Figure 4.5 as a guide when developing yours.

"A Day-in-the-Life": a Guide to What Customers Do

How much time do your customers spend online in a typical 24-hour day? Is it at their desk, on a laptop, or on a handheld while driving? Your success depends on becoming a regular part of the customer's day, whether for information, social networking, play, or e-commerce. But what's the source of the "newfound" time they'll spend on your new site or using your new app?

Will they sleep less? Will they spend less time on Facebook or eBay? Will they spend less time goofing off at work to spend time at the new site?

What's the source of the "newfound" time they'll spend on your new site or using your new app?

Be sure to understand how they find out about new products. Are they religious readers of TechCrunch or *People*, game-review sites or news feeds? Do they Tweet often, and do they read Tweets from two people or 50? Text twice or 100 times a day, and to whom? Where do they go for information about products in general and products like yours, and how often and for how long?

Where will you find your customers? On the web, your customers can be anywhere: at niche websites, reading blogs, on Facebook and other social networks, or on social news sites. The could be Tweeting or reading Tweets, texting or engaging with other similar customers on forums, wikis, and more.

"Day in the Life" Highlights	Customer Acquisition Guidance
• Under 15 min/day on social nets	Facebook, social media a low marketing priority
• 3 texts daily, mostly with spouse	Forget Twitter for this audience
• Read cooking magazines, sites	Big PR push in this arena: recipes, press releases, etc.
• Watch celebrity chefs 2-3x/week	Try to get founders as guests on shows; co-promote
• Hour a day reading news sites	Reach food/lifestyle editors at news publications
• 20 min/day online not for work	Test before spending on e-mail blasts, online ad campaigns
• 45 min/day listening to NPR	Consider weekend sponsorship, send press releases, call in
• Talk/e-mail 15-20 same friends	Provide recipes, ideas, discounts to circulate to friends

A Guide to Using A Day-in-the-Life to Drive Strategy (Figure 4.6)

Create a "day in the life" scenario using 15- or 30-minute increments from wakeup to bedtime, paying close attention to time spent on web/mobile devices, specifying not only which device but what your customer is actually doing on the device and for how long: texting with friends, reading blogs (note which ones), playing mobile or social games (note which ones), shopping for shoes (note where), or posting pictures of her cat on Facebook?

Use the detailed example in Figure 4.6 as a guide when developing yours.

Summarize the archetype and day-in-a-life in a tight bullet-point format. Use those bullets to evaluate the potential value of activities you'll use to "get" customers when developing the upcoming Customer Relationships hypothesis. Figures 4.5 and 4.6 offer an example for a company selling down-loadable gourmet-cooking lessons targeting working couples who cook together, and try to do it creatively.

When the customer archetype and "day in the life" are complete, you now know what your customers look like, what they do with their days, and how to find them.

This example illustrates how the archetype and "day in the life" efforts can focus "customer acquisition" activity. While there's no such thing as perfect targeting in mass-marketing efforts, fine-tuning every "get customers" activity to "fish where the fish are" helps maximize the return on every customer-relationships dollar you'll spend.

Here's How to Create a Consumer Web Influence Map:

In the web/mobile world, influence maps (described on page 92) are as daunting and complex as they are influential. Think of the number of ways a consumer can be influenced online, and how your efforts can also influence the influentials themselves as part of the marketing process. "Dots" on the online influence map include blogs and chat rooms, authoritative websites, social networks, pundits, and referral or reference sites. In addition to delivering direct exposure, these influencers are often significant sources of "natural search" clicks that bring people to the website.

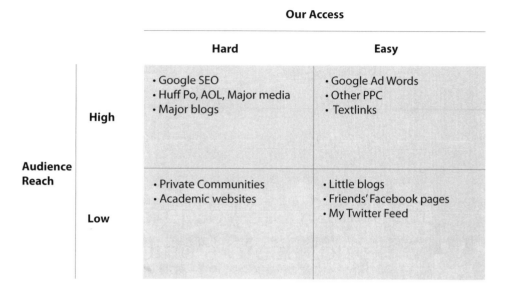

Consumer Web Influence Map (Figure 4.7)

Finally, recognize that in web/mobile apps, you may have multiple customer segments in a multi-sided market. In this case, "customers" can be users who may pay nothing for the product or service but provide a value to the supplier that it can resell to others. Google is the canonical "multi-sided" example: billions of "customers" search at Google for free, and millions of advertisers pay to reach them. Most social-network and content sites operate this way.

Channels Hypothesis (Physical)

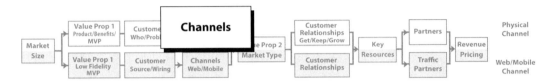

The channel brief describes how the product gets from company to customers.

The difference between physical and web/mobile channels is dramatic. In one, physical goods move from a loading dock to a customer or a retail outlet. In another, no human involvement is required, as the product is offered and sold online. (If the product itself is bits, it's both sold and delivered online.)

Physical channels have been around for centuries. They're an "intermediate customer" the startup has to deal with, and the barriers can be significant: high cost, long lead times, lack of control, and lack of promotion, to name a few. However, the rewards can be great. In the 20th century, physical distribution was especially important. Back then, the pinnacle of distribution was to be sold at Walmart, which welcomes 20 million Americans every day.

Consider whether your product fits the channel.

Most companies use both web/mobile and physical channels today. For example, even with some 10,000 massive physical stores, Walmart also invests heavily in walmart.com, an alternate channel, as most national retailers do. Most channel strategies, particularly for physical goods, today involve both physical and web/mobile channels. Whether a company uses a physical or web channel, it must generate customer demand and drive it into the sales channel. Physical and web channels employ very different demand-creation activities.

Consider Whether Your Product "Fits" the Channel

Different sales channels support different product price bands. For example, a salesperson selling enterprise software needs to bring in more than $1.5 million in annual revenue. On the other hand, few Smartphone applications sell for more than $10, minus the typical 30 percent app-store fee. Other e-tailers such as Amazon and bestbuy.com regularly sell products for hundreds if not thousands of dollars, sometimes keeping as much as half the gross revenue for themselves.

Be sure to factor all channel costs into the pricing hypothesis, since many channels charge for distribution, promotion, and even sometimes for placing products on the shelves or returning unsold merchandise to the company. Channel selection changes the company's revenue model, often dramatically, so be sure to revisit and update the revenue stream hypothesis based on the company's costs and net revenue when making the channel selection. (Always compute the revenue stream on a "net" basis, reflecting only revenue that will arrive in company coffers once the dust settles.)

Physical Channel Choices

Each physical distribution channel has its own unique set of strengths, weaknesses and costs. Some channels are "indirect," with a company selling to intermediaries sometimes called "resellers" (distributors, value-added resellers, dealers, etc.), who then sell to an end user. For example, when a handheld video-game maker wants to use local independent toy stores as a channel, those toy stores buy merchandise from a local or national distributor. Your company calls on the distributor but can't possibly afford to visit every independent toy store in America. In general, physical distribution is as complex as it is costly. Here are some of the most common alternatives.

Direct sales: These are salespeople you employ to either call on end users (consumers or businesses) or sell to other resellers.

Strengths: superb oversight and control; sales force focused on/dedicated to your company's products.

Weaknesses: Most expensive alternative; hard to find great talent and even more difficult to manage. The product price/margin may not support the expense.

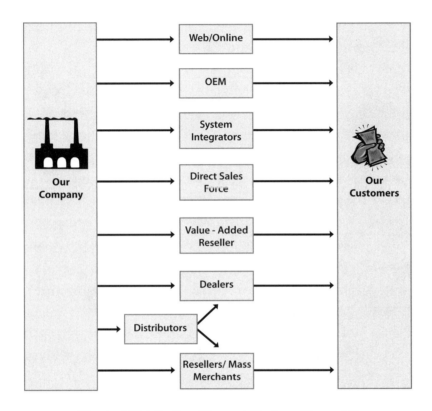

Physical Distribution Channel Choices *(Figure 4.8)*

Independent sales-rep firms: Independent salespeople represent multiple companies to a particular channel or chain, generally on a geographic basis (although some rep firms are national). They typically handle compatible but not competing product lines. They often work on commission, less often on retainer or a per-sale fee.

Strengths: Fast way to get national distribution at a variable cost with little upfront spending.

Weaknesses: They're loyal to their customer, not to you, the selling company; they're more of a conduit than a proactive marketer.

Systems integrators/value-added resellers (VARs): Unlike independent sales-rep firms, systems integrators/VARs add value to the products they sell (consulting, installation, or integration of additional products from other manufacturers). These organizations sell principally in technology industries in business-to-business sales. Systems integrators can be as small as a one- or two-man local IT consultant or vast global networks like Accenture and IBM.

> *Strengths*: Fast way to get national distribution and "whole product integration and installation" at a variable cost with no upfront cost to the company.

> *Weaknesses*: They're loyal to their customer, not to you; they are more a conduit than a proactive marketer. They require immense care and feeding such as promotional effort, hand-holding, training and incentives and as a rule are challenged to organize into a consistent national footprint and harder still to motivate.

Distributors/Resellers: Mid- and low-volume business and consumer products are often sold through distributors—intermediaries between manufacturer and retailer who do little more than stock the product locally and make it available in modest quantities to local stores. Some distributors (think CDW for computers, Arrow for electronic components, McKesson for pharmaceuticals) are national in scope and carry literally thousands of items. It's difficult and costly to get a distributor to promote a particular product.

> *Strengths*: They provide personal attention and can showcase and promote products they like.

> *Weaknesses*: Expensive. Generally have an "order taker" mentality and are rarely marketing/promotion partners. They may have the rights to return your product. Typically don't pay until the product is "sold through."

Dealers (aka Retailers): Unlike a distributor, a dealer has bought the product. Whether they're selling to businesses or consumers, dealers are usually independent retailers or small chains that display and promote what's generally a limited selection of products. Typically, they take a large markup (often double their cost, called a "keystone") on the wholesale price to compensate for higher operating costs and smaller volumes. Dealers seldom deal directly with "the factory" (your company), instead buying goods from a distributor or similar intermediary, in more modest quantities than, say, Costco. Consumer products are also still sold in "mom-and-pop" food and convenience stores.

Strengths: They provide personal attention and can showcase and promote products they like.

Weaknesses: It's hard and costly to build a new business using dealers as the principal channel.

Mass merchandisers: In the U.S., national chains from Walmart to Costco and Home Depot to 7-Eleven move massive amounts of merchandise to consumers. As a result, they wield enormous influence over manufacturers and extract their "pound of flesh" by often charging 50 percent of the retail price for carrying the product. They seldom launch new products without a successful "test market" in a modest number of stores. And when that test succeeds, the retailer asks for "slotting allowances" in the tens of thousands of dollars (in addition to their markup) for agreeing to display the product.

Strengths: Massive distribution and advertising/marketing potential.

Weaknesses: Long lead time to sell into (at times a year or more), extremely high cost, little marketing control and less opportunity to influence. May have the right to return unsold product months later. Pay painfully slowly, sometimes taking six months or more.

Original Equipment Manufacturers: OEMs buy a product to make it part of their larger product. A PC maker buys hard drives, semiconductors, circuit boards and keyboards from scores of manufacturers and assembles those products into a larger, usually more complex product for sale to end users. Issues a startup should consider:

The startup's brand, image and identity are subsumed by the OEM and often invisible to the end user. ("Intel inside" is a rare exception where the component's brand and reputation add value); your startup's success depends completely on the success of the OEM's product, not the startup's; and the OEM's sense of customer needs, issues, and reactions can obscure the startup's understanding of customer needs.

Strengths: Massive volume potential.

Weaknesses: Typically low-margin; no "branding benefit" or visibility for your startup.

Which Channel Should I Use?

A tragic mistake many startups make is to overreach on initial channel efforts. Until the company completes customer validation, it should pick a sales channel representing the greatest potential and focus on it to the exclusion of all others. Your company is still testing and expanding its hypotheses and needs to focus on learning. Don't try to launch a product via direct sales, chain stores and direct mail all at once—it's almost impossible to succeed at all three. The big exception, of course: physical-channel launches with simultaneous web-marketing (and sometimes sales) support.

Decisions about channel and pricing are interrelated, so develop the channel hypothesis while working simultaneously on the revenue and pricing hypothesis (page 180). For example, retail distribution cuts the company's revenue dramatically while direct sales may deliver more sales dollars but do so more slowly. When considering which channels to adopt, keep these criteria in mind:

- Are there established buying habits/practices in the product category?
- Does the channel strengthen the sales process? At what cost to the company?
- What are the price and complexity issues surrounding sale of the product?

Startups seldom get the channel strategy right the first time. Most technology startups, for example, assume that a direct sales force is the way to go, a hypothesis that's often proved wrong. It's almost always smartest—and safest—to first observe existing buying patterns and habits for similar products and product categories, since customers are demonstrating their preferred channel by spending their money there.

Channels Hypothesis (Web/Mobile)

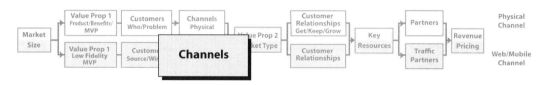

⇨ The distribution-channel brief describes how a web/mobile product gets from company to customers.

Begin this hypothesis development by reading the introduction to the physical channel section, just prior to this one. It addresses general channel strategy and costs of various channels and how they affect revenue.

Web/mobile channels can reach billions of wired people worldwide via computer, tablet, or handheld device. These channels are "always on," and never sleep, often literally in the palm of a consumer's hand and usually within arm's reach 24 hours a day. The reach, persistence and accessibility of the mobile channel has only just begun to affect the way people live, work, buy, and do.

A storefront or service solution accessible to literally billions of people every single minute of every day is a marketer's dream. Web/mobile products can be built quickly and enable a near-instant presence at potentially minimal cost—as little as $5 a month for a small online Yahoo store, for example. The company retains complete control, keeps nearly 100 percent of the revenue from its direct sales, and can change pricing, promotion and more in mere moments.

But the downside of this is that no customers "walk by" the website, and the burden and cost of generating awareness, traffic, and sales falls entirely on the company. (This is discussed in greater detail later in the customer relationship hypothesis on page 144.) Whether it's a website run by the company itself or Amazon.com or Apple's App Store, success in the web/mobile channel is almost entirely dependent on creating demand, attracting visitors to the site cost-effectively, and persuading them to engage with the product or buy it.

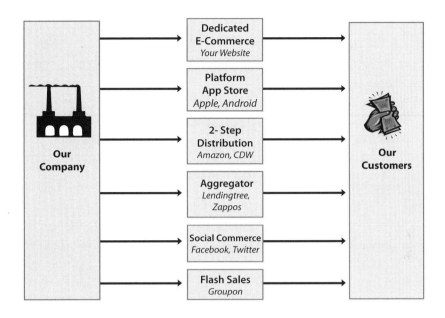

Web/Mobile Distribution Channel Choices (Figure 4.9)

Web/Mobile Channel Choices

Much like the physical distribution channel, each web/mobile channel has its strengths, weaknesses, and costs. (Increasingly, physical products are sold both online and in a physical channel.) As a startup you should pick *the one distribution channel* that provides the optimum balance between the company's value proposition, its costs and revenue model, and how customers prefer to buy. (You can add additional channels as you scale and grow.)

Pick one distribution channel. You can add additional channels as you scale and grow.

Dedicated e-commerce: Your company offers its products for sale directly on your own "dedicated" e-commerce website (which can be hosted anywhere). Customers access the site via a web browser. Whether the product is physical or web/mobile, consumers and businesses can learn details, see products, compare features, and complete the transaction at the single URL.

Strengths: Basic sites are easy to create, and deliver complete control of price, product presentation, inventory and more.

Weaknesses: Company must bear all challenges and costs of traffic-building and converting visitors to buyers.

Two-step e-distribution: This is how your company can reach many more customers by simultaneously selling your products on e-commerce sites that help generate awareness and demand. It is the most common web/mobile channel, encompassing every conceivable retailer from Amazon.com BestBuy.com, the Android and Apple app stores to small e-commerce sites. Distribution costs vary, with Amazon.com at the high end, charging 55 percent of retail prices to sell a physical book. For that hefty sum, this channel maintains inventory, packs and ships the goods, and collects payment. As a rule, the more the retailer does to generate consumer demand, the more it earns for making the sale.

Strengths: Fastest way to get national distribution at a variable cost with little upfront spending.

Weaknesses: Little control of on-site promotion or product visibility, except with extra spending.

Aggregators: The online equivalent of a physical shopping mall, usually in a single category. They aggregate consumers with common areas of interest and direct them through a web/mobile supermarket of products. Customers access the site via a web browser. Hundreds of mortgages and related financial products are available through LendingTree.com, while cloudshow-place.com provides a buyer's guide to hundreds of SAAS software tools, many of which can be purchased with a few clicks on the showplace. Diapers.com and Zappos (both owned by Amazon) aggregate baby and shoe products, respectively, from hundreds of manufacturers. Online trade shows for business-to-business products work in a similar way, creating the look and feel of a typical trade show and selling booths to marketers who provide demonstrations, white papers, and literature and can take orders in their virtual "booths."

Strengths: Fast way to get national distribution at a variable cost with little upfront spending.

Weaknesses: Hard to get visibility, on-site promotion and marketing; can be very costly.

Platforms that Operate as Channels

Mobile-app commerce: A web/mobile application distribution platform behaves in many ways just like a physical channel's retail stores. Mobile apps and many web apps and games are sold on web/mobile platforms. For example, Zynga's Farmville and other online games use Facebook, with hundreds of millions of users, as a "platform." Facebook offers its platform to thousands of other companies, turning its social network into a sales channel. Apple and Google's Android offer app stores that allow mobile users to buy everything from games to expense-account software for their iPhone or Android phones.

Dedicated marketplaces like the iPhone app store or the Android are the primary "platform-as-channel" marketplace for smartphone app. The Apple App Store charges 30 percent of retail pricing for downloadable iPhone applications. Smartphone apps dominated sales in this channel, but sales-force.com opened its AppExchange for business-to-business applications and other companies will follow.

Strengths: Massive reach in a fast-growing channel for games, software, shopping applications and more. It's a channel that's "always on" and quite handy (for literally many millions of consumers). This is an explosive business opportunity.

Weaknesses: Costly intermediaries, file-size constraints, product-presentation and payment challenges, operational complexity, extremely difficult to get consumers' attention or promote app or its marketing messages.

Social commerce: Social networks like Facebook and Twitter have moved quickly to turn their platforms into commerce to monetize their vast audiences. Customers access the site via a browser or dedicated app. Web/mobile currency and items for enhanced online gaming are already maturing, with many more vertical markets following in its lucrative footsteps.

Strengths: Fast, potentially massive distribution; great for product launches, awareness-building, and fast cash.

Weaknesses: Hard to create awareness and draw attention. Platforms take 50 percent or more as a cost of sales.

Flash sales: Flash sales offer a list of consumers deep discounts on branded merchandise with offers expiring in 24 or 48 hours. Gilt.com, Groupon and scores of clones assemble massive e-mail and social networking lists of consumers eager to obtain product discounts in specific categories or geographies. These social-commerce sites deliver the revenue and a volume of customers.

Flash sales can generate massive red ink in a hurry.

Strengths: Fast, potentially massive distribution; great for product launches, awareness-building, and fast cash.

Weaknesses: Often painfully expensive. End users often expect 50 percent discounts from retail price; manufacturer then pays 50 percent of its 50 percent sales price to the social-commerce site. Can generate massive red ink in a hurry.

Free-to-paid channel: While it's hard to say whether this is a platform, a channel, or a demand-creation strategy, it's an increasingly powerful way to create customer relationships, particularly among companies with web/mobile products that require little or no customization. A few fast-growing companies such as Zynga have used social networking to create vast audiences of free users of games like Farmville and MafiaWars. They provide a certain amount of game play for free—sometimes even all of it—but sell lots of web/mobile goods for real cash as they "hook" their users on the game.

If they don't convert and pay, you're dead.

Other game companies offer free, limited versions widely or full versions for a limited time ("seven-day free trial with your credit card") only to aggressively upsell free users to a more elaborate paid version. Recently, online tax-software companies have begun offering free federal-tax-return preparation online for simple tax returns, only to create a channel from which they can upsell people with more complex returns to prepare or charge them for state and municipal returns.

Strengths: Accelerates trial and adoption at relatively low cost. Terrific as a launch strategy.

Weaknesses: Free-to-pay is sexy but dangerous. You can get tons of users fast, but if they don't convert and pay, you're dead. Mapping profitable conversion of free to paid users makes or breaks the company.

Tests Can Help You Pick the Channel

For some products, the channel choice is obvious. There's one channel for an iPhone or iPad app, and another equally obvious channel for social games. Many products, however, will need to test both the cost-effectiveness and volume potential of several channels to determine where to put their energy, focus, and marketing dollars. A simple downloadable app, for example, might simultaneously test as many as three channels: an app store, the freemium model, and online retail. Design the test to spend roughly the same amount of money on each one, and—at a bare minimum—look to generate at least $2 in revenue if not more for every dollar spent on marketing (you can always improve it later). Then see which program delivers customers at the lowest cost per customer, and which delivers the greatest absolute number of customers.

Multi-Sided Markets Need Unique Channel Plans

At about the same time a physical channel company begins thinking about its sales channels, startups in multi-sided web/mobile markets should develop a hypothesis about their "other" side or, in this case, the "revenue channel."

Most multi-sided revenue channels function quite simply: they attract a large number of users and advertisers pay to reach them via textlinks, banner ads, in-game visibility or traditional online advertising. So the goal now is relatively straightforward, identify potential advertisers or agencies, and estimate how much they're willing to pay, how the sales process works, and whether the hypotheses about the revenue "side" of the market is valid. Beware the two deadliest advertising-related problems for multi-sided marketers: small and indistinct audiences.

The more distinct the audience—and the harder it is to aggregate—the more valuable it will be.

Small audiences: Advertising agencies like to spend big piles of their client's money with as few insertion orders (the advertising equivalent of a purchase order) as possible, and they want to reach massive numbers of people with each one. Getting an insertion order or even the opportunity to make a sales pitch to an advertising agency generally requires monthly page views in the many millions. Make sure the "payer" channel's potential is clear as part of the channel validation process.

Indistinct audiences: The online advertising world is so littered with unsold inventory that many advertisers buy huge volumes of banners, skyscrapers and textlinks through online advertising "networks" that aggregate dozens or hundreds of sites appealing to a specific group, such as teenagers. They collect all the unsold inventory at a very low, distressed price and roll it into one package that often includes hundreds of millions of impressions for one or several advertisers.

The more distinct the audience—and the harder it is to aggregate— the more valuable it will be. "Working mothers" and "generation Y" consumers can be aggregated easily, for example, while very frequent fliers or luxury-car owners are harder to aggregate. Other high-value audiences: orthodontists, owners or renters of private aircraft, gamers who spend more than $100 a month on gaming, and high-roller casino gamblers. The more distinctive a group, the more a multi-sided market can charge the "other side" to reach the group with ads.

Value Proposition 2: Market-Type and Competitive Hypothesis

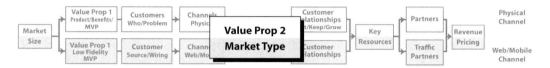

The market-type brief describes which of the four market types the company fits into. (Refer to Chapter 2, Rule 7, in the Customer Development Manifesto.) It also adds a competitive brief.

Regardless of the channel they choose, startups adopt (or pursue) one of four market types. The consequences of choosing the wrong market type are severe (prematurely burning cash on marketing and sales before it's needed), but unlike decisions about product features, the market-type choice is a "late-binding" decision. While a final decision can be deferred until customer creation, it's wise to develop and test an initial market-type hypothesis while moving through the customer discovery phase. In the next chapters, we'll come back to the market type selection process many times, and refine and deepen the analysis after further discussing customers and market.

In this brief, seek a provisional answer to just one question: is the company entering an existing market, re-segmenting an existing market, creating a new market or cloning a market?

Market type drives marketing spending, sales timing and cash need.

Market Type

For some startups, the market-type choice is pretty clear. When entering a market that has a ton of competitors, whether it's smartphones, social networks, glucose meters or airplanes, the choice has already been made for you: it's an existing market. On the other hand, if your company invents a new class of product no one has ever seen before, it's most likely in a new market. However, most companies have the luxury of choosing which market type to use. So how to make the decision? A few simple questions begin the process:

- Is there an established, well-defined market with large numbers of customers? Do customers know the name of the market and do competitors exist? Does the product have an edge (better performance, features, service) over competitors? If so, it's an existing market

- Would some part of an existing market buy a product designed to address its specific needs? Even if it cost more? Or even if it had worse performance in an aspect of the product irrelevant to this niche? If so, think re-segmented market/niche strategy

- Another type of re-segmentation answers the question: Are there customers at the low end of an existing market who will buy "good enough" performance if they can get it at a substantially lower price? If yes, think re-segmented market/low-cost strategy

- Without an established and well-defined market, there are obviously no existing customers or competitors and a new market is being created

- Startups in Russia, India, Indonesia, Brazil, Japan and China (where they have large local markets and language and cultural barriers) have an additional market type: the clone market. Can you adopt/borrow/copy an already-successful business model and company from the U.S. and adapt it to local language and buying preferences. (Not too long from now, ideas from those countries will be cloned in the U.S.)

When you talk to customers, they'll have lots of opinions about where the product fits. Don't worry about wavering among the market-type choices. For now, just look at each market type and pick the one that best fits the company's vision today. The Table 4.1 summarizes of the trade-offs.

	Existing Market	Resegmented Market (niche or low cost)	New Market	Clone Market
Customers	Existing	Existing	New/New usage	New
Customer Needs	Performance	1. Cost 2. Perceived need/ problem	Simplicity & Convenience	New idea already proved overseas
Product Performance	Better/Faster	1. Good enough at the low end 2. Good enough for new niche	Low in "traditional attributes," improved by new customer metrics	Good enough for local market
Competition	Existing Incumbents	Existing Incumbents	Non-consumption/ Other startups	None, foreign originators
Risks	Existing Incumbents	1. Existing Incumbents 2. Niche strategy fails	Market adoption	Cultural adoption

Market Type Trade-Offs *(Table 4.1)*

One of the best tools for sorting out existing market entry strategies is derived from military operations research. It suggests a few simple rules that companies can use to analyze an *existing market*:

- If a single company has 74 percent of the market, the market has become an effective monopoly. For a startup, that's an unassailable position for a head-on assault. (Think Google in search or Facebook in social networks.)

- If the combined market share for the market leader and the second-ranking company is greater than 74 percent and the first company is within 1.7 times the share of the second, it means a duopoly commands the market. Its position is impervious to attack by a startup. (In the telecom sector, Cisco's and Juniper's combined share of the core router market fits this description.)

- If a company has 41 percent market share and at least 1.7 times the market share of the next-largest company, it's the market leader.

For a startup, this too is a very difficult market to enter. Markets with a clear market leader offer an opportunity for re-segmentation.

- If the biggest player in a market has at least a 26 percent market share, the market is unstable, with a strong possibility of abrupt shifts in the company rankings. Here there may be some existing market entry opportunities.
- If the biggest player has less than 26 percent market share, it has no real influence on the market. Startups that want to enter an existing market find these the easiest to penetrate.

If you decide to attack a market that has just one dominant player, you need to be prepared to spend three times the combined sales and marketing budget of that dominant player. (Ouch—so much for going head-on with Google or Facebook.)

In a market that has multiple participants, the cost of entry is lower, but you still need to spend 1.7 times the combined sales and marketing budget of the company you plan to attack. (To enter an existing market, you must steal market share from an incumbent, hence the war analogy.) Table 4.2 summarizes the existing market cost of entry.

	Market Share	Cost of Entry (vs. Leader's Sales/ Marketing Budget)	Entry Strategy
Monopoly	>75%	3x	Resegment/New
Duopoly	>75%	3x	Resegment/New
Market Leader	>41%	3x	Resegment/New
Unstable Market	>26%	1.7x	Existing/Resegment
Open Market	>26%	1.7x	Existing/Resegment

Market Type—Cost of Entry (Table 4.2)

Competition in an Existing Market

Now that you understand the type of market you're in, the competitive landscape becomes clearer. If you believe your company and product fit into an existing market, you need to understand how your product outperforms your competitors'. In an existing market the customers can tell you what the basis of competition is.

It nearly always has to do with key product attributes, but sometimes it's other components of the business model—e.g., channel or price. Strive for a product or feature or improvement that can get a customer to say, "I'll pay anything for that."

Positioning the product against the slew of existing competitors is accomplished by adroitly selecting the basis of competition *where you can win*. Remember it's not always features. It can be convenience, services, brand, etc., where the new entry is clearly better. Summarize the thinking in a brief. When entering an existing market, good questions to address in the brief include:

- Who are the incumbents and which ones drive the market?
- What is the market share of each competitor?
- How many marketing and sales dollars will the market leaders spend to compete?
- What will the cost of entry be against incumbent competitors?
- What performance attributes have customers said are important? How do competitors define performance?
- What share of this market does the company want to capture in the first three years?
- How do the competitors define the market?
- Are there existing standards? If so, whose agenda is driving the standards?
- Does the company seek to embrace these standards, extend them, or replace them? (If the answer is to extend or replace them, this may indicate a re-segmented market.) When you enter an existing market, though, also fill out the competitive brief discussed later in this section to shape the positioning further

One way to plan your attack in an existing market is to refer to your business model canvas. What jobs are your customers asking your product to fill? What problem is your value proposition solving?

Re-segmenting an Existing Market

In an existing market, your startup is the weakest player with the least resources. Therefore, attacking the strongest players head-on is foolish. You want to choose strategies that acknowledge your weaknesses and play to your agility. If there's a dominant player with more than 74 percent market share, don't attack that market head-on. Why? Because you need three times the resources of the market leader. Instead, target your attack at the point where your limited resources can make a difference. You'll segment the existing market to create a submarket where your product can be unique or substantially different. Or if you can create a new market, you can define a space the market leader doesn't address at all.

If your enemy is superior in strength, evade him. If angry irritate him. Pretend to be weak, that he may grow arrogant.

If the dominant player has between 26 percent and 74 percent market share, pick your battles carefully. Remember the cost of a head-on attack: three times the budget of a single competitor or 1.7 times that of a competitor in a crowded market.

Most startups don't have access to those financial resources. Therefore, re-segmenting the market or creating a new market is almost always the default when faced with a dominant incumbent. All the marketing tricks for nipping at the heels of an entrenched competitor can be used here. Most of them were invented 2,500 years ago by Sun Tzu and described in his book *The Art of War.* Paraphrasing about: "All warfare is based on deception. If your enemy is superior evade him. If angry irritate him. If equally matched, fight, and if not, re-evaluate".

Your goal is to become No. 1 in something important to your customer. It could be product attribute, territory, distribution chain/retailer, or customer base. Keep segmenting the market (by age, income, region, etc.) and focusing on the competitors' weak points until you have a battle you can win. Remember, any company can take customers away from any other company—if it can define the battle.

When re-segmenting an existing market, positioning rests on either:

(a) finding a unique niche where some product feature or service redefines the market, creating a clear competitive advantage

(b) being the "low-cost provider" or

(c) combining differentiation and lower operating cost into a Blue Ocean Strategy that creates an uncontested market space and makes the competition irrelevant while creating and capturing new demand. Southwest Airlines was among the first to re-segment air travel this way, followed by many copycat failures and much later by JetBlue. Cirque du Soleil is an example of a Blue Ocean re-segmentation, offering product differentiation as well as lower operating costs

In an existing market, your startup is the weakest player with the least resources.

When re-segmenting for a unique niche, address these questions in this brief:

- What existing markets are customers coming from?
- What are the unique characteristics of those customers?
- What compelling needs of those customers are unmet by existing suppliers?
- What compelling product features will get customers to abandon their current suppliers?
- Why couldn't existing companies offer the same thing?
- How long will it take you to grow a market of sufficient size? What size?
- How will the company educate the market and create demand?
- Given that no customers yet exist in the new segment, what are realistic sales forecasts?
- How can this forecast be tested?
- Can parts of the business model be changed to differentiate the company?

For this type of startup, draw a "market map" (a diagram of how this new market will look) as shown in Figure 4.10, to illustrate why the company is unique. Draw the market map with the startup in the center. A re-segmented market assumes that customers flow from an existing market(s). Draw the existing markets that customers should flow from (remember that a market is a set of companies with common attributes). Draw the product features and functions that, when assembled, best describe the new product (think Hershey bar, now with peanut butter and zero calories—each attribute draws different customer groups).

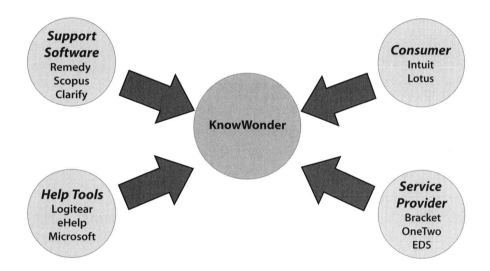

Example of a Market Map (Figure 4.10)

When re-segmenting based on low cost, questions to address include:

- What existing markets are customers coming from?
- What are the unique characteristics of those customers?
- What price will it take (known as "switching cost") to get those customers to spend time online with or buy from the new company?
- What features are customers willing to give up to get the lower price?
- How can this hypothesis be tested quantitatively?

Finally, visualize why thousands of new customers will believe in and move to this market. And beware the "low-price provider" re-segmentation, since competitors can reprice in a matter of days if not hours, eviscerating the positioning that everyone just bet the new business on.

⇨ The market map is particularly important for new web-based businesses. Consider how much time you expect consumers to spend on the site, whether for personal accounting, online gaming or social networking. Then consider where the time will come from: will they abandon Site A or B, sleep less, or do all their e-mail on the new social network? It's a market map based on minutes, not dollars.

Where will the minutes come from, and how and why will they come to the new company. For social networks, it's the "Facebook question:" what can people do on the new social network that they can't or don't already do on Facebook, the market leader, and why will they do it elsewhere?

It's the web/mobile equivalent of market share. Explain how and why consumers will "trade in" time they currently spend elsewhere for time on the new site. If a new online game won't cut back on someone's playtime with Farmville or Mafia Wars, where will he or she find the time to play an additional new game? Figure it out and map the "time source."

What could be better than a market with no competitors?

Entering a New Market

What if there are no competitors? What if, after talking to all your early customers, you continue to hear, "There's nothing else like what your company is offering"? What if, after looking at all the quantitative data, you can't find other companies with comparable products? Congratulations—you're creating a new market. At first

Value Proposition 2: Market-Type and Competitive Hypothesis

glance, a new market has great appeal. A standing joke is that every new market has its own descriptive TLA (three-letter acronym). What could be better than a market with no competitors? And absence of competition typically means that pricing isn't a competitive issue but an issue of what the market will bear. Wow, no competitors and high margins!

A company creating a new market is a radically different type of company from one entering or reframing an existing market. While there are no market-share battles with competitors, there are also no existing customers. If there are no existing customers, even an infinite demand-creation budget at the point of product launch won't garner market share. *Creating a new market is about long-term customer education and adoption.*

New-market entries are by far the most expensive demand-creation challenges, particularly since the marketer can't say "tastier than Yummies" or "faster than Porsche" or "cheaper than Brand X," since no such comparables exist. At the risk of sounding pedantic, creating a new market means a market doesn't currently exist—there are no customers. When entering a new market, good questions to address include:

- What are the markets adjacent to the new one being created?
- What markets will potential customers come from?
- What's the company's vision and why will lots of people care?
- What "never could have been done before" will make customers use/buy?
- How long will it take to educate potential customers to grow a market of sufficient size? What size is that?
- How will the company educate the market? How will it create demand?
- Given that no customers yet exist, what are realistic sales forecasts for the first three years?
- How much financing will it take to soldier on while educating and growing the market?

- What will stop a well-heeled competitor from taking over the market once the startup develops it? (This phenomenon is the source of the phrase "Pioneers are the ones with arrows in their backs.")
- Is the product better-defined as one that will re-segment a market or enter an existing one?

New-market entries are by far the most expensive…

Companies compete in new markets not by besting other companies with product features but by convincing a set of customers that the new company's market vision is real and solves a real problem a different way. A few classic examples: Snapple, Toyota Prius, Siebel, Groupon, and Facebook. However, who the users are, and the definition of the market itself are both clearly unknown. This brief defines the new market and its users with the startup at the center.

One last thing to consider: startups creating new markets won't create a market of sufficient size to generate a profit until three to seven years from product launch. This sobering piece of data is derived from looking at the results of hundreds of high-tech startups of the last twenty years. While you may be convinced your startup is the exception, the odds say that unless you're in a "bubble economy," it takes time for new ideas and products to diffuse and catch on. (A bubble economy is defined as a time of irrational exuberance in a market when all normal rules are repealed.)

Market type, in summary: Market type is one of the most important choices founders need to make and agree on with investors, since it drives spending, timing and competitive analysis. The choice doesn't need to be made during customer discovery, but an initial hypothesis is needed. If investors are expecting substantial revenue in Year One, thinking they've invested in an existing-market company, the outcome is typically a new CEO. Market type selection drives spending and budget as well as revenue expectations.

Competitive Brief

Once you understand your market type, it's relatively simple to assemble a competitive brief. This will help you understand how you'll compete in the market.

When entering an existing market or re-segmenting one, your first instinct may be that the basis of competition is simply the product features of your value proposition. That may be, but you may be missing a bigger competitive advantage. Is there something about partners, the channel, resources, etc. that would be a game changer? Think of Apple and the original iPod. It combined a hardware player, which lots of vendors had, with an easy-to-use software application, iTunes, which no one had (but others could have built) and then added partners at the record labels (which required Steve Jobs' reality-distortion field). The business model canvas is a perfect vehicle for brainstorming some of these ideas.

In a new market, it's tempting to say, "We have no competition." But you'll be wrong.

Explain how and why your new product is better than its competitors. Other items the competitive brief should consider:

- How have existing competitors defined the basis of competition? Is it in terms of product attributes? Service? What are their claims? Features? What makes the new company and its product stand out as dramatically different? Features? Performance? Price?

- Will customers care if the new product lets them do something they couldn't do before?

- In a retail store, which competitive products will be shelved next to the new entry?

- For web/mobile apps, assess competitors' product quality, features, sales or user data, and traffic levels.

- What's strongest about each competitor's product? What do current customers like most about those existing products? What would customers change about them?
- What is a customer's "reason to buy" or use the product, app, or site? And which competitors will they abandon to do so, and why?

If you're in a new market, it's tempting to say, "We have no competition." But you'll be wrong. The new product itself may not yet exist, but what do people do today without it? Do they simply not do something, or do it badly or inefficiently? What will your new product enable them to do that they couldn't do before. Why will they care?

It's only natural that startups compare themselves with other startups around them, but it's important to remember a key tenet of Customer Development: Don't make a list of all competitors' features to simply make a bigger list. A few incremental features or improvements seldom result in a great, scalable company. What's more, in their first few years, startups seldom put one another out of business.

Winners understand why customers buy.

While startups compete for funding and technical resources, *winners understand why customers buy. The losers never do.* Competitive analysis starts at why customers will buy and then looks at the whole market, including new and established competitors.

PROCEED WITH CAUTION:
This is not the time to broadly launch your product to a wide audience or get a ton of press. (You'll be under enormous peer pressure to do so.)

Customer Relationships Hypothesis (Physical)

This customer-relationship brief describes how you *get* customers into your sales channel, *keep* them as customers and *grow* additional revenue from them over time.

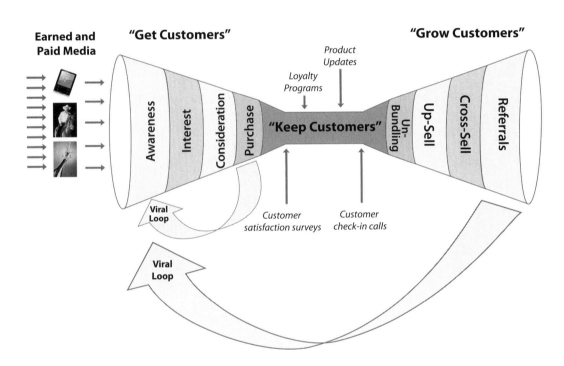

The "Get, Keep, Grow" Funnel in Physical Channels *(Figure 4.11)*

While Figure 4.11 illustrates the flow through the process, Table 4.3 provides an overview of the most widely used activities, by channel, for each step in the "get, keep, grow" process. In this hypothesis we'll focus on the column on the left: the physical channel.

Every company, whether its product or channel is physical or web/mobile, can summarize its mission in three succinct phrases: build great products; "get, keep, and grow" customers; and make money directly or indirectly from these customers. Customer relationships are the strategies and tactics to *get, keep and grow* customers.

Getting customers, sometimes called demand creation, drives customers into your chosen sales channel(s).

Keeping customers, or retention, gives customers reasons to stick with the company and product.

Growing customers involves selling them more of what they've bought as well as new and different products and encourages them to refer new customers.

"Get, Keep and Grow" are among the most important hypotheses for any startup.

"Get, keep and grow" are among the most important hypotheses for any startup. You will die without customers and these are most expensive parts of any company. The diagram in Figure 4.11 provides an overview of the entire customer relationship life cycle. This hypothesis will "dissect" the diagram, starting on the left from "awareness," the first step, and proceeding through each of the many steps in the "get, keep, grow" process.

> **PROCEED WITH CAUTION:** There is no way you can implement all this or even process it in one sitting. What follows is an overview of all the things you need to consider as you shape a marketing strategy that's best for your startup.

Developing Customer Relationships in the Physical Channel

	Physical Channels	**Web/Mobile Channels**
GET customers (demand creation)	*Strategy:* Awareness, Interest, Consideration, Purchase	*Strategy:* Acquire, Activate
	Tactics: Earned Media (pr, blogs, brochures, reviews), Paid Media (ads, promotions), Online tools	*Tactics:* Websites, App Stores, Search (SEM/SEO), email, Blogs, Viral, Social Nets, Reviews, PR, Free Trials, Home/Landing Page
KEEP customers	*Strategy:* Interact, Retain	*Strategy:* Interact, Retain
	Tactics: Loyalty programs, product updates, customer surveys, Customer check-in calls	*Tactics:* Customization, User Groups, Blogs, Online Help, Product Tips/Bulletins, Outreach, Affiliates
GROW customers	*Strategy:* New Revenue, Referrals	*Strategy:* New Revenue, Referrals
	Tactics: Upsell/Cross/Next-Sell, Referrals, (maybe) Unbundling	*Tactics:* Upgrades, Contests, Reorders, Refer friends, Upsell/Cross-Sell, Viral

Customer Relationship Tools for Physical Channels *(Table 4.3)*

Think of the "get customers" process as a "funnel" in which the greatest number of potential customers—those on the left—have awareness of the product. The number of potential customers declines as their interest grows, as they consider buying, and then as they make the actual purchase. During customer discovery, you'll launch a series of small-scale, inexpensive "get customers" experiments to determine the tactics that move customers into and through the funnel in a repeatable, scalable, and cost-effective way. Later, once you have customers, you'll begin customer retention activities to *keep* the customers and use upselling, cross-selling and customer referral programs to *grow* the number of customers and the revenue.

"Get Customers"

Getting customers, or demand creation, has four distinct stages in the physical channel: *awareness, interest, consideration,* and *purchase.* See Figure 4.12.

"Get Customers"

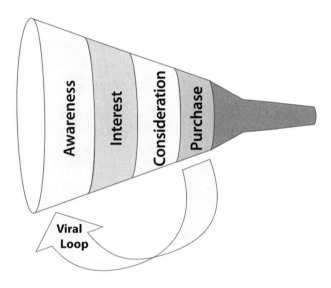

The "Get Customers" Funnel for Physical Goods (Figure 4.12)

PROCEED WITH CAUTION: There is no way you can implement all these alternatives at once or even process them in one sitting. What follows is an overview of all the things you need to consider as you shape a marketing strategy that's best for you.

Awareness lets potential customers know about your product or service (think TV commercials shouting "new airline" or radio ads saying, "Now you can fly cheaper"). It gets people thinking about the product or service.

Interest means the message is no longer being ignored even if the prospect isn't ready to act. Think of people saying, "I should try one of those low-cost airlines sometime," as a result of the initial awareness effort. One more push could move this prospect to the consideration step.

Consideration follows interest when the message is powerful enough or contains a convincing offer that might lead to the thought, "Why don't I take JetBlue on my trip to Florida next month?" Consideration may take the form of a free trial where it's offered.

Purchase follows consideration. It's clearly the desired result of "get" activities.

Creating demand for a consumer electronics product sold on Walmart's shelves is different from opening a chain of pizza parlors or selling a new type of semiconductor. And while the description of customer relationship activities may seem simple at first, it's actually the result of a complex interplay among customers, the sales channel, the value proposition and the budget for marketing activities. When you get it right, it all comes together in a repeatable, scalable, profitable business model.

Develop Your "Get Customers" Strategy

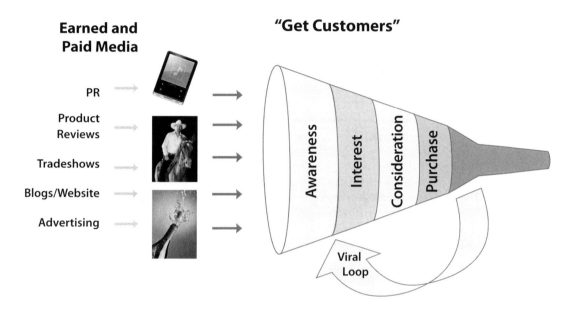

Earned and Paid Media Feeding the "Get Customers" Funnel *(Figure 4.13)*

The first three funnel stages—awareness, interest, and consideration—happen in the consumer's mind, out of reach of anything other than your advertising messages. The first two stages—awareness and interest—are out of your control until the customer identifies herself or himself to some channel like a retailer, a direct-sales rep, or a website and says, "I'm interested." (This could happen when the customer leaves a business card at a trade show, requests more information online, or talks with a company representative.) The "get customers" activity moves customers as far into the funnel as possible until the customer self-identifies and the channel takes over the "consideration" and "purchase" activity. But it all starts with awareness.

	Physical Channels	Web/Mobile Channels
GET customers (demand creation)	*Strategy:* Awareness, Interest, Consideration, Purchase *Tactics:* Earned Media (pr, blogs, brochures, reviews), Paid Media (ads, promotions), Online tools	*Strategy:* Acquire, Activate *Tactics:* Websites, App Stores, Search (SEM/SEO), email, Blogs, Viral, Social Nets, Reviews, PR, Free Trials, Home/Landing Page
KEEP customers	*Strategy:* Interact, Retain *Tactics:* Loyalty programs, product updates, customer surveys, Customer check-in calls	*Strategy:* Interact, Retain *Tactics:* Customization, User Groups, Blogs, Online Help, Product Tips/Bulletins, Outreach, Affiliates
GROW customers	*Strategy:* New Revenue, Referrals *Tactics:* Upsell/Cross/Next-Sell, Referrals, (maybe) Unbundling	*Strategy:* New Revenue, Referrals *Tactics:* Upgrades, Contests, Reorders, Refer friends, Upsell/Cross-Sell, Viral

"Get Customers" Tools for Physical Channels *(Table 4.3a)*

An important caution: be aware of the way the physical-channel has changed in the past decade. Whether a product is sold at a car dealership, a gravel pit, a 7-Eleven or the trendiest retail boutique, 21st-century consumers begin their search for products online. So online marketing is every bit as important to marketers in the physical channel as it is to their web counterparts. Your job as a marketer is to be sure customers can easily find your product or service on the web. This means that physical-channel marketers need to pay almost as much attention to the next section of this chapter—"Web/Mobile Customer Relationships"—as they pay to this one.

(For best results, read both sections before beginning the tasks outlined here.) Marketers in the physical channel must embrace basic web-marketing tactics at every opportunity—websites, AdWords, online advertising—even in the unlikely event that your product isn't for sale online. Online, your job is to "pull" customers to your product so they can discover it online, even if they then buy it at your warehouse, at Walmart or face-to-face from a sales representative.

Awareness, interest, and consideration in the physical channel are primarily driven by two types of communication tactics: *earned (or free) media* and *paid media*.

Earned media is the free exposure a company generates. In the physical channel, it includes press releases, product reviews, editorial features and a range of "guerrilla marketing" tactics such as handing out fliers at trade shows where the company doesn't buy a booth. These tactics are often favored by startups because they're far less expensive than paid media efforts. Many consumer products find their first customers through free sample or trial programs or by handing out samples or discount coupons on street corners.

The downside of earned media: unlike paid media, which run on specific dates and locations, editorial coverage is unpredictable and runs—or doesn't—as editorial space or the product's news value allow.

Online marketing is every bit as important to marketers in the physical channel as it is to their web counterparts.

Paid media is exactly what it sounds like: media exposure that's purchased on TV, blimps, direct mail or the web. This kind of activity can cost literally millions of dollars when rolled out, so customer discovery employs small-scale tests to see which tactic will deliver the best results later, at product launch.

Other paid-media awareness-creation tactics that aren't free include advertising, trade shows, direct mail, catalogs, events, telemarketing, and in-store promotion. Most physical-channel marketers also promote their products online, of course. During customer discovery your spending will be low until you successfully test a tactic and prove that it generates leads and sales cost-effectively.

Simple "Get Customer" Tactics to Consider

Build a "get customers"-hypothesis spending spreadsheet that lists:

- the free and paid media programs
- what the company hopes to achieve and at what cost

Before conducting these or any other tests of customer-relationship tactics:

1. Create a "pass/fail" metric for each "Get" test that defines whether it worked and should be expanded. An example: will we get one sales call for every 30 phone calls made to prospects?

2. Consider a methodology for improving the results of each test, such as: If the call blitz doesn't work, we will e-mail first and then call each prospect twice.

3. Be sure the tests are objectively measurable so that the big spending decisions that follow aren't made based on the fact that "it felt good" or "seems to work well." JetBlue's metric for radio ads might seek to generate reservations-hotline calls at a cost of $1 each. The logic: they can spend $3 on marketing (sometimes called customer acquisition cost) to sell a round-trip ticket, and one caller in three buys a ticket on average.

4. Don't forget that people buy from people. Create, don't avoid, opportunities to talk via phone or in person with potential customers. There are few more powerful sales tools!

Most companies selling through the physical channel will use a variety of web/mobile marketing tactics...

---

5. Remember that most companies selling through the physical channel still use a variety of web/mobile marketing tactics to gain awareness and sales for their products, so be sure to include elements of web/mobile "Get" programs from the next section.

The sample spreadsheet in Figure 4.14 charts the costs and expected results of the "get" efforts for a startup's new heavy-duty, $2,500 printer sold to businesses through office-products stores. The spreadsheet is used to be sure the program tests are affordable.

Sample Customer Relationship Program Spreadsheet

Earned Media

Program	Cost	Pass/Fail
Get 5 new product releases/trade mags	$2,000.00	50 inquiries
Hand out 1,000 flyers at biz show	$ 100.00	10 inquiries
Offer free trial loaner machines at 5 law offices	$ 500.00	2 sales
Install demo unit at 3 tech pub offices/get reviews	$ 100.00	3 sales

Paid media

Direct mail $50 coupon to 1,000 office managers	$3,000.00	20 sales
Ad in local computer-user magazine	$ 500.00	10 sales
Google AdWords drive to mini-website	$ 500.00	5 sales
Test local in-store promo with 3 Staples stores	$2,000.00	10 sales
Total spending	$8,700.00	50 sales

Program goals 50 sales plus 60 inquiries, 10% of the inquiries convert

Total 56 sales, 54 prospects

Total cost/sale = $140.00 (8700/56) vs. profit/sale of $300.00

√ This is a good test

***Sample Customer Relationship "Tactics to Test" Hypothesis
with Return on Investment Analysis*** *(Figure 4.14)*

"Keep Customers"

As the "Get" customers exercise clearly illustrates, getting a new customer is an expensive process. Thus it's important to think now about how the company will *keep*, or retain, customers it's worked so hard to get. When customers cancel a subscription, never return to a supermarket, or close a corporate purchasing account, it's called "churn" or "attrition" (the opposite of retention!).

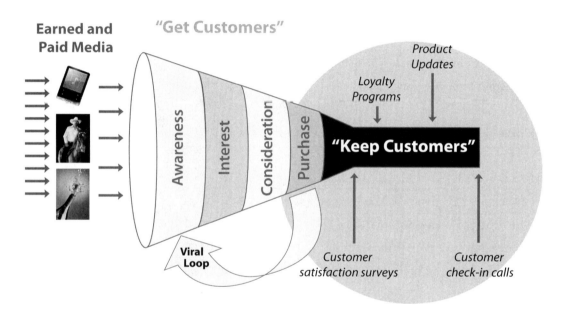

The "Keep Customers" Funnel *(Figure 4.15)*

Develop Your "Keep Customers" Strategy

	Physical Channels	Web/Mobile Channels
GET customers (demand creation)	*Strategy:* Awareness, Interest, Consideration, Purchase *Tactics:* Earned Media (pr, blogs, brochures, reviews), Paid Media (ads, promotions), Online tools	*Strategy:* Acquire, Activate *Tactics:* Websites, App Stores, Search (SEM/SEO), email, Blogs, Viral, Social Nets, Reviews, PR, Free Trials, Home/Landing Page
KEEP customers	*Strategy:* Interact, Retain *Tactics:* Loyalty programs, product updates, customer surveys, Customer check-in calls	*Strategy:* Interact, Retain *Tactics:* Customization, User Groups, Blogs, Online Help, Product Tips/Bulletins, Outreach, Affiliates
GROW customers	*Strategy:* New Revenue, Referrals *Tactics:* Upsell/Cross/Next-Sell, Referrals, (maybe) Unbundling	*Strategy:* New Revenue, Referrals *Tactics:* Upgrades, Contests, Reorders, Refer friends, Upsell/Cross-Sell, Viral

"Keep Customers" Tools for Physical Channels *(Table 4.3b)*

For any customer retention strategy to work, first the company must deliver on all its promises that got the customers to buy in the first place. Customers need to love the product or service, and every customer-facing aspect of the business model has to perform exceptionally, from customer service and support to complaint-handling, delivery, billing, and more. First, a steady stream of product upgrades and enhancements should always keep the product ahead of competition. By their nature, these are core-value-creation activities and should be addressed in the value proposition hypothesis.

Next, begin to think about programs that reach out to customers proactively to strengthen or bolster retention. This can be as simple as placing (often quite powerful) outbound calls to be sure customers are happy or as complex as a multi-tiered loyalty-points program to reward repeat purchases. In a startup's early days, it's hard to test the impact of loyalty programs, since the results need to be measured over long periods of time.

In a startup's early days, it's hard to test the impact of loyalty programs...

In addition, consider loyalty programs such as points, rewards and discounts as well as long-term retention incentives like multi-year contracts. Make them part of the hypothesis, and test them where possible during customer validation.

Finally, consider other parts of the business model canvas. Are there things your partners can do to help you keep customers? Other resources you can use?

Simple "Keep Customers" Tactics to Consider: During customer discovery, put together plans and then test some basic, inexpensive "Keep" activities to see how they perform. Use the test results to guide future plans in customer validation and creation. Some simple programs to test and consider:

- *Loyalty programs:* How you will use loyalty programs to retain customers. Read more about loyalty programs in the customer validation section (on page 396) and address them in this hypothesis.
- *Customer check-in calls:* Put together a plan to call every customer, or every fifth customer, once a month or once a quarter simply to thank them for their business and see how they like the product. While you have them on the phone, probe for questions they have about the product, features or functions. (By the way, e-mail is still a poor substitute for a voice or Skype connection.) Over time, target at least a 15 percent improvement in repeat sales or renewals from customers who've talked.

- *Launch a customer-satisfaction survey:* Whether on the web or by mail or e-mail, plan to check with customers about their use of and satisfaction with the product or service. (Probe for complaints or lack of use, and reach out to any who express problems. Look for at least a 15 percent reduction in churn from those who've been contacted.)

- *Send product-update bulletins:* Create simple tip sheets or user notes on how customers are making the most of the product. (Send them to all users, and offer a prize for users whose tips are published later. This is difficult to measure precisely but inexpensive to implement.)

- *Monitor customer-service issues:* Customers who complain frequently are most likely to churn. (Get proactive with these customers, fix their problems, and make them happy. Far fewer complainers should leave if they've had their problems addressed.)

- *Customer lock-in/high switching costs*: If it's relatively easy for your customer to switch from your products to your competitors', you'll probably have a higher churn rate. You may want to consider tactics for "locking in" customers to your product or solution (through long-term contracts, unique technology, or data that can't be easily transferred).

It's 5–10x cheaper to keep a customer than to acquire one.

Longer-Term Customer Retention: Customer retention is effective only when the customers self-identify so they can be contacted by the salesperson, channel partner, or company representative charged with keeping them happy and coming back to buy more. As you learn more about individual customers over time, retention becomes increasingly individualized and targeted based on the observed and measured customer behavior. This subject is more fully addressed during customer validation, when there are more customers to think about keeping.

Specific retention metrics to monitor and act on include:
- purchase patterns: volume, frequency, slowdowns or halts
- participation in "grow customers" programs (described in the next section)
- number of complaints to customer service, refund requests, problems, and the like
- participation, activity levels, redemptions in loyalty and incentive programs

Retention programs live or die by a close monitoring of customer behavior to learn who's staying and who's leaving and why. You'll organize the metrics around "cohorts," or common groups of customers (such as "new customers signed in January"). Three-month customers, for example, may behave one way while nine-month customers may be more or less active than their newer brethren. (This is addressed in detail in the retention-optimization discussion on page 397.)

"Grow Customers"

Once a company has a customer, why not sell them more, since it costs less than acquiring new customers? Most startups think only about the revenue they receive in their first sale to a customer, but smart companies think about the revenue they can get over the lifetime of the relationship they have with a customer. Measuring customer lifetime value can be important when computing a startup's potential. Describe how the company will get more revenue from its existing customer base with programs that sell more and encourage customers to refer new ones to the company.

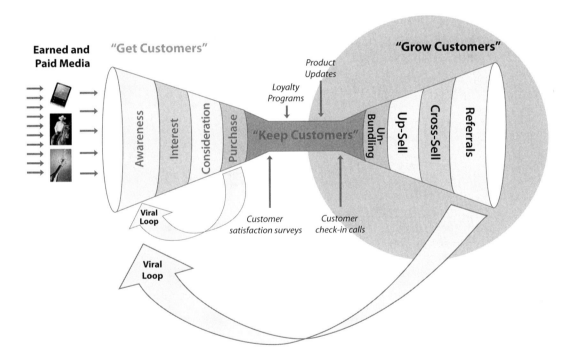

The "Grow Customers" Funnel (Figure 4.16)

Develop a "Grow Customers" Strategy

	Physical Channels	**Web/Mobile Channels**
GET customers (demand creation)	*Strategy:* Awareness, Interest, Consideration, Purchase *Tactics:* Earned Media (pr, blogs, brochures, reviews), Paid Media (ads, promotions), Online tools	*Strategy:* Acquire, Activate *Tactics:* Websites, App Stores, Search (SEM/SEO), email, Blogs, Viral, Social Nets, Reviews, PR, Free Trials, Home/Landing Page
KEEP customers	*Strategy:* Interact, Retain *Tactics:* Loyalty programs, product updates, customer surveys, Customer check-in calls	*Strategy:* Interact, Retain *Tactics:* Customization, User Groups, Blogs, Online Help, Product Tips/Bulletins, Outreach, Affiliates
GROW customers	*Strategy:* New Revenue, Referrals *Tactics:* Upsell/Cross/Next-Sell, Referrals, (maybe) Unbundling	*Strategy:* New Revenue, Referrals *Tactics:* Upgrades, Contests, Reorders, Refer friends, Upsell/Cross-Sell, Viral

"Grow Customers" Tools for Physical Channels *(Table 4.3c)*

Your "Grow" strategy will have two key components: get the customers you have to buy more, and get them to refer other customers to you. A few "Grow" tactics only work in the physical channel, such as:

- "Upsell" offers such as "spend $25 more and get free shipping"
- In-pack promotional mailers of offers, coupons, and samples
- Specials or premiums only available to customers who meet with a sales rep

Direct mail is also an effective customer growth tool, of course. Increasingly, however, physical channel marketers are turning to online marketing rather than postal mail because of its speed, lower cost, and the ability to target better. *You should also study the discussion of "Grow" strategy and tactics in the web/mobile section that begins on page 164 for many more ideas.* This will help you shape your initial programs to grow your customer base through additional sales and referrals.

It's difficult at this time to think through and test extensive "Grow" customers programs because you have very few customers to test them with. Far more detail is provided in the customer validation step (see page 400), when there are enough customers aboard your "Grow" programs.

Customer Relationships Hypothesis (Web/Mobile)

⇨ This customer relationships brief describes how you get customers to your website or mobile app, keep them as customers and grow additional revenue from them over time.

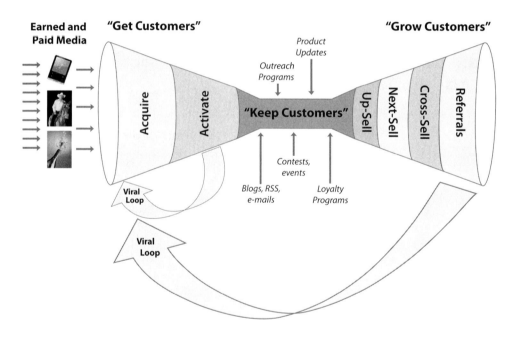

The "Get, Keep and Grow" Customers Funnel in Web/Mobile (Figure 4.17)

PROCEED WITH CAUTION: This is not the time to broadly launch your site or app to a wide audience. You are writing the briefs here, not implementing tactics with your MVP!

Review the previous section on customer relationships for physical products before starting this one. The web/mobile customer funnel in Figure 4.17 is quite different from its physical counterpart in Figure 4.11. Getting customers here is simpler, having only two steps. It also includes a "viral loop" where early customers invite friends and colleagues to explore the new product. Finally, not visible in the diagram is the fact that web/mobile startups can test tactics faster, market less expensively, and reach out to far more customers than companies in the physical channel.

The test of "Get, Keep and Grow" activities during customer discovery is small-scale, exposing the "rough and dirty," or low-fidelity, minimum viable product to a modest number of customers, perhaps a few hundred or so, to gauge their reaction to the business model (including value proposition, price, and product features.) Discovery explores which tactics work and gauges initial reactions to the MVP.

	Physical Channels	Web/Mobile Channels
GET customers (demand creation)	*Strategy:* Awareness, Interest, Consideration, Purchase	*Strategy:* Acquire, Activate
	Tactics: Earned Media (pr, blogs, brochures, reviews), Paid Media (ads, promotions), Online tools	*Tactics:* Websites, App Stores, Search (SEM/SEO), email, Blogs, Viral, Social Nets, Reviews, PR, Free Trials, Home/Landing Page
KEEP customers	*Strategy:* Interact, Retain	*Strategy:* Interact, Retain
	Tactics: Loyalty programs, product updates, customer surveys, Customer check-in calls	*Tactics:* Customization, User Groups, Blogs, Online Help, Product Tips/Bulletins, Outreach, Affiliates
GROW customers	*Strategy:* New Revenue, Referrals	*Strategy:* New Revenue, Referrals
	Tactics: Upsell/Cross/Next-Sell, Referrals, (maybe) Unbundling	*Tactics:* Upgrades, Contests, Reorders, Refer friends, Upsell/Cross-Sell, Viral

Customer Relationship for Web/Mobile Channels (Table 4.4)

The right-hand column of Table 4.4 provides an overview of web/mobile "Get, Keep and Grow" strategies and tactics. It focuses first on getting customers, since the company first has to *have* customers before it can work to keep them, sell them a second time, or grow them.

Many web/mobile products operate as multi-sided markets; Google and Facebook are canonical examples. Consumers use the product at no cost. Advertisers pay the company to reach those customers with ads, AdWords, textlinks and other marketing messages. That revenue is why Google can afford to build massive data centers and offer search for "Free."

Multi-sided marketers need two separate, parallel "Get" approaches—one for the users and another for the payers, since the value proposition for each is quite different. Almost universally, multi-sided marketers focus first on efforts to get users. A company that has aggregated an audience of many millions can almost certainly find marketers eager to pay for the privilege of communicating with that audience.

Getting Customers: Acquisition and Activation

Develop the company's hypothesis about how it will "Get" customers.

There are a million-plus apps for sale on mobile app stores and an infinite number of commerce, social and content websites, so the mere fact that you've launched a new one doesn't make it a successful business. *Building your product is the easy part. The hard part is getting customers* to find your app, site or product. It's a daunting, never-ending challenge to build customer relationships, quite literally, one customer at a time.

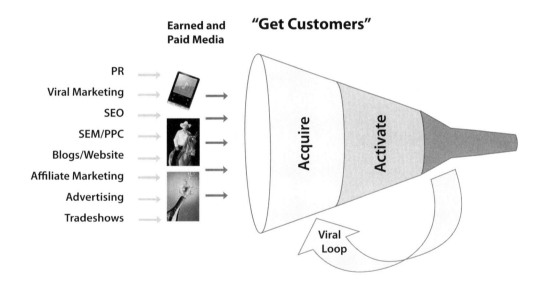

The "Get Customers" Funnel in Web/Mobile Channels (Figure 4.18)

Building your product is easy.
The hard part is Getting Customers.

Acquisition vs. Activation: What's the Difference?

Let's get started with the first two steps for "getting" customers: acquisition and activation.

	Physical Channels	**Web/Mobile Channels**
GET customers (demand creation)	*Strategy:* Awareness, Interest, Consideration, Purchase *Tactics:* Earned Media (pr, blogs, brochures, reviews), Paid Media (ads, promotions), Online tools	*Strategy:* Acquire, Activate *Tactics:* Websites, App Stores, Search (SEM/SEO), email, Blogs, Viral, Social Nets, Reviews, PR, Free Trials, Home/Landing Page
KEEP customers	*Strategy:* Interact, Retain *Tactics:* Loyalty programs, product updates, customer surveys, Customer check-in calls	*Strategy:* Interact, Retain *Tactics:* Customization, User Groups, Blogs, Online Help, Product Tips/Bulletins, Outreach, Affiliates
GROW customers	*Strategy:* New Revenue, Referrals *Tactics:* Upsell/Cross/Next-Sell, Referrals, (maybe) Unbundling	*Strategy:* New Revenue, Referrals *Tactics:* Upgrades, Contests, Reorders, Refer friends, Upsell/Cross-Sell, Viral

"Get Customers" Tools for Web/Mobile Channels (Table 4.4a)

Customer *Acquisition*: The acquisition phase equates to the "awareness," "interest," and "consideration" steps in the physical channel, where customers learn about and explore a product before they buy. In web/mobile apps, the "Get" effort focuses on bringing as many customers as possible to the company's online "front door"—the landing page. There, they're introduced to the product and hopefully buy it or use it. Since the number of people who come to a landing page and look but don't buy or use is often very high, web/mobile "Get" plans must reach lots of people—for a consumer website, that can be millions.

Customer *Activation*: This second step in the "Get" process is much like the "purchase" step in the physical channel. Here the customer shows interest through a free download or trial, a request for more information, or a purchase. *A customer should be considered activated even if he doesn't purchase or register, as long as the company has enough information to re-contact him* (whether by e-mail, phone, text, etc.) with explicit permission to do so.

Overview: How Customers Shop Online

Unlike the door-to-door salesmen of yesteryear, your job on the web is to "pull" customers to you rather than to push your product at them. The web offers a near-limitless tool set to help you pull customers in.

Your job on the web is to "pull" customers to you…

Your first step in customer acquisition and activation is understanding how people buy or engage with your product. Here's how it happens:

Step one: *People discover a need or want to solve a problem.* They say, "I want to throw a party," or feel lonely and decide to find a hot party or a dating site. Then what?

Step two: *They begin a search.* Overwhelmingly, in this century, that search begins online. It often happens at Google.com, but it can happen on Facebook, where they ask their friends, or on Quora, where they solicit opinions, or on hundreds of other special-interest "recommendation" sites from Yelp to Zagat to TripAdvisor.com.

Step three: *They don't look very hard.* People don't just "find" you online, and in fact they often only pay attention to the first few things they uncover (how often do you search beyond the first page of results on Google?). You must make your site, app or product as visible as humanly possible, in as many of these places as possible where your customers are likely to begin the search. (The entire "Get" section ahead will guide you in doing just this.)

Step four: *They go where they're invited, entertained or informed.* You don't "earn" interest from your customers with hard-boiled sales pitches or bland information. In a typical Google search, you're one of many thousands of options the customer can click on. So you have to earn that click by providing inviting, helpful or entertaining information in lots of formats (copy, diagrams, white papers, blogs, videos, games, demos, you name it) and by participating in the communities and social media your customers are likely to be.

Develop your "Get Customers" Strategy

Make your information as rich and inviting—and widely available—as possible and cast the widest-possible net when people begin their search. Provide helpful, non-sales-y information that leads them back to your product, app, or site. Then the selling process begins.

Use the way people make decisions to guide your acquisition and activation strategy:

1. *Determine who your audience* is, then your goal is to be prominent wherever they spend time on the web. Skateboarders don't read *The Wall Street Journal* or TechCrunch very much, so focus on skateboarding sites, blogs and the like.

2. *What kind of content* will they find attractive? Our skateboarders probably prefer illustrations, games, and videos over long essays and white papers. Reach them with the kinds of content they'll find most interesting and helpful, such as tips on safer skateboarding or bolder tricks, not long essays on the finer points of boarding.

3. *Make sure your content works* in the location. Quora, Twitter, and Facebook users expect short, interesting items and get bogged down

with or ignore long ones. Social networks don't have much use for lengthy sales pitches. Be sure your content "fits" where you put it.

4. *Participate in the communities* your customers are a part of. Answer questions, provide feedback, offer tips, and gently invite people to explore your product.

5. *Create content that people want to link to.* Whether it's helpful tips, FAQs, cartoons or fun videos, make your content the kind of content your customers want to share with friends. The result extends your invitation to those friends more often than not.

Customer Acquisition Tactics to Test

The best way to get this started is to put your initial acquisition test plan into a spreadsheet outlining the activities, their costs, and each program's goals. See a sample acquisition-plan spreadsheet in the "Activate Plan" section of Chapter 9, page 319. Acquisition begins by using free or earned web-media opportunities to acquire customers, since "free" is obviously the best cost. The web offers many free crowd-sourcing or acquisition opportunities (SEO, social media, viral marketing, buzz and more).

Earned or free acquisition tactics:

- *Public relations:* Generate small "test" amounts of news and feature coverage about the problem (not the product itself) on websites, blogs and social nets. Don't publicize the product or solution until customer validation, it's just too early. (Public relations doesn't mean hire an expensive outside agency. During customer discovery, you should be learning this firsthand.)

- *Viral marketing:* This often-confused term refers to three types of acquisition marketing, each used in different web/mobile channels. The three are perhaps the most important customer acquisition tactics for web/mobile marketers, because they're all free or inexpensive to implement. This is discussed in "grow" customers (on page 164) where viral activity encourages customers to refer others

- *Search engine optimization* (SEO), an unpaid, or "natural," search option, directs consumers to the product or service
- *Social networking* encourages friends and early customers to blog about a product or a company, use Facebook to "like" it, or use Twitter and other tools to broadcast personal recommendations

After you get the free acquisition programs going, you should start to test paid tactics.

Paid acquisition tactics:

It's hard to determine how much money to spend on acquisition tactics, in part because there are so many variables: how much funding you have, how confident you are in your hypotheses, and how hard it is to find your customers are three of the key considerations. Obviously, free tactics are better than paid tactics when they deliver quality customers with strong LTV in sufficient numbers to create a great business. As a rule, however, life is seldom that easy, and you'll need to test a blend of paid tactics along with a wider variety of free ones.

Here are some of the most common web/mobile paid acquisition tactics you should consider:

- Pay-per-click (PPC) advertising: targetable, accountable paid search advertising on Google and other search engines drives targeted traffic to the company
- Online or traditional media advertising: often used to introduce a new product or service
- Affiliate marketing: other related websites are paid to drive traffic to the product site or app.
- Online lead generation: purchase of permission-based e-mail lists to solicit interest (much trickier and more highly regulated for direct-to-mobile-phone messaging)

Review the list of "get" customers tactics from the physical channel to see which ones warrant testing for your web/mobile startup. Candidates certainly include advertising, direct mail, and everything from zany on-street promotions to blimps, billboards and more.

Some quick and simple acquisition tests:

In Phase 2 of customer discovery you'll run some small-scale acquisition tests with the free and paid tactics described above to test your understanding of the customer *problem/need*. In Phase 3 of customer discovery, you'll again use acquisition tools to gauge initial customer reaction to the MVP and discover whether the MVP is a compelling solution to the problem. These are limited and targeted tests, not a product launch. Press releases make no sense here, for example, since wide dissemination could either bring too many customers or create the false impression that the product is "launched" and finished.

Your Phase 2 & 3 acquisition tests should be limited to controllable, inexpensive, easily measured tactics like these:

- *Buy $500 worth of AdWords* and see if they'll drive customers representing five or 10 times that amount in potential revenue to the site or app and at least get them to register. Test at least two different headlines and as many calls to action, carefully monitoring the performance of each. Drop ineffective ones and refine the best

---

Viral marketing can't start until there is a customer base to viralize.

- *Use Facebook messages or Tweet* to measurable audiences to invite at least 1,000 people to explore the new product. Test several different messages or invitations to be sure the messaging about the product is clear. If none of the messages delivers engagement or registrations, the product or offer may well be the problem

- *Viral marketing*: Getting customers can't start until there's a customer base to viralize. There are several types of viral marketing, so review the viral discussion in the previous section (and also on page 167). Network-effect businesses should consider viral activities sooner

- *Post referral banners* using Commission Junction to get sites offering your offer. Spend $1,000 in referral fees to relevant websites (usually $12 per referral). If the banners run and the money's largely unspent, move on

- *Buy an e-mail blast list* of targeted customers for $500 or $1,000. Send at least two versions of the offer and expect to generate at least three times the potential revenue to at least sign up, if not a purchase

- *Traffic partners* are another important source of users or customers that fuel the "Get" effort. These are typically contractual relationships with other companies that provide predictable streams of customers or users to your company while you provide either customers or fees to the partner. This is so important to most web/mobile businesses that it's addressed in its own "traffic partners" hypothesis on page 178

Who's Creating This Content?

Successful web/mobile startup teams have a combination of skills: great technology skills (hacking/hardware/science), great hustling skills (to search for the business model, customers and market), and great user-facing design. The co-founder who's the user-interface/design expertise owns content creation. Ideally he or she is talented enough to create it without legions of hourly-rate agency folk around. Use guru.com and craigslist.com to find talent, cost-effective freelancers with good references.

Customer Activation Tactics to Test:

Activation is the second step in getting customers. As discussed earlier, this is where the customer either makes a purchase or, at a minimum, raises a hand and says, "I'm interested, contact me." Activation could be an exploratory visit your website or free mobile app to see how a game is played, a comment posted on a blog or social network, or the use of a free search engine. At the other end of the spectrum, low-cost mobile apps and other products find transactions to be the best initial activation, since the product may be a free version or cost only 99 cents.

Activation is the choke point...where customers decide whether they want to participate, play or purchase.

For web/mobile businesses, *activation is the choke point*—the make-or-break place where customers decide whether they want to participate, play, or purchase. Here, unlike the physical channel, the "product is the salesman," encouraging visitors to explore, try, or read about the product on their own, without pressure or patter from a sales representative. Activation is always encouraged by a compelling value proposition, well-communicated and coupled with a good, clear offer and a low-fidelity (in discovery) or hi-fidelity (in validation) MVP. Start by creating an activation-tactics plan in simple spreadsheet form as in the example on page 319.

Many startups falsely assume that because their customers are online, online communication is all their customers want or expect. Very often, even a single phone call can make a dramatic difference in acquisition and activation rates. In some instances, as few as half the customers who discover a product online will activate or buy without human-to-human contact. And the presence of a phone number is known to communicate the company's authenticity. Just the presence of the company's phone number—even if never called—can increase its online click-through rate by five percent to 30 percent. (When adding a phone number, be sure it's answered promptly, knowledgeably, and effectively by someone with incentives to activate the caller.)

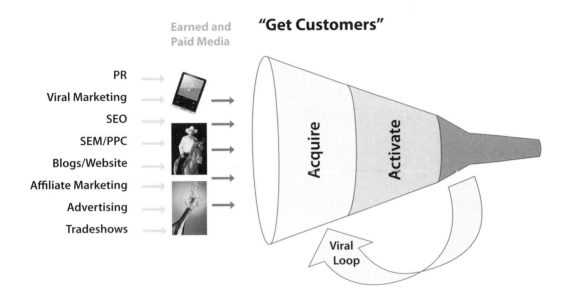

Acquisition and Activation in Web/Mobile Channels (Figure 4.19)

Some quick activation tests:

- *Capture the customer's e-mail address* and get permission to follow up with further information. Follow up with 1,000 customers and expect at least 50 or more to agree to activate

- *Offer incentives for activation:* Offer a free trial, download, or white paper or a significant discount to 500 or 1,000 customers. Try this with at least three different offers, hoping to find at least one that generates a 5 percent or greater response rate. Keep testing until you do, and then calculate the revenue model based on response rates, and costs

- *Call 100 prospects who don't activate immediately.* See if the phone calls generate enough of a response-rate improvement to warrant the cost. Three times the response rate is probably needed

- *Free-to-paid conversion:* Offer a seven- or 14-day free trial of an app, service, or web/mobile product. Then compare the total 60-day acquisition revenue with the Get results of the typical paid offer. Or offer the use of some but not all of the site or app's features. eHarmony.com, for example, lets people find their ideal matches for free but requires paid enrollment to tell your dream date that you've discovered him or her

---

Even a single phone call can make a dramatic difference in acquisition and activation rates.

- *Use free-download websites* to offer free downloads or trials. Make sure the revenue generated over a 90-day period exceeds that of the standard activation offer

Monitor the results of all tests and, when you're not satisfied (or it fails your pass/fail test) revise the program and test again.

Keeping Customers (Customer Retention)

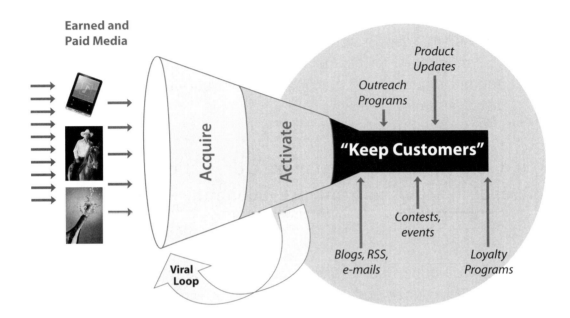

The "Keep Customers" Funnel in Web/Mobile Channels (Figure 4.20)

Keeping customers in the web/mobile channels has the same goal as retention efforts in the physical world: to minimize customer churn/attrition by providing great products and services, and interacting with customers often. (At this point in customer discovery, there aren't customers to retain, so identify retention programs to test in the future.) Retention is done more easily online, where companies have the incredible power and ability to track and monitor every single prospect's or customer's individual behavior or lack of behavior (without violating their privacy).

	Physical Channels	**Web/Mobile Channels**
GET customers (demand creation)	*Strategy:* Awareness, Interest, Consideration, Purchase *Tactics:* Earned Media (pr, blogs, brochures, reviews), Paid Media (ads, promotions), Online tools	*Strategy:* Acquire, Activate *Tactics:* Websites, App Stores, Search (SEM/SEO), email, Blogs, Viral, Social Nets, Reviews, PR, Free Trials, Home/Landing Page
KEEP customers	*Strategy:* Interact, Retain *Tactics:* Loyalty programs, product updates, customer surveys, Customer check-in calls	*Strategy:* Interact, Retain *Tactics:* Customization, User Groups, Blogs, Online Help, Product Tips/Bulletins, Outreach, Affiliates
GROW customers	*Strategy:* New Revenue, Referrals *Tactics:* Upsell/Cross/Next-Sell, Referrals, (maybe) Unbundling	*Strategy:* New Revenue, Referrals *Tactics:* Upgrades, Contests, Reorders, Refer friends, Upsell/Cross-Sell, Viral

"Keep Customers" Tools in Web/Mobile Channels (Table 4.4b)

Loyalty and points programs and other tactics borrowed from the physical channel can also play a significant role here, as can elegant personalized customer service and support, conducted digitally as much as possible. Strong digital help tools, FAQs, user blogs, clubs, and newsletters help with retention as well.

Customer Retention Strategy

Retention programs live or die by a close monitoring of customer behavior to learn who's staying and who's leaving and why. It's critical to instrument the product not in order to track everything but in order to follow the most important customer behaviors you want to improve.

For example:

- Track start dates and sources of each customer (referred by a blogger, another site, etc.)
- Track customers' activity level individually. How often do they come? How long is each visit? What's the time span between visits?
- When do customers abandon, and what were they doing that caused them to do so?
- Monitor customers' behavior on-site: what do they click on, what don't they click on?
- Track customer referrals to others and the sources and activity level of referred visitors
- Track the results of each promotion, whether outbound or on the site itself

> **PROCEED WITH CAUTION:** Remember, this is an overview/tutorial. There's no way you can implement all this or even process this in one sitting.

Keep the following guidelines in mind as you test:

- E-mail is easy to ignore and at times feels like spam, so be careful about overly relying on it. At least four of five e-mails are never opened, and consumers often unsubscribe from self-serving marketing e-mails
- Consumers often resent "faux" personalization. People appreciate legitimate, helpful personalization if they've opted in for example ("Here are the sneakers we have in your size, 11D" is far better than "Great buys for Bob")
- Don't get lazy and make automated marketing and e-mail programs your only customer-retention efforts. Focus on great product, product enchancements, terrific service and other core retention initiatives

- Embrace social networks as points of retention. Use them to keep visibility high and to invite customers and friends back often

The key for retention for web/mobile channels is that the data customers have given you make personalized retention efforts easy. But you need to collect it. Observe each customer's behavior and interact with customers based on what they do or don't do.

Track the behavior of each customer individually. Use that data to create a personal one-to-one relationship that guides him to the next steps the company wants him to take. (But always respect personal-data privacy.)

Retention programs live or die by a close monitoring of customer behavior.

Simple Retention Tests to Consider:

The hypothesis should include some core initial retention efforts that will be discussed during discovery and tested on a modest scale later, during customer validation. Be sure to include digital versions of relevant programs outlined in the physical section (page 136). Some specific tactics to test:

- *Outreach programs,* including welcome e-mails, how-to guides, and phone calls thanking the user for coming aboard and offering simple tips on how to get more out of the product. Consider retention e-mails like these:

    ○ We haven't seen you visit in two weeks. Is everything OK?

    ○ I've noticed you've had a few problems. How can we help?

    ○ Have you seen some of the new features on our site?

    ○ Here are five "power user" ideas for getting more out of your time at XYZ.com

- *Blogs, RSS* and news feeds to further engage customers or users with the product or site

- *Loyalty programs* that encourage and reward repeat visits, purchases, or referrals borrowed from the physical channel

- *Contests and special events:* webinars, special guests, new features, and other reasons for current customers to come back

- *Mobile app push notifications:* iOS/Android gives developers the ability to push messages to users even when the app is closed. For app developers, getting this right is critical to retention and customer engagement

- *Product updates and enhancements* to the actual product itself always drive loyalty and retention (and communicating them to customers helps)

Getting new customers is painful and costly, so keeping those already on the roster is easier and more cost-effective.

- *Placing live phone calls to users* several weeks or (if annual) a month or more before contract renewal is a good option if you have a subscription revenue model. Make them friendly, service-oriented calls, but always listen for signs of potential churn and be ready with a deal, discount or offer to save the customer. Remember: getting new customers is painful and costly, so keeping those already on the roster is easier and more cost-effective

- *Tips-and-tricks newsletters*, time-triggered e-mails every seven or 14 days based on users' on-site behavior or lack of visits

- *Personalized customer service and support*, conducted digitally as much as possible. Strong digital help tools, FAQs, user blogs, clubs, and newsletters help with retention as well

- *Customer lock-in/high switching costs*: If it's relatively easy for your customer to switch from your products to your competitors' (in an existing market) you'll probably have a higher churn rate. You may want to consider tactics to "lock in" your customer to your product or solution (through unique technology, data that can't be transferred—think Facebook and LinkedIn—or high startup costs with a new vendor.)

Monitor Specific Retention Metrics

Monitor and act on at least these basic retention metrics:

- signs of dwindling visits, page views or time spent on the site or app

- increased time between visits

- average customer life (how long they stay active) and, if possible later, lifetime value

- increases in complaints, help or support tickets

- reduced response rates or open rates on company e-mails

Organize the metrics around "cohorts," or common groups of customers (like "those who joined in January"), since, for example, three-month customers may behave one way while nine-month customers may be much more or less active than their newer brethren. (This is addressed in detail in the retention-optimization discussion in Chapter 10.)

Growing Customers (New Revenue and Referrals)

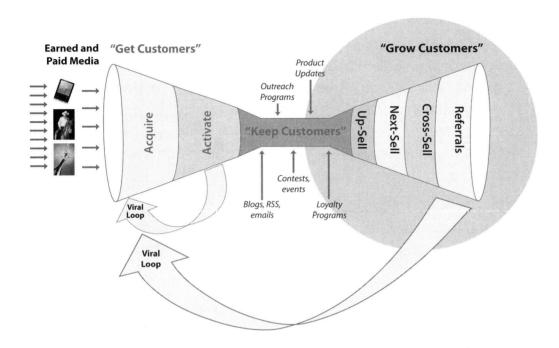

The "Grow Customers" Funnel in Web/Mobile Channels (Figure 4.21)

There are two ways to grow existing customers: get current customers to spend more money or encourage them to send more customers to the company. These programs are detailed in Chapter 10 (Optimize Getting More Customers, page 380). By then your company should have a sizeable number of customers to grow!

> **PROCEED WITH CAUTION:** Remember, this is an overview/ tutorial. There's no way you can implement all this or even process this in one sitting.

	Physical Channels	**Web/Mobile Channels**
GET customers (demand creation)	*Strategy:* Awareness, Interest, Consideration, Purchase *Tactics:* Earned Media (pr, blogs, brochures, reviews), Paid Media (ads, promotions), Online tools	*Strategy:* Acquire, Activate *Tactics:* Websites, App Stores, Search (SEM/SEO), email, Blogs, Viral, Social Nets, Reviews, PR, Free Trials, Home/Landing Page
KEEP customers	*Strategy:* Interact, Retain *Tactics:* Loyalty programs, product updates, customer surveys, Customer check-in calls	*Strategy:* Interact, Retain *Tactics:* Customization, User Groups, Blogs, Online Help, Product Tips/Bulletins, Outreach, Affiliates
GROW customers	*Strategy:* New Revenue, Referrals *Tactics:* Upsell/Cross/Next-Sell, Referrals, (maybe) Unbundling	*Strategy:* New Revenue, Referrals *Tactics:* Upgrades, Contests, Reorders, Refer friends, Upsell/Cross-Sell, Viral

"Grow Customers" Tools for Web/Mobile Channels (Table 4.4c)

1. Get Current Customers to Spend More

Getting current customers to buy more starts by making sure they're satisfied with the product, performance and price. Then you try to sell them more product, upgrade their service, or extend their contracts. These activities are important for the long-term, so test at least a few during customer validation. Some of the basic approaches to Grow Customers include:

- *Cross-sell programs* that encourage buyers of a product to buy adjacent products. Getting buyers of toner cartridges, for example—to buy paper, pencils, and other office products

- *Up-selling programs* that promote the purchase of "more" of higher-end products. For example, buying cases of toner rather than single cartridges, or the purchase of copiers, fax machines and other office machines along with the toner

- *Next-selling programs* that concentrate on the next order: can the company encourage a long-term toner contract, sell the customer envelopes to put the copies in, or become his primary office-products supplier? These basic customer growth strategies work in consumer goods as well as business-to-business

- *Unbundling*, which sometimes grows revenue. If a product is complex or multi-featured, split it into several products, each sold separately. This works well in many tech, software, and industrial product areas

For now, develop a hypothesis about how the company will grow its customers, and test those ideas with—who else?—customers.

Some simple "grow" programs to consider:
- Every "thank you" or confirmation page should suggest multiple items the customer may also find interesting, and ideally provide an incentive for doing so

- New items, special offers, and discounts for increasing the order size should be prominent and integrated with the checkout process for high visibility

- e-commerece companies should have "recommendation engines." "If you bought X, you'll love Y"

- e-commerce companies should include special offers and discounts in each shipment

- e-mail customers to introduce new and different products or "add-on" features to buy

- Promote special sales and offers on new products or services the customer hasn't bought

- *Customer referrals* are the most common type of viral marketing, although they obviously can't begin until you actually have customers (so it's discussed in the "Grow" section). Viral marketing stimulates referrals of customers from other happy customers. Generate attention among the largest audience possible. Consider tools like YouTube and conferences you can attend and perhaps speak or promote at. Encourage friends of the company and its team to invite their friends to learn more. Consider contests, sweepstakes and promotions to drive the reach of viral efforts

- *Viral products* help sell themselves. Hotmail, Gmail, Facebook and many other web products end every customer communication by saying, "Invite a friend to use our service." When used, it's powerful and virtually free viral marketing

- *Network-effect virality* boosts usage of products like Skype, Photobucket, and even fax machines. You can't talk via Skype with a friend who doesn't have it or fax someone without a fax machine, so customers encourage others to join, expanding the network for their own benefit. In the process, they get new users for the company

---

Customer referrals are the most "honest" source of new business...

---

2. Get Customers to Send More Customers to the Company

There are lots of different viral marketing tools and tactics that help you get customers to refer other customers to the company. Here are the six most powerful viral marketing techniques to consider:

- Encourage customers to "like" the product on Facebook
- Offer customers discounts or free trial offers to share with friends

- Enable customers to e-mail their friends using their address books to create mailing lists

- Create contests or incentives to encourage Tweeting, "liking" and other viral activities

- Highlight social-networking action buttons on the site to make viral efforts easy

- Encourage bloggers to write about the product, and reward them for doing so

(The customer relationship hypotheses should also address how the "Get, Keep and Grow" programs will be optimized once they're under way. For guidance in these areas, see Optimizaton Plans/Tools, page 362.)

Key Resources Hypothesis (Physical and Web/Mobile)

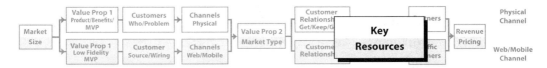

This brief identifies external resources critical to the company's success and how you'll find and secure them.

Key resources fall into four main categories: *physical*, *financial*, *human* and *intellectual property*. In each relevant category, create a list of the key resources you'll require, what you expect to pay, and where you'll go to find them.

Physical resources: These fall into two types: company facilities and product/service resources. Examples of company facilities are office space and company location (near mass transit to more easily attract lots of employees, in a city with great restaurants, etc.). Product/services may include a steady supply of superthin silicon wafers or iron ore or thousands of feet of warehouse space or specialized lab or manufacturing space. Many resources are capital-intensive, particularly where physical goods are concerned—manufacturing equipment, raw materials, and the like.

...many of the capital-intensive resources have become utilities or can be outsourced.

In the 21st century, many of the capital-intensive equipment or services resources companies used to need to physically own and pay for have become utilities or can be outsourced. For example, startups that need computing and server capacity can buy processing power and storage, in the cloud, from Amazon.com and many others (slashing the cost of a software startup by a factor of 10 or more). Manufacturing that used to be a capital-intensive is now outsourced to Asia (with an equally significant reduction in cost). IT and services can be done cheaper in India, etc.

Financial resources: Money is the lifeblood of startups. You stay in business until you run out of it. This book is about how to reduce startup infant mortality by making everything you do less wasteful and more cash-efficient.

There are tons of articles, websites and entire books on how to raise money for a startup—and whom to raise it from. Friends and family, crowd funding, angels, venture capital and corporate partners are the usual suspects. But don't overlook government grants as an alternative funding source for new ventures. In the U.S., the grants.gov website is the first stop for a number of sources such as SBA (Small Business Administration) and SBIR (Small Business Innovation Research) grants.

Companies selling physical products have additional sources of capital:

- *Equipment lease line.* This lets you finance the entire purchase price of business equipment or commercial vehicles. Typically offered by a bank, a lease line can be a great solution whether you need to preserve working capital for other expenses or you're in an expansion phase and need financing

- *Factoring.* If you've sold product to a customer who takes a while to pay, you can sell your accounts receivable (i.e., the invoices) to a third party (called a *factor*) at a discount. It provides your company with immediate cash

- *Vendor financing.* This is a loan arrangement that takes place between your company and a vendor that supplies large volumes of their product to you. The vendor lends money to you so you can buy products from it

Don't forget the *Human* Resources

Human resources fall into three categories: personal advice (mentors, teachers, and coaches), company advisors, and qualified employees.

Teachers, coaches, and mentors are people you'll need to help you advance your *personal* career. If you want to learn about a specific subject, find a teacher. If you want to hone specific skills or reach an exact goal, hire a coach. If you want to get smarter and better over the course of your career, find someone who cares about you enough to be a mentor.

Advisors are people you'll need to help advance your *company's* success. Founders fail when they believe their visions are facts. Listening to advice based on experience can help you sort through whether your vision is a hallucination. Getting an advisory board (by expanding your circle of accumulated wisdom beyond your investors) is so important that it's an explicit step in the Customer Development process.

Qualified and motivated employees are the difference between a good idea that never goes anywhere and a billion-dollar firm. Will your company need dozens of specialized engineers or coders or designers as it grows? If so, where and how will you find them? Is your city or location a magnet for world-class talent? Is there a shortage of talent? Will offshore teams be required as the company scales, and how will you select and manage them? In more specialized industries (think avionics, chip design, and biotech) this may be even more challenging if scaling the team quickly is important, especially if the company is headquartered in a smaller or off-the-beaten-path location to where you'll have to relocate much of your talent pool in order to employ them. If you're in a part of the country or the world where the number of potential employees is limited, how can you be more creative to get them? Identify what the human resource needs are now and what they will be two to three years later to be sure that growth won't be constrained.

Intellectual Property is a Key Resource

Intellectual property gives you rights to stop others from using your creativity. The assets you can protect may include your "core technology," such as source code, hardware designs, architecture, processes, and formulas. Or it can be your brand, logo or domain name. You can protect business processes, know-how, customer information, and product roadmaps. Protection is also available for content such as music, books, and film. Some of these assets are protected automatically. For other classes, it's wise and sometimes mandatory to go through a registration, application or examination process to get full protection.

Trademark: A trademark protects branding and marks and gives you the right to prevent others from using "confusingly similar" marks and logos. Trademark protection lasts as long as you use the mark. The more you use the mark, the stronger your protection. Trademark registration is optional but has significant advantages if approved.

Copyright: A copyright protects creative works of authorship, typically songs, books, movies, photos, etc. Copyright gives you the right to prohibit others from copying, distributing or making derivatives of your work. It protects "expressions" of ideas but doesn't protect the underlying ideas. (If your product is software, copyright is also used to prohibit someone from stealing your software and reselling it as machine and/or source code.) Copyright protection lasts practically forever. Registration is optional but is required for suing for infringement.

TYPES OF INTELLECTUAL PROPERTY PROTECTION

Type of IP	What is Protectable	Examples
Trademark	Branding (i.e. Nike swoosh)	marks, logos, slogans
Copyright	Creative, authored works; expressions (not ideas)	software, songs, movies, website content
Trade Secrets	Secrets with economic value (i.e. the Coke recipe)	non-public technology customer lists, formula
Contract, NDA	As defined in the contract	technology, business information
Patent	Inventions	new technology

Types of Intellectual Property Protection *(Table 4.5)*

Contract: A contract is a binding legal agreement that's enforceable in a court of law. There's no official registration process; you have whatever protection is defined in the contract (e.g., a nondisclosure agreement gives you certain rights to protection of your confidential information). The protection lasts for the time period defined in the contract.

Patents: A patent is a monopoly the government grants to prohibit others from making, using or selling your invention, even when the other party's infringement is innocent or accidental.

Just about anything can be patented—circuits, hardware, software, applied algorithms, formulas, designs, user interfaces, applications, systems. Scientific principles or pure mathematical algorithms may not be patented. Your invention must be "nonobvious." The test for whether it's nonobvious is: given the prior art at the time of the invention, would a typical engineer 1) identify the problem and 2) solve it with the invention? You must be "first to file." You must file in the U.S. within a year of sale, offer for sale, public disclosure or public use. Your patent application has to include a written description with details of the claims of the invention. The details have to allow others to duplicate your invention from your description and have to use the "best mode" in describing critical techniques/technologies. And it has to identify all prior "art," or solutions to the problem.

Patent protection typically lasts 15 to 20 years. There is a formal application and examination process. Each patent filing will cost your company $20,000 to $50,000 and take one to four years to complete. Filing of patents is frequently of major interest to people funding your company. (There's something called a "provisional patent" that's an alternative to a full patent. It allows you to claim "first to file" and use the term *patent pending*. Provisional patents get into the patent office quickly and cheaply. However, they automatically expire after one year, and no patent rights are granted. Provisional patents are a good placeholder because they're cheap to file and don't get in the way of your other patent efforts.)

Intellectual Property Creates Value

Intellectual property is an asset for your company. You need to acquire, protect and exploit it. You can map out an intellectual property strategy by asking:

- Who are the key players and technologies in its market(s)?
- What are the most important ideas and inventions that need patents (or provisional patents)? Start filing these early!
- What are the important patent applications that come next?

Four Common Intellectual Property Mistakes Startups Make

1. *Founders didn't make a clean break with previous employer:* Do your employers or university own or have a claim on your inventions? It's a very subjective standard, and since startups don't often have resources or time to spend on lawsuits, large companies and universities may use threats of litigation to ensure that you don't take anything. Therefore the best advice is to "take only memories."

2. *Your startup cannot show that it owns its intellectual property:* Take the time to create a clear, well-documented chain of title (think lab notebooks) to your intellectual property. If you're using independent contractors, make sure you have written agreements assigning work created. Make sure you have Employee Invention Assignment Agreements. (If you hire subcontractors or friends to do some work, get assignment agreements as well.)

3. *You lost your patent rights due to filing delays/invention disclosures:* In the U.S., patent rights are forfeited if you wait more than a year after:

   - disclosure in a printed publication (white paper, journal/conference article, website)
   - offer for sale in the U.S. (start of sales effort, price list, price quotation, trade-show demonstration, any demonstration not under NDA, public use in the U.S.)

   In most foreign countries, there is no one-year grace period.

4. *Your company grants "challenging" licenses to intellectual property:* Startups acquiring their first customers may give special licensing terms in key markets, territories, etc.—e.g., a grant of "most favored nations" license terms or other licensee-favorable economic terms. This can make your intellectual property less valuable to future buyers of your company. Or you may cut a deal that you can't assign or transfer (or can't get out of) if you get acquired.

There May be Other Key Resources

Consider other external business elements that are vital to the company's success. Celebrity websites need a steady stream of "hot" gossip (this one shouldn't be a problem) and MarthaStewart.com wouldn't be much without Martha. Overstock.com would fail without a stream of good-quality discount merchandise.

Dependency Analysis

The company's dependency analysis basically answers the question "To sell our product in volume, what has to happen that's out of our control?" Things out of a company's control can include other technology infrastructure that needs to emerge (all cell phones become web-enabled, fiber optics are in every home, electric cars are selling in volume). Dependencies also include changes in consumers' lifestyles or buying behavior, new laws, changes in economic conditions, and so on. Specify what needs to happen (let's say the widespread adoption of telepathy), when it needs to happen (must be common among teens by 2020), and what happens if it doesn't happen (the product needs to use the Internet instead). Note the benchmarks you'll use to measure whether the change is happening when needed.

Identify all key resources in this hypothesis, and explain how the company will make sure those key resources are readily available. Be sure to identify the risks of their unavailability, as well as alternatives that will minimize impact on the company's business model. Be careful not to confuse partners (to be discussed next) with resources.

Partners Hypothesis (Physical)

Key partners often provide capabilities, products, or services that the startup either can't or would prefer not to develop itself. Batteries for a flashlight maker or design services for a website are two simple examples. But the most famous is Apple and the iPod. Without the record labels providing music as content, the iPod and iTunes would simply be another hardware/software player. The partners made the business model the juggernaut it is today.

The key-partners hypothesis names the essential partners your company will require, along with the "value exchange" with each one (as in "we give them money, they send us customers"). Partnerships generally fall into four key areas: *strategic alliances*; *"coopetition,"* or cooperation between competitors; *joint new business development efforts*; and *key supplier relationships*.

Think of this hypothesis as a simple three-column spreadsheet. The headings: partner name (list primary and runner-up candidates), "what they provide," and "what we provide." Don't feel bad when the word *money* appears repeatedly in the third column. It's fairly typical for startups, at least in their early days.

Strategic alliances, generally between noncompetitive companies, can often shorten the list of things your startup needs to build or provide to offer a complete product or service. For physical products, alliance partners might provide product training, installation or service, peripherals or accessories, whether they're sold under your startup's brand name or not. Specialized service firms in many industries (law, accounting, engineering, IT) can often market a wider range of services by combining their services with those of other specialists. Alliances can also be used to broaden a startup's footprint, making its product more available in geographies where the startup itself can't support sales or service.

Joint new business development efforts generally happen later in a startup's life, but can be important once the startup has established its own identity and brand. Dell and HP sell lots of software and products made by others, but seldom do so until they're confident the product has significant consumer demand. Think of these as longer-term opportunities to investigate as part of your customer discovery process.

"Coopetition" similarly happens later in a startup's life, as a rule. It's a form of working with a direct competitor to share costs or market together. New York City's "fashion week" is a good example of coopetition for established fashion houses. While they're fiercely competitive, they work together to coordinate fashion show schedules so the top buyers can attend all the key showings. Word for Mac is perhaps the greatest coopetition example of all time, but both companies were well-established before the product was developed and launched.

Key supplier relationships can mean life or death for a startup. Imagine how tough it would be to churn out millions of iPhones without Foxconn, the massive Apple manufacturing partner in China, or to make Ben & Jerry's famed Cherry Garcia without an uninterrupted supply of delicious cherries. Suppliers can be instrumental to any company's success, but tight, flexible partnerships can be absolutely critical. Many startups outsource a variety of "back office" functions, ranging from warehousing and fulfillment of physical goods to HR, payroll, benefits and accounting. These outsource suppliers act as extensions of the company that leverage the suppliers' expertise to improve the startup's efficiency and cost structure.

Will the partner flex its delivery times, order-size requirements, credit terms or even its price in your startup's early days? How will the partner ensure a steady supply that rises (quickly, we hope) or falls in line with customer demand? Identify the key suppliers in this hypothesis, along with what you'll need from them. You'll visit with them later to validate this hypothesis and understand your role and theirs in forging a mutually beneficial relationship.

Traffic Partners Hypothesis (Web/Mobile)

⇨ In addition to the four types of partnerships in the previous section, there's a fifth, vitally important type of partner for web/mobile startups: *traffic partners*. Traffic partners deliver people to websites and mobile apps several ways:

- on a "cross referral," or swapping, basis
- on a paid-per-referral basis
- by using textlinks, on-site promotions and ads on the referring site
- by exchanging e-mail lists

As detailed later in Phase 3, these traffic deals are as difficult to negotiate as they are important. Develop your hypothesis by identifying the target partners, what you want them to do, and how your startup will reciprocate in cash or in kind.

Partnerships can sometimes be the lifeblood of a startup. Some examples to consider in thinking about traffic partnerships of your own:

- *Zynga*, the online-gaming juggernaut, is overwhelmingly dependent on its partnership with Facebook, the only place where Zynga's popular Farmville and other games are played. Without the partnership, Zynga would have little traffic or revenue
- *YouTube* got much of its early traffic through a partnership with Google, so much so that Google bought the company
- *Salesforce.com* drives traffic and revenue to web/mobile sales and CRM applications through its AppExchange
- *Mobile apps* get much of their traffic from dot.com partners
- *Niche content* retail sites often have similar active partners

Other partnerships unique to web/mobile channels can also be quite important: App stores and marketplaces are critical partners for mobile apps, since they're the apps' principal channel. (Learn much more about this in the channels section.) Understand how they work, their willingness to partner, and the costs. And credit card issuers are often overlooked as partners. They sometimes look askance at web content, social networking, gaming and e-commerce businesses (particularly startups and sellers of web/mobile goods), since the card issuers have been burned so many times by un-scrupulous entrepreneurs. The result: rigid rules that are often biased against startups.

Identify traffic partners your startup will need initially and as it grows. Develop a prioritized list of the must-have and best-to-have partners in each category. Later, in Phase 3, you will conduct meetings with prospective partners to determine if they're interested and what they will need to make the partnership a mutual success.

Revenue and Pricing Hypothesis

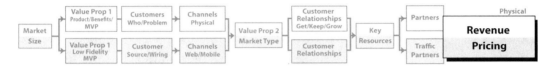

The revenue and pricing brief may well be the toughest of all, but it's critically important, since it ensures that the business model makes financial sense. In a way, this brief is elegantly simple, since it asks only four questions:

1. How many of these things will we sell?
2. What's the revenue model?
3. How much will we charge?
4. Does this add up to a business that's worth doing?

Channel

	Web	**Physical**
Bits	• Freemium add-ons • Mailing list rentals • Virtual goods • SAAS sales • Upsells • Ancillary revenues	• Products • Subscriptions • Referrals • Add-on services • Upsells
Physical	• Upsells • Mailing lists • Warranties • Service • Ancillary revenues	• Products • Leasing • Service • Upsell/Next Sell • Referrals

Product (label on left axis)

Revenue Sources (Figure 4.22)

While some of the issues differ from channel to channel, the process of computing your company's revenue is fundamentally the same, regardless of channel. The good news: much of the work for this brief is already complete.

Question 1: How Many Will We Sell?

In the physical channel, companies generate revenue by selling their product, collecting revenue either as a one-time sale, via time payments, or through such financial tools as leasing or subscriptions. They also solicit referrals from current customers, often rewarding customers for referring others.

Collect the following revenue stream components from hypotheses completed earlier:

- Market size and market share hypotheses, which should translate into the anticipated number of customers (as in 10 percent of a million-person market = 100,000 customers)

- Channel hypotheses, along with estimates of their volume potential and channel costs

- Be sure to include (subtract, really) the channel's cost of sales, which can be enormous, since the company only gets to "count," or keep, net revenue received after channel costs are subtracted. (Enthusiastic entrepreneurs make this mistake far too often)

➾ Question 2: What's the Revenue Model?

Web and mobile products in particular have a wider variety of potential revenue sources than their physical channel cousins. (Product sales are the prime revenue source for physical products.) Direct revenue sources to review and estimate include:

- Sales: Product, app, or service sales are the principal revenue source for many web/mobile startups, typically in a one-time transaction that may also lead to follow-on sales

- Subscriptions: Software, games, and other online products are often sold by a monthly subscription

- Pay-per-use: Some web products (travel sites and eBay are two simple examples) earn revenue on a "per use" basis, with subscription or discounted volume purchases optional

Other web/mobile resources may include:

- *Referral revenue*: payments for referring traffic or customers to other web/mobile sites or products
- *Affiliate revenue (revenue sharing)*: finder's fees or commissions from other (typically e-commerce) sites for directing customers to them
- *E-mail list rentals*: subscription and membership sites often rent their customer e-mail lists to carefully selected advertiser partners
- *Back-end offers*: add-on sales from other companies offered as part of registration or purchase confirmation processes,

When it comes to advertising sales, two fundamental rules apply. First, the more distinctive, unusual, or hard to reach an audience actually is, the more a marketer will pay to reach it. Private pilots or people who travel on private jets are far more valuable than "travelers," and "active multiplayer gamers" are worth considerably more than teens.

Rule number two: very few marketers or advertisers will be interested in small audiences, even if the product or site is destined for huge audiences down the road. The "friction" costs of research, contracts, and paperwork required just to reach a few thousand (or sometimes half a million) people is often just not worth it to an advertiser. Research this question with prospective revenue sources and factor the responses into the revenue calculation.

Question 3: How Much Do We Charge? (Pricing Tactics)

This is a two-part question. Part one assesses the costs of doing business. For physical products, this is often far more important. If you're selling canned peas or microwave relay towers, there's a clear, sizeable cost of the physical product itself: parts, assembly, packaging, shipping, and more.

In business-to-business and some consumer sales, other issues warrant consideration, such as total cost of operation (if rent is high or staff is huge, or the electric bill is a high component of product cost).

Part two of the "how much will we charge" question is simple: "what's the price?" You will start testing your pricing hypothesis later in discovery, but first there's a bit more work to do.

A good pricing model recognizes Market Type, accommodates manufacturing costs, the value the product delivers, market beliefs, and competitive prices. It also charges "as much as the market will bear" to maximize profits. For best results, start with a deep understanding of competitive pricing.

⇨ In web/mobile channels, pricing is much more transparent and almost always easily found online, which heightens the need to monitor competitive pricing.

Startups have lots of choices in selecting their pricing models. Among the most popular pricing models:

- *Value pricing*: Based on the value delivered by the product rather than the cost itself. Investing or accounting software tools, unique patented products and pharmaceuticals can sometimes optimize profits with this model

- *Competitive pricing*: Positions the product against others in its competitive set, typically in existing markets

- *Volume pricing*: Designed to encourage multiple purchases or users, in situations ranging from office supplies to SAAS software

- *Portfolio pricing*: For companies with multiple products and services, each with a different cost and utility. Here the objective is to make money with the portfolio, some with high markups and some with low, depending on competition, lock-in, value delivered, and loyal customers

- *The "razor/razor blade" model*: Part of the product is free or inexpensive, but it pulls through highly profitable repeat purchases on an ongoing basis. (Think of the cost of ink-jet printers compared with the cost of the ink.) Often challenging for startups due to the upfront cost

- *Subscription*: While now thought of as a software strategy, the Book of the Month Club pioneered this for physical products

- *Leasing*: Lowers the entry cost for customers. Provides constant earnings over a period of years

- *Product-based pricing*: Based on a multiple of actual product cost. Usually for physical goods. (Typically priced for maximum revenue/profit versus volume)

⇨ This calculus is very different for a web/mobile product, where the incremental cost of a new customer is practically zero, as it is for a multiplayer game app that adds, say, 50 new customers to its system at a cost measured, at most, in pennies per customer.

Two Business-to-Business Pricing Issues

Total Cost of Ownership/Adoption (TCO): More an issue in business than in consumer sales, the TCO analysis estimates the total cost to customers of buying and using the product. For business products, do customers need to buy a new computer to run the software? Do they need training to use the product? Do other physical or organizational changes need to happen? What will deployment across a whole company cost? For consumer products, measure the cost of "adopting" the product to fit consumer needs. Do customers need to change their lifestyle? Do they need to change any part of their purchasing or usage behavior? Do they need to throw away something they use today?

Return on Investment (ROI): When setting prices for sales to corporations, your company may have to prove to them the purchase price was "worth it," or that they got "a good deal," which may be less about price than about the total return on their investment. As a rule, companies focus more on ROI than consumers do, partly because of the size of and oversight on large transactions. ROI represents customers' expectation of their investment measured against goals such as problem-solving, productivity, time, money and resources. For consumers, return often includes status or style and sometimes even just plain fun.

When selling to businesses, prepare a hypothetical ROI in advance of initial customer meetings. (This is often a good subject for a helpful white paper.) If the solution doesn't return a meaningful multiple ROI, sales may be difficult. That $50,000 robot vacuum system as a replacement for a $5,000 annual cleaning bill may be a tough sell, especially after a good job on the TCO (maintenance, electricity, parts and more) as part of the ROI computation.

Question 4: Do Revenues Point to a Business Worth Doing?

You have to do more than multiply the volume by the average selling price to get the answer to this question, but don't worry—this answer doesn't need to be precise just yet. Remember, the goal of customer discovery is to refine a business model enough to test it on a larger scale in the next step, customer validation. So at this point, with a rough view of the gross revenue and all the fixed and variable costs involved, make a rough computation of the following:

- Is the revenue adequate to cover costs in the short term?
- Will the revenue grow materially if not dramatically over time?
- Does the profitability get better as the revenues get bigger?

Again, this is a rough, back-of-the-envelope calculation used only to decide if what you found in discovery moves your forward to customer validation. It's not an accounting exercise.

Web/mobile markets are often multi-sided.

⇨ How Single and Multi-Sided Markets Affect Financials

Companies with physical products most often have "single-sided" markets: customers who buy the one product the company makes.

Web/mobile markets are often multi-sided. When a web/mobile startup plans to first focus on amassing huge numbers of users, eyeballs, or clicks and to "figure out the revenue model later," this implies a multi-sided market.

Multi-sided markets have a different business model for each side of the market. Typically, the business model components that change include value proposition, customer segment, customer relationships and revenue stream.

One side, the users, is measured in eyeballs, page views, referrals, or hours rather than dollars. The other side of the market, the customers, consists of advertisers who pay to reach the users. Hundreds of millions of

Facebook users think of it as a free social network, and indeed, Facebook makes its money from a completely different customer segment (advertisers) with a completely different value proposition through a different channel (direct sales and online self-service).

Calculate the revenue model for that second side of the market—the payers—right now. Understanding what an advertiser is willing to pay to reach your startup's audience is vital to the business model.

Remember, you have limited resources. Focus first on the one key, big source of revenue before expanding into secondary sources, which can be distracting to the company.

Two More Revenue Issues to Consider

Distribution Channel Affects Revenue Streams. Calculating revenue is easy for a product sold directly by your own sales force: You simply deduct any discount you gave the customer from the list price of the product. When you sell through indirect channels, revenue calculations might be harder. Selling to Walmart is wonderful, but most retails channels have "return rights." (If your product doesn't move off their shelf, you have to take it back.) Are you selling to OEMs where the discount is steep and the revenue to your company doesn't appear until the OEM begins selling in volume?

Consider Lifetime Value: How much will the customer ultimately spend not just in the first sale but over the life of his or her relationship with the company? SAAS software, dating websites, and online gaming focus on customer lifetime value. Customers can sign up for salesforce.com, for example, sometimes for a few dollars a month, but the company no doubt spends several times that amount to attract and sign a new user. Why? Because it understands that the average salesforce.com subscription lasts many months, making the new customer worth a multiple of the monthly cost—provided, of course, that the company stays in business long enough to collect the revenue. (On the other hand, the lifetime value of a demolition contractor's typical customer often approximates his first invoice.)

Customer lifetime value dramatically affects revenue stream and pricing strategy, online or off, although other than magazine and newspaper subscriptions, which are declining rapidly, there are scant few subscription products beyond gym memberships among physical products.

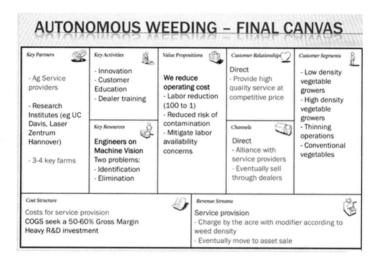

Final Draft of a Business Model Hypothesis *(Figure 4.23)*

Tie the Components of Revenue Together in a Hypothesis

Revenue stream and pricing interact with the value proposition, the channel, customer relationships, and the other business model components. That means there'll be lots of iterating and pivoting. The revenue stream hypothesis will be tested repeatedly before it's cast in stone, first in customer discovery discussions and again with more customers as part of customer validation. When the draft of the revenue stream brief is complete, re-validate it to see that the math adds up. Ultimately, only one answer matters: can we generate enough revenue, profits and growth to make this business worth our time and energy?

Completing the Hypothesis Development Process:

This brief completes the company's only large-scale paperwork exercise. The action now moves outside the building so you can start to understand what potential customers need and to qualify or refine the initial hypothesis assumptions. But before doing that:

- Convene a team meeting where a large copy of the latest business model canvas and briefs are taped to a wall. A summary of each of the briefs should be adjacent to the canvas
- All participants should read each of the business model briefs
- Look at the summaries on the canvas, read the details in the briefs, discuss them as a team, and look for obvious conflicts or inconsistencies.
- Founders, product development, engineering and operations teams should again validate cost assumptions and changes
- Return to the first hypotheses developed to be certain there's no conflict from one to the next. Does the sales channel make sense, for example, in light of the pricing, need for installation, etc.? Will fewer customers still adequately fund overhead and development?
- Review and agree on the final versions of each hypothesis
- Make certain the hypothesis summaries agree with the summary in the appropriate business model box
- Update the business model as appropriate
- For more detailed checklists, see Appendix A

Now it's time to move ahead and get out of the office, where customers and facts live.

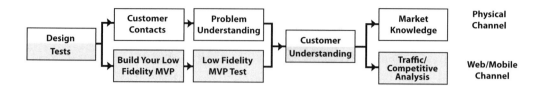

CHAPTER 5

Customer Discovery, Phase Two: "Get Out of the Building" to Test the Problem: "Do People Care?"

PHASE 2 GETS THE TEAM "OUT OF THE BUILDING" to test the problem and to answer three key questions:

- Do we really understand the customer's problem?
- Do enough people really care enough about the problem for this to become a huge business?
- And will they care enough to tell their friends?

The next section, Phase 3, will test to see whether the product offers a compelling solution to customers who have said there's a problem. When the "problem" and "solution" questions are answered with a resounding "yes," product/market fit is achieved and it's time to move on to customer validation.

⇨ This problem phase is markedly different for web/mobile startups, where product development time is far shorter and feedback comes far faster. Problem discovery is conducted with the development of a low-fidelity MVP website or mobile app (as discussed on page 200). Sometimes as simple as a PowerPoint diagram or a single web page, this early MVP helps gather immediate feedback about the problem. Later, the solution is tested with a hi-fidelity MVP.

This phase includes five key steps:

- designing experiments for customer tests
- preparing for customer contacts and engagement
- testing customers understanding of the problem and assessing its importance to customers
- gaining understanding of customers
- capturing competitive and market knowledge

As this phase gets under way, here's a reminder of the key rules from the Customer Development Manifesto in Chapter 2:

- Customer discovery is done by the founders
- Hypotheses require testing. Testing requires experiments to be designed
- Web surveys are nice, but always correlate them with face-to-face customer feedback, even for web businesses
- Customer meetings aren't about learning whether customers love the product, at least not yet. They're about understanding the problem and how urgently your potential customers need to solve that problem. You'll focus more on the product itself once you're certain the problem it solves is big enough to create a market worth going after
- Initial hypotheses rarely survive feedback without iterations or pivots

Design Tests and Pass/Fail Experiments

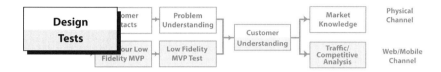

At this point, your Phase One business model hypotheses are still just "guesses." In this phase you'll turn those hypotheses into facts by getting out of the building and *testing* them in front of customers.

Here's an easy way to visualize this: think of a three-layer business model. The bottom layer represents your initial vision of the startup. The second layer outlines the detailed hypotheses you just developed in Phase One. The third layer shows the tests you'll conduct to verify and measure each hypothesis, turning guesses into facts as you do, so that the business model can be verified and measured.

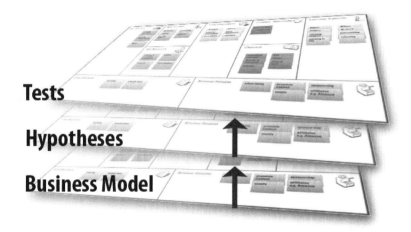

Business Model/Hypotheses/Tests (Figure 5.1)

But how do you test? Rule number 6 of the Customer Development Manifesto says to *design experiments* and Rule 9 says to do it with *speed, tempo* and *fast cycle time*. So the first step in running a test of your business model hypotheses is to design simple pass/fail experiments for each test. Next you run the tests, and then you gather the data and not only try to learn something from the test but also try to gain some insight. The Hypotheses/Experiment/Test/Insight loop is shown in Figure 5.2 below.

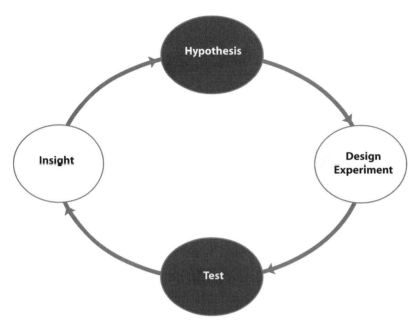

Hypothesis/Design Experiment/Test/Insight *(Figure 5.2)*

Regardless of whether it's a physical or web/mobile product, Customer Development experiments are short, simple, objective pass/fail tests. You're looking for a strong signal in the noise. The pass/fail tests give you a "good enough" signal to proceed.

Start by asking yourself, "What do I want to learn?" Then ask, "What's the simplest pass/fail test I can run to learn?" Finally, think about, "How do I design a pass/fail experiment to run this simple test?"

For example, a Customer Relationships hypothesis for a physical product may have assumed that for every 10 sales calls three people would move into active consideration of buying. The experiment might be as simple as making the same presentation to 30 prospects and having the experiment "pass" by coming away with nine or more orders or letters of intent.

⇨ A web business model hypotheses for Customer Relationships and Revenue Model may have assumed that you can acquire 5,000,000 customers by spending $1 million on Google AdWords. Your pass/fail experiment might take the form "we believe we can acquire visitors with Google AdWords at a cost of 20 cents per click." Your experiment would create three different landing pages, allocating $500 in AdWords to each, and sequentially testing each landing page (using the same AdWords) every other day. A "pass" would get 2,500 clicks per page. Anything less, the hypotheses failed. (A secondary test that falls out of this is which page got the customers the fastest!)

Most of the time you can mock up the web page or create a demo or prototype to elicit valuable learning.

Tests

One of the things that trips up engineering founders is thinking that these hypotheses tests have to be actual code, hardware or the real product. Most of the time you can mock up the web page or create a demo or physical prototype to elicit valuable learning. Nor do the tests involve large sums of money or large amounts of time. When you get a strong "grab it out of your hands" on, say, from four of your first ten customers, it's OK to stop the test and declare it a success. The goal is speed, learning and looking for a global maximum (not a local maximum).

What's a global maximum? Let's say you run a free trial offer for three days on your great new weekend getaway website and you get 50, then 60, then 80 signups in the first three days. You might say, "Wow, 80, that's great," and end the test. But on day four, the sun comes out. Had you run the test for only two more days, you might have discovered your "global maximum," 500 signups a day. Only experience and good guesswork can tell you how long to run a test, and while shorter is always better, be sure you've given yourself the opportunity to reach your global maximum.

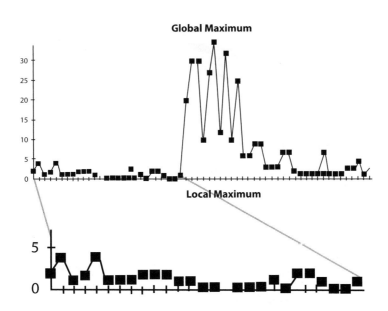

Global Maximum versus Local Maximum Response Rates *(Figure 5.3)*

The next steps in Phases 2 and 3 and in customer validation provide details on how to set up tests for both web/mobile and physical products.

Insight

The goal of these experiments/tests is not just to collect customer data. Nor is it to simply get "pass" on the pass/fail experiments. And it's not just to learn something, though we hope you will.

It's something more profound, intangible and what makes entrepreneurship in the end still an art. It's the fact that *you're looking past the data – you're looking for insight*. Did you get thrown out of sales calls time and again but you remembered someone said, "Too bad you don't sell x, because we can use a ton of those."

Prepare for Customer Contacts (Physical)

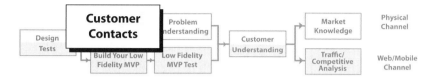

The next step in qualifying your business model hypotheses is to leave the safe confines of your office and conference room and venture out to the real world, where the people who will pay your bills live. Regardless of whether you're selling to large corporations or consumers at home, your friendly first contacts are the people who will start your education about customers and their problems. Better yet, they may *become* your customers.

Start with 50 Target Customers

The first step in this phase will be the hardest: contacting potential customers who don't know you, persuading them to give you some of their time, and looking them in the eye.

At this stage, you're less interested in big names and titles or the "exactly right" consumers.

Start by gathering a list of 50 potential customers you can test your ideas on. Fifty names sounds like a lot, but as you'll soon see, you'll go through them quickly. A solid discovery effort will usually involve 10 to 15 customer visits a week, and getting face-to-face with 50 people will probably require contacting 200 customers or more. Where do the names come from? Start with the people you know directly. Next, expand the list by scouring your cofounders' and employees' address books, social-network lists (Facebook, Google+, Twitter, LinkedIn, Jigsaw, etc.). Then call in every favor possible, from friends, investors, founders, lawyers, recruiters, accountants to add names to your list. Finally, use conference-attendee lists, trade media, and any other source you can think of.

Even if you're selling to businesses, right now your customers' titles and their levels in the organization are irrelevant. And if you're selling to consumers, whether they currently have the slightest interest in your product or not is also inconsequential. What matters is what you will learn from them. At this stage, *you're less interested in big names and titles or the "exactly right" consumers*. You're interested in finding people who will give you some of their time and who you think even loosely fit the profile embedded in your customer hypotheses. (In fact, calling on high-level execs now is a waste of a great lead. You really have no idea what you're saying yet, with nothing more than untested guesses, and will regret making the call. Wait until your business model and story stop changing on a weekly basis.)

While you're building your contact list, simultaneously begin to develop an *innovators list*. What's an innovator? These are the most innovative companies, departments in companies, or individuals in your field who are smart, well-respected and usually out in front of a subject. For consumer products, they may be the "gadget freaks" everyone asks for advice or the group of people others look to for help spotting a trend. You'll use this list two ways. First, you need to find and meet with the visionaries who are known to "get" new ideas. Unfortunately most people view innovation as a dangerous virus that must be kept out of their companies, while few others look forward to hearing about and understanding what's new. The few are the people to talk to. Second, your innovators list will give you a great contact list of industry influencers and potential advisory board members.

It's hard if you've never called on someone you don't know, but it's a lot easier if you carefully prepare a *reference story* that gets you in the door.

Develop a Reference Story

The first step in customer contacts is coming up with a reference story.

A reference story emphasizes the problems you're trying to solve, why it's important to solve them, and the solution you're building.

The story typically starts with an introduction: "Hi this is Bob at NewBankingProduct Inc. I was referred to you by (insert helpful reference name here), who said you were the smartest person in the (name your market/industry)." Now give the potential customer a reason to see you: "We're starting a company to solve the long-teller-line problem, and we're building our new Instanteller software, but I don't want to sell you anything. I just want twenty minutes of your time to understand if you have the long-teller-line problem and learn how you and your company solve your own teller problem."

The best introduction to a prospect is through a peer.

What's in it for your contact? "I thought you might give me some insight about this problem, and in exchange I'll be happy to tell you where the technology in this industry is going." Exhale.

Obviously, you'll need to vary and tweak the story, but the goal remains the same: get meetings scheduled (you can do this via e-mail but it's a lot less effective). This may sound easy on paper, but if you aren't a professional salesperson, it can be very hard. Nobody likes calling people they don't know. First-time practitioners of customer discovery stare at the phone, walk around it, pick it up, and put it down without calling. But eventually you have to "bite the bullet" and place the calls. And you know what? There's nothing more satisfying than hearing a potential customer say, "Why, yes, that's exactly the problem we have. I can spare twenty minutes to chat—why don't you come in Tuesday." Yes!

Start the Appointment-setting Process

First, a few pointers:

- The best introduction to a prospect, when you can manage it, is through a peer within his or her company. For consumer products, it can be just as challenging—how do you get hold of someone you don't know? But the same technique can be used: a reference from someone the prospect knows
- Start with an introductory e-mail or LinkedIn, Twitter or Facebook message—preferably sent by whoever gave you the contact—explaining the

reason for the call that will follow and why the time spent in the visit will provide value to the customer

- Always start by mentioning the referral source, as in, "Steve Blank said I should call"

- Tell them that the meeting is not a sales call and that someone said they were the smartest person in the industry and you want to get their feedback.

- Ask for a short amount of time: "I just need 15 minutes of your time." (You'll get more)

- Don't talk product or features. Explain that the goal is an understanding of the problems or issues in the market or product category, and explain why the person's time will be well used

- Sometimes the best "meeting" is a friendlier, less "threatening" cup of coffee that's clearly intended to be an information exchange and not a hard-boiled sales pitch. Guests will be more likely to accept and often more relaxed, receptive, and open to talking

---

One of the mistakes entrepreneurs make is confusing motion with action.

Companies that succeed in this phase often spend an entire week setting up the meetings and at least several weeks conducting them. It's a small price to pay when compared with the years the team will spend driving toward success. Each founder needs to have at least 10 (yes, 10) conversations a day until you book enough meetings to fill your calendar.

One of the mistakes entrepreneurs make in this step is confusing motion with action. Motion is a sent e-mail, a left voice-mail message or a note on LinkedIn. Action is a two-way conversation. So 10 conversations may require 25 e-mails, voice mails, Tweets, etc. Keep calling until the schedule's booked with three customer visits a day. Get used to being turned down, but always ask, "If you're too busy, who else should I talk to?" It's helpful to keep hit-rate statistics (were any lead sources or job titles better than others?). The same approach works for consumer products. As a rule of thumb, every 50 calls should yield five to 10 visits. Before going out, plan the call from icebreaker to conclusion and rehearse.

Build a master calendar of booked appointments and assign members of the founding team to each one. Geography, proximity and logistics challenge the time efficiency. Research the company in advance to personalize the visit as much as possible. Don't expect every customer to be able to react thoughtfully to every question or have a valid opinion on every aspect of the need or problem. Instead, plan to assemble a mosaic of answers that ultimately provide depth of feedback on every question on your list.

Build Your Low Fidelity MVP (Web/Mobile)

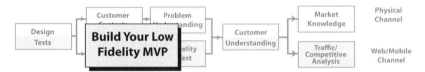

⇨The tests to qualify your web/mobile business model hypotheses will have you engage thousands of customers in discussions about their problem or need. You'll do this by developing a *low fidelity* minimum viable product that answers two critical questions: do you understand the customer problem or need, and when you do, do lots of customers care?

This low fidelity MVP test makes sure the problem or need your company will address is an urgent one for customers.

You'll build the low fidelity MVP in this step and run the actual tests in the next step.

The *Low Fidelity* MVP Strategy

As discussed in Phase 1 (page 82), the low fidelity MVP can be as simple as a landing page with your value proposition, benefits summary, and a call to action to learn more, answer a short survey, or preorder. Or it can be a quick web-site prototype in PowerPoint or built with a simple landing-page creation tool. More experienced web developers can build a functional user interface with a wireframe prototyping tool and build a working low-fidelity website. No matter what, this is a very basic website without fancy U/I, logos, or animation.

Get the MVP live as quickly as possible (often the day you start the company) to see if anybody shares your vision of the customer need/problem. Start with a low-fidelity website that:

- describes the problem's severity in words or pictures ("Does your office look like this?")
- describes the problem, encouraging users to "sign up to learn more"
- shows screen shots of the solution ("pay your bills this way")

Consider other simple MVP components like a YouTube video showing or discussing the problem, a short online survey on the issue, or a blog asking visitors their opinion.

In the next step, you'll invite consumers to respond as thoroughly as possible, giving them several options for doing so. Start by asking for a response as simple as signing up to learn more. The next most important measure is whether they'll rush to tell lots of their friends, which tests the visitor's view of the importance or magnitude of the problem, or the excitement around the thought of a new online game, for example.

The third step invites more detailed feedback via an e-mail or a survey tool or by asking the viewer if she'd welcome a call to discuss the new product or company. Remember: the more a visitor is asked to do, the less likely it is she will respond. So be sure to have the simplest, most basic response mechanism—like "sign up to learn more"—most prominent on the MVP.

> The tools listed in this section are examples. That are not recommended or preferred, just representative of what's available. New tools appear daily. Do your homework and check www.steveblank.com for the latest tools.

How to Build a *Low Fidelity* MVP

For non-coders:

- Make a quick prototype in PowerPoint or use Unbounce, Google Sites, Weebly, Godaddy, WordPress or Yola
- For surveys and preorder forms, Wufoo and Google Forms can easily be embedded within your site with minimal coding

For coders (tips for building the user interface):

- Pick a website wireframe prototyping tool (i.e. JustinMind, Balsamiq)
- 99 Designs is great for getting "good enough" graphic design and web design work for very cheap using a contest format. Themeforest has great designs

- Create wireframes and simulate your low-fidelity website
- Create a fake sign-up/order form to test customer commitment. Alternatively, create a "viral" landing page, with LaunchRock or KickoffLabs
- Embed a slide show on your site with Slideshare, or embed a video tour using YouTube or Vimeo
- Do user interface testing with Usertesting or Userfy

By the way, don't underestimate the long-term value of design and the importance of user interface. At times even friends and relatives would look askance at an MVP that's so crude it seems like the person who created it is totally out of his depth. But the goal at this stage is not U/I perfection. It is to test a problem. It could be done with a sock-puppet if the test were set up correctly.

Consider Using Multiple MVPs

Many startups develop multiple low-fidelity websites to test different problem descriptions. For example, a simple online accounts payable package can be simultaneously tested three different ways: as fastpay, ezpay, and flexipay. Each addresses three different accounts payable problems—speed, ease of use, and flexibility. Each landing page would be different, stressing the "ease of use" problem, for example. As a simple test of the problem, first buy Google AdWords for each URL and present the problem three different ways, in the AdWords space and on the landing page. Next, you would rotate the listings so each is on top of the Google stack exactly one-third of the time. (If nobody clicks, return to the start of this chapter.) Which approach generates the most clicks? Which yields the most sign-ups? The most referrals?

In the next step, you'll turn on the low fidelity MVP you've built, and see what happens in the next step. Good luck!

Test Understanding of the Problem and Assess Its Importance (Physical)

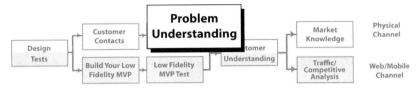

With your customer meetings scheduled, it's time to get out of the building and measure how serious and important the customer problems, passions or needs are in the customer's eyes. Are you solving an urgent "hair-on-fire" problem or something that it would be nice to fix "someday?" Obviously, one of those suggests a far larger market opportunity.

Develop a Problem Presentation

In contrast with a product presentation, a problem presentation is designed to elicit information *from* customers. The presentation summarizes your hypotheses about customers' problems and about how they're solving the problem today. It also offers some potential solutions, to test whether your assumptions are correct. This presentation is your icebreaker when you meet customers. (You may have to do this for each "side" in multi-sided markets, where the issues differ for buyers and sellers/users and payers.)

In contrast with a product presentation, a problem presentation is designed to elicit information *from* customers.

Developing a problem presentation is easy. Your hypotheses about customer problems and their solutions were articulated in the value proposition hypothesis in Phase 1. Put these assumptions into slides. Consider something as simple as a single-slide presentation (see Figure 5.4) listing the perceived problems first, the current solutions in Column 2, and your proposed solution in Column 3.

List of Problems	Today's Solution	New Solution
1.	1.	1.
2.	2.	2.
3.	3.	3.

Customer Problem Presentation *(Figure 5.4)*

Hopefully you'll never get to use your presentation. Your goal is to get the *customers* to talk, *not you. This is the biggest idea in Customer Development.* The real goal of the problem presentation is for you to capture your hypotheses about what you believe, but unlike an existing company, you aren't trying to convince anyone you're right. You're there to listen.

Get the *customers* to talk, *not you.*

The Problem Meeting

When you have the slide done, be prepared to present it using a whiteboard or simply one-on-one across a table. Remember, though, that "presenting" in this context really means inviting the customers' responses. So, after describing your assumed list of problems in column 1, pause and ask the customers what *they* think the problems are, whether you're missing any problems, how they would rank the problems, and which are must-solve rather than nice-to-solve. You've hit the jackpot when the customer tells you they will do anything to solve the problem.

The presentation must encourage discussion. Most people enter a meeting room expecting to be "talked at," especially in a first meeting with someone viewed as a potential vendor. When using slides, at least half the slides should create a "pause" that requires more than a yes/no response. Better still, use no slides and perhaps a printed handout or two instead. These kinds of questions stimulate a problem discussion:

- We think these are the five top problems facing the industry. How would you rank them as they affect your company?

- If you have three major problems to solve (in this area) in the year ahead, what are they and why do they make the "top three"?

- How does your company evaluate new products? (price? performance? features?)

What if a customer tells you that the issues you thought were important really aren't? Instead of feeling as if you've failed, realize you've just obtained great data. While it may not be what you wanted to hear, it's wonderful to have that knowledge early on.

Summarize this discussion by asking two questions: "What's the biggest pain in how you work? If you could wave a magic wand and change anything about what you do, what would it be?" (These are the "IPO questions." Understand the answers to these questions and your startup is going public.) Casually ask, "How much does this problem cost you (in terms of lost revenue, lost customers, lost time, frustration, etc.)?" You'll use this number later in the customer validation step, when you develop a presentation.

Understand How They Solve the Problem Today

With agreement on the problems and their cost, you can display Column 2 (in Figure 5.4), the solutions available today. Again you pause, ask the customers what they think the solutions to the problem are, whether you're missing any problems, and how they would rank the viability of the existing solutions. What you're looking for here is an understanding of how customers solve this problem today or how they think others do. If the problem is painful or important enough, you'll get interesting answers. While you're at it, another critical piece of information is who shares these problems. Are there other consumers who do x or y? Other people in the same company? Others in an industry? Others with the same title? A set of people with common problems equals a common value proposition. This means you can describe the value of your product in a message that's understood across a broad audience.

"If you could wave a magic wand and change anything, what would it be?"

Finally, for both corporate and consumer products, introduce the company's solution (not a set of features but only the big idea) in Column 3. Pause and watch the customers' reactions. Do they even understand what the words mean? Is the solution evident enough that they say, "If you could do that, all my problems would be solved?" Alternatively, do they say, "What do you mean?" Then do you have to explain it for 20 minutes and they still don't understand? Ask how your solution compares with the current solutions you just discussed. Once again, the point is not to deliver a sales pitch but to get their reaction and a healthy discussion.

Of course, what you learn from these discussions depends on what sticks after the meeting. Responses tend to blur together, so it's helpful to take hypothesis briefs along on visits. Look at the entire set. Before each call, shorten the list to "What are the three most important things I need to learn in the call?" Get at least those three questions covered. Take notes and listen actively. Over time, as response to key issues crystallizes, begin to ask different questions.

Think about ending a meeting with "Who are the three other smart people like you I should talk to?" I want my contact list to always be getting bigger. Another favorite closer is "What is it that I should have asked you?" The answers have been known to keep meetings running for another half-hour.

The *Problem* Meeting in a New Market

Using the problem presentation can be daunting in new markets, which lack context, since it's tough to solicit feedback on a problem folks don't recognize or realize they have. The classic (and tired) example of this is the likelihood that if Henry Ford had asked customers what they wanted, they would have said, "A faster horse." Unlike an existing market where there are customers who can name the basis of competition (features, price, needs, etc.) new markets have no existing customers. But that doesn't mean you should sit in your office and simply build your vision.

Always ask, *"What should I have asked?"*

Problem meetings in new markets use the problem–and-solution presentation to inform an entrepreneur's *vision*, not to specify features. In a new market, customer responses should provide additional insight, not numerical data. In a new market one of the warning signs that you may be hallucinating rather than have a vision is if you can't find any earlyvangelists who share your vision. (They share it by giving you an order, not a pat on the back.)

Collect Information on Everything

Before concluding the visit, ask yourself, "What else can I learn?" Never leave meetings, even bad ones, without learning three new things. I ask a series of seemingly innocuous questions. What conferences or trade shows do they attend? What blogs, journals, and magazines do they read? Who's the best salesperson they've ever seen? How do they hear about new ideas? Imagine asking these questions across 100 or more contacts and you can see yourself building a "customer order of battle"— a deep understanding of who they are and how to reach them. Keep detailed records of all responses. Develop a Customer Discovery Scorecard, described on page 241.

Avoid the Big-Company Meeting Trap

There's a special trap to watch out for when you call on big companies, where employees tend to attend meetings en masse, Clearly detrimental to open, freewheeling conversations with potential earlyvangelists that could have been rich in feedback. To ensure maximum feedback at big companies:

- Arrange one-on-one meetings with key targets (decision-makers, key influencers, and heavy users) before and/or after group meetings to gather individual feedback

- Try to get the "big boss" alone since others are often reluctant to speak up when he or she is in the meeting. They may also defer to him or her, minimizing important "outlier" feedback

- A possible approach to discovery with a big company is to bring your entire startup "brain trust" to a peer-to-peer meeting with the company's leadership so the two senior teams have a forum to discuss the opportunity

- Always state the goal upfront: we want a better understanding of how a trendsetter or industry leader confronts problems or challenges that might be solved by a new product (flattery never hurts)

Amalgamate and "Score" the Customer Data

When the first "out of the building" problem phase is complete, summarize the data, in a Customer Discovery Scorecard (Figure 5.5). The scorecard provides a sense of whether there's enough customer excitement around the product to warrant further forward motion. The analysis should help gauge whether the right people were contacted and whether enough earlyvangelist candidates were identified. "Weight" the data to adjust the findings' importance to company goals. In the process, some customers will be pursued aggressively, others will be put on "hold" until the product becomes mainstream, and some will be abandoned.

Don't lose or ignore outlier comments. They may lead to new features or different ways of selling or provide other suggested iterations for the business model. Look at both the summary data and specific or unusual comments from prospective customers.

Customer	Excited	Urgent Need	Business Impact	Work-around	120 day	Key Decider	120 x 2	TOTAL
A	3	3	3	2	2	3	2	18
B	2	2	2	1	2	2	2	13
C	2	2	1	1	1	2	1	10
D	3	2	1	1	3	2	3	15
E	1	3	1	1	1	1	1	9
F	1	1	1	1	1	1	1	7
Average	2	2.16	1.5	1.16	1.6	1.8	1.6	

Sample Customer Discovery Scorecard *(Figure 5.5)*

The scorecard rates six customers' views on a new industrial battery, using a score of 1 to 3, with 3 being highest. Rating checkpoints in this example include:

"Excited" and **"urgent need"** are self-explanatory.

"Business-Impact" reflects how important or transformative will the adoption of this technology be on the customer? Nice to have? Impacts a division? Changes their entire business model?

"Work-around," indicates that the customer has been solving the problem with a home-grown solution.

"120 day" indicates how likely it is that the customer will sign a purchase order in 120 days. Since this hypothetical company requires more funding within six months, 120-day purchases are double-weighted (thus the 120x2 column).

"Key decider," indicating that the conversation was with an empowered buyer.

The actual scorecard might have tens, hundreds or thousands of lines, but on this sample scorecard we're just looking at a handful of customers. If the six are representative, our sample scorecard suggests the need for more discovery data. Why? Only Customers A and B reflect both excitement, and an urgent need, for the product. Of those, only Customer A is an earlyvangelist candidate, experiencing enough pain to attempt a work-around solution. Even then, Customer A's score is only 18 of a potential 21 points, and he reflects uncertainty about buying the product within 120 days, neither of which are signs of a rabid enthusiasm for the product. Some other observations:

- Customer A is likely to buy within the 120-day goal period
- Forget Customer E for now, since excitement is poor despite the urgent need. And conversations with a decision-maker are a long way off, as is a buying decision
- Approach Customer C in hopes of meeting the decision-maker, and request another meeting with the decision-maker at Customer B
- Don't abandon any of the customers, since each acknowledges some significant need for the product. Those not selected for further discovery should be kept on ice and made part of the pipeline at a later date. Take your time calling back Customer F

Develop a viable mechanism that properly weights the key issues.

The average scores are also informative. The high "urgent need" average suggests there may be non-product problems, such as an inadequate problem presentation, ROI justification, or the need to reach higher-level folks during customer discovery in general, since everyone recognizes a need for the product but few are eager to buy. The poor 120-day score reinforces the likelihood that product benefits weren't described well and that the price/value message was unclear, or perhaps the price/value itself needs a pivot or an iteration.

Every product has a different set of variables to consider and score in aggregating and assessing the customer discovery findings. The key is to develop a viable mechanism that properly weights the key issues. Once the scores are impartially applied, discuss the system's accuracy. If it's accurate, score the entire set of customers. Don't forget to study the outlier comments.

Low Fidelity MVP Problem Test (Web/Mobile)

⇨ Now it's time to see if anybody cares about the problem you're solving or the need you're fulfilling. It's time to gradually invite people to the MVP you built in the previous step, see how they respond, and measure how and what they do.

> **WARNING!! PROCEED WITH CAUTION.** This step should be taken gradually, as your new product is meeting the public for the first time. Please resist the temptation to "go live" until you've read the next few pages.

Just because the MVP is live doesn't mean anyone will find it (remember that the web is a vast place with zillions of sites). So start inviting people to experience the MVP (at most, a few hundred at a time). Follow the plan outlined in your "get customers" hypothesis, accelerating the pace of customer acquisition slowly and watching every action or inaction closely. After all, this is the first time your product hypotheses will actually meet real customers, and the learning is likely to be intense.

Some of your hypotheses might be shot down in flames in the first hour or two. For example, most entrepreneurs would change something if they invited 50 friends to an MVP "problem" page and not a single one clicked or signed up. Imagine your surprise if you bought a list of 1,000 mothers of toddlers and three just accepted your invitation to join "toddlermom.com."

The customer relationships hypothesis developed in Phase 1 details how you'll "get" potential customers to the MVP, app, or site. Review it and take mini-bites of several acquisition and activation tactics you believe will bring you hordes of customers. (Think of each tactic you're planning as a jug of fuel. Start with an eye-dropper full and check the results. If they look good, as outlined in your hypothesis, pour in a tablespoon, a pint, or maybe a quart.) Remember that this is a small-scale test to determine whether your startup is solving a problem or need that customers care a great deal about.

There are three basic ways to invite people to engage on your site, and you should likely use all three: push, pull or pay.

Push people toward your site or app by using e-mails, their friends, or social media to get them there; *pull* them with SEO and pay-per-click or other devices; and *pay* is just what it says—buy lists, clicks, or other tools that deliver eyeballs.

"Push" Contacts Need Referral Sources: Reach out to friends and contacts using e-mails, texts, and social messaging tools such as Twitter, Facebook and LinkedIn. Encourage them to e-mail friends and colleagues and to use their Twitter, Facebook, Google+ and LinkedIn accounts to reach as many other people as possible. Obtain the longest possible list of e-mail addresses. Worry less about the details in these efforts and more about getting a big list. An invitation always works better when it comes from someone known to the recipient.

Provide a draft message your friends can use when reaching out on behalf of the company. It should express support for the idea and the value of exploring the problem. The e-mail should be short and as personal as possible and should indicate a strong relationship between founder and sender.

"Pull" Strategies: Pull can be ads, textlinks or AdWords and natural search driving people to the MVP, app or site. Pull solves three problems:

- There's no need to cajole everyone for e-mail addresses
- Only people interested in the issue, problem or need will respond
- People who are pulled are more likely to respond, perhaps repeatably

Here are some ways to pull people into the discussion:

- Google AdWords
- display ads or textlinks on social networks (Facebook, et al.) or relevant websites
- press releases with links to a survey or site about the problem
- getting bloggers to blog about the problem and invite commentary
- exploring the many online feedback tools available

"Pay" for Contacts: Buy lists of targeted business or consumer prospects. Typically the least attractive startup option for obvious (cash) reasons, this is usually the fastest option. A few to consider:

E-mail lists: Buy permission-based e-mail lists. The more narrow or focused the targeting, the greater the cost. Response rates are still challenging with this approach

Online survey tools: Buy a package of respondents, survey design, implementation and a guaranteed number of targeted responses from one of many suppliers such as Markettools

Established mobile data vendors: Vendors with credentials, high-quality clients and high ethical standards are a must in this channel. Check references thoroughly, since it's easy to violate federal laws

Hire a publication: Some trade and online media will survey their readers for you at a cost. It's expensive but helps with targeting and response because of the medium's credibility

Missteps to Avoid when Testing the Low Fidelity MVP:

- Customer discovery slips from the hands of founders and becomes a task for specialists (consultants, employees, etc.)
- Comments are summarized, averaged, and amalgamated, which tends to blur or hide the most distinct "outlier" comments that often lead to iterations and pivots

- National laws on mobile messaging and privacy need to be understood and respected. Penalties are substantial
- Online tools provide very little chance for context and dialogue that "drill down" in key discovery areas
- As a rule, people pay far less attention when filling out online surveys than they do in face-to-face conversation
- Online feedback is not a substitute for leaving the building and talking directly to customers, some of whom can be initially identified online. Don't let online interaction stand alone

You Don't Have Real Data Until You See Their Pupils Dilate

People lie on the web. And if you're depending only on web data, you'll never know it. Correlate response you get online with "ground truth." The best way to do that is to interview some of the sources of your web data in person. You don't have real data until you've seen their pupils dilate.

In addition, in-person interviews can test how well your MVP is explaining the need or problem, particularly if you show the customer several MVPs and learn which they like best and why. Can the customer "play back" the value proposition or problem statement after a brief explanation? Do they get palpably excited, or do they politely meander through the discussion? Talk about how extensively this problem affects their friends or coworkers and whether they'd be likely to buy a problem that solves it. Keep a close ear to the ground for outliers and comments like "It'd be much more important if you did this" or "Isn't that the same as product x, which never works right?" Those one-off comments are where pivots and iterations in the business model are most often found.

Drive Traffic and Start Counting

As soon as you can, begin e-mailing, Tweeting, calling, and inviting everyone you know to come visit and react to the MVP. One of the strategies of a web or mobile app is to instrument the product and measure and analyze everything. Use web analytics to track hits, time spent on-site, and source. For your initial site, Google Analytics may provide adequate information with the fastest setup. Once you've moved beyond your initial MVP, you'll want to consider a more advanced analytic platform (Kissmetrics, Mixpanel, Kontagent, etc.). Create an account to measure user satisfaction (GetSatisfaction, UserVoice, etc.) with your product and to get feedback and suggestions on new features.

Measure how many people care about the problem or need and how deeply they care. The most obvious indicator is the percentage of invitees who register to learn more. Next you need to learn if visitors think their friends have the same need or problem, so include widgets for forwarding, sharing and Tweeting the MVP.

Focus on the conversion rates. If the MVP got 5,000 page views and 50 or 60 sign-ups, it's time to stop and analyze why. If 44 percent of the people who saw an AdWord or textlink to the MVP signed up, you're almost certainly on to something big. What percentage of people invited to the test actually came? What percentage of people in each test (a) provided their e-mail address, (b) referred or forwarded the MVP to friends, or (c) engaged further in a survey, blog, or other feedback activity? Of those who answered survey questions, how many declared the problem "very important" as opposed to "somewhat important?"

Specific questions, such as "Is there anything preventing you from signing up?" or "What else would you need to know to consider this solution?" tend to yield richer customer feedback than generic feedback requests. If possible, collect e-mail addresses so you have a way to contact people for more in-depth conversations.

A powerful way to test a problem uses the Net Promoter Score™, developed by Satmetrix as a gauge of customer interest in the problem or need. The Net Promoter Score asks customers to answer a single question on a 0-to-10 scale, where 10 is "extremely likely" and 0 is "not at all likely": "How likely is it that you would recommend our company to a friend or colleague?" Based on their responses, customers are categorized into one of three groups: Promoters (9-10 rating), Passives (7-8 rating), and Detractors (0-6 rating). The percentage of detractors is subtracted from the percentage of promoters to obtain a Net Promoter Score. An NPS of +50 is considered excellent.

Analyze the results carefully. Dissect the numbers finely to determine if some customer segments or media drove particularly enthusiastic customers to engage with the MVP. For example, if 92 percent of teen girls forwarded the information to all their friends while nobody else expressed any serious interest, your business may still be quite viable.

Consider the Scalability: Not only is finding customers who care a daunting challenge, you need lots of them to be successful. What if your startup reaches break-even at 1 million activated users, for example (a modest goal for many venture-backed web businesses)? In the customer creation phase, you might need to invite 500 million people to visit—a potentially backbreaking expense if you hope to activate a million users.

Here's the math:

Number of people exposed to the site or product	500,000,000
2% of those exposed are actually acquired (1 in 50)	10,000,000
10% of those acquired become activated customers (1 in 10)	1,000,000 customers

Unless customer acquisition is almost totally viral in this hypothetical company, the costs of reaching 500 million people will result in running out of money. To avoid it, be sure you've found an important, painful problem or a serious customer need (then solve the problem or fill the need). The ability to attract large numbers of customers will make or break the business. If response rates don't at least approach those in the customer relationships hypothesis, it's time to revisit the business model.

The "Just Do It" Scramble

Increasingly, even at this early stage of customer discovery, some investors encourage startups to break all the rules and "just do it"—launch the product even if it doesn't exist. (Entrepreneurs are legendary rule-breakers anyway.) That's always an option, however your investors have a portfolio of 10, 20 or more startups like you. Their bets are across the entire portfolio. You, on the other hand, make a bet on a portfolio of one. There are times when tossing this book out and "going for it" makes sense (market bubble, incredible customer reaction to the concept, etc.), but make sure you understand why.

Gain Customer Understanding

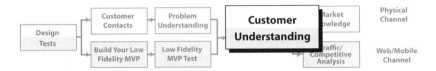

In addition to checking your assumptions about customer problems, you need to validate your hypotheses about how customers actually spend their days, spend their money and get their jobs done. Whether the product is for corporate customers, a social network, or a new consumer electronic device, you want to understand in detail how their lives or jobs work, how their work/design flow happens and how they currently solve the problem or fill the need.

If they're in a business, are their jobs done in isolation? If not, how do they interact with other departments? What other products do they use? Is the problem they've identified limited to them, or do others in the company share it? Is it possible to quantify the impact (dollars, time, costs, etc.) across the entire organization? The same questions work for consumers. Will they use the product themselves? Does it depend on others or their friends and family using it?

You'll want to check your assumptions about whether and how much people will pay for your solution. What would make customers change the way they do things? Price? Features? A new standard? If the customer's eyes haven't glazed over yet, dip your toe into the hypothetical product spec. "If you had a product like this (describe yours in conceptual terms), what percentage of your time could be spent using the product? How mission-critical is it? Would it solve the pain mentioned earlier? What would be the barriers to adopting a product like this?" (If you're a founder who has been in the industry you're entering, you may already be a domain expert and already bring deep customer understanding.)

Since someday soon your startup will have to create demand to reach these customers, use this opportunity to find out how they learn about new products. Who are the visionaries in the press/analyst/blogging community whom they read? Whom they respect?

Finally, never pass up an opportunity to spot talent. Can these customers be helpful in the future? For the next round of conversations? For an advisory board? As a paying customer? To refer you to other customers?

Your goal, after enough of these customer conversations, is to be able to stand up in front of your company and say, "Here were our hypotheses about our customers, their problems, and how they worked. Now here's what they're saying their issues really are, and this is how they really spend their day."

Your goal is to understand the customer in depth. What does *in depth* mean? It's impossible to know their jobs as well as they do, but you should be so thoroughly conversant with what truly matters to customers that you can discuss their issues convincingly.

In business-to-business companies, experience the customer at work, or at the very least observe it. Spend a day behind a cash register, at a trade show, or at a conference the target customers are likely to attend. Buy lots of coffees and have lots of casual conversations. Your goal should be to know the customer you're pursuing, and every aspect of his or her business, so deeply and intimately that they start to think of you and talk to you as if you were "one of them."

Know the customer you're pursuing so deeply they think you're "one of them."

⇨ Understanding customers for web/mobile applications starts with this strategic view:

For consumer applications, the web is replacing the face-to-face social interactions that people have had since we came down from the trees. Friendships are taking on new meaning, having essentially moved online, to social networks. Texting has replaced conversations, photo sharing has eclipsed the sharing of snapshots, and online games have replaced board games. "Traveling" salesmen spend more time on Skype and WebEx than on the road and network through LinkedIn, Jigsaw and Facebook. Even grandparents often video-chat as much as they visit.

Business applications have gone the same way.

So as you gather customer data, ask yourself, "What are we replacing? Why? How will it change what people now do physically?"

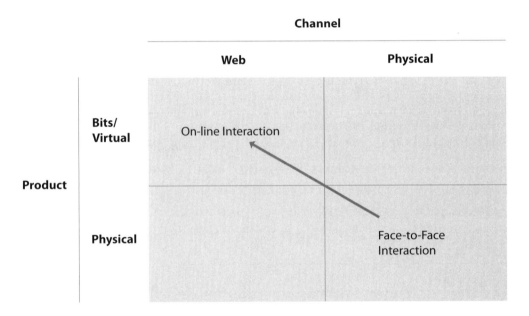

Understanding Customer Interactions *(Figure 5.6)*

Tactically, it's equally important to "become a customer" of existing web/mobile products to get a feel for how customers are getting their jobs done or needs fulfilled today. To do so, start to act like a customer:

- Participate in their culture. Read their websites and publications, watch their favorite videos, movies and TV shows, and share as many customer experiences as possible

- Get to know real live customers, not just in focus groups but in the places where they really spend time. Observe when they're online and when they're off and what they're doing each time they pick up their handheld: what app are they using, who are they texting or talking to, why did they choose this minute to play game A instead of game B, and how did they learn about games A and B in the first place?

- Play the games they play, use the apps they use, participate in their social networks and regularly visit the sites they regularly visit. You can internalize the customer's experience by observing it in depth and understanding his behavior and motivation

- Seek to understand, quantitatively, how and where they discover new ways to spend their time. From friends? From the "top seller" lists on an app store? On the airplane or the school bus?

The goal is to "become the customer."

Capture Market Knowledge (Physical)

With a better customer understanding under your belt, it's time to round out your understanding of the overall marketplace. Meet with companies in adjacent markets, industry analysts, people in the press, and other key influencers. Go to industry trade shows and conferences to understand the shape and direction of the market you're about to create.

When you start a company, you should have some vague notion of what companies are in adjacent markets or are part of the infrastructure or ecosystem of your business. Through your own contacts, but usually through introductions, take peers out to lunch. In exchange, gather information—not competitive information but answers to questions such as: What are the industry trends? What are key unresolved customer needs? Who are the key players in this market? What should I read? Whom should I know? What should I ask? What customers should I call on?

What will motivate these people to meet? Most won't do it out of the goodness of their hearts; rather, they'll meet to make a "trade." They'll learn about a key problem and its solution in exchange for providing their industry knowledge and insights.

Just as you did with your problem presentation to potential customers, don't present or sell—just listen and learn. Spend the time to take a few of the friendliest customers to lunch and ask them who they see as potential competitors, both internally and externally. Who do they think has similar products? Who else is an innovator in this space? Has this solution been tried elsewhere in their company? Is anyone else inside their company trying to build this product? It's amazing how much you can learn from the people who will eventually buy your product.

Ask the same questions of peers in adjacent markets, and after practicing on them, try to make contact with the key industry influencers and recommenders listed in Phase 1 and ask them the same set of questions.

It's a rare company that doesn't have a website. These provide a treasure trove of information, literally available at one's fingertips, about competitors, the market, and the industry where the company plans to compete. Start by Googling the problem and reading perhaps the first few hundred links. Be as specific as possible in selection of search terms, and try several different searches for maximum information. This effort leads to a wealth of market information, including news about the category, companies providing solutions, key blogs and websites addressing the industry, industry experts, and consultants.

Take competitors to lunch.

Then dive deeper into each competitor uncovered in the initial search. Find out not only what they say about themselves but also what others say about them—positive and negative. Try to discern key product features and selling points, which help differentiate the new offering from competition. Collect industry and competitive press releases, studies, and reports, and follow the thread to the consultants, researchers or pundits who wrote them to see what else they've said.

Next, start gathering quantitative market data. More than likely, Wall Street analysts issue reports on the market or adjacent markets. Get copies of all of these reports. More important, actually read them. Understand what the analysts believe are the trends, the players, business models, and key metrics.

Finally, industry conferences and trade shows are invaluable and essential. Never say, "I'm too busy to attend." Attend at least two key conferences or trade shows (the important ones picked in Phase 1). Not only do they provide great trinkets, but conferences and trade shows are the prime areas for both talent- and trend-spotting. Ask usual questions about trends and players, but this time accomplish a few things that can't happen anywhere else. Get demos of competitive and adjacent products. Get your hands on the products themselves, get competitors' literature, talk to their salespeople, and generally immerse yourself in your new industry. Attend as many conference sessions as possible, listening to others describe their products. What are their visions of the future, and how do they compare with your own newly developed value proposition?

After testing the customer problem (or need) and gaining a complete understanding of the customer, it's time to expose the product itself to potential customers for the first time. Not to sell to them but to get their feedback. Before doing so, be sure to update the hypotheses and business model wherever changes are indicated.

Traffic/Competitive Analysis (Web/Mobile)

⇨ The tools and tactics for developing market knowledge in the physical channel work equally well in the web/mobile channels. Start by searching the web and attending conferences, trade shows and other events to uncover great market insights. In addition, meet-ups of local groups focused on certain industries, particularly in the tech world, can be a great source of market knowledge, as can webinars conducted by competitors.

Web-market knowledge should deliver a complete understanding of the company's competitors and how potential customers solve the problem or address the need.

Use free traffic-measurement tools to compare and understand the traffic generated by each competitive product...

Use free traffic-measurement tools like Alexa and Compete to compare and understand the traffic generated by each competitive product or website, along with the traffic sources, growth trends, and demographic information where available. Much of this information is available for free, including the keywords driving traffic to the site, specific lists of sites linking to it and, in some cases, demographic and income data on site visitors. Compete.com offers side-by-side comparison of multiple url's, for example. Visit "answer" sites like Quora.com and start asking questions. This will cause more market information to surface and probably lead to new sources of expertise on product, category or market.

Mobile startups should visit every app store for each appropriate platform to identify competitors and their categories. Where do the competitors rank within the category, and is that rank ascending or descending? Try to determine at least approximate sales volumes wherever possible. And read the product reviews both at the stores and in category-specific review sites. There are particular challenges posed by the Apple app store. Their review process and lack of transparency in distribution (how many people see your app, how many click through, how many download) make accurate measures of acquisition/engagement difficult to come by.

Summarizing the results and reviewing them with the management team is helpful, ensuring that everyone is well-versed in the competitive arena the product is about to enter. Organize the competitive findings themselves into a competitive grid and a market map (described on page 119) to help position and market the new product.

CHAPTER 6

Customer Discovery, Phase Three: "Get Out of the Building" and Test the Product Solution

STEVE'S PHONE RANG AND THE VOICE ON THE end said, "You don't know me but I just read your book and think I need your help." That was the day we got to know one of the most innovative startups within a "Fortune 500" corporation (#6): General Electric's Energy Storage division.

Prescott Logan, the unit's brand-new general manager, recognized that his unit's new sodium industrial battery was a disruptive innovation, which GE traditionally does well, but aimed at a market where the end users were unknowns. Logan realized his division looked more like a multimillion-dollar startup with all the usual startup uncertainty, but located within a huge, execution-oriented company. He needed a framework or architecture to help his team deal with a "white space" market and apply startup "search" and customer discovery principles at a company known for "six sigma" execution.

Energy Storage was buying capital equipment, breaking ground on a massive factory, and out making sales calls—in full "execute" mode, the way most big companies work—based on a ton of diligence and an external consultant's 30,000-foot view of the opportunity, but not likely having had enough face-to-face end user conversations.

Soon after the call, the customer-facing team came to the ranch to map a customer discovery plan. They had a clear fix on the "customer problem" (life cycle, wider range of operating temperatures, etc.), and knew how they'd take the well-vetted innovation from the lab to manufacturing, but one question remained. Who would buy it in volume, and why? In two days of brainstorming, the Customer Development process offered GE the following initial observations:

- The new GE battery should serve dozens of market segments, not just the two they'd selected: backup systems for cell towers and data centers
- They needed to look many more customers in the eye to validate the market selection
- Product managers were spending too much time in Schenectady, N.Y. headquarters, where there were no customers and no answers. Customers were outside the building
- With an existing global customer base, GE had plenty of access to potential customers
- They needed to find earlyvangelists, essential when launching new technology like GE's, and determine the earlyvangelists' characteristics as well as how to find them
- They needed a formal process to review what discovery data they'd gathered to date to understand how different the value proposition was for each market segment—and where the opportunities might be greatest for a high-performance, more expensive alternative to lead-acid industrial batteries (far bigger versions of the one in your car)

- What other business model "boxes" would customers like them to change in order to sign a purchase order? The GE team uncovered several including changing the product features themselves, making the product somewhat configurable, and offering leasing and other alternative financing models

Prescott grasped Customer Development faster and better than anyone we had ever seen. The Energy Storage division was a startup. All the rules for managing and launching product line extensions—business plans and revenue models—didn't work. They needed instead to first test their basic hypotheses about their business model.

Leaving the ranch, Prescott and team joined the million-mile club as they flew across the U.S. and to Asia, Africa and the Middle East, meeting face-to-face with dozens of prospects, suspects, and influentials to explore multiple potential new markets and applications. They did their best to leave PowerPoint decks behind, and listen to customers' problems, needs, and frustrations with the battery status quo. Unscripted, open-ended discussions with a wide range of prospects were conducted worldwide to listen about how prospects bought their batteries, how often they used them, and the operating conditions. In one target market, Prescott actually relocated a top customer development team member and his family to India and said "don't come home til you get a purchase order signed," which he did, learning immensely about how his target segment customers might use the battery and—more important—how they'd evaluate and buy.

Talking to a wide range of prospects, the team soon found more market segments, and even though they aren't huge businesses yet, they're promising because the product's unique capabilities "unlock" far more value for users in certain segments. For example, the battery's small footprint and environmental friendliness make it a far better choice as a backup to computer systems in high-rise office buildings, where real estate is expensive and the floors often can't hold the weight of massive lead-acid battery arrays. In one case, they found an architect who said "I don't really care what it costs, I want it."– the precise definition of an earlyvangelist!

It was customer discovery and early validation on steroids, driven by a passionate entrepreneurial CEO (though Jeff Immelt has that particular title) who'd stand up against any valley startup leader. Prescott's boss, GE VP Tina

Donikowski, provided cover while the team executed the thorough, honest search process any startup must have, rather than the six sigma execution drills that made GE so famous. And Prescott chose people who didn't fit the typical big company mold: "white space" thinkers who lived for the search and embrace the unknown.

While the jury is still out, and the business is a long way from its huge revenue goals, this team of passionate entrepreneurs hiding in a *"Fortune 6"* company have just about posted a "sold out" sign on the factory for its first six months of operation. We think that sign has a good chance of being up for a while.

"Test the Solution:" an Overview

The previous phase tested the customer *problem* or need and explored customers' passion for it, This phase tests whether the *solution* to that problem—the value proposition—gets customers' enthusiastic enough to buy/use the product. This phase has five steps:

- Update the business model and team—a Pivot or proceed point
- Create the product solution presentation (physical channel) or the high fidelity MVP test (web/mobile)
- Test the "product solution" (physical channel) or begin to measure customer behavior (web/mobile channel)
- Yet again, update the business model and team
- Identify the first advisory board members

⇨ Web/mobile startups find it hard for customers to visualize the proposed solution without a minimum viable product. (Most startups should have at least their low fidelity MVP up by now.) The MVP illustrates the product for customers so they can see whether the minimally featured product solves the problem. Feedback takes the form of online and in-person discussions. (Screen shots and mock-ups are no longer viable stand-ins.)

Update the Business Model and Team (a Pivot-or-Proceed Point)

With a far deeper understanding of customers and their problems, it's time for an important pivot-or-proceed pause in the Customer Development process. While some startups have already pivoted, every entrepreneur should use this step to take a pause and review the collection of customer feedback about the problem and its importance. Those findings, coupled with extensive customer, industry, and competitive research, have taught the company a great deal about its customers, how they work or play, the market, and the problem the company has been founded to solve. This learning makes it a near-certainty that at least some business model hypotheses need to change. (When a substantial change is made to one or more business model hypotheses, it's a pivot.)

Start this phase by gathering as much of the company management as possible (not just the founders and VPs but directors and managers as well), along with key investors, for the pivot-or-proceed review. Share everything that's been learned, with a focus on customer feedback regarding the importance or severity of the problem or need—the potential product/market fit. The group also reviews new findings that may affect hypotheses or assumptions made in Phase 1, adjusting them where appropriate. These can often include the value proposition or product specs, customer segments, pricing, and revenue model assumptions.

Start by Assembling the Data

Before the meeting, the Customer Development team gathers all the customer data and builds a work-flow map of the prototypical customer. At the meeting itself, the spokesperson for the team diagrams and describes how customers actually do their job and whom they interact with. This provides a reality check of the customer hypotheses. Keep diagramming and drawing until it's easy to explain how customers' businesses and lives work today, including how they spend their time and money. Compare this description with the initial hypotheses. (While corporate customers may have more formal organization to diagram, a consumer will have more external influencers to track.)

With the customer work flow and interactions fully described, dive into the real news. What problems did customers say they have? How painful are these problems? Where on the "problem scale" are the customers you interviewed? How are they solving these problems today? Draw the customer workflow with and without your product. Is the difference dramatic? Did customers say they would pay for that difference? In general, what did you learn about customers' problems? What were the biggest surprises? What were the biggest disappointments?

Question *Everything*

Once the Customer Development team has presented its findings, the fun begins. You can now ask the most difficult question. Given all that's been learned from talking to customers, how well do the preliminary product specs solve their problems? Dead on? Somewhat? Not exactly? If the answer is "somewhat" or "not exactly," this meeting becomes a soul-searching, company-building exercise. Is it because the right people weren't interviewed? Failed to talk to enough people? Because nobody asked the right questions? This assessment is critical because of a fundamental assumption of the Customer Development model: before changing the product, keep looking for customer enthusiasm. If and only if no customers can be found for the product, discuss changing the feature list.

People who talk to customers tend to collect a list of features that, if added, will get one additional customer to buy. Soon there's a 10-page feature list just for selling 10 customers. In contrast, in Customer Development the goal is to have a single-paragraph feature list that can be sold to thousands of customers.

What if everyone believes you're talking to the right customers but the feedback says you're building the wrong product? Something has to change. Don't continue building the product and think miracles will happen. Either get back outside the building and find a different set of customers who will buy the product or consider changing the features.

Assuming the product is at least a partial fit for customers' problems, continue examining the product assumptions and specs. Based on customer feedback, review the Phase 1 feature list. Prioritize the features in terms of their importance to the customer. Can the Customer Development team match each feature to a customer problem? If not, why not? While figuring out what features to ship is important, knowing which features don't matter is equally important. Which features did customers not care about? Can any features on the product spec be deleted or deferred? Remember, in a startup the Customer Development team isn't supposed to be adding features; it's supposed to be finding out the *minimum* feature set, based on input from visionary customers.

Next, review and get agreement on the delivery schedule, again revising Phase 1 assumptions as necessary. As noted earlier, visionary customers, particularly in corporations, will be buying into the entire vision, not just the MVP. *They will need to hear what the company plans to deliver over the next 18 months.*

Earlyvangelists need to hear about the 18-month product roadmap.

Finally, as a group, review the other Phase 1 hypotheses. (Now it's clear why writing them all down was important.) Given all the feedback from customers, which of the four market types is the company in? Why is it different? What are its competitive advantages? Do the initial pricing and delivery channel assumptions hold up? What was learned about influencers?

⇨ While this step is largely the same for web/mobile startups, they have the advantage of more behavioral data to assess. Web/mobile startups can quantify customer interest in and enthusiasm for solving the problem or filling the need. The analysis shouldn't care whether 2.5 percent or 3.2 percent of the customers were interested but should instead assess whether this is a big, serious "hair-on-fire" problem that many customers are eager to solve. Customer discovery data is limited because online problem discovery is conducted on a small scale, so right now your analysis is simply direction-al in nature. Some signs that the problem or need is sizable or serious:

- At least 10 percent (25 percent or 50 percent is even better) of customers exposed to the problem somehow indicate their interest in solving it

- Many of those exposed to the problem pass information along to friends or coworkers

- A Net Promoter Score of at least +50 or, ideally, far higher (see page 215 for details)

- Some clear segment of the total market is particularly passionate about the problem or need

Pivot or Proceed

Regardless of channel, this step concludes with the first of many pivot-or-proceed discussions. Management and investors affirm they're confident the company has uncovered a problem in which a sizable enough universe of customers is clearly eager to solve. If not, it's time to rethink the value proposition and attack a more severe problem or a need of greater interest or urgency to a larger customer universe. If the universe is eager to solve the problem, the group moves on to present   its potential product solution to customers.

...summarizing customer findings is not an accounting problem.

One last thought: Collecting and summarizing customer findings is not an accounting problem. You aren't simply adding up the number of responses. You're looking for learning, meaning and insight in the data. And more than anything, you're looking for hordes of customers who will try to rip the product right out of your hands so they can have it before their friends or competitors.

Create the Product "Solution" Presentation (Physical)

Once product development and Customer Development teams agree on the revised hypotheses, the next step is to assemble the first product "solution" presentation. This presentation is emphatically *not* the presentation used for fundraising or recruiting. Nor is it the problem presentation just used with customers in Phase 2. Toss those slides out and start over. This presentation tests the revised assumptions about the product itself. It's a *solution presentation* confirming that the product fits a serious customer problem or need. Customers confirm their interest by expressing interest in buying or using the product.

The presentation should cover the five (no more!) key product features and the problems they solve. Include a story about "life before the product" and "life after the product" where appropriate. Draw the customer's work flow or the consumer's day "before" and "after" the product. Leave out all the marketing, positioning and fluff. Close with the product vision (from the value proposition "vision" hypothesis) at least 18 months out.

Leave plenty of room and "cues" in the presentation to prompt customer feedback. Rehearse. Remember that this is still not "selling," but an effort to uncover whether the product is salable. Learn enough so that when selling begins, the team is confident that customers will be eager to buy.

Here's the product/solution presentation outline:

Review the problem. Start by reminding the audience about problems the product is designed to solve and why a solution is important if not urgent. Pause here to re-validate the importance of solving the problem. As surprises emerge, return to Phase 2.

Describe the solution. Demonstrate the product if possible; even sketches or prototypes of key concepts or features help customers understand. Pause to probe for a reaction. Do customers agree it solves the problem?

Draw the customer work flow before and after the new product. Validate the "before and after" work flow. Describe who else in the customer's organization the solution might affect.

Understand the value equation: Some customers will pay almost anything for a product that solves a serious business problem. Sometimes, third-party features enhance value when added. Keep pricing discussions fluid, and identify the key values a prospect sees. Watch for pleasant upside pricing opportunities.

The product/"solution" presentation should take no more than 20 minutes. In the next step, you'll present it to customers and *listen to their feedback.*

If an MVP doesn't exist, a demo or prototype will make the discussion more effective. This is why fashion designers make one actual dress and show it to buyers, car companies build one "concept car" to display, and why toy companies make one or two nonworking Styrofoam prototypes of the latest toys and games to show buyers. The more an MVP looks, feels, and works like the product, the more informed the customers' reactions will be. Obviously, this is far easier in some product categories than others. (Try prototyping the new 787 jetliner, for example.) Equally obvious: the closer the MVP is to a touchable, usable prototype, the fewer slides are needed for the solution presentation.

High Fidelity MVP Test (Web/Mobile)

⇨ The "Low Fidelity MVP Test" (page 211) probed the intensity of customer interest in the problem or need. Now it's time to determine whether customers will engage with or buy the product or use the site or app.

This "solution test" is not a live launch or even a "soft" launch; rather, it simply invites a limited number of customers to experience the MVP (which is a continuously improving work in progress). That "limited number" can be measured in thousands, and if even more show up that's a very good sign, since they've probably been sent by friends who think highly of the solution.

This "solution test" is not a live launch or even a "soft" launch.

Large-scale testing isn't the goal here. At this point, you're opening the "front door" and inviting a modest number of customers in. It's discovering enough passionate, enthusiastic earlyvangelists who clearly believe the product solves their problem. (For guidance on home and landing page MVP development, see pages 320-321.)

More than anything else, watch for the "velocity" of customer activation. What's velocity? In a car, it's how fast it's moving. In a web/mobile business, velocity means several things, often at once:

- how many visits before someone activates
- how many tell their friends

- how fast those friends activate, and
- how quickly—and how often—visitors return

Two rare exceptions to this quest for velocity may be niche vertical sites like "lefthandedprobowlers.com" and high-value products like enterprise software or extravagant jewelry, where fewer high-value customers may be just fine.

Stealth or No?

It's impossible to launch a hi-fidelity MVP test in "stealth" mode, since the product and its website are being exposed to customers and prospects to test their reactions. Customer Development and stealth are mutually exclusive. If you believe your idea is so fragile that it cannot be exposed to non-employees without a signed non-disclosure agreement, you shouldn't be reading this book.

A completely open, public site or app invites competitors, so you may want to consider an "invite-only" site to control access as you test your solution.

In most markets and industries the trade press is not investigative journalism (you have to set yourself on fire to get noticed). As a reminder, now is not the time for press releases, interviews, blogs or public demos (other than to potential investors). You simply do not know enough yet to say what business you are in. If you do get noticed by the press, simply don't return their e-mails or calls.

Test the Product Solution with the Customer (Physical)

With the solution presentation complete, decide which customers to visit. Earlier, your "problem discovery" visits should have reached at least 50 potential customers. Try to deliver this solution presentation to every qualified prospect who heard the problem presentation. Expand the original set of customer contacts to include at least 10 potential customers for complex products like enterprise software, and many more for consumer products. These new contacts keep the momentum going and lay the groundwork for selling something during customer validation.

This time, test previous assumptions about the titles of people who will make the purchasing decision. Return to the customer types described earlier (page 87), and interview several of each type to get a full spectrum of feedback. Find prospective saboteurs wherever possible, with an eye to spotting patterns in their job titles. With the call list in hand, create an introductory e-mail, reference story and sales script, and then get out of the building.

Solution Presentation

Begin by reminding the audience what problem the product is designed to solve and why the company believes solving the problem is important. With agreement on the problem and its significance, it's finally time for the solution presentation you developed earlier (most entrepreneurs have wanted to do this since Day One, so you should be ready by now). Demonstrate the product, rough prototype or MVP wherever possible for maximum impact.

Now it's time to listen. After hearing the solution description, how do customers think it solves their problem. Do they think it's different? Do they think the product is creating a new market, or is it a better version of an existing product (and, if so, better in what way)? Or do they yawn or shrug? Check other hypotheses. What do customers think about the proposed revenue model and pricing? What are comparable prices for this kind of product?

Use a post-visit "report card" (see a sample on page 241) to consistently record feedback. Remember, this isn't a sales call, but an exploration to see whether customers believe the product is a strong solution to an important problem—and to gauge whether the solution is strong enough to get them to buy when the product's ready.

"Show Me the Money" Questions

When talking to visionary customers about big-ticket b-to-b products, ask several questions to test adoption. "Would you deploy our software enterprise-wide if it were free?" Tests the seriousness of a potential customer. If the customer isn't ready to deploy the software even for free, you're obviously talking to the wrong person. When a customer is willing to visualize the pain of rolling out your product, ask how they would deploy it, how many users would use it, what groups would get it first, the criteria they'd use to measure its success, and so on. By the end of this visualization exercise, potential customers are sometimes mentally installing and deploying your software.

Be sure to get to the "who has the money" question. There's nothing more frustrating than having a series of great customer meetings for months only to find out very late in the sales cycle that no department has the budget or that new capital purchases are made on an annual cycle that just closed. Ask if a current budget exists for products like this and which department or individual would have the budget. The information will be critical when assembling the sales roadmap.

Pricing Questions

Explore the pricing boundaries. Ask, "Would you pay $1 million for our software?" The answer is usually instructive. Suppose customers said, "we couldn't see paying more than $250,000 for the first set of applications." In their minds, they had already bought the product and the bill just came due. The first number out of their mouths was usually what they had in their immediate budget or the initial purchase price.

AJAX Customer Discovery Report Card
Company Name_____ Date_____
Contact Name_____ Job Title_____Interviewed by_____
Years in field____with company___ reports to _ (circle one) approves/buys/influences sale
Key problems in my industry: (in priority order, as customer tells it)
1._____
2._____
What our product solves/doesn't solve for customer:
_____
Key solution elements: price-features-easy to get-easy to use-training-support
Rate customer pain with key problem/need (5 is torture): 1 2 3 4 5
How they solve problem today:_____
Customer satisfaction with current solution (5 very happy): 1 2 3 4 5
(Circle:) Has workaround /Has budget to fix /Has tried and failed /Pressure to fix from above
New/different problem(s) customer faces/needs solved/wishes we solved:
_____
Key features desired/not needed in new product/solution:
_____
"If I had a magic wand, a product would appear that…"
_____
Company process for testing/buying new products
(people/approvals/timing/bidding/other):
_____
How/where they'd buy:_____
Where they go/read/learn about new products: _____
Key decision-maker/where to start/who else to see:_____
_____
Price considerations: range/customer estimate/similar products:_____
_____
BEST ESTIMATE/number of units (initial range):_____ to _____ year two:_____ to __
BEST GUESS price_____ % probability_____ sale month_____ direct/channel___
Is interview subject (circle)
Earlyvangelist Advisory Board Industry Influential Saboteur C-Level
Referrals to others "like him or her ": (name)_____ (company)_____
                                        (name)_____ (company)_____
Others to see at this company: (name)_____ (company)_____
                                        (name)_____ (company)_____
Follow-up opportunities:
_____
(Circle) return with product/return meet others/provide data, specs/sample/write order

REMEMBER: referrals to other companies…can I call you again…send thank-you note

Sample Customer Discovery Report Card (Figure 6.1)

Once you get a first number, ask, "How much more would you expect to pay for professional services (the customization and installation)?" Most of the time they'll say that that cost was included in their budget number, but some add to that figure. Then push and see whether they would spend those extra dollars every year or ask, "What would we have to do to get you to spend twice that? Three times that?"

After a few of these customer exercises, you'll understand your average selling price and sense the lifetime value of a customer.

Channel Questions

What about distribution? Test these assumptions by asking customers how they would most likely buy. Retail store? Online? Direct sales? Distributor? From there, as time allows, explore how marketing might reach the customer with questions like:

- If you were interested in a product like this, how would you find out about it?
- How do you find out about other new products like this?
- Do you ask others for their opinions before buying? If so, whom?
- Do you or your staff go to trade shows?
- What industry-specific magazines or journals do you read? What business publications?
- For consumer products, ask what general-interest publications, newspapers, bloggers or websites would best connect with the consumer

"Get/Keep/Grow Questions"

Next, probe the customers' product acquisition process. For corporate products, ask, "How does your company buy products like this? Walk me through the approval cycle. Who is involved?" Software entrepreneurs should be forewarned that many Fortune 500 companies, too often burned, automatically reject software offerings from startups that haven't reached their fifth birthday. If it's a consumer product, understand the buying process. Is this an impulse buy? Do they buy only known brands? Items advertised on TV?

Presentation Tips

A few tips to smooth the way:

- Don't attempt to ask every question in each solution interview. Some customers will know more about one aspect of the product than another
- Opt for one-on-one discussions over large-group meetings. You'll get more detail and more thoughtful opinions
- Convert the discussions into a rough sales pipeline based on people's interest in buying
- It's better to find and stop work on or delete unnecessary features than features to add new ones. The goal is an MVP now!

It's optimistic to expect customers to share all this information at the first presentation or to expect every customer to know enough to answer every question. Try to accumulate answers to all the questions over the course of all the customer visits. Completing this phase signifies a complete understanding of customers' problems and a solid grip on their level of product interest.

Meet the Channel

If any form of indirect sales channel will be involved, one more group needs to see the solution presentation your potential channel partners needs to see. While it's too early to sign up channel partners with formal commitments, meet them now and understand what it would take to get them to sell the product.

- What do channel partners need to hear or see from early customers?
- How do customers access their channel?
- Is it the kind of product they'd sell proactively?
- Do they want articles in the business press, product reviews and customers calling them and asking for the product?
- Do they seek financial inducements such as shelf-stocking fees, guaranteed returns or—worse—a "guaranteed sale" policy that allows them to return unsold merchandise?

Channel partners won't magically know how to position or price the new product. For products in an existing market, it's easy to tell them, "It's like that other one you sell but faster." For re-segmented and new markets, indirect channels have a harder time understanding how to position products. Spend time understanding channel partners' motivations and incentives, and soliciting their feedback about features, pricing, sales opportunities and more.

Understand each channel partner's business model. Why? There's no way to understand how much channel partners should order or how much they should charge customers unless *their* business model is clear. See how other companies do it. Take other executives to lunch and ask about margins and discounts. The worst that could happen is that they won't disclose the information. Keeping all this in mind, assemble a channel/service partner presentation and stress what's in it for the partner. Partners are usually fondest of things on which they make more than just margin—some like products that require installation, service or ongoing supplies, such as paper and toner for copiers. Finally, hit the streets to start a dialogue and learn about their business:

- How do companies establish a relationship with them?
- Do they hear their customers asking for a product like yours?
- How does a potential partner make money? (By project? By hour? By reselling software?)
- How does their business model compare with others in their business?
- What is the minimum dollar size for a transaction of interest to them?
- Understand each channel partner's business model well enough to draw it on a whiteboard

Measure Customer Behavior (Web/Mobile)

⇨ The high-fidelity MVP test launched in the previous step began inviting customers to engage with your product, site or app. The goal is not to sell them anything (even though that may happen more than once) but instead to gauge the extent of their enthusiasm for the product. As customers arrive, each one of their actions should be measured: where they come from, what they click on, what they do and how long they stay, to name a few. It's not a statistical exercise at all, but a process that begins by knowing the right metrics to measure.

> **PROCEED WITH CAUTION:** Remember, this is an overview/ tutorial. There's no way you can implement all this or even process this in one sitting.

Measure Enthusiasm Most of All

These metrics are key "enthusiasm indicators" for almost any product, app, or site:

Purchase: Obviously a favorite among e-commerce and subscription sites, this action is the easiest to measure if the product or service is available for sale, even as an MVP, at this very early stage. If not, an acceptable substitute is customers' willingness to register so they can be notified when the product is available or simply to learn more about it.

Engagement: Once a user visits for the first time, how often does he come back? Multi-sided market and other ad-supported sites need to know users will come back often, generating page views that lead to revenue. If a user comes back five times a day or a week, that's promising. Five times a month probably won't deliver a scalable business. If 1,000 customers come once, how many of them return often, as opposed to those who seldom or never return? Dig deep to determine the level of user engagement:

- how often do users visit?
- how long do they stay?
- how active are they when using the site or app?
- What are the characteristics of frequent returnees (are they gear heads, teens, retirees or housewives)?
- Can more of them be found cost-effectively?

At low-engagement sites like Weather.com and bing.com, and apps like tip calculators or Foursquare, customers hit the app or site, find what they want, and depart in a matter of moments. These sites and apps need to measure frequency of use to determine enthusiasm. If users visit once a month, they're of little value; if they use an app dozens of times a day, it's probably a strong multi-sided market product. Low-engagement sites should measure frequency of use first.

Look for significant visit frequency or time spent on the site...

High-engagement sites like multiplayer games, social networks, and rich niche-content sites need to look for significant time spent on the site: a solid percentage of visitors:

- registering
- filling out profiles, posting
- comments
- uploading photos
- inviting friends to engage

Retention: for almost any app or site, retention is a critical measure of customer enthusiasm. It's tricky to measure retention during the customer discovery phase, when time spans are relatively short. After all, if discovery is under way for two months, retention can be measured for only that brief period. Look for behavior patterns. Measure both of the most obvious form of attrition (the opposite or enemy of retention): unsubscribes and terminations. Inactivity is the most insidious form of attrition, particularly in mobile apps. People don't delete the app, but they also never use it.

Referral: Do site visitors or MVP users refer their friends?
- what percentage refer others?
- do they refer one or two or six or 10?
- whose referrals engage better than others?
- which referrals become heavy users or referrers?

The operators of freecash.com would no doubt get a near-infinite number of referrals if the site lived up to its name. Greater referral volume indicates enthusiasm for the product and also should point toward a lower customer acquisition cost, since many customers may come via referrals from other customers. Both are good indicators of success potential.

Conduct Pass/Fail Tests

For each test, you should have a pass/fail metric developed earlier. But look for great or massive response and activity, not just a passing grade.

The answer to pass/fail tests is binary, by definition: Do (more than 50% of) customers love it? Is the product exciting to "enough" customers (insert your number here) for the startup to move forward to the customer validation step?

How many customers are "enough" is a multipart question for entrepreneurs, not accountants.

Detailed spreadsheets and analyses will help immensely during customer validation, when the behavior of tens of thousands of visitors will be measured in painstaking detail. For now, job No. 1 is to be sure the test is valid, with the success criteria established upfront and factored into the business model. For example, if you need to spend $50 on Facebook ads to get an order, that's great if the product costs $200, but not so good if it sells for $49.95. So when you "pass" a test, you're moving closer with each passing grade to a successful business model.

How many customers are "enough" is a multipart question for entrepreneurs, not accountants.

The question of Earlyvangelist volume needs a convincing answer: yes, enough interested, passionate earlyvangelists can be found to buy the product. (They will guide product development and marketing through the next stages of Customer Development.)

Don't stop driving people toward the product until you're certain of:

- How many people who expressed serious interest in the need or problem actually accept an invitation to explore the product, and how many engage or accept the call to action?

- How many less interested or uninterested people are willing to explore and engage?

- For each of those groups, how many will tell others, and how many will they tell?

- Answer each question on both an absolute and a percentage basis. If, for example, 1,000 people show up, were invitations sent to 2,000 or 200,000? The implications are obvious

Whether via e-mail, AdWords, Twitter or carrier pigeon, each set of invitations should be sent multiple times (read about e-mail cascades on page 326) for maximum impact. Consider changing the messaging if traffic or engagement are inadequate. Otherwise, nobody will ever know if the messaging was bad or the product was uninteresting.

Measure Test Results Carefully

It's crucial to measure customer behavior with the MVP itself. While user volume will probably be small, measure not only the traffic and user activity but also the traffic sources and acquisition and activation rates. How much time did users spend with the product or on the site? Did visitors register on the first, second, or third visits? Referral rates, perhaps the most critical measure of enthusiasm, should be closely measured as well. (Guidelines are found in Chapter 4, beginning on page 167.)

But look for great responses and activity, not just a passing grade.

Assemble the data and mine it deeply, looking for insights into sources of traffic, most or least engaged customer types, those who referred the most customers, and other clues. The data will be reviewed in depth in the next phase, but focus on one simple thing: have we found enough people interested in the product to move forward to customer validation?

Study channel data: In the web/mobile product arena, channels may be resellers like amazon.com, an app store or iTunes or aggregator reseller websites like GameStop, CDW or yugster. Interact with these channels to understand their regulations governing new products, how long it takes from initial contact until actual live sales begin on their sites, payment terms and more. Since they deal with massive volumes of app and software sales, the execs at these resellers can be extremely helpful on such key issues as pricing and positioning.

In the customer discovery phase, numbers themselves often aren't strong or exciting. Before abandoning ship, dig deeper to determine whether the app or site has hit a nerve among a customer cohort or segment (teenage girls, first-time site visitors, old golfers). Mine the data from the most frequent users (easy if there aren't too many of them) to see if they share any common traits. Might they all be Democrats or gourmet cooks or young urban professionals? If so, consider iterating the marketing messages and the audience targeting in hopes of getting far more excitement and engagement from a smaller subset of the total population.

Multi-sided markets should also conduct initial conversations with the other "side" of their market: the people who will pay to reach the audience aggregated by the site or application. How do the "payers" buy advertising? What are they willing to pay? How long does the process take, and at what point should conversations begin? (For a more detailed discussion of the "other side" of multi-sided markets, see page 110.)

Update the Business Model Again
(Another Pivot-or-Proceed Point)

Here you'll update the business model to reflect the latest round of customer discovery "solution" findings and how they do or don't affect the elements of your business model. Think of it as a "tune up," since you'll conduct a thorough business model review in the next phase.

Your focus here is totally about customers' enthusiasm for the product, and the conversation should be about pass/fail test results, not opinions.

⇨ For web/mobile startups, data plays an even greater role in this conversation, as discussed below.

Your business model should undergo regular updates.

Look for Massive Customer Enthusiasm

This is the time to remember that *lukewarm response to any product or the problem it solves is a serious, red-alert danger signal* that calls for an iteration or a pivot rather than an automatic step forward into customer validation. Discuss the percentages as well as the number of customers visited who express rabid or significant enthusiasm for the product and high confidence that it solves an important business problem or fills a high-priority consumer need. What's the team's honest appraisal of how many customers would run out and buy it immediately? How many would tell all their friends or associates? Did any or, better, many declare the best possible vote of confidence, "I don't care if it's not complete or perfect—I want it now"? Start the conversation by sorting customer reactions into the following main categories:

Category 1: Customers unequivocally love the product, and no changes are needed.

Category 2: Customers like the product, but we've heard consistently that they want this or that additional feature at launch.

Category 3: Customers can understand the product after a long explanation, but no one was jumping over the table to buy it.

Category 4: Customers don't see much of a need for the product.

If most of the customers fall into Category 1, congratulations! If the business model components "add up," as reviewed in the next step, it may well be time move on to customer validation.

Regardless of channel, customer discovery sought a market for the product as originally spec'ed. The most dangerous customer responses lie in Category 2: "We need more features." As emphasized earlier, knowing which features don't matter is as important as knowing which features to ship first. Balance customer reactions with development time, since it may take much more product development effort to earn a convincing Category 1 answer. Why? Because the joke is true: "Normal people believe if it isn't broke, it doesn't need to be fixed. Engineers believe if it isn't broke, it doesn't have enough features yet."

The natural instinct of Engineering is to keep adding features. But customer discovery is a race to get the MVP into paying customers' hands as quickly as possible, so fewer features or an MVP that's just "good enough" are far better than losing a month or even a week's worth of customer feedback. Ask whether any features can be deferred. Let early customers help determine which features and functionality to add and in what sequence. Listening carefully to the right customers delivers a product strategy with a high likelihood of success in any channel.

⇨ In the web/mobile channels, the team is reviewing granular behavior data from a larger universe of early customers. Qualitative discussions about features should happen, but almost every discussion is augmented with hard, cold facts about customer behavior, and data is central to almost every discussion point. Some of the facts to discuss, always in absolute numbers as well as percentages:

- Page views per day or week and the growth rate of those page views over time
- Average time spent or page views with the site or product
- "Rate of gain," or the time it takes people to increase time/page views on subsequent visits
- Number of repeat visits for avid and average users; time lag between repeat visits and "rate of gain," or the measurable decrease in time between visits
- Number and percentage of invited or aware customers who were acquired
- Conversion rates of visitors-to-acquired, acquired-to-activated, and activated-to-active-users
- Referral rates and virality: number and percentage of early users who refer their friends, how many they refer, and how many friends are acquired/activated/actively engaged

---

Lukewarm customer response can indicate a profound problem.

While the numbers are probably small in many of the categories above, the discovery process is more directional than finite. To be honest, it's a search for rampant customer enthusiasm—the kind that delivers blockbuster business success. Determine whether there's enough customer enthusiasm and positive feedback to warrant a move forward to more rigorous testing in customer validation.

This is where entrepreneurial experience and "gut" guide the go/no-go decision. And the most convincing arguments for "go" involve statistics that show lots of activation, many people visiting and coming back again and again, and many more telling more and more of their friends or colleagues. So while the statistics drive the conversation, the leaders' instincts make the decision. This is where seasoned entrepreneurs, advisers, and investors have the potential to make important contributions.

Answers in Categories 3 and 4—customers aren't jumping over the table or don't see a need—are typical during a first round of customer discovery. At a minimum, they require serious thought and probably a pivot that involves restarting Phase 1 from the beginning rather than continuing forward on a death march to failure. This makes for a challenging board meeting but is often a critical turning point for investors and company alike. For technology products, lukewarm customer response can indicate a profound problem, usually characterized as the lack of product/market fit: not enough of a market for the product or a lack of robust demand for a product in a vast market.

Repackaging the Product—A Pivot Strategy

Other issues are sometimes referred to as positioning but more accurately described as "product repackaging." Product repackaging is a problem most technology startups have to deal with at some point. A technology-driven startup's first product is usually determined by the founding product development team. Often the product development team has a perfect feel for what the customers' needs are and how the customers want to buy the product. But most of the time they don't. If they haven't been intimately connected to the customer, the initial product configuration needs further refinement by the Customer Development team. While the core technology might be spot-on, its match for customer needs or purchase preferences can be off. A single monolithic software package might be too expensive or too complex to sell that way. Technology repackaging might solve the problem by reconfiguring the product features. Perhaps it can be sold as modules, or as a subscription service, or with increasingly featured versions, without requiring Product Development to completely reengineer the product. This problem must be caught and dealt with in customer discovery or it may affect the company's ability to survive.

Update the Business Model Canvas Again

Regardless of channel, this series of analyses and discussions will almost certainly affect some of the business model hypotheses. Most likely to be affected is the value proposition, since this first "solution discovery" effort helps shed light on whether people think the product solves the problem in a way that compels them to buy. When it doesn't, the value proposition is the most likely suspect for adjustment, whether features are added or subtracted as a result.

Customer segments should be reviewed, since the product may have resonated well with some segments and not others. If, for example, the product generates excitement only among a subset of the intended market (men, not women; managers, not staff people), that discovery will affect the revenue stream hypothesis as well. The team will conduct a thorough review of the business model in the next phase, so this is best thought of as a tune-up that updates the model to reflect the latest round of customer discovery "solution" findings.

Identify First Advisory Board Members

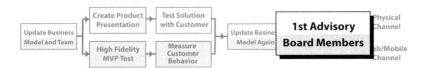

As good as any founding team may be, invaluable people outside the company who can't be hired full time will often be willing to help in an advisory capacity. These advisers can help solve technical problems, introduce key customers, provide domain-specific knowledge, and share business expertise and wisdom. Throughout customer discovery, when meeting customers and analysts, prospecting for advisory board members should always be in the back of everyone's minds.

Product Development should engage some advisers for specific help in designing and building the product, and a business mentor, someone who's been through the startup grind before, may also be helpful. One or two customer voices typically stand out from the crowd. Engage these people by asking them for advice, taking them to lunch or dinner, and seeing if they're interested in helping. Formalize the advisory board process later, during customer validation.

Read more about the advisory board structure and organization on page 352.

CHAPTER 7

Customer Discovery, Phase Four: Verify the Business Model and Pivot or Proceed

HAS YOUR CUSTOMER DISCOVERY EFFORT turned your hypotheses (or guesses) into hard facts? Do you believe it's time to proceed to customer validation, when you test whether your business model can scale?

There are three critical questions to answer:

1. *Have we found a product/market fit?* Is there sizable demand for solving the problem, and does the product fill that demand well in the customers' eyes?

2. *Who are our customers and how do we reach them?* Do we understand the demography and archetypes of our key target customers and enough about their behavior to know how to find them cost-effectively?

3. *Can we make money and grow the company?* Can we grow predictably and large enough to make a great company?

If your answer to this analysis is "proceed," remember that it's still not time to launch. This go/no-go decision answers only one question: do we have enough confidence in customers' enthusiasm and the product/market fit to proceed to customer validation and see if our business model scales by five times, 10 times or more? It's often frustrating to entrepreneurs who make the "go" decision, since they're rarin' to get out and start doing and selling. After all, that's what entrepreneurs do. It's also a dangerous trap: customer validation accelerates spending, which—if unsuccessful—can cost you your job, your equity, or both. (As we've said, this process isn't easy.)

Is This Business Worth Doing? *(Figure 7.1)*

Bring your team and investors to a "full stop" to answer the questions above. At a bare minimum, whether you Pivot or Proceed is the subject of an entire board meeting. Generally this assessment forces at least one return trip back to the start of the discovery process. This is the norm! (It's far better to find out now, before more years of 100-hour workweeks are invested.)

⇨ The three questions you're answering are virtually identical, regardless of whether the product and channel are physical or web/mobile. But web/mobile startups should have far more customer feedback and have implemented more product iterations than their counterparts in the physical world. Web/mobile startups should already see some measurable "velocity" in their rates of customer activation (which may not be as clear-cut in physical channel startups). If your web/mobile startup isn't seeing strong early signs of customer activation (sign-ups, referrals, return visits, upsells), it's almost certainly time to stop right here and start exploring changes to the business model.

Have We Found a Product/Market Fit?

Product/market fit has three components:

- Is the problem or need that's addressed urgent or vital to *lots* of customers—i.e., is there a market? (Replace "lots" with a real "pass/fail" number.)
- Does your product solve the problem or fill the need at a price customers will gladly pay? (Insert real number from business model, of course.)
- Are there enough customers (insert number) "out there" to deliver a sizable (insert number) business opportunity?

This checkpoint is important enough to take these questions one at a time. (If you're uncertain or want more data, there's a deeper exploration of this set of questions at the end of Chapter 12.)

Are you attacking a serious problem or filling a compelling need?

This question should have been thoroughly probed directly with customers both online and, more important, face-to-face. Have you consistently heard enthusiastic responses like "This is a high-priority problem (or need) near the top of my list?" If they add comments like "I'd pay anything to solve this problem" or "My patchwork solution isn't good enough," even better. Probe only for a high level of consistent enthusiasm. That defines a market opportunity.

Key questions to review and discuss:

- Did your customers have friends or colleagues with similar problems or needs, and did they think the problem was important enough to discuss it with, or refer it to, their friends or coworkers?

- Were many of the customers you met attempting home-grown or work-around solutions to the problem your product will solve?

- Did most customers rate the problem or need's severity at 8, 9, or 10 on a scale of 10?

- Did most customers rate the pain caused by the problem at or near 5 on a scale of 5?

- Review the before-and-after customer work-flow diagram.

- Was the difference dramatic after buying the product?

- Were customers palpably excited?

- Did customers say they would pay for that difference?

⇨ Web/mobile startups should look closely at customer or user referrals to gauge the problem's magnitude and importance. If only tens or hundreds of users have the problem or need or nobody thinks it's of interest to their friends or associates, this is an "acid test" of the problem's seriousness. If inquiries from referred potential users yield few or no activations, it's equally serious. Stop and get on the phone with as many of those users (nonusers, really) as possible to understand their lack of interest. Perhaps it's the messaging, an easy fix. Don't "sell" them in the call—probe for their genuine interest and listen for opportunities to change the message, the product, or the activation incentives.

Does your product solve the problem or fill the need for your customers?

Review all the customer feedback report cards, summaries, and analysis—there should be quite a pile of it. Here again, as with validating the problem question, be sure there's robust enthusiasm for the product, even in its MVP form. Look for comments like "I have to have this now" or "Everyone I know will want one" or "When can I get it?" Lukewarm or average enthusiasm seldom delivers scalable startups. Be objective and park entrepreneurial enthusiasm at the door.

Key questions to review and discuss:

- Did the minimum viable product generate significant "buy" or "engage" enthusiasm?
- Was the product exciting enough to stimulate significant customer referrals? Did those referred customers buy or engage at an encouraging rate?
- Did the long-term product vision generate highly positive customer feed-back?
- Is the latest product-features-and-benefits hypothesis still appropriate and profitable?
- Did the long-term product-delivery schedule generate purchase enthusiasm?

Also review the delivery schedule, revising assumptions as necessary. Customers are buying into the entire vision, not just the MVP, and need to hear how and when the product will evolve.

⇨ One of the telltale symptoms of a bad "solution" fit for web/mobile startups is easy to spot: tons of acquisition but very little activation. Your potential customers agree that you've hit on a problem or a need they care about, so they came to learn more, but when they arrived, they didn't like your proposed solution.

Customer feedback is vital here. First probe customers' feelings about the product, site, or app and what they liked or didn't like about it. Then probe the messaging. Did the product not deliver on the message (as in "Lose 20 pounds tomorrow") that got them to the site in the first place? Was it their lack of confidence in the product, a lack of evidence (claims, testimonials, diagrams or demos), or poor messaging? Get to the bottom of these questions before proceeding, gathering as much one-on-one feedback from both activators and non-activators. What led the activators to sign up? What was missing in the pitch—the product, the "sales pitch" or the company that might have changed the minds of non-activators?

Are there Enough Customers to Deliver a Sizable Business Opportunity?

Did customers verify that they'd buy at the level you expected? Did any competitive or other data emerge pointing to larger or smaller market share? Review your initial TAM (total addressable market) and SAM (serviceable market) hypotheses and compare those estimates with what customers actually said. How much do they buy, how often, and are their friends or colleagues similarly inclined? Check findings against market knowledge and competitive analysis data gathered in Phase 2.

Key questions to review and discuss:

- Have you validated the TAM and SAM for your market?
- Is the market size as you expected, and is it verified by customer feedback and industry data?
- Is the market growing significantly, with strong growth prospects?
- Do customer conversations verify that they'll buy repeatedly and refer others to do the same?
- Did any unexpected competitive threats emerge?

The hard question to answer here is how many customers are "enough." This question must be answered by founders and investors together, with everyone on the proverbial "same page" about longer-term goals for the company and whether results to date point toward achieving those results. These results differ widely by channel and product type. A few generalizations:

- *Enterprise software:* Three or four earlyvangelists showing very strong interest might well be enough, provided that the team has at least as many more enthusiastic prospects in the pipeline. Where possible, customers should come from multiple segments, and few or no segments should be far behind the others in terms of interest in the product
- *Capital equipment:* The "three or four" enterprise software rule applies here, too, as a rule, but a closer look at results of customer discovery with a broader range of customers is helpful. Are most prospects interested in the

product largely as spec'ed, or does everyone want some form of customization? Do discovery results point to a robust pipeline, acknowledging that the sales cycle for capital goods can be quite lengthy

- *Consumer products:* Whether it's a new skateboard or a flat-screen TV, more than a handful of earlyvangelist customers is almost certainly required—perhaps 20 or 30 or more. It's also important to establish serious interest in the channel where you expect to sell the product. If 15 people want to buy your skateboard, that's probably not convincing enough for the Walmart buyer, for example

- *Web/mobile applications:* Since customer discovery efforts should reach at least several thousand prospective users or customers, a web/mobile app should almost certainly activate at least 100 apps or downloads to say it's seen "enough" customer response. You should also watch the percentages, to be sure the conversion rate is encouraging

- *Social networks and "network effect" startups:* These should probably attract at least 500 if not 1,000 active, engaged users to be able say they've attracted "enough." If the site or app is free or a freemium (free-to-paid), that number should be at least three times—preferably five times—larger, since it's so much easier for a user to say "yes" to something that's free. Monitor the activation rate, and look as well at the percentage of users who are returning regularly—say, three times a week—since they're not only an indication of customer volume but also point to the customers' quality and engagement

If the team is talking to the right customers but feedback says the product is wrong, something has to change. Reassess your customer segments and get back outside to find a different set of customers, or consider changing the features, product configuration, pricing, or other business model elements.

Do We Know Who Our Customers Are and How to Reach Them?

The previous step assures that there are customers "out there" who want your product. But do you know how to find them and sell to them with an affordable marketing or "get customers" budget? This verification step starts by ensuring that you know "what a customer looks like."

- Can you draw a customer archetype for each of your key customer segments? Does it clearly point you to places where you can find them?
- Can you draw a day in the life of a customer so you know how to pitch the product to him?
- Did some segments respond better, faster, or with larger orders than others?
- Did any new segments emerge, or should any be eliminated?
- Do customers recognize big improvements in a "day in the life" of users?
- Do you know what your customers read, trade shows they attend, gurus they follow, and where they turn for new product information?
- Can you draw your channel map, showing how the product moves from your startup to its end user, along with the costs and marketing/sales roles of each step in the sales channel?

Try to measure your "get customers" cost and response rates objectively. Review the real, "all in" costs (including staff time, overhead, whatever) of activating or selling, say, 50 customers. When you add up all the costs (not just the ad or AdWords costs themselves, for example), are you still confident of your ability to get lots more customers at roughly the same cost per customer?

Look beyond your total "Get" budget to identify which programs were most cost-effective, and do some homework to be sure that if, for example, you quintupled your e-mail marketing budget, results would quintuple as well. This is the time to figure out how much you really need to spend to get one (or 50) good customer(s), since you're about to head to customer validation, where spending will increase by a factor of 10 if not more!

If a significant amount of customer feedback has given you high confidence in all these answers, there's one more step—determining whether you can consistently acquire customers at the costs outlined in your "Get" hypotheses. Your early tests of the Get programs should have given you a good sense of that, so review the data collected. Don't worry if the costs are a little high, since you'll be optimizing those programs as you ramp them up during validation.

⇨ Web/mobile startups should be far smarter about answers to these vital "Get" questions, partly because they can be. Is the response best on Facebook, Twitter or Foursquare? Do people who eventually activate find the site or app most frequently via AdWords, textlinks, natural search or when they read about it on blogs or hear about it from friends? You should know this quite well based on even the earliest customer discovery testing you've done.

Remember to look beyond mere customer acquisition statistics and identify the activated users or buyers by *source* so that you know where to find lots more of them. Often you'll discover that nothing works better than person-to-person referrals, so look at that "Get" approach more closely. And always look at the data for each customer segment or cohort separately, since some customers will usually prove far easier to acquire than others.

Be sure to update the business model based on any changes in customer acquisition costs discovered in this review, since they're often the largest costs your startup will confront.

Can We Make Money and Grow the Company?

Assemble Revenue Model Data

By this point, the team has assembled a massive amount of hard data about pricing, revenue, costs and acquisition and marketing costs, among others. The data needs to be verified, with any gaps filled in along the way, which may entail returning to learn more in further customer, channel, or product development discussions. The most important hard data to review includes:

- summary of customer report cards, indicating potential sales revenue expectations over time

- market size estimates

- channel cost and revenue potential summaries

- pricing plan

- customer acquisition costs

- detailed information about the industry, the customers, and their behavior

- competitive product and pricing information

Combine this data to create an accurate net revenue forecast for at least the next four quarters of the company's existence—the customer validation phase—and, if possible, another year beyond that. This shouldn't be a precise, to-the-penny estimate by any means. Instead, it's more of a rough "gut check" to be sure that the company will emerge from customer validation as a growing, profitable business. Take a close look at Figure 7.2, a hypothetical analysis of a company selling both via its own website and through a physical channel. Average cost of customer acquisition is 40% of revenue in this example. The data assembly is a four-part process:

1. Compute the "best estimate" of total gross revenue the company will receive *directly* from customers, quarter by quarter. Review results of customer discovery report cards and "get customers" program tests as well as market

size estimates to estimate the company's direct revenue from customers quarter by quarter.

2. Next, compute the amount of *channel* revenue (other than direct revenue for sales to end users, from which the company receives 100 percent). Review the channel costs (margin, rep fees, promotional costs, etc.) and deduct them from channel revenues.

3. Add the net channel revenue to the total direct revenue by quarter to figure total company revenue. Deduct quarterly operating costs from the revenue.

4. Compute all the costs of acquiring customers, recognizing that they will most certainly change quarter by quarter, both as the company spends more money on its "get customers" effort and as it acquires customers more cost-effectively.

category	q1	q2	q3	q4	TOTAL
direct revenue	500,000	750,000	1,000,000	1,200,000	3,450,000
net channel revenue	200,000	300,000	400,000	500,000	1,400,000
TOTAL revenue	**700,000**	**1,050,000**	**1,400,000**	**1,700,000**	**4,850,000**
less acquisition costs	-280,000	-420,000	-560,000	-680,000	-1,940,000
less basic operating costs	-800,000	-800,000	-800,000	-800,000	-3,200,000
CASH BURN	**-380,000**	**-170,000**	**40,000**	**220,000**	**-290,000**
Cash at quarter end	20,000	*-150,000*	*-110,000*	100,000	

Sample Financial Analysis *(Figure 7.2)*

The computation should deliver a reasonable rough estimate of the company's revenue expectations across its next four (or, preferably, eight) quarters. Consider developing this entire exercise three different ways, using a "good/better/ best" approach that delivers three different forecasts or business cases: high, best guess, and worst case.

This analysis all by itself may stop the pivot-or-proceed process in its tracks, as it often does, if the computation shows the company running out of money within the year. The spreadsheet is a simple example of a rough "cash burn" computation that should be enough to send any smart founder back through the discovery and validation processes, considering that the company runs out of money 90 days from moving forward.

Looking at an analysis like this, the founders and investors should be highly nervous about proceeding to spend nearly $2 million on customer creation activities. The startup in this example has several options:

- Raise another few hundred thousand dollars immediately in order just to survive the year ahead
- Reduce the spending on operations or customer acquisition costs
- Cut staff or reduce founder salaries until break-even is achieved

Without taking any of these steps, the company will clearly not survive, and it must return to refine its business model.

Key questions to review and discuss:

- Have you translated market and market share findings into potential unit sales and revenue?
- Have you validated your pricing model with customers?
- Are volume, demand, and purchase-frequency hypotheses validated?
- Were any unanticipated channel costs uncovered, such as sales reps' salaries or promotional fees?
- If the market is multi-sided, have all costs of generating "buy"-side revenue been estimated?
- Does this rough forecast point to a scalable, profitable business with substantial exit value?

Pivot or Proceed?

This is either the beginning of the end or, more likely, just the end of the beginning. It's where you must acknowledge that an estimated one idea in thousands morphs into a scalable, profitable big company with an exit value of $100 million or more. The company has put a stake in the ground with a series of hypotheses and tested its assumptions. Potential customers have validated the product, and a base of prospects has evolved. And all the learning is captured in writing in the updated business model canvas and its supporting hypothesis documents. Now it's time to honestly assess if the modified hypotheses provide a sound foundation for moving forward—not to launch—to a larger-scale test in customer validation.

Summary questions to review and discuss:

- Have we identified a problem lots of customers will eagerly pay to have solved?
- Does our product solve these needs distinctively, cost-effectively and profitably?
- If so, do we have a sizable market and a viable, scalable and profitable business model?
- Can we draw a day in the life of our customer before and after purchase of our product?
- Can we create an organizational chart of users, buyers and channels?

The hardest question is simple and needs an honest answer: do the customer discovery findings point to a big enough market that's hungry for the product? This is often a painful question and, sadly, more often than not leads back almost to the beginning of customer discovery. While it's a defeat of sorts, it's far better to confront this question honestly and candidly, ensuring that the business model, properly executed, points to a repeatable, scalable, profitable business opportunity. Without one, the company faces a painful road to ignominy.

Exhausting as the customer discovery process is, it often requires multiple iterations to fully understand the market and discover customers who can't wait to buy. However, it's never been easy to find the Holy Grail. Until you do, take everything learned in Phases 1 through 3 to heart, modify the presentations, go back to Phase 1 and do it again. Try out several markets and users. Does the team need to reconfigure or repackage the product offering? If so, modify the product presentations and go back to Phase 3 (solution presentation) and do it again.

If the team votes "all systems go," there are two more steps to complete before taking a deep breath and moving forward into customer validation.

Determine the Validation Checkpoints

It's wonderful to have lots of soft, fuzzy metrics of success, but they seldom deliver success to startups. Be sure that every hypothesis has a clear, measurable "validation checkpoint" and that those checkpoints tie into the business model. A few examples of the kinds of checkpoints to test in the customer validation phase:

Physical channel/business-to-business checkpoint examples:
- We can close a sale in three meetings
- One of six prospects will buy if we get to talk to VPs of finance
- Customers will expand the number of users of our service by 25 percent after six months
- Customers will place an average of two orders per month

Web/mobile checkpoint examples:
- Every new customer invites 10 friends, half of whom sign up
- A third of our visitors will return to the site within a week
- A quarter of our visitors will refer an average of 1.5 friends within a week

- Average session duration will be 10 pages or minutes per visit
- Average order size will be $50 in the customer's first month
- One hundred websites will promote traffic to our site at a CPM of less than $X
- One hundred websites will run our banners on a CPA basis

On to Customer Validation? Congratulations!

If you've gotten this far, you've changed your hypotheses many times. Some were iterations, others were pivots. One of the best techniques to see how far you've come is to show the canvases as a series of snapshots over time. You can do this by putting them up on the wall or clicking through a series of PowerPoint slides. Either way, this visual presentation of the hypotheses and your tests to turn those guesses into hard, cold facts, is the final step in determining whether it's time to move on to the next of the four steps, customer validation.

If it's time to move to the next step, congratulations! This is a major achievement and warrants celebration. Customer discovery is the most challenging, powerful step you'll encounter in Customer Development: defining a product, an offer, a channel and pricing for a product that consumers are eager to buy. Hold on to all the information collected from customer interviews for use throughout the phases of customer validation, when actual selling will develop a sales roadmap for the company.

Customer discovery is an exhausting, sometimes-frustrating process. However, it's the foundation of Customer Development and thus the foundation of a successful, scalable business. The checklists in appendix A recap the phases of this step, the goals of each phase, and the deliverables proving that the goals have been met. With that done, take a well-earned vacation or a long weekend to celebrate. You'll need to rest up before moving on to customer validation.

III

Step Two:
Customer Validation

Overview of the Customer Validation Process

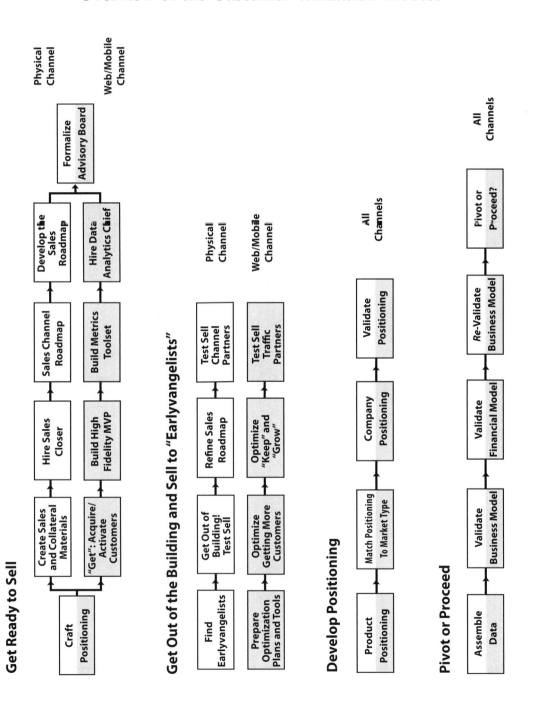

Get Ready to Sell

Craft Positioning → Create Sales and Collateral Materials → Hire Sales Closer → Sales Channel Roadmap → Develop the Sales Roadmap → Formalize Advisory Board (Physical Channel)

Craft Positioning → "Get": Acquire/Activate Customers → Build High Fidelity MVP → Build Metrics Toolset → Hire Data Analytics Chief (Web/Mobile Channel)

Get Out of the Building and Sell to "Earlyvangelists"

Find Earlyvangelists → Get Out of Building! Test Sell → Refine Sales Roadmap → Test Sell Channel Partners (Physical Channel)

Prepare Optimization Plans and Tools → Optimize Getting More Customers → Optimize "Keep" and "Grow" → Test Sell Traffic Partners (Web/Mobile Channel)

Develop Positioning

Product Positioning → Match Positioning To Market Type → Company Positioning → Validate Positioning (All Channels)

Pivot or Proceed

Assemble Data → Validate Business Model → Validate Financial Model → Re-Validate Business Model → Pivot or Proceed? (All Channels)

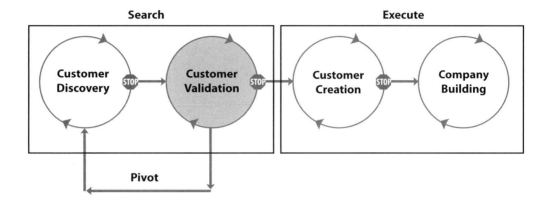

C H A P T E R 8

Introduction to Customer Validation

Along the journey we commonly forget its goal.
—Friedrich Nietzsche

E.PIPHANY'S FOUNDING HYPOTHESES WERE typically pretty straightforward and "investable" in the mid-1990s, when software companies were automating everything from accounts payable to network security, sales force processes and even wine-cellar inventories. "Why not automate the marketing department?" asked the founders, meeting in their modest living room. "After all, most of the tasks like press releases and data sheets and customer letters are repeatable processes." Venture capital was raised and the company began to build its product based on the founders' vision.

However, the company's initial idea of who the customer was and the problem they wanted to solve was just plain wrong. The company's later success was due to the four passionate entrepreneurs' willingness to listen to customers and to the three painful pivots driven by customer feedback.

The Browser Breakthrough

During the '90s, large corporations acquired different software applications to automate each part of their enterprise—finance, customer support, manufacturing, and sales among them. But the data these applications collected were accessed via reporting tools from the IT organization. More important, the data existed in "virtual silos," with each functional system walled off from the other. The finance system didn't talk to the sales system, which didn't know that the manufacturing system even existed. Queries like "Compare the sales data of green dresses versus blue ones with current inventory for each by store, and contrast the gross margin by region to calculate discounts" were virtually impossible to answer to because they required combining data from three incompatible applications. As a result, it could often take days or even weeks to get a simple inventory-detail report.

E.piphany's then-radical notion was to provide managers anytime/anywhere drill-downs and analysis in real time, without IT, through a revolutionary new technology called a web browser. One of the company's key hypotheses was that the product should be a great fit for companies with lots of customers, tons of data on each one, and a recurring need for fast new data-driven, microsegmented marketing campaigns.

An Epiphany at E.piphany

Early on, E.piphany assembled an advisory board. A key adviser was the VP of database marketing at Schwab. She was incredibly generous with her time and said the system might work in their application. She introduced the company to five other database marketing executives, who essentially said, "If you get a system working at Schwab, we'll have to buy one as well." You couldn't get much better than that. E.piphany had found its first earlyvangelist and first market.

But each time Schwab's people looked at the system's technical details, they politely said our product was missing a key feature for database marketing. It took two meetings before the founders realized they understood her problem, all right, but the solution—the underlying database schema of the software—was missing the most important feature for solving it. It didn't include "householding," and without this feature, she could never buy the E.piphany system. (Householding, well-known among database marketers, recognizes that two or more people at the same physical address live together and, in Schwab's case, often invest together. This feature was crucial to direct-marketers who didn't want to send multiple or differing ads to the same address.) And no amount of sales and marketing hand-waving was going to fix the problem.

It was a major mistake. Until this meeting, the founders hadn't understood the customer problem well enough to provide the correct solution.

E.piphany's co-founders, Ben Wegbreit and Steve Blank, joined the Schwab VP, and her engineering team in a deep technical discussion of what the software needed to do for Schwab's business and what was needed. Ben asked five or 10 questions, everybody nodded and the meeting ended. On the long ride back to E.piphany's living-room office, Steve asked, "Ben, how do we solve Schwab's problem?"

After a moment of silence, he replied, "Show them page 6 of our product spec."

"What do you mean page 6? Our spec only has five pages!"

Ben looked at Steve and smiled. "Not anymore."

They had just pivoted the product and refined the minimum feature set. E.piphany's first order from Schwab came the week after they demo'ed householding. Other orders followed soon after. A week later, the founders sat down to figure out what other feature they would toss out to make room for this one.

E.piphany would go through two additional equally painful pivots before its initial public offering, but that "householding" pivot sold the founders on the "power of the pivot" value.

The meeting and car ride from Schwab to the company headquarters illustrates the customer validation process every startup needs: a method for validating the business model with real customers and orders.

Customer validation turns hypotheses into facts about basic questions like:

- Do we understand the sales/user acquisition process?
  - Is it repeatable?
  - Can we prove it's repeatable? (If our business model is single-sided commerce, the only acceptable proof is enough full-price orders.)
  - Can we get these orders/users with the current product?
- Have we tested sales and distribution channels?
- Are we confident we can scale orders/users into a profitable business?
- Have we correctly positioned the product and the company?

The Customer Validation Philosophy

Customer validation attempts to "test sell" at every stage. It runs a continuing series of quantitative pass/fail tests to *determine whether there's strong enough product/market fit to justify scaling sales and marketing spending.* Most of your testing effort will be asking people to give you an order or engage with your app or website. At this point, you're testing the entire business model, not its individual components, even as you learn more details about some, like price or channel.

Just as customer discovery was disorienting for experienced marketers, the customer validation process turns the world upside down for experienced salespeople and, in particular, those with sales responsibility. All the rules sales executives learned while selling in physical channels at large companies are *not* applicable to startups. In fact, they're positively detrimental. It's not all about the launch party!

In the customer validation step, *you are not going to hire and staff a sales team.* You are not going to execute to a sales plan or "the sales strategy." The reality is that you don't know enough yet to do any of these things. At the end of customer discovery, you have in hand firm hypotheses about who will buy, why they will buy, and at what price they will buy. But until those hypotheses are validated—with customer orders—they're all little more than educated guesses, even with the work invested to develop them.

From Business Model Canvas to the Sales Roadmap

In customer discovery you tested some of the hypotheses of your business model:

- *Value proposition:* You affirmed it with a few dozen to a few hundred people
- *Customer segments:* You have a hypothesis about customer archetypes
- *Customer relationships:* You tested several "get, keep and grow" activities
- *Channel:* You understand your key channel partners, and some have expressed interest
- *Revenue model:* The company has an idea of how to price its offering

A sales roadmap uses all you've learned from customer discovery to guide the creation of a sales funnel specifically for your company. It answers:

- Who influences a sale? Who recommends a sale?
- Who is the decision-maker? Who is the economic buyer? The saboteur?
- Where is the budget for purchasing the type of product you're selling?
- How many sales calls are needed to make one sale?
- How long does an average sale take from beginning to end?
- What is the selling strategy? Is this a solution sale?
- If so, what are "key customer problems?"
- What's the profile of optimal visionary buyers, the earlyvangelists every startup needs?

- Where will the traffic come from? Will it stick?
- Will the product be strong enough to grow virally?

Unless a company has proven answers to these questions, few sales will happen, and those that do occur will result from heroic single-shot efforts. Of course, on some level, most sales VPs realize they lack the knowledge they need to draw a detailed sales roadmap, but most believe they and their newly hired sales team can acquire this information while simultaneously selling and closing orders. This is because most executives new to startups confuse *searching for a business model with the execution of a known business model*. A sales roadmap is part of the *search* for a business model. Only after it's built can it be executed. Startups can't learn and discover while they're busy executing. As we can see from the rubble of any number of failed startups, attempting to execute before you have a sales roadmap in place is pure folly.

Building a Sales Roadmap Versus Building a Sales Force

Given how critical the validation step is, a CEO's first instinct is to speed up the process by spending more on customer acquisition or adding salespeople. The reality is, this doesn't speed up the validation phase. In fact, it most often slows it down. Instead, you'll build a roadmap to figure out how to get repeatable sales (by explicitly testing product/ market fit). Once that's done, *then* build a sales organization.

Developing a sales roadmap is part of the search for a business model.

In an existing market, customer validation may simply validate that the sales VP's rolodex or contact list is relevant, and that product performance metrics the company identified in customer discovery were correct. In a re-segmented, clone or new market, even a rolodex of infinite size (or tripling the AdWords budget) won't substitute for a proven business model and a tested sales roadmap.

For an experienced sales or business development executive, these statements about customer validation are heretical. All the actions in Customer Development we consider to be mistakes are what traditional sales professionals have been trained to do. It seems counterintuitive and disorienting. So let's look more closely at why the first sales in a startup are so different from later-stage sales or selling in a large company.

Founders Must Lead the Customer Validation Team

Founders who complete customer discovery often mistakenly ease up and delegate customer validation activities to Sales, Business Development, Marketing or Product Management. This is a bad idea. Middle and junior managers aren't likely to be good at customer validation, which requires creative searching, probing, and turning on a dime—not execution of a repeatable process.

Why must the founders lead? First, founders and only founders call the shots on pivoting. To do so, they must hear about flaws in the product or business model *directly from the customers.* Nothing else has the same impact. Anyone other than a founder who learns of a serious product or business-plan flaw faces two challenges: he or she doesn't have the authority to pivot, and he or she seldom has the courage to report bad customer feedback to the founder.

⇨ In web/mobile channels, where there's much more feedback to process, the founders still make the call about pivots, but the company needs to have data junkies, A/B testers, statisticians, and SEO/PPC experts, as well as at least one or two wildly creative online marketers. (This might be physically embodied in the founder and one or two amazing people.) This team will measure, assess, manage and improve the acquisition, or Get Customers, funnel described in Chapter 3. As they're getting "out of the building" digitally, a customer development team also leaves physically for face-to-face customer validation, and for deal-making that drives traffic or referrals.

Validation Proceeds at Different Speeds in Different Channels

It takes far more time to set up visits in a physical channel with prospects in cell-phone companies in Asia and Africa than to get customer feedback electronically for a website. And more customers can be reached via web/mobile channels than can ever be met face-to-face.

⇨ Customer validation for web/mobile startups always proceeds faster with many more iterations than it does with physical channels and goods. Why? It's all bits that can be changed. Regardless of speed, the fundamental principles of customer validation are identical across all channels.

Make Early Sales to Earlyvangelists

In customer validation you will target Earlyvangelists as your first paying customers. (If you can't sell to them, it doesn't get better over time.) The earlyvangelist's profile was described in detail on page 58. Review it before you proceed.

Constrain Spending in Customer Validation

A typical failure scenario for startups is *premature scaling*, when there are more salespeople in the field burning cash than are needed while your business model is still unproven. Or running expensive demand-creation activities before you're sure who your customers really are. Too often those sales people are fired and their marketing programs killed when the startup faces a major pivot after scaling too early. Customer validation delays sales-and-marketing hiring and spending until validation is nearly complete. This constraint is central to the process, which assumes startups will fail and iterate often. The spending constraint keeps enough cash in the bank to fund multiple pivots on the road to success.

Prioritize What Needs to be Validated

Prioritizing the business model elements that need validating is essential at the start of customer validation. Every startup business model has a zillion moving parts. Validation can't possibly measure and affirm every variable or the founders will be 100 years old by the time they're ready to scale—or, worse, exit—the business.

The business model canvas is an excellent guide here. Most startups will focus on the four core elements: value proposition, customer relationships, channel, and revenue model. This list works for many businesses but not all. Multi-sided markets need to prioritize all sides of the market. Think about the five or fewer things that will make this a huge, successful business—or not.

Why Accountants Don't Run Startups

With all the process steps involved, it's sometimes hard to remember that the Customer Development process isn't a giant focus group. The goal is not to add up all the customer feedback and vote on what features to implement. Founders who are artists at heart run startups—the true purpose of Customer Development is to *inform their vision.* (In a new market, there's no data at all!) A great entrepreneur may consider all the customer data, listen to his instincts and say, "Here's why I'm going to ignore what we just heard."

And Finally: Don't Be Afraid to Let Go When Lightning Strikes

Occasionally, fast-scaling web/mobile startups with viral or network-effect drivers find the business suddenly blasting off, even if this book doesn't suggest that it should happen yet. This occurred at Google, YouTube, Facebook, and Twitter, to name an elite few. If you're lucky enough to hit a consumer nerve as hard as they did, put this book down and hold on to the rocket ship. After all, that's what entrepreneurs do! (Skim the book another time on your private jet or yacht or Sunfish.)

The Customer Validation Philosophy, in Summary

Customer discovery first tested your hypotheses about the company's business model with a relatively tiny group of customers who were asked for opinions, not orders. Discovery itself didn't deliver any proven, hard facts about who would buy or how scalable the business was.

Customer validation goes to the next step and *determines whether a product/market fit can be validated by orders or usage.* It does so by further developing the MVP as well as the company's sales and marketing plans and materials. Then it gets founders out of the building (physically, virtually, or both) to test the MVP and every other key business model hypotheses, including product features, pricing, channel, and positioning. How? By asking for orders (or downloads, logons, or clicks)!

Test the MVP.
How? By asking for orders.

Customer validation is complete when the company has answers to these three questions:

1. *Can the business scale?* Will a dollar spent on customer acquisition yield more than a dollar's worth of incremental revenue, page views, downloads or clicks?
2. *Is there a repeatable and scalable sales roadmap?* Does the company know the right prospects to call on or acquire, and what to say to them to consistently deliver sales?
3. *Is the sales funnel predictable?* Do the same sales programs and tactics consistently deliver an adequate, profitable flow of customers through the funnel?

Now let's get started.

Overview of the Customer Validation Process

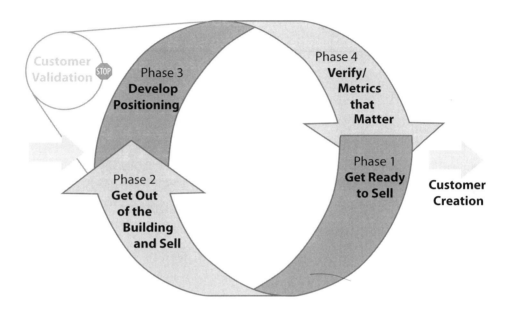

Customer Validation: Overview of the Process *(Figure 8.1)*

Customer Validation has Four Phases

Phase 1 consists of six "get ready to sell" activities; product positioning, sales/ marketing materials for "test selling" efforts, the hiring of a sales closer, the creation of a distribution channel plan, refining a sales roadmap, and creating an advisory board. These activities make your team the best prepared early stage venture ever to hit the streets.

⇨ Companies in web/mobile channels also have six "get ready to sell" activities: Product Positioning, assembling Acquire/Activate Plans, building the high-fidelity MVP, building the metrics toolset, hiring a "data chief" and creating an advisory board. They help deliver lean, cost-effective customer acquisition programs.

Phase 2 gets founders out of the building to put the product to the ultimate test: will customers validate your business model by buying your product? You'll attempt to actually sell customers an unfinished and unproven product without a professional sales organization. Getting feedback is as important as getting orders. Startups in the physical channel do this with brochures, PowerPoints, sales materials and, where possible, product demos or mockups. Dozens if not hundreds of meetings help refine the product presentation and channel plans, validate the sales roadmap, prove the predictability of the sales funnel, and validate that the business model is repeatable, scalable and profitable in a real-world test.

⇨ Web/mobile startups "go live" and get out of the building virtually to see if their plans and tools to acquire customers actually attract customers who activate or buy. Do more than a handful of real customers behave as the hypotheses suggest they will? Acquisition and activation activities are measured and optimized.

Startups in multi-sided markets (physical or web/mobile) need to get out of the building to test each side of the market. Web/Mobile marketers first test users and then validate a different set of hypotheses (value proposition, segment, revenue model, etc.) with the "payers," who are marketers or advertisers willing to pay to reach people using the site for free.

Phase 3 happens once you have a couple of orders under your belt and enough customer information to develop and refine your product and company positioning. The positioning is tested in meetings with industry pundits and analysts and face-to-face with the expanded customer audience.

⇨ Web/mobile startups refine their "Get" program tactics. Then they conduct initial product positioning, next they gather and organize the customer behavior data collected in Phase 2: customer responses to "Get" activities and metrics summarizing their initial on-site behavior. They collect feedback about the MVP itself and the effectiveness of acquisition tools.

Phase 4 stops all activity for long enough to conduct a detailed pivot-or-proceed analysis and verify that, regardless of channel, customer validation is complete and the company knows how to scale. If so, it's ready to reap the rewards for founders and investors alike. But first there are lots of tough questions and hard work to verify.

In sum, the question is simple: "is this a business worth doing," and devoting several years of backbreaking work? Will it generate enough revenue, growth and profits to achieve the founders' and investors' goals? And has the team learned enough to make it happen?

Odds are overwhelming that the optimum business model won't be found on the first or second try in validation.

The moment customer validation is over is when it's clear that there are real orders, users, or clicks—not surveys or chats. Customer validation confirms that customers will accept the minimum viable product, proves that the customers exist, figures out how to reach them predictably, and crafts a scalable plan to engage and sell many more. It's often called the "epiphany moment."

The roadmap to that moment begins on page 291.

CHAPTER 9

Customer Validation, Phase One: "Get Ready to Sell"

PHASE 1 OF CUSTOMER VALIDATION PREPARES the tools to test the company's ability to acquire customers. In this phase, you'll craft your product positioning, which guides how you write the marketing, and online materials needed for the sales effort. For companies in the physical channel, other steps in this phase include development of collateral materials, channel sales plans, and a sales roadmap. Sometimes, a "sales closer" is also hired at this point. And you'll finalize your advisory board.

⇨ Web/mobile channel startups develop their plans and tools for customer acquisition and activation as well as a dashboard or toolset for monitoring the results. They create a hi-fidelity MVP to be sure the acquisition efforts are valid.

Steps in this first phase are markedly different for each channel, so physical and web/mobile channels are addressed separately, as outlined in Figure 9.1.

When all these steps are in place, it's time to get out of the building and start selling, in Phase 2. Here are the steps each channel requires before you are ready to sell.

Physical Channel	Web and Mobile Channel
Product Positioning	
Develop Sales Materials and Collateral	"Get": Acquire/Activate Plans/Tools
Hire Sales Closer	Build High Fidelity MVP
Develop Channel Action Plan	Build Metrics Toolset
Refine the Sales Roadmap	Hire "Data Chief"
Create Advisory Board	

Phase 1 – Get Ready to Sell (Figure 9.1)

Get Ready to Sell: Craft Positioning Statement

From your customer's perspective, what does your company stand for, what does your product do, and why should they care? You probably had an idea when you started the company, but now you have some real experience in interacting with customers. It's time to revisit the product vision, features and competitive information in light of what you've learned in customer discovery.

Can you reduce all that you've learned into a single clear, compelling message explaining why your company is different and the product is worth buying (or spending time with). That's the goal of a unique selling proposition. A unique selling proposition builds the bond between you and your customer, focuses marketing programs, and becomes the focal point for building the company. More relevant for this step, it gets the company's story down to a short "elevator pitch" powerful enough to raise a customer's heart rate. It'll appear in lots of different places from billboards to banners and business cards from here on out and helps focus sales and marketing efforts. Don't worry about getting it perfect, because it will change with feedback from customers, analysts, and investors. For now, take a first best shot.

While positioning messaging seems straightforward, it can be a challenge to execute. It takes serious work to get to a pithy statement that's both understandable and compelling. It's much easier to write (or think) long than to write (or think) short. Start by revisiting what customers said they valued during customer discovery. What were the top problems? Did a phrase keep coming up to describe the problem or solution? Where does the product affect customers most? How significant is the product's impact? What does the new offering provide that competitors can't or won't? What does it do better? Think simple and short at all times. This may be a place where outside creative resources are worth the investment.

In technology startups, one of the biggest challenges for engineers is to realize the need for a simple message that grabs customers' hearts and wallets, not their heads and calculators. It's not about the product features. Seek a simple sentence that condenses the entire value proposition into a few pithy, catchy words that say it all: "Think Different," from Apple; "Don't Leave Home Without It," American Express; "Just Do It," Nike; "We Try Harder," Avis; "Earth's First Soft Drink," Perrier; "The Ultimate Driving Machine," BMW.

The exercises, in Figures 9.2 and 9.3, developed by Geoffrey Moore (of *Crossing the Chasm* fame) early in his career as a marketing consultant, can help evoke the necessary elements:

PRODUCT POSITIONING STATEMENT TEMPLATE

- **For** [target end user]
- **Who wants/needs** [compelling reason to buy]
- **The** [product name] **is a** [product category]
- **That provides** [key benefit]
- **Unlike** [main competitor]
- **The** [product name] [key differentiation]

Product Positioning Statement (Figure 9.2)

Here's how a mobile expense-reporting application, *Mobiledough,* might have used the product position statement:

PRODUCT POSITIONING STATEMENT EXAMPLE

- *Mobiledough* is **FOR** busy executives who travel a lot
- **WHO WANT/NEED** to do expense reports accurately in the least possible time
- And Mobiledough **IS AN** easy-to-use tool for receipt tracking and expense tabulation
- **THAT PROVIDES** a detailed weekly expense report in under 10 minutes
- **UNLIKE** expense report packages, Mobiledough scans, sorts and totals receipts and presents a near-final report draft for review in 11 popular expense reporting formats

---

Product Positioning Statement Example (Figure 9.3)

What might Mobiledough's tag line be? A few candidates:

- "Your dough, on the go. Fast, accurate, online"
- "Track your expenses while you're makin' tracks"
- "Mobiledough. It just adds up, instantly, online"

Use the Geoff Moore outline or one like it to brainstorm positioning statements with the Customer Development team. Consider a companywide contest or creative session. To see if the positioning is emotionally compelling, think about the following:

- Do customers' heart rates go up after they hear it?
- Do they lean forward to hear more? Or do you get a blank stare?
- Is it understandable in the users' language or unique in their minds?
- For B-to-B products, does the positioning imply a cost or competitive advantage for the product?
- For consumer products, does it save time or money or provide fun or love, glamour or status?

Finally, does the positioning pass the reality test? Claims like "lose 30 pounds in a week" or "increase sales 200 percent" or "fall in love tonight" strain credibility and probably legality as well. Moreover, it's not only the claim that needs to pass this test. Is your company a credible supplier for the product you're describing? When selling to corporate customers, there are additional hurdles to think about. Are your capabilities congruent with your claims?

One last thing to keep in mind is our continual question about what market type you're in (see page 39 for details). If you're offering a product in an existing market, your unique selling proposition is about better, faster, or higher performance. It's framed by what you've learned from countless customer interviews about the basis of competition..

If you're creating a new market or trying to reframe an existing one, you'll probably come up with a transformational unique selling proposition. Transformational unique selling propositions deal with how the solution will create a new level or class of activity—i.e., something people could never do before.

Get Ready to Sell: Sales and Marketing Materials (Physical)

Acquiring customers in the physical channel evolves in a four-stage process: awareness, consideration, interest, and purchase. To facilitate this sales process, you'll use the unique selling proposition you created in the last step to produce sales and marketing materials—product data sheets, presentations, a website, etc.—called "marketing collateral." Your sales team will hand or present this collateral to potential customers and/or on your website to communicate the reasons customers should buy.

"Get Customers" Funnel

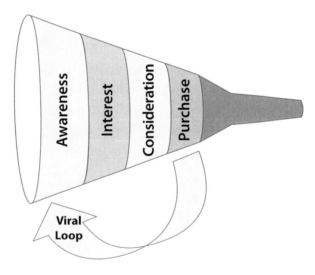

The "Get Customers" Funnel in Physical Channels (Figure 9.4)

In the physical channel, the job of marketing materials is not to close the sale but to drive prospective customers into the sales funnel, where physical locations, live salespeople, and supporting selling materials take over and effect a transaction.

The material should give people enough information to raise their curiosity and spark an interaction with sales—but not so much information that they can decide *not to buy* without first interacting with the channel! Human helpers need a variety of tools to close the deal, and this step plans and creates a first version of the tool set that helps close the deal.

This section describes online tools, physical sales tools and how to tune both for your audience.

Much of the information for the materials (product features, benefits, specs) is found in the hypotheses developed and refined during customer discovery. Don't spend money on flashy design or large print runs, but keep the materials crisp and professional, knowing they'll change based on customer feedback.

	Physical Channels	Web/Mobile Channels
GET customers (demand creation)	*Strategy:* Awareness, Interest, Consideration, Purchase *Tactics:* Earned Media (pr, blogs, brochures, reviews), Paid Media (ads, promotions), Online tools	*Strategy:* Acquire, Activate *Tactics:* Websites, App Stores, Search (SEM/SEO), email, Blogs, Viral, Social Nets, Reviews, PR, Free Trials, Home/Landing Page
KEEP customers	*Strategy:* Interact, Retain *Tactics:* Loyalty programs, product updates, customer surveys, Customer check-in calls	*Strategy:* Interact, Retain *Tactics:* Customization, User Groups, Blogs, Online Help, Product Tips/Bulletins, Outreach, Affiliates
GROW customers	*Strategy:* New Revenue, Referrals *Tactics:* Upsell/Cross/Next-Sell, Referrals, (maybe) Unbundling	*Strategy:* New Revenue, Referrals *Tactics:* Upgrades, Contests, Reorders, Refer friends, Upsell/Cross-Sell, Viral

"Get Customers" Tools for Physical Channels (Table 9.1)

Physical Sales Collateral and Materials

Once they arrive in the physical channel, whether they're driven by the web, Twitter, or an old-fashioned newspaper ad, the customer eventually gets face-to-face with a salesperson. When he does, sales materials and tools are often required. Instead of randomly writing product specs and presentations, develop a "collateral plan" listing all the items needed at each sales-process stage (see Table 9.2 for an example). A basic minimum collateral checklist for almost any company should include the following items:

- website (see page 302)
- PowerPoint sales presentation
- Demos, prototypes and videos
- Data sheets
- Price lists, contracts and billing systems

Don't forget the more obvious items: white papers, company press clippings, customer testimonials, letterhead, presentation folders and business cards!

Sales Presentations

Sales presentations should deliver an updated, integrated version of the problem, solution and product presentations developed during customer discovery, guided by the new positioning. The core audience during customer validation is earlyvangelists, not mainstream customers. Cover a brief outline of *the problem*, possible *existing solutions*, and *your proposed new solution*, and then product details. The presentation should run no more than 30 minutes. In customer discovery, you may have found that different presentations were required, depending on the type of people who played a role in purchase decisions inside a company or with different types of consumer audiences. Were separate presentations required for senior management and lower-level employees? How about for a technical audience? How about for different companies in different industries? For consumer products, was there a different presentation based on demographics? Income? Geography?

A worthwhile investment at this stage of Customer Development is professional help in developing a PowerPoint template. It gives the company a professional, established appearance even if the office remains a garage or a basement.

Demos/Prototypes/Video

Most people you're trying to sell to don't have your skill in visualizing products that don't exist. It's why you're the founder and they're not. For many people, most product concepts are too hard to understand without some kind of demo or prototype. Wherever possible, prepare some kind of prototype, working or not, that illustrates how the product operates and its key selling points. At a minimum, provide a slide-based, nonworking illustration or a short video. Ideally, the presentation illustrates the old way and the new way of solving the problem. It can be made of cardboard or Styrofoam, or it can be a series of simple sketches, but it should "bring the product to life" wherever possible. Product development teams in physical-product startups sometimes confuse demos with working products. They're not.

It's these demos that "turn on the lightbulb" over the heads of many earlyvangelists and get their passionate about the product.

Data Sheets

It's easy to confuse product data sheets, which detail product features and benefits, with solution data sheets, which address customer problems and big-picture solutions. Which ones you need depend on market type. When entering an existing market, your focus is on the product and why yours is better. Here, product data sheets are the best way to illustrate that. However, if you're creating a new market or cloning a market, the solution data sheets are more appropriate. If you're re-segmenting a market, both types of data sheets are essential.

Price Lists, Contracts and Billing System

Hopefully by now, someone has asked, "How much does it cost?" Prepare price lists, quote forms, and contracts. These documents makes a small startup look like a real company. They also force codification of assumptions about product pricing, configurations, delivery, discounts, and terms. Consumer products require a way to take early orders, usually involving credit card processing, e-commerce tools, and more.

Collateral Needs to Be Tuned to the Audience

In validation, startups selling in business-to-business markets have two different audiences for collateral materials: the earlyvangelist, the technology gatekeepers and each require different messages and materials (see Table 9.2). Earlyvangelists buy the vision first and then buy the product. Therefore, make sure materials are clear and detailed enough about vision and benefits to help earlyvangelists sell the idea by themselves, after the presentation ends, inside their companies or to friends or family.

Most business-to-business selling situations require a technical overview with a distinctly deeper level of information for other players in the sales cycle. Issue-specific white papers can address particular areas of interest or concern. Develop these as they become necessary but not before. Customers will tell you what they need. Especially in tight economic climates, business customers might require a return-on-investment (ROI) white paper. It's a customer's fancy way of saying, "Show me how I financially justify this purchase. Will it save me money in the long run?" Much of the development work for this was done as part of the customer discovery process. Earlyvangelist champions will usually have to pitch the product to others in their company—often without startup spokespeople present—before someone agrees to sign the check. For consumers the issue is the same; just imagine kids trying to make the ROI issue for an iPad. "I won't have to carry DVD's in the car, and promise to read more books if you buy them for me."

On the other hand, startups selling in business-to-consumer marketers focus the collateral on materials for the sales channel: shelf-talkers, retail packaging, coupons, and ad slicks. The collateral plan distinguishes objectives, targets for, and timing of each piece.

Test-drive all the collateral, because what's written in the confines of an office often has little relevance in the field. A/B-test online "collateral" such as landing pages, checkout pages, and product feature/benefit statements as ambitiously as possible (more on this in the next section). Consumers and business buyers have no obligation to memorize the company's jargon or understand "inside jokes." Keep the collateral plan handy. Update and add to it along the way.

	Awareness	Interest	Consideration	Sales
Early-vangelist Buyers	Corporate website Brochure	General sales presentation(s)	Tailor presentations to each customer	Contacts
	Solution data sheets	White paper on business issue	Analyst report on business problem	Price list
	Influential bloggers	Product Presskit		
	Tech websites	Product brochure	ROI demonstration	
	Direct mail pieces	Viral marketing/ e-mail tools	Follow-up e-mail	
		Product data sheets	Pricing quote form	Thank-you note/e-mail
Technology Gatekeeper	Influential Bloggers	Tech presentation	Tech presentation on specific customer issues	Thank-you note
	Tech websites	Tech white paper	Tech white paper	
		Analyst report on technical problem	Tech overview data sheets with architecture diagrams	

Example of a Business-to-Business, Direct-Sales Collateral Plan (Table 9.2)

Online Tools for Physical Channel Marketers

Even if the company's principal channel strategy involves physical distribution customers still search for products online, you'll need an array of basic online tools to generate awareness and trials and to provide product information on the web. These tools almost always include a website, some kind of viral marketing program to find customers, and digital forms of brochures or other selling materials. In addition, social networks have become huge sources of customers, even for the most mundane physical goods, and lots of new product ideas surface every day in Twitter streams.

Even the most complicated "old world" products are promoted through websites and online marketing.

Even the most complicated "old world" products like construction equipment and materials are promoted through expansive websites and massive online marketing programs. As a result, marketers in the physical channel must explore and develop online customer-acquisition and marketing plans even if their pumps, bushings and gravel are sold only over the counter in a dingy warehouse. Warehouse or not, today's buyer will often search for those products online.

Modern marketing is as much about "pulling" customers to a product as it is about "pushing" that service at them. For example, an e-mail in your inbox or a sales rep at your desk is there to push a product at you. Samples at a Costco display or search engines invite, or pull, you toward the product, encouraging you to explore it voluntarily because it's aroused your interest. Strong marketing campaigns and tools should be blended to do a good job of both push and pull marketing.

Here are some guidelines to consider in preparing those materials.

Websites

At this stage, websites for companies using the physical channel should provide clear information on the company's vision and the problem it was founded to solve. Your job in this step is to learn how much detailed product information can pull the customer in to facilitate a sale. At a minimum, the website's job is to arouse interest in and spark consideration of the product or company and to drive interested prospects into the physical sales channel. (For low-dollar-item products, you can even have the website close the sale.) However, the website shouldn't provide customers with reasons *not to buy* (it shouldn't display details about price, installation requirements, etc). It should instead encourage interested prospects to interact with the company. Use the site to collect as much information as the prospect will provide. (Remember, response rates drop in direct proportion to the number of "required fields" in a sign-up form.)

Social Marketing Tools

Many companies that sell physical products exclusively in a physical channel use Facebook pages, Twitter streams, and other social marketing tools to spread the word and attract customers. They also use these online tools to invite customers and prospects to introduce products to their colleagues and friends. Making all this readily available and promoting it ambitiously is a relatively inexpensive way to accelerate the Get process. (Details about these tools are found in Chapter 3, page 131, and beginning on page 313 later in this chapter.)

E-mail and e-mailable Marketing Tools

E-mail messages are an important tool for communicating with prospects and customers online, since they can be targeted and often individualized based on what you know about them. When crafted carefully to provide useful information beyond a flat-out sales pitch, they can break through the cluttered inboxes of even the most cynical prospects. Create e-mail messages and campaigns that reflect what you know about the individual and design multi-e-mail campaigns for optimum impact. Create digital versions of brochures, white papers, and other sales materials to accompany the e-mails themselves. (Learn more about e-mail campaigns in the customer-relationships section of Chapter 4.)

Get Ready to Sell: Acquire/Activate Customers Plan (Web/Mobile)

➪ In customer discovery, you developed a rough plan to acquire and activate customers (see Chapter 4, page 144). Now it's time to refine those plans and build the acquisition and activation programs and tools. As a reminder:

- *Acquisition* is where prospects first learn about, experience, or visit the product, site or app. This is the widest point in the company's sales funnel and the customer's first interaction with the company

- *Activation* gets newly acquired customers to sign up, participate or buy, or at the very least to identify themselves and move through the "Get" funnel

Remember that "Get" activity is very different in web/mobile: you must attract customers to your site, app, or product or they won't even know you exist! Review page 150, which, in brief, says: figure out where your customers go when they're searching for a solution; be visible and inviting in as many of those places as possible; and "earn" their visit to your product with helpful, friendly information, not hard-boiled sales pitches.

> **PROCEED WITH CAUTION:** Remember, this is an overview. There's no way you can implement all this or even process it in one sitting. It's a plan. Implementation happens later.

	Physical Channels	Web/Mobile Channels
GET customers (demand creation)	*Strategy:* Awareness, Interest, Consideration, Purchase *Tactics:* Earned Media (pr, blogs, brochures, reviews), Paid Media (ads, promotions), Online tools	*Strategy:* Acquire, Activate *Tactics:* Websites, App Stores, Search (SEM/SEO), email, Blogs, Viral, Social Nets, Reviews, PR, Free Trials, Home/Landing Page
KEEP customers	*Strategy:* Interact, Retain *Tactics:* Loyalty programs, product updates, customer surveys, Customer check-in calls	*Strategy:* Interact, Retain *Tactics:* Customization, User Groups, Blogs, Online Help, Product Tips/Bulletins, Outreach, Affiliates
GROW customers	*Strategy:* New Revenue, Referrals *Tactics:* Upsell/Cross/Next-Sell, Referrals, (maybe) Unbundling	*Strategy:* New Revenue, Referrals *Tactics:* Upgrades, Contests, Reorders, Refer friends, Upsell/Cross-Sell, Viral

"Get Customers" Tools for Web/Mobile Channels (Table 9.3)

The "Acquire" Plan and Tools

The Acquire plan is short, to-the-point, and tactical in nature. The plan helps you find tools that predictably deliver large numbers of "good" customers (who engage with or spend heavily on the site or app) into the widest point of the funnel (at the left) at the lowest cost per customer.

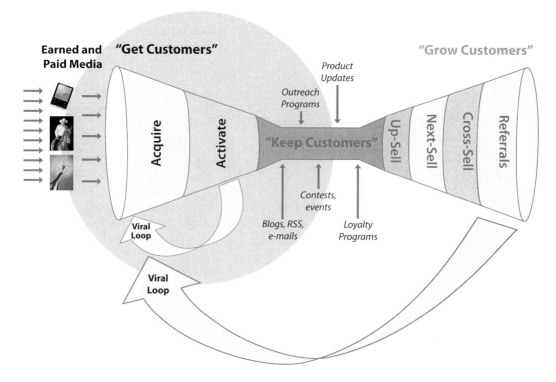

The "Get Customers" Funnel in Web/Mobile Channels (Figure 9.5)

> **WARNING**: There is no possible way you can read, process and act on this section in one read. There's a lot here. Skim it first, then go back and read each section. Then think about what action you need to take for your startup.

The Acquire plan (see sample plan on page 308) should fit on a single page. It details the first set of Acquire activities to test and includes:

- *Who*: Who's responsible for driving the program; who will add support or expertise
- *What*: Describe the tactic and its parts (see below for a list of tools)
- *Budget*: Estimate of spending for the first round of testing
- *Timing*: Outline the steps needed to launch (our example in Figure 9.6 uses a four-week cycle)
- *Why*: Specific, measurable acquisition goals of each plan element
- *Multi-sided or not:* Do you have users, or users and payers?

The acquire plan and tactics will change repeatedly, since in customer validation they're basically a series of experiments.

**The acquire plan and tactics will change repeatedly...
they're basically a series of experiments.**

In a physical consumer channel like Walmart, marketers seldom know which consumers see, touch, or buy any particular product. But in the web/mobile channels, every aspect of consumer behavior can be instrumented, analyzed and, often as not, optimized to improve business performance. Be sure your product is instrumented to track every consumer action or inaction. Without building the instrumentation upfront, optimizing your acquisition activities is more challenging, if not downright impossible.

A Sample Acquire Spreadsheet

Shown in Figure 9.6 is a sample of part of an Acquire plan for a web startup with a small budget. The plan is built around a few key assumptions:

Who: Two staffers are needed, one full-time and one half-time

What: The tactics, chosen by the team, seem best-suited to maximizing leads and sales (see next section for a list of tools)

Budget: The startup has about $25,000 to spend for this

tool	who	what	element	cost	week-4	week-3	week-2	week-1	launch
e-mail blitz campaign	joe	friends/ bought lists	3 e-mail invites each	2,000	buy 3-4 test lists; e-mail platform	outline mails, offers, headlines	finalize creative, lists (x6)	set up, test blast system	launch
small biz ad banners	sue	free trial offer	CPA, banners, e-mails	5,000	identify sites, get rates, ad ideas	start creative, negotiate rates	final ads, need IAB sizes	a/b tests, cut POs	launch
CPA e-mail campaign	sue	free trial offer	mailer gets $5 per	5,000	talk to mailers, start creative	test first creative with 2 mailers	pick lists, set a/b tests	final, creative cut POs	week 3
public relations	sue	new product news	releases, demos	1,000	call media, offer online demo	more demos start blasts	launch event? Bloggers	interviews, more blasts	keep going
PPC/ adwords	joe	small biz tax savings	2-3 test campaigns	8,000	Brainstorm-ing, shop competitors	layout word track (test jargon)	finalize 3 test campaign	Rotate	
SEO/natural search	joe	optimize website		1,000	select vendor, start asap	change text, metatags	collect links keep adding	optimize	optimize
flyer distribution	all	flyers to small offices	addresses, numbers	500	find bldgs w/small cos, list	draft flyer, offer	book staff, hire temps	plan routes, print flyer	blitz
small biz conference	sue	small booth/ free cd	demo cd at show	2,000	order space, find cheap booth	figure demo CD vs. flyer costs	signage, staffing plan	invite press, get ready	attend

A Sample Acquire Plan and Timetable (Figure 9.6)

Timing: The team is allowing itself four weeks to prepare all elements for the launch of validation

Why: The goal is to get 30,000 to 35,000 customers to download a free trial and to get 15 percent of them to convert to paying customers. This would achieve a customer acquisition cost of about $5, as suggested in this plan's revenue model hypothesis

Multi-sided or not?: Does your product have both users and payers? If so, a multi-sided market requires a separate plan for each "side" of its market. Users will be acquired one way, while reaching and selling advertisers will demand a totally different approach. (Our sample is a single-sided market)

Guidelines for Developing the Acquire Plan

Determining whom to acquire (i.e., which customers,) what promotional tactics to use, and what to say and how to say it (the content and messaging) is made easy because you did most of the research and planning in customer discovery. Start this plan by referring back to three hypothesis documents you devised when you created and tested your original business model canvas hypotheses:

- *Customer segments:* customers to be reached (which guides e-mail, targeting of marketing activities, ads, and PR)
- *Customer relationships:* how customers will be reached (SEO, PPC, e-mail, PR, etc.)
- *Value proposition:* what will excite customers and persuade them to engage, visit or buy

Don't be afraid to update or change the hypotheses based on the latest feedback or even instinct at this point, since they're still just "best guesses" confirmed by only a few customers. Other guidelines to keep in mind:

- *Remember that this is a test* to figure out which tools work and cost-effectively when they're launched during customer creation, the next step. *This is not a company or product launch.* Your goal is learning, *not revenue,* so don't be afraid to test lots of alternatives

- *Define success upfront* for each test, using a pass/fail metric (such as "one in five people will click"), and monitor results

- *Be the greatest, friendliest, coolest thing going.* Your job is to attract or invite customers to your product, site, or app, so be interesting and welcoming (and, if appropriate, even fun or funny) rather than not just offering a hard, cold sale. Think like your customers, and be prominent and visible where you think they'll be searching for a solution like yours. (Think about forums and online communities)

Running tests without collecting data is a cardinal sin.

- *Instrument everything.* Running tests without collecting data is a cardinal sin. Engineering needs to spend the extra effort to collect all customer behavior data so it can be measured and optimized continuously. Confront this upfront, as it's hard to "bolt on" later

- *Don't start everything at once,* since that will create chaos both in the market and in the company. For example, start search engine optimization and pay-per-click tests on Day Five, and add e-mail and affiliate marketing programs two or three weeks later. The individual, program-by-program results will be easier to identify and measure

- *Don't spend more than $2,000 or, if well-funded, $10,000 to test any one thing.* The startup usually can't afford it at this stage, and the risks of guessing wrong are too great

- *When a test seems to be working, ramp it up* to be sure it withstands the test of scale. If a $2,000 e-mail marketing campaign is performing, double it, refine it and do it again

- *Choose agency partners very carefully, if at all.* The costs and management time needed to hire a pr, ad, or web agency this early in your startup make it a very risky proposition. Most often, agencies are great at execution of programs but not at developing and testing strategies. Rely on founders and staff where possible, as they know the product and the business model best. Consider freelance talent specialized in developing tests and strategies or those who specialize in specific tasks (e.g., pay-per-click, demos and other specialized skills) if they don't exist within the company

- *Don't launch the Acquire effort by itself.* Activation programs must be ready to "catch" the customers you've acquired, so if there's copy saying, "Sign up today and get a free box of chocolates," for example, the site's back-end system has to be operating, the chocolates have to be ready to ship, and copy for the thank-you e-mail must be ready to go. If you're taking customers' money, all back-end systems need to be working, including such elements as receipts, credit-card processing, and customer service. Similarly, site and app instrumentation must be up and running, tested and feeding the management dashboard so it can measure the behavior of every customer who passes through the funnel. Remember that acquisition by itself is one of several integrated pieces of the "Get" strategy (there's also activation, retention, and "grow customers," to name a few).

The acquisition plan is managed through close monitoring of every step customers take as they move through the sales or "get customers" funnel. That monitoring, generally in a dashboard (read about them on page 343), enables constant effort to improve performance or "throughput"—customers movement from one step to the next—at every step of the funnel, using tools detailed in the next section, "optimizing the acquire plan."

Acquire Plan Tools

Acquisition tools you can buy

The list of customer acquisition tools you can buy and use is virtually endless, but their customer impact and effectiveness vary over time. Acquisition is a numbers game based on your ability to cost-effectively deliver large volumes of customers to your site or app. Basic tools include:

- search-engine marketing
- e-mail marketing
- outreach to bloggers
- affiliate marketing
- online lead generation
- customer incentives

Use the web (and www.steveblank.com) to identify the latest innovations and to select vendors. Most tools are discussed in detail in Customer Relationships, page 126.

> **WARNING**: There is no possible way you can read, process and act on this section in one read. There's a lot here. Skim it first, then go back and read each section. Then think about what action you need to take for your startup.

Acquisition Tools You Engineer Into Your Product

In addition to the tools you buy and deploy, build social network and viral components into your product itself to create the most powerful acquisition tool of all. First, it's fundamentally free, making it obviously the most cost-effective! Second, it can be remarkably fast, as seen in the skyrocketing growth of social-media and photo-sharing sites, among others. As a bonus, it's highly likely that the first customers attracted to the new product will know others who are also interested and will personally endorse and refer the product, app, or site to them.

Three distinct types of social networks and network effects aid acquisition:

Word of mouth, the most prevalent, encourages happy customers to share news of their new-found product or service with friends and business associates. It brings a personal friend-to-friend endorsement that's extremely powerful

Sharing allows others to use and share articles, demos, and sample code so people can re-Tweet and use it on social media, RSS feeds, etc.

Direct network effects: People who want to share photos, make free calls, or have free video chats with friends need their friends to use the service, so they invite them to join

A great test of how your product fits is asking your early customers, "On a scale of 1 to 10 (with 10 being the best), would you recommend this product to your friends?" If your product doesn't rank 9 or 10, it has little word of mouth or network effect.

Some products are inherently *viral*...

Some products are inherently *viral,* some aren't. Some can be engineered to do so. For example, every sent Gmail message ends with the tag line, "Invite (recipient) to Gmail." It uses the e-mail "send" process to expand the network and Gmail's user base.

Encourage early customers or visitors to promote the product and your company to friends and business colleagues at every opportunity. Give them materials (e-mails, mailable links or demos), and consider rewarding them for doing so, as many online marketers do. This tactic is highly cost-effective and credible when done right, in large measure because it brings with it the sender's implied endorsement.

Develop simple widgets or links that make it easy for early visitors or customers to "like" the product, company or both on Facebook or to Tweet about it. Create YouTube videos and other shareable content that encourages exploration of the product. People respond to their friends' likes and dislikes and are more apt to explore something recommended by a friend than something they see in an e-mail or an ad. Create robust profiles of company, product and users wherever possible on Facebook and other relevant social-networking sites. Provide valuable information of interest to prospective customers rather than purely self-serving messages.

You might also want to consider creating separate, unbranded experiences (sites, blogs) that are specifically geared toward the problem your product or service is intended to solve. For example, a game startup might create a site dedicated to "cheats" hints and tips. A medical-device company selling gastric bands might have a site dedicated to weight loss.

The Activation Plan and Tools

While the previous step, acquisition, brings prospects to the doorstep (your home page/landing page,) activation gets them to engaged with a sign-up, a free or paid download, a click on something, game play, or a post on a site. However you engage the user, activation is the critical choke point in the sales funnel, where the customer begins a relationship with the product or company as a member, user, subscriber, player, or buyer. Whether you're asking for sharing, playing, participation or an order, this is the place where a first-time visitor crosses the threshold to become an active user of your site or app.

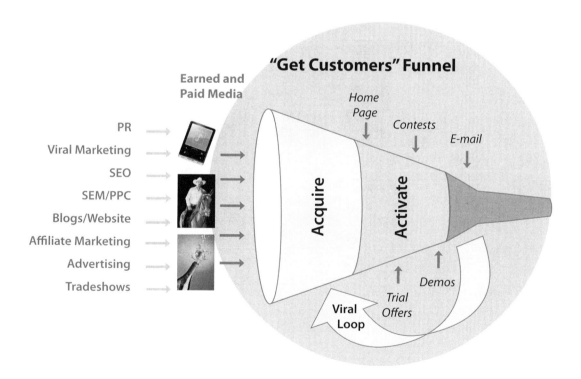

The "Get Customers" Activation Activities in Web/Mobile Channels (Figure 9.7)

In the activation step, users decide—all by themselves—whether to engage with or buy your product, and the decision is often made in a matter of seconds. So the home or landing page must work hard and fast to activate newly acquired "lookers," converting them into buyers, users, or tryers. (Activation sometimes happens in an app store, via e-mail, through the channel, or by telephone.) If you can't get people to activate at once, ideally you can get them to at least sign up so they can perhaps be persuaded to try, engage, or buy later.

The landing page is where activation most often begins. *(Figure 9.8)*

Wherever the customer arrives, he or she typically knows little if anything about where he or she has just landed. Here's what you need to address to activate a customer, using an oversimplified example of what goes through the visitor's mind on arrival:

- *Why* am I here? They want me to buy this new online multiplayer game
- *What* makes it special? Oh, here's a feature list and reasons to buy
- *How* do I know it's any good? Here's a demo, list of endorsements, user quotes, etc.
- *Where* do I get more information? I see buttons pointing to free trials, more info, etc.
- *Next?* What does the company want me to do? Oh, click here to try/ buy/sign up

Guidelines for Developing the "Activate" Plan

In the customer validation phase, the activation plan is really a test plan, A/B-testing every key aspect of the home/landing page, from color and copy to offers and navigation. It's OK to start with approximations or guesses, but they should iterate rapidly based on measured customer responses.

Should a landing-page offer scream "free" or subtly ask for a credit card? Should the "buy now" button be elegant and on top or bright orange and huge in the lower right-hand corner? Does an animated product demo activate more users than a simple graphic? There are scores if not hundreds of variables on almost any home page, and many tests must be repeated more than once to confirm results. Outside information architects and design professionals can help. They understand the range of tools available as well as the latest tricks of the trade in this highly creative process.

The list of tools, tricks, and variables to try is nearly endless, and it's hard to predict which ones will win. That's why repeated testing and measurement are so important, following the "test, measure, tweak" approach discussed earlier.

Here's what an activation plan should include:

- *Two types of action steps*: Activation happens both on and off the home page, so create two separate lists of the "Get" customers activities you plan to test (like offering a premium with every signup)
- *First/second test*: This is customer discovery, where you're running small-scale tests of your activation programs. Each of those programs needs to be tested at least twice, if not far more frequently, as you try to find the program that'll generate the most users or customers. Identify at least the first two tests
- *Pass/fail test*: Every test should have a "pass/fail," or an expectation that defines what "success" will look like if you have it. Based on experience, trials, or research, identify the metric that'll determine if the experiment was a success

An "Activate" Plan Example

Most activation happens on the home or landing page, where you're doing anything you can to get a user or customer you've acquired (he or she came to your page) and trying to engage them—get them to click, sign up, post a comment, play, or buy.

The home page is "where the action is" for activation.

And while the home page is "where the action is" for activation, there are other things you can also do—like send follow-up e-mails, for example—to further engage someone who's expressed more than a passing interest.

Table 9.4 is a simplified example of what an activation plan might look like for a social network where new golfers can offer and solicit improvement tips. In this example, since the business is in a multi-sided market, activation goals include such non-monetary actions as registration, inviting friends, asking a question or answering one.

Home Page Action	First Test	Second Test	Pass/Fail Test
"Join now" button	Large/ugly vs. small	Change color/blink	>8% improvement
Make comment now	Use large box/button	Add as a pop-up	3% make comments
"Better golf" demo	It's 100% of page	large green box	>5% better signups
"See today's tips"	Present on page	Click to view	>5% better signups
Join-free golf balls	Three balls	Six balls	>25% more signups
"Free forever" offer	Flash/link to signup	Show $29/year price	10% of views signup

Off Home Page	First Test	Second Test	Pass/Fail Test
3 e-mail followups	"Free forever" offer	3 free golf balls	>8% or >25% better
Phone followup	Thanks for visiting	Sign today/get balls	>20% conversion
Lead gen websites	Come visit/no offer	Signup/get balls	>8 or >25% better
Golf radio ads	Find a tip today	Post a tip today	Users @ <$1.00 per
Tourney program ad	Get/give tip image ad	You can win $5000	Users @ <$0.50 per
Flyers at golf clubs	Post and win prizes	Join and win prizes	Users @ <$0.50 per
E-mail demo to lists	Post tips and win	Just join to win	Users @ <$0.50 per

Sample Activation Plan for a Golfers' Social Network (Table 9.4)

Tools for the Activate plan

Activation happens both on and off the home page. Key tools to consider for each are in the bullet points that follow.

On the home or landing page

The landing page itself offers lots of ways to drive activations, including content, look and feel, and navigation. It can also showcase these activation tools:

- product demos
- free trials
- customer contact tools
- animation

Non-home page acquisition tools

While the home page is the primary activation tool, consider these others too:

- e-mail cascades
- price/incentives
- traditional tools

On the home or landing page itself:
Start with Content, Look and Feel, Functionality and Navigation

Good landing pages bear little resemblance to online brochures. They're invitations to "activate now," working hard to invite customers to engage or interact with—or buy—the product. This must happen literally at once, often in seconds. Otherwise the customer (and the money spent to acquire him or her in the previous step) vanishes with the click of a mouse. Develop the home/landing page along four axes:

1. *Content:* Does the site present everything for a customer needs to make the "activation" decision simply, in multiple places (for example, does every page say "join now")? Is it friendly, informative, and inviting?

2. *Look and feel:* Does the appearance relate to the audience ("corporate" for business apps, "serious" for financial sites, "edgy" for

teen or skateboarding products)? Does it match the typical style of the demographic or their country?

3. *Functionality:* What tools, widgets, configurators, demos or other devices can quickly engage customers, get them experimenting with and experiencing the product itself, and figuring out what it costs, how much time it would save, or how the game plays?

4. *Navigation/structure:* How is information organized? How accessible is it? How easy is it for users to complete high-value tasks (ordering, searching, etc.)?

Here's how to approach each area.

Home/Landing Page Content:

- *Tell me how I got here!* Users arrive at the home/landing page in a variety of ways (clicks, e-mails, referrals), but don't assume they know where they've landed. Welcome them; explain the site ("Welcome to the No. 1 online gaming portal.") to avoid fast abandonment

- *Reinforce the "scent"* of the e-mail, ad, or tool that drove the customer to the page. Use similar verbiage (and look and feel) to increase confidence that the viewer has come to the right place

- *Issue a clear call to action.* The "pitch," or call to action, tells the customer what you want him or her to do. It should reflect positioning developed in Stage 1 of validation, whether it's "buy now," "sign up," or "attend a seminar." Use redundant calls to action wherever you can, but be sure they're not confusing. Clearly tell visitors what to do and why doing so delivers value to *them*. The landing page should always accomplish the following:

  ○ Explain what problem the product solves and why it's important to users and worthy of their attention

  ○ Communicate ease of use and installation for the product

  ○ Clearly explain how the product works

  ○ Provide fast proof that it works (user quotes, competitive analysis, demos, etc.)

Calls to action appear three ways on a home/landing page: hyperlinks, buttons, and forms. They should stand out and be obvious to every visitor. Highlight product features that make the most powerful pitch for activation or purchase, and always provide easy access to more information about all the above.

Some guidelines for home or landing page content development:

- *Encourage me to "experience the offer:"* Never think of the landing page as a brochure. It's effective only if it encourages customer engagement, trial, or purchase. All content should invite involvement, and offers should be judiciously sprinkled throughout headlines, graphics and text, including "try now" textlinks embedded at least occasionally in body copy

- *Offer multiple calls to action* ranging from "buy now" and "learn more" to "download our white paper" and "talk to someone." Remember to make one of these far more prominent than all the others—the action most desired by the company

- *Write short!* Web visitors are very fragile, temporary guests. Respect their short attention spans and get to the point before they depart. The best calls to action are generally written in 10 or fewer words and displayed in an easily readable font

- *Be specific.* One of the most powerful page elements should be the core product-positioning statement developed in Step 1 of customer validation. Succinctly tell users why they should buy or use what the company's selling

- *Use bold graphics* such as snipes or bursts on the landing page to promote a mobile site.

- *Deploy contests, promos and sweepstakes* to encourage mobile downloads. These are highly valuable in the online space—both for users, who can redeem such offers immediately, and for startups, which can test and adjust offers on the fly

Manage your content inventory. Content should build credibility for the company, presenting it as solid, established, and ready to do business. Information on most of the following should be accessible from the landing page:

- product detail and information about the solution
- customer lists and success stories
- customer resources and support
- vendor partners
- company background
- current news and events
- company contact information (postal, phone, and e-mail)
- the company's privacy policy

Look and Feel

Design the home or landing page for maximum impact and minimal confusion. Always provide the user with multiple pathways to the desired "activation" action, whether it's subscribing, posting, playing or buying. Strive for fewer, crisper design elements, not more, keeping national cultural differences in mind when designing. (The advice below is for the U.S., where users expect websites to look clean and simple.) In some other countries, including China, users expect more design elements, which may look cluttered to a Western eye.

- *Keep it clean and simple,* without too many distractions from the call to action
- *Pick one promotional message and drive it the hardest* at the expense of others. Make it more prominent, supported by other things on the page, and compelling, along the lines of "free trial download" or "special introductory pricing this month"
- *Leave plenty of white space.* Crowded pages are clearly a turnoff. An overbearing number of graphic elements (art, type, buttons, etc.) will frustrate and distract users

- *Use visuals.* Whether using graphics, videos, demos, or diagrams, don't rely on copy itself to maintain user interest. Web visitors have extremely short attention spans. Keep the diagrams, charts and graphics simple. Use animation carefully to add interest

- *Use interactivity.* The web allows customer interaction with the brand, something no other medium allows. (If these kinds of tools aren't on the site, you're not using the web to its fullest potential)

- *Use big buttons.* "Download" or "buy now" or "sign up" should be graphically interesting, sizable and easy to spot

Navigation and Functionality

Navigation is really about two things: the logical organization of information and the shortest routes to task completion.

"Friendly" navigation provides users several "routes" to the call to action. Routes might take a user to a demo, to customer testimonials, to a white paper, or to a list of product features. Since nobody can predict what a customer wants to do next, each pathway should easily lead to "buy now" or another call to action.

Confusing navigation is the "foe," offering too many choices, confusing buttons, textlinks and a hodgepodge of options a user might choose. This often leads to higher abandon rates.

Overall Website Functionality:

- *Use tools to invite customer engagement.* Video, animation, demos, configurators and other devices should provide customers multiple ways to engage with the product itself, any way they'd like. "Take a tour (of our product)" and "play now" and "forecast your retirement needs" are typical engagement invitations, and each is far more powerful than offers like "read more" or "learn about …" Some examples:

  1. "Enter your age/answer three questions to learn how little this insurance costs"

  2. "Click here to see Facebook friends' photos on our site"

3. "Pick your character and start talking to him now"
4. "Find young single women in your neighborhood right now"
5. "What's your favorite golf ball? Click here for deep discounts. Free shipping!"

- *Use a demo* to engage users with the product and show off its features and ease of use. Make the demo more compelling (and under a minute long) than a PowerPoint. When possible, draw users into an actual, functioning component of the product ("put your data here" or "play this brief version."). The demo should end at the call to action

---

Engage users with the product and show off its features.

- *Offer free trials.* Not to be confused with a *freemium* pricing strategy, a free trial offer can be restricted by limiting the free version's functionality or duration (as in "try it free for two weeks"). Follow up with a series of e-mails that introduce features, offer tips, and provide reasons to buy. Where it makes sense financially, follow up with telesales
- *Click to contact.* Particularly for commerce and paid subscription sites (and probably too costly for freemium or multi-sided startups), offer several ways for prospects to contact the company. This can be as simple as a clickable link that spawns an e-mail to the sales department or a form for requesting more information or a call from Sales. Many commerce sites use real-time live voice and chat technology to engage quickly with prospects and enhance the chances of activation
- *Use animation.* Interactive configurators, calculators, animated demos, microsites, and many other utilities can bring the product to life and engage the customer. These can be developed inexpensively by outside sources found online. Some websites launch brief welcome

videos or quiet, animated demos that load automatically when a user gets to the site, but only play on demand (so it doesn't annoy the visitor or drive her away). Use animation sparingly, as it can be jarring

- *Incorporate source-driven pages:* Create multiple landing pages and match each one to the source of the click that brought users to the page. "Welcome, Yahoo friends" would almost certainly increase the visitor's comfort and click-through rate, as would a "special offer for Yahoo e-mail customers" that, oddly enough, is the same offer presented to Gmail customers or on a slightly different landing page

---

An entire industry has emerged around tools to encourage customers to take action.

An entire industry has emerged around tools to encourage customers to take action while at a company's website. New home-page tools are developed regularly, and some grow in popularity while others fade. This is an area where a modest amount of time spent on online research about the latest tools can pay off. In addition, freelance or small-agency experts in activation tests might be helpful (just remember that you don't want to run major programs yet, just experiments). Check www.steveblank.com for the latest tools.

Beyond the Home Page itself, Consider these Additional Activation Tools:

E-mail cascades: E-mail addresses are difficult to acquire, since customers resist registering, knowing that sales e-mails will follow. Think of customers' e-mail addresses as valuable assets: prospects willing to be sold. Develop sequences of three e-mails that strike a balance between brevity and enthusiasm for the product and its features, and stress key elements of the value proposition. Each e-mail should highlight different features or other reasons to buy and, where possible, tailor the message to reflect the source of the sign-up (referring site, location on website). Every e-mail should have multiple calls to action, both in textlinks and via a visible graphic "action" button, along with offers of further information and, of course, an easy way to unsubscribe. Compare the tradeoffs of HTML and text e-mails, since many mail servers block HTML e-mail.

Price/incentives: As discussed in detail in the section on revenue model hypotheses in Chapter 4, pricing can be another activation tool: free, freemium, special offers, and volume discounts can all be used. To avoid cannibalization of the company's revenues, consider making the special discount offer as a follow-up, after the prospect has declined the full-price offer at least once.

Traditional tools: Don't overlook a wide range of traditional, non-digital marketing tools when it comes to activating customers. Contests are often used ("win 500 frequent flyer miles" or "get a free tote bag," for example), as are sweepstakes ("you could win a free trip"). Outbound telemarketing can be a powerful tool to active folks who register. Direct mail can sometimes be used cost-effectively, as can traditional media advertising, where you can consider using QR codes.

Whatever the tool, test it during customer validation and measure the result as well as the resulting cost per activation. Compare the costs of acquiring active users with traditional vs. online tools and consistently optimize for the lowest cost per active user. If your test seems to work in a controlled test, expand the test and try again to see if the program scales. Much more on this in Phase 2, page 365.

Managing the Activate Plan

Close management of activation tests step is vital. In the next step, optimization, we'll discuss the use of dashboards to measure performance and cost-efficiency of each activation program individually. However, as a first step, a simple "funnel" can be used to monitor activation. Here's an example:

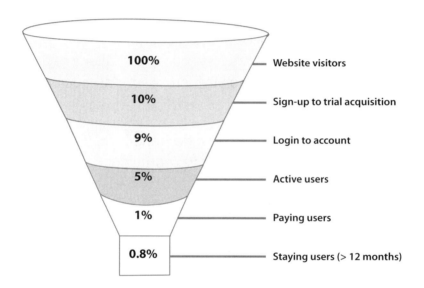

Example of a Simple Activation Funnel (Figure 9.9)

This funnel monitors prospects as they move through each step of the activation process. In this example, only one website visitor in 10 (10 percent) signs up for the free trial. Worse, only 9 percent of that group actually activates, becoming users of the product. And only a very small subset of that group moves on to become active users of the product or service. In this simple example, the company will need to attract literally millions of "free trial" sign-ups in order to build a sizable number of active users—a daunting challenge indeed.

Get Ready to Sell: Hire a Sales Closer (Physical)

In most startups, the founding team is typically product-oriented and rarely includes a sales professional. While founders often do just fine at finding earlyvangelist customers by themselves, they often lack the skill or experience to turn those relationships into orders. As sales efforts get under way, it's time to honestly determine whether someone on the founding team has the necessary experience to close deals. Does the team know how to negotiate with a buyer or a purchasing manager? Negotiate deal terms with a CFO? Are the founders willing to bet the company on their ability to close the first sales? If not, it's time to hire a sales closer.

A sales closer is not a sales VP who wants to rush out to build and manage a large sales organization. Good sales closers are aggressive, love early markets, want great compensation for success, and have no interest in building a sales organization. Typically, closers are experienced startup salespeople noted not just for their rolodexes in the target market but also for fabulous listening, pattern-recognition and collaboration skills. They also love finding new markets and closing deals and aren't ready to retire behind a desk.

While the closer will be an integral part of customer validation, the founders and the CEO still need to actively lead the process. Together, the founders and the sales closer are the core of the Customer Development team. It's their job to learn and discover enough information to build the sales and channel roadmaps. Going once around the customer validation loop without a sales closer may make sense unless it holds back progress. At that point, hire the closer. *A closer is invaluable in setting up meetings, pushing for follow-up meetings, and closing the deal. Having a sales closer is in no way a substitute for getting founders personally out and in front of customers.*

Get Ready to Sell: Build a High Fidelity MVP (Web/Mobile)

⇨ Customer discovery used your two MVPs to rapidly test and iterate prototypes to learn about the problem/need and solution. The goal of the MVP in customer discovery wasn't sales, just customer feedback.

This step tests the high fidelity minimum viable product. It's a more featured complete and polished functional version of the one used in Phase 3 of customer discovery. It still does not offer all the features and functionality the ultimate product vision will deliver. Why hi-fidelity? As customer validation invites more users to the product to test acquisition and activation tactics, the hi-fidelity MVP improves the test results, since visitors don't feel as if they're looking at a second-class product even if the MVP is an incomplete rendering of the product, as is often the case.

What does "part" of a product look like? It might be a multiplayer game with five levels of play instead of the 20 or 50 that will eventually be included. A social network could have limited features that don't allow photo sharing or provide users' locations but facilitates easy interaction and navigation. An online shoe store might have only women's casual shoes as a start, or it might not offer odd sizes while providing a superb e-commerce experience. If features aren't live for the customer validation tests, consider a page or several highlighting features that are "coming soon," but don't make it too prominent, since the objective is to test-sell the MVP now, not to give customers a reason to wait.

Note that a hi-fidelity MVP doesn't just magically appear in this step. You don't just stop at this step and write one. Instead, it's the result of agile development with continuous deployment and continuous product and feature refinements that have been made since the company opened for business (one of the many reasons you can't do Customer Development with waterfall engineering). You haven't gotten this far unless your product development team has continually iterated, deployed, tested and improved the high fidelity MVP since you left Phase 3 of customer discovery.

Now if not earlier, the hi-fidelity MVP must be architected for instrumentation that delivers a stream of customer and product behavior data used at the company every single day to further develop the business model and the product. Ensure that the dials, meters and gauges are working, and then hold onto your seat because we're about to move those needles. Think of instrumentation for a software application as gauges and instruments on the business model canvas, providing information about what's happening in the application.

Get Ready to Sell: Sales Channel Roadmap (Physical)

This sales channel roadmap section assumes that, in Customer Discovery, your team evaluated the distribution channel alternatives and is focused on one specific sales channel. Get one channel right first, then expand later.

Rather than spreading yourself thin, focus on one channel first.

What if you're not sure this is the right channel? It's OK, this is just a test. Rather than spreading yourself thin, testing multiple distribution channels at once, focus on one channel first, whether it's direct sales, chain stores, or mail order. Based on test results, other channels are easily added later. The one exception to this rule: companies using their own website to sell directly to end-users should also test that in parallel.

Elements of a sales channel roadmap are:

- channel "food chain"
- channel responsibility
- channel discount and financials
- channel management

Sales Channel "Food Chain"

For a distribution channel, the food chain is the link of organizations between you and your customer (from your vp of sales to a sales rep to a distributor to a retailer, for example). The food chain describes each of the organizations in the chain, and its relationships with the company and with one another.

Here, for example, is the food chain showing how books move from a publisher to a book-buying customer at an e-book publishing company. The food chain diagram might look as simple as Figure 9.10 below.

Direct e-book Publishing Food Chain *(Figure 9.10)*

However, selling through the traditional physical distribution food chain for printed books, it's far more complex, as shown in Figure 9.11.

Book Publishing Physical Channel Food Chain *(Figure 9.11)*

To get ready to sell, create a visual representation of your channel food chain. It may include these or other "links" in the chain:

- *National wholesalers*: Stock, pick, pack, ship and collect, and then pay the publisher for orders received. They fulfill orders but don't create demand
- *Distributors*: Use their own sales force to sell to bookstore chains and independents. The distributor makes the sale; the bookstore actually orders from the national wholesaler
- *Retailers*: This is where the customer sees and can buy books

Review the channel hypothesis (page 98) to see what needs to be included in your diagram.

Channel Responsibility

A channel-responsibility map diagrams the relationships in a complex distribution channel. A written description of these responsibilities, created in describing the "food chain," should accompany the diagram. It helps everyone on the team understand why the channel was selected and what to expect from it.

One of the mistakes startups often make is assuming their channel partners invest in creating customer demand. Most do not. For example, in Figure 9.12, don't assume the book wholesaler does anything other than stock and ship books. The same is true for the distributor. It takes orders from bookstores and in some cases may promote book sales to bookstores, but it doesn't bring customers into the store to buy. (Unfortunately nowadays most publishers don't create demand either.)

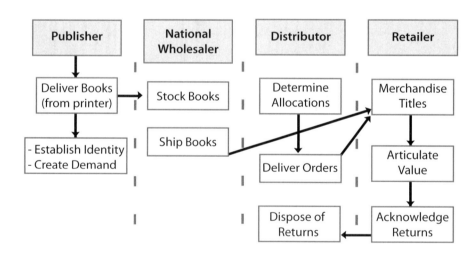

Channel Responsibility Map (Figure 9.12)

Channel Discounts and Financials

Each tier in the "food chain" costs the company money, since each tier charges for its services. In most channels, these fees are calculated as a percentage of the "list" or retail price consumers pay. To understand how the money flows from the customer to company, first calculate the discounts each channel tier requires.

Continuing with our book-publishing example, we can construct a diagram, as shown in Figure 9.13, detailing the discount each tier requires.

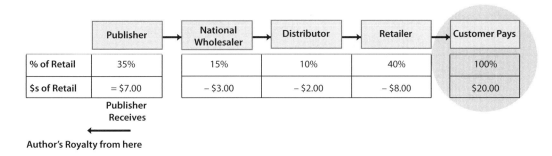

	Publisher	National Wholesaler	Distributor	Retailer	Customer Pays
% of Retail	35%	15%	10%	40%	100%
$s of Retail	= $7.00	– $3.00	– $2.00	– $8.00	$20.00

Publisher Receives

← Author's Royalty from here

Channel Discounts (Figure 9.13)

As you can see, a book retailing for $20 would net our publishing company $7 after everyone in the channel took his cut. From this $7, the publisher must pay the author a royalty, market the book, pay for the printing and binding, contribute to overhead, and realize a profit. Out of the $20 a customer pays, there's only a dollar or two for the author! No wonder authors are ditching print and going directly to e-books.

Channel discounts are only the first step in examining how money flows in a complex distribution channel. For example, in the book channel and many others (software, media, more), sales are on a *consignment* basis with 100 percent return rights. This means your product (the unsold books in the example) can be returned to your company for full credit (and to add insult to injury, you have to pay the return freight for returned products). Why is this a problem? A mistake that startups frequently make when they use a distribution channel is to record the sale to the channel (in this case the national wholesaler) as revenue. The sad truth is that orders from a channel partner don't mean that end customers bought the product; it only means they hope and believe they will.

In addition, some channels have a stock rotation-returns policy (outdated food, old versions of software or hardware) requiring allowances for a proportion (or all) of your "sold" products to be returned.

Your channel financial plan should include a description of all the financial relationships among tiers of the channel (see Figure 9.14).

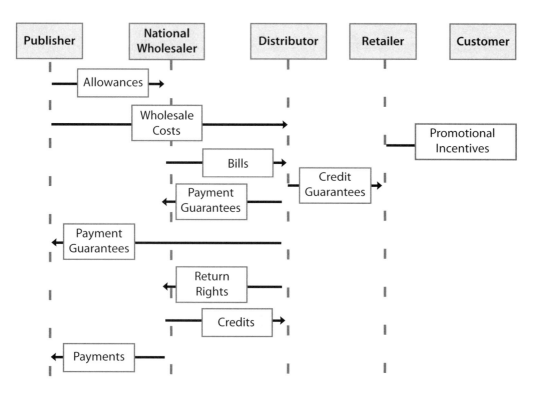

Channel Financial Relationships *(Figure 9.14)*

Channel Management

Although every company's goal is a well-managed and carefully selected sales channel, failure to select the right channel or to control the channel often results in miserable sales revenue and unanticipated channel costs. Much like instrumenting a website, you need to monitor your channel inventory levels, sell in and sell through. In a direct-sales channel, it's straightforward: no goods leave your company until there's a customer order. In an indirect channel, however, the biggest risk is knowing how much end-user demand actually exists. Why? Your company has a direct relationship only with the tier of distribution closest to it. You're dependent on channel-partner reports, which are often months out of date, to learn how much product has "sold through" the channel or how much has actually been purchased. Another risk is the temptation in an indirect channel to "stuff" the channel. *Stuffing* means getting a tier of the channel to accept more product on consignment than sales forecasts reasonably expect the channel to sell. This tactic can provide a temporary but imaginary inflation of sales, followed by a debacle (or in the case of public companies, lawsuits) later. All these potential issues need to be documented and discussed in the channel-management plan in order to avoid surprises later.

Multi-Sided Markets

Multi-sided markets are more common in the web/mobile channels but exist in the physical channel as well. Medical devices are a good example of a "physical" channel with a complex multi-sided market. An artificial hip may be approved by the FDA, recommend by a doctor, implanted inside a patient, bought by a hospital, installed by a surgeon but paid for by an insurance company. (See Figure 9.15 below.) In this case, just focusing on patients or doctors or hospitals without understanding who the payers are and how they reimburse for hip implants would be a fatal error. Startups in multi-sided markets need to validate *all sides* of their channel hypothesis.

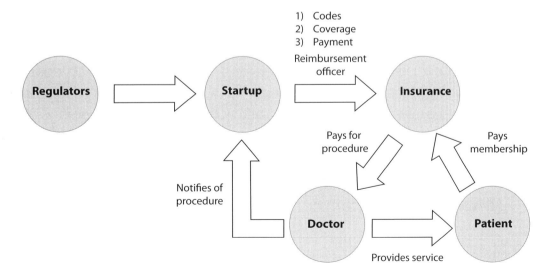

Channel Diagram for a Complex Multi-Sided Market (Figure 9.15)

Get Ready to Sell: Build a Metrics Toolset (Web/Mobile)

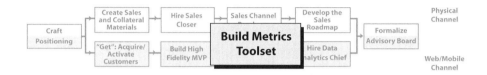

⇨ Web/mobile businesses focus on data collection, analysis and optimization from the day they go live till the day the doors close. A web/mobile startup's conversion funnel monitors customers through their entire life cycle. The entire process is driven by a never-ending campaign to test, measure, and optimize every step in the funnel, from awareness to purchase. It's a 24/7 process of "try it, measure it, tweak it."

Web/mobile businesses focus on data collection, analysis and optimization from the day they go live til the day the doors close.

The products you build should be instrumented to measure every click on the website or app, its source, and the action it causes or doesn't. As a result, the management team should have at its fingertips a dashboard that summarizes every key, actionable user behavior, and delivers insights and trends that drive continual business improvement. There are two parts to building a metrics tool set:

- determining which key business metrics need to be measured
- developing a dashboard or system to collect and monitor the data

Key Metrics to Measure

Long before the web was born, 19th-century retailer John Wanamaker of Philadelphia summarized the challenge that online and mobile marketers would face nearly two centuries later: "I know I'm wasting half of my advertising budget. I only wish I knew which half." In the web/mobile channels, this process is far easier than it was for Wanamaker's newspaper and radio ads, because every click and consumer action can be recorded. Determining what to measure is where the process begins.

Using your customer relationships hypotheses, identify the metrics for success in the business model. Prioritize and limit the number of metrics to fewer than a dozen, and the only metrics to be measured are those that can be acted on or improved. Think: "how many, how fast, how much, and how good?"

- *How many* customers are acquired, and how many of those are activated? (And how many are lost? And where in the purchase process do you lose them?)
- *How fast* do they arrive and how fast do they activate? After one page view or visit, or 20 of either?
- *How much* does each acquisition and activation cost?
- *How good* are the customers who are being acquired? Active users/ spenders who return again and again or visitors with no "stickiness" at all?

"Get Customers"

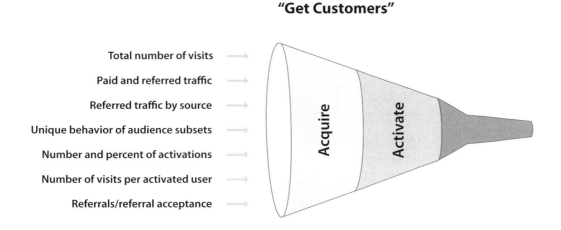

Metrics to Measure, in the "Get Customers" Funnel Web/Mobile Channels (Figure 9.16)

For consistency's sake, consider organizing the metrics the way the sales funnel is organized—by acquisition and activation metrics. For example:

Acquisition metrics:

- *Total number of visits* by visitor type, time of day, and source, and page views per visit
- *Paid and referred traffic conversion rates* by source (how many links or banners, and at what cost, to generate one visitor or user) and cost per acquired/activated user
- *Quantities and percentages of referred traffic* by source
- *Unique behaviors* or actions of subsets or segments of the customer universe

---

I know I'm wasting half of my ad budget.
I only wish I knew which half…

Activation metrics

- *Total number of activations:* another percentage of hourly/daily/weekly acquisitions
- *Number/percentage of activations,* tracked back to the original source
- *Number/percentage/cost per activation,* based on quality (heavy users and big spenders or modest spenders and inactive users?), wherever identifiable, preferably by source
- *Number of visits, page views,* referrals per activated user, by source and by cost

Activation metrics also capture user behavior for assessment and improvement. Typical behavior metrics include the number and percentage of people who download or otherwise activate, register or engage within a certain number of visits or page views.

Monitor people who take an activation action, like watching a demo, and then don't activate, as well as those who abandon during the enrollment or registration process. Again, the list is endless, so be careful not to measure more than the team can manage or improve on effectively.

This list is the tip of a huge iceberg. Focus on the ones that help you understand customer behavior to efficiently drive acquisition and activation and ultimately drive revenue!

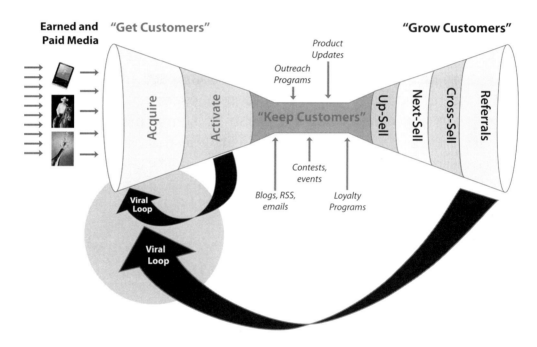

"Grow Customer" Referrals happen through "Viral loops." (Figure 9.16b)

Referral Metrics

Referral metrics are important because recommendations from existing customers are the most cost-effective source of new customers. Key referral metrics are:

- number and percentage of users referred
- average number of prospects existing customers
- referral acceptance rate

Assess referral incentive programs to determine which incentives motivate the most new users to refer others and the cost per referral.

At this point in the customer validation process, it's too early to worry much about customer retention (discussed in depth in Phase 2), since the company's overwhelming early focus is on getting its first customers. When designing the metrics system, make sure it can accommodate metrics that will be needed later to monitor retention and referral, including user cohorts described in detail in Phase 2.

Use a dashboard or system to collect and monitor data

Your startup's future lies in its customer acquisition, activation and retention data. This is so important that many web businesses actually display their real-time site-performance data on a jumbo flat-screen monitor in the office so that it's always the center of attention. Off-the-shelf dashboard systems are available, and home-grown solutions are readily built using tools as simple as Excel.

Be careful not to overdo it with metrics. A small number of metrics tell the overall "health" story of the business.

Be careful not to overdo it with metrics. Generally, a relatively small number of metrics tell the overall "health" story of the business, so resist the temptation to generate complex, overwhelming collections of data that take management eyes off the key issues. Those issues usually revolve around "how many, how much, how fast": how many customers are activated (or lost), at what cost, and how quickly. Good CEOs have these key statistics as well as their improvement trends and key drivers at their fingertips and can recite them almost on cue. Equally important, they can be measured on a whiteboard or a simple spreadsheet.

The metrics you use to measure and monitor your business ought to be the same ones you and your board are looking at during board meetings. If they're *only* asking you for income statement, balance sheet and cash flow and not looking at these numbers, you've failed as a CEO. It's your job to get your board to agree that the numbers you're worrying about are the numbers they're worrying about.

Figure 9.17 shows a dashboard for a simple content site where the business goals are increased page views, customer referrals, and e-mail delivery.

Example of a Simple Dashboard (Figure 9.17)

In the next step, if your startup doesn't already have one, you'll recruit and install a "data chief" to manage the data and its interpretation. He'll also quarterback the company's plan to use that data to drive continuous improvement in the way customers discover, engage with, and use the product and how they help sell it to their friends and colleagues.

Get Ready to Sell: Develop the Sales Roadmap (Physical)

A classic startup flaw is hiring a sales force before you've figured out how to sell. At the start, a fog of uncertainty hangs over you. It's the founders' job to gather enough information to illuminate how to proceed one step at a time, and then assemble that information into a coherent picture of the right path to take. We call this the "sales roadmap."

Your goal is to determine who your true customers are and how they'll buy your product. You build a sales team only when you completely understand the process that transforms a prospect into a purchaser and know you can sell the product at a price that supports your business model. With the sales roadmap in their hands, the members of your sales force will be able to focus on actual sales instead of the hit-and-miss experimentation you'll undertake as you move through the customer validation process.

With the sales roadmap in their hands, the members of your sales force will be able to focus on actual sales.

A sales roadmap details every step from the first call to a prospective buyer to the contract signing. It should also show how those steps vary from one company, buyer or job title to the next. The initial sales-road-map hypothesis developed in customer discovery should be updated based on customer feedback and revisited before sales calls begin. Don't worry—it will change further based on field experience with customers.

The roadmap's complexity depends on the customer's size, buying cycle and budget as well as the product's price, the industry, and the distribution channel selected. The roadmap for selling the CEO of a midsize company is clearer, say, than the route to selling a Fortune 500 VP. And roadmaps to Safeway, Intel or Toys "R" Us are far tougher than those leading to local florists or pet stores. Good roadmaps are hard work, but they're the difference between success and failure. Refine the roadmap while the company is lean and small, before dozens of sales reps find themselves lost on the road, selling without a map.

Three other key sales-planning tools support the sales roadmap: company organization and influence maps, and customer access maps.

Organization and Influence Maps

Remember those organization and influence map briefs you created in the customer discovery step? It's time to pull them off the wall and study your findings. By now your early hypotheses have been modified to reflect the reality you encountered as you spoke with potential customers. Use this information to develop a working model of the purchase process for your target customer. You'll also want to take a closer look at the notes from your encounters with possible earlyvangelists. You might also want to bring in customer information from other sources such as a company's annual report, Hoovers, Dun & Bradstreet or press articles.

The E.piphany sales cycle is a good example of how the influence map for a complex sale can be developed. Given the six- to seven-figure cost of E.piphany's software, buyers had to feel a significant pain, recognize it as a pain, and be committed to making the pain go away for E.piphany to get a sale. The product also required "top down" selling to senior executives first who would use their authority to mandate agreement/acquiescence from their staffs. In a large enterprise the alternative is working "bottom to top," up from low level employees, with each trying to convince the boss, a much more difficult process for costly systems. Further, E.piphany changed the status quo inside companies. It required several organizations to reconfigure their business processes and job specs. While an improvement for the company, change engenders resistance, and resistance creates saboteurs—always an unwelcome surprise.

The bad news: multiple "yes" votes were required to get an E.piphany order. Other enterprise sales, such as manufacturing-process controls or customer support, sometimes need endorsement from only one key executive or user community to close a deal. With those packages, Information Technology executives personnel generally had input into selection, but the actual users enjoyed substantial power in the decision. An E.piphany sale was different, since IT wasn't the driver, but it *was* an active participant—often with veto power. Likewise, experience showed it was necessary to sell both "high" and "wide" on the user and technical sides of an account. After getting thrown out of multiple accounts, we built a simple two-by-two matrix that shows where support and approval were needed:

	Operational	**Technical**
High	Executive	CIO or Division IT Executive
Low	End Users	Corp. IT Staff or Division IT Staff

Support/Approval Matrix (Figure 9.18)

This matrix said that even with a visionary executive in an operating division supporting the E.piphany purchase, it was necessary to sell to four constituencies to close a deal. Without support in an operating division of the company and IT/tech "approval," we couldn't close a deal. Early on, it became apparent that if the IT organization was determined to derail an E.piphany sale, it would often succeed. This insight was a big deal. It was one of the many "aha's" that made Epiphany successful. We figured out how to solve the problem because a founder and the sales closer were present to witness the initial sales strategy failure, and spent time figuring out how to pivot the sales strategy.

Early sales efforts fell short because they ignored the fact that selling E.piphany into the enterprise was different from the sale of other enterprise products. The most glaring oversight was failure to enlist the support of the IT organization. In sales calls, it was easier to get people on the operational side excited than it was to excite IT about a suite of applications to serve sales, service or marketing. In some cases, E.piphany took the excited prospects in operating divisions at their word when they said they could make CIO and the IT department "fall into line" and approve the purchase. In other cases, necessary steps were skipped and it was assumed that several enthusiastic users could do our deal. Rarely did this prove true.

	Operational		Technical
High	Executive	**1** ⟶ **2**	CIO or Division IT Executive
Low	End Users	**3** ⟶ **4**	Corp. IT Staff or Division IT Staff

Example of an Influence Map *(Figure 9.19)*

We assembled that sales failure and success data into an "influence map." We had already established that a) we needed the support of four groups to get a deal done, b) IT would often be harder to win over than users and c) low-level IT personnel would oppose the concept. The critical question became "How to proceed?" The influence map, as shown in Figure 9.19, delineates the players and the order in which they need to be convinced and sold. Each step leveraged strengths from the step before, using momentum created by groups that liked the company and the products to overcome objections from groups that didn't. More often than not, shortcutting the process or skipping a sales stage meant losing the sale.

When understood, the Influence Map set the execution strategy for sales. Call on: (1) high-level operating executives (VPs, divisional GM's, etc.) first. Then, use that relationship as an introduction to (2) high-level technical executives (CIO or divisional IT exec), then (3) meet the operational organizations' end users (the people who will use the product), and finally, (4) use that groundswell of support to present to, educate, and eliminate objections from the corporate or divisional IT staff.

Customer Access Map

With the influences understood and written down, turn your attention to answering the perennial sales question of how to get the proverbial foot in the door. For corporate sales, purchasing or procurement is about the worst possible place to start, particularly when offering disruptive innovation. Varying with the prospect's size, corporate sales often require agile maneuvering through different layers or departments to set up meetings with the people identified in the organization and influence maps. Sales calls to actual customers help fill in blanks in the access map, adding information and suggesting behavior patterns. Figure 9.20 illustrates an access map in a corporate account.

For consumers, finding the right entry to early customers can be equally difficult. Rather than making random calls, think of organizations and special-interest groups that can be reached inexpensively. Can you reach customers through organizations they belong to, such as the PTA, book clubs, or antique car clubs? Are there web-based groups or meetups that might be interested?

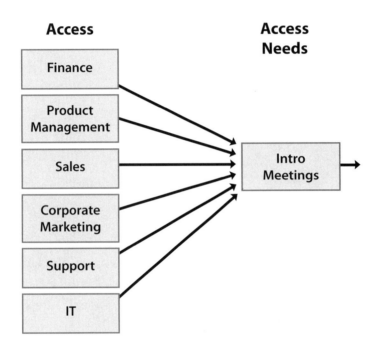

Example of an Access Map *(Figure 9.20)*

Sales Strategy

Understanding the influence map is step one in finding a repeatable sales process.

Lay out your corporate/consumer organization map, influence map and your access map side by side. For a corporate sale, your challenge is to move beyond the names and titles of the people you'll call on to develop a strategy for approaching them. As you begin to develop a sales strategy, here are some questions to consider:

- At what level do you enter the account? For example, do you sell high to executives? Or low to the operational staff?

- How many people on the organizational map need to say yes for a sale?
- In what order do you need to call on these people? What's the script for each?
- What step can derail the entire sale? Who are the potential saboteur?

Similarly, if you were trying to reach twentysomethings with a new consumer product, the questions might be:

- Do you need to get access to a specific demographic segment? For example, do you sell to college students? Parents? Families?
- How many people need to say, Is this an individual sale or family decision?
- If this sale requires that multiple members of a family or group agree, in what order do you need to call on these people? What's the script for each?
- What step can derail the entire sale?

Again, as you move out into the marketplace to sell your product, you'll learn what works or not. As predictable patterns emerge, your strategy will become clear.

Implementation Plan

A common first time founder mistake is getting a "thumbs up" from an earlyevangelist and opening the Champagne to toast the first sale. As any of you with experience in sales will know, don't do it yet. Unfortunately, much can happen between the time the decision-maker agrees to make a purchase and you actually receive the check. The goal of the implementation plan is to write down all the things left to happen before the sale is finalized and the product delivered and to determine who will follow up to manage them. For example:

- Does the CFO or the CEO or both need to approve the sale?
- Does the board need to approve the sale?
- Does Mom or Dad need to approve the sale?
- Does the customer need to get a loan to finance the sale?
- Must other vendors systems/components be installed and working first?

Get Ready to Sell: Hire a Data Analytics Chief (Web/Mobile)

⇨ In a startup that's selling physical goods, it was the founders who first had to find the sales roadmap and then hired a sales closer to assist them. Likewise, a web/mobile company needs a dedicated data analytics chief after the founders have discovered the key customer acquisition and activation metrics. The analytics chief will drive "continuous improvement," not just in the customer validation process but in perpetuity.

The analytics chief will drive "continuous improvement," not just in the customer validation process but in perpetuity.

At first, one of the founders may take on this role. (Extra credit if he's an experienced "data junkie," statistical analyst, or "quant" who loves to collect and pore over data, looking for anomalies, opportunities, trends and weaknesses.) Whether the person's called the chief marketing officer, the data analytics chief, the database or online marketing director, or just plain "founder" is irrelevant. Agility with numbers and tools are critical job skills, as is innate curiosity. Also required: the "clout" to make things happen in the company once the data shows that something isn't happening per plan and requires a pivot. Responsibilities include:

- online optimization of targeted campaigns, managing all aspects of customer behavior reporting, tracking, analysis, and optimization
- management of all internal research, sponsorship, lead generation, and promotion programs

- development and management of plans, budgets costs and results of marketing programs
- management of budgets, forecasts, tracking and administration of program costs and results
- assuring the data is available to all key team members

If this person is not a founder, he or she must be a part of the senior management team, reporting to and updating it regularly. He or she should be hired as early as possible, ideally in time to participate in development of the dashboard system and selection of the metrics it will track. He or she must fully understand the business model and key business drivers, as he or she will be a loud voice driving pivots and iterations. The person must be a good collaborator, easy to work with, and highly creative—a rare combination.

This person must be a part of the senior management team.

Agree on how often the CEO should be briefed. The management team? The entire staff? Remember to focus the person on prioritizing and collecting only key, actionable data, not reams of useless information. Craft both compensation and confidentiality/no-compete agreements with this person, who will know more about the company's business drivers than virtually anyone else. Losing this person prematurely can be a major setback.

Get Ready to Sell: Formalize the Advisory Board
(All Channels)

Hopefully, you've asked for help from advisers on an informal basis in customer discovery. In this phase, it's time to formally engage them. There are no hard and fast rules for how large an advisory board should be or whether it should be a "board" at all. Basically, you want two things from advisors: great introductions you can't get any other way to key customers, talent or investors; and bold, out-of-the-box business model design thinking that will have dramatic impact on your strategy. All the rest is window dressing.

Think strategically, not tactically, about advisors' reach and sphere of influence. Recruit only advisors who will make a serious impact on the company in one way or another—think quality, not quantity. (If you're raising money having a cloud of "impressive names" may help, but don't confuse them with these people.) Formal advisory board meetings aren't required, at least for now, but this process should deliver access to experts who can help.

Begin by assembling an advisory board road map, much like the collateral roadmap developed earlier. As shown in Table 9.5, the roadmap is an organized list of the key advisors needed. (Don't feel compelled to put advisors in every box on the chart.)

In this example, the roadmap differentiates how each advisor will be used (technical, business, customer, industry or marketing). Usually, the most important advisors your startup can have are the ones with "golden rolodexes" who can make high-level introductions to early customers, channel partners, or partners who can deliver significant web traffic. Product Development may need technical advisors as early as Phase 1 of customer discovery. The technical advisory board is staffed with advisors from academia or industry who can offer technical advice and pointers to technical talent. As the company begins to sell product, these advisors are used as technical references for customers.

Where possible, particularly in enterprise sales situations, put key potential customers on the customer advisory board. These are people met in customer discovery who can advise about the product from the customer's perspective. I always tell these advisors, "I want you on my advisory board so I can learn how to build a product you'll buy. We both fail if I can't." They'll serve as a customer conscience for the product, and later some will be great references for, or introducers to, other customers. Use them for insight and one-on-one meetings with the company's business and Customer Development staff—and don't be afraid to ask them for specific introductions.

	Technical	**Business**	**Customer**	**Industry**	**Sales/Marketing**
Why	Product Development advice, validation, recruiting help.	Business strategy & Company Building advice.	Product advice & as potential customers. Later as customer conscience & as references.	Bringing credibility to your specific market or technology through domain expertise.	Counsel to help sort out sales, PR, press, and demand creation issues.
Who	Brand name technical luminaries for show, plus others with insight into the problems you are solving and are OK with getting their hands dirty.	Grizzled veterans who have built startups before. Key criteria: you trust their judgment and will listen to them.	People who will make great customers, who have good product instincts, and/or who are part of a customer network.	Visible name brands with customer and press credibility. May also be customers.	Experienced startup marketers who know how to create a market, not just a brand.
When	Day one of company founding and continuing through first customer ship.	Day one of company founding & ongoing.	In Customer Discovery. Identify in phase 1, begin inviting in phases 2 & 3.	In Customer Validation. Identify in phase 1, begin to invite in phase 3.	In Customer Creation. Need diminishes after Company Building.
Where	One-on-one meetings with Product Development staff at company.	Late-night phone calls, panicked visits to their home or office.	Phone calls for insight & 1-on-1 meetings with business and Customer Development staff at company.	Phone calls for insight & 1-on-1 meetings with business and Customer Development staff at company.	One-on-one meetings and phone calls with marketing and sales staff.
How Many	As many as needed.	No more than two or three at a time.	As many as needed.	No more than two per industry.	One for sales, one for marketing.

Advisory Board Roles (Table 9.5)

Two other sets of advisors to consider: an industry advisory board of domain experts who bring credibility to the company's specific market or technology; and an advisor to the CEO who's a "been there, done that" CEO type who can bring practical, how-to advice.

Make sure that, for people that count to you , you count to them.

The number of advisors for each domain will obviously vary with circumstances, but there are some rules of thumb. Both sales and marketing advisors tend to have large egos. You can usually only manage only one of them at a time. Industry advisors like to think of themselves as *the* pundits for particular industries. Have them give you their opinions without being in the same room or showing up on the same day—this allows you to sort through whose advice you want to follow. Business advisors are much like marketing advisors, but some have expertise in different stages of the company. Consider keeping a few on hand to make you smarter. Finally, our product development team could never get enough of the technical advisors. They'd come in and make us smarter about specific technical issues. The same was true for the customer advisors. Be sure to learn something new every time they come by.

Compensating Advisors

The Oracle of Omaha, Warren Buffet, says it best: "Make sure that, for people that count to you, you count to them." That about sums it up. Advisers typically receive common stock without precise correlation to the hours they'll give your company or exactly what they'll do to help. The stock typically vests over time, in monthly increments, so it's easily adjusted based on the adviser's value to the company.

**The best advisors of all *pay you* to become advisors.
They often make a modest cash investment.**

The best advisors of all *pay you* to become advisors. They often make a modest cash investment of, say, $20,000 or $100,000 for some of the company's preferred stock, and their investment is "boosted" with a generous allocation of common shares that pay for the advisory services. Sophisticated investors recognize the importance of advisors' willingness to not only lend their names but also invest some personal cash in what they clearly believe is a significant opportunity.

Find Earlyvangelists	Get Out of Building! Test Sell	Refine Sales Roadmap	Test Sell Channel Partners	Physical Channel
Prepare Optimization Plans and Tools	Optimize Getting More Customers	Optimize "Keep" and "Grow"	Test Sell Traffic Partners	Web/Mobile Channel

CHAPTER 10

Customer Validation, Phase Two: Get Out of the Building and Sell!

IN THIS PHASE OF CUSTOMER VALIDATION, it's time to try to sell. Customer discovery had you get out of the building twice, first to understand customers' problems and how they work and second to determine how well the new product solves that problem. And while you've no doubt conducted hundreds of tests to iterate and pivot your business model, there is no better "pass/fail" test than asking a customer to give you an order or spend time with your app or website.

In a physical channel, nothing validates a hypothesis better than a signed order, especially when it's signed before the product is either complete or actually shipping. In the web/mobile channel, the equivalent validation is attracting users or payers at the rate your hypotheses said you would. (In a multi-sided market, even if you're getting great traffic and growth, be sure the "other" side, usually the advertisers or payers, are eager to spend to reach your traffic.)

Your job in this phase is not to scale a revenue plan but to validate your business model hypotheses with pass/fail tests that feel an awful lot like selling or building web traffic. But revenue or traffic at full scale doesn't happen until the next step, customer creation. Customer validation is the *test* sales process that—while it makes real sales—is principally aimed at answering a long list of questions, including:

- Are customers enthusiastic about the product's value proposition?
- Does the company understand its customer segments and their needs?
- Do customers truly value the product features? Are any key features missing?
- Is the product pricing right, and can the product be sold at a reasonable cost?
- What's the purchasing and approval process inside a customer's company?
- Are the sales roadmap and channel strategy valid for scaling the sales team?
- Are there enough customers to make this a real business?

"Get out of the building" means one thing for companies with physical goods or those primarily using the physical channel, and it means something radically different for companies in the web/mobile channels. Since the activities and their relative speed of iteration can vary so widely, this chapter addresses each channel separately, as outlined in Figure 10.1.

In customer validation, the testing process is a series of elegantly simple pass/fail tests where the answer is binary, and never "it feels good" or "they like it." Some examples:

If your physical channel business model says...
- you will close two sales for every 10 sales calls, do you?
- an average customer will buy six widgets in three months, do they?
- $5,000 at spent at a tradeshow (or in direct mail) will generate 25 leads, does it?
- 2/3 of the prospects you pitch will refer you to three friends each, do they?

⇨ *If your web/mobile channel business model says…*

- two of five acquired users will activate, do they?
- four in 10 activators will pass your free trial offer to five friends, do they?
- $100 spent on AdWords will generate 50 clicks to your site, does it happen?
- one in four advertisers in your multi-sided market will sit still for your advertising sales pitch (even though they probably won't buy till you have lots more traffic), do they?

Here are the next steps you'll undertake, by channel:

Physical Channel Startups	Web and Mobile Channel Startups
Find Earlyvangelists, Get Appointments	Prepare Optimization Plans and tools
Get out of the Building to "Test Sell"	"Get Out of the Building" Activation Tests
Refine Sales Road Map	Measure and Optimize the Results
Test Sell Channel Partners	Test Sell Traffic Partners

Steps for "Get Out of the Building and Sell" by Channel *(Figure 10.1)*

Get Out of the Building: Find Earlyvangelists (Physical)

The biggest sales challenge in customer validation is finding the right people to call on. This involves first identifying and then spending time with true visionary customers, not mainstream customers. The biggest danger is that not all visionary customers are alike. As a rule, there are visionaries with budgets (we like these) and "strategy," "long-term planning" or "technical visionary" people without the power to write checks. Table 10.1 describes the differences. We shouldn't need to tell entrepreneurs this, but just in case: focus on buyers with checkbooks. They're called earlyvangelists, as you should know by now.

Earlyvangelists have budgets, period. And while all visionary customers may recognize they have a problem, only the earlyvangelist candidate is (a) motivated enough to do something about it, (b) perhaps already trying a home-grown solution and, most important, (c) has the clout and the budget to solve the problem. Often, earlyvangelists have already visualized a solution something like the one being presented. They're partners in this sales process and will often rationalize or explain any missing features to their own management. Never ever embarrass or abandon them.

Review the key earlyvangelist characteristics identified in customer discovery. Do they point to other, additional prospects? Create a target earlyvangelist list and repeat the appointment-generation techniques used in customer discovery: generate a customer list, an introductory e-mail, and a reference story/script. (For a refresher, return to customer discovery Phase 2.) Even with thorough preparation, assume one of 20 prospects will engage in the sales process. In other words, be prepared for 95 percent rejection! That's OK; it's early in the process and 5 percent will do just fine. Of those few, depending on the economic climate, one of three or fewer will actually sign a purchase order. That's a lot of sales calls (which defines a startup). Good news: A sales closer is aboard to handle all the tedium of making contact and arranging meetings, which founders should always strive to attend.

Distinguish your earlyvangelist targets from other major customer types, including early evaluators, scalable customers, and mainstream customers. Scalable customers may be earlyvangelists as well, but they tend to buy later. Instead of buying on a vision, they buy for practical reasons. These will become target customers in six months but are still more aggressive buyers of new products than mainstream customers.

Finally, mainstream customers are waiting for the finished product and generally need an off-the-shelf, no-risk solution. They might say, "We look forward to testing your product when it rolls off your production line. We don't test proto-types." Remember their names, since they'll become customers in one to two years.

	Early Evaluators	Earlyvangelists	Scalable Customers	Mainstream Customers
Motivation	Technology evaluation	Vision-match. Understand they have a problem and have visualized a solution you have matched.	Practicality. Interested in a product that can solve an understood problem now.	Want to buy the standard, need the "whole product" delivered.
Pricing	Free	Using their pain threshold, you get to make up the list price and then give them a hefty discount.	Published list price and hard negotiating.	Published list price and harder negotiating.
Decision Power	Can OK a free purchase	May be able to OK a unilateral purchase. Usually can expedite a purchase. Internal cheerleader for a sale.	Buy-in needed from all levels. Standard sales process. May be able to avoid competitive bake-off.	Buy-in needed from all levels. Standard sales process. Competitive bake-off and/or RFP.

Four Types of Customers (Table 10.1)

Get Out of the Building: Prepare Optimization Plans/Tools (Web/Mobile)

⇨ The job of optimization is to squeeze more out of each of the "get, keep and grow" steps. Squeeze more of what, you ask? More of everything. For example:

- If 6 percent of visitors activate at launch, try to increase it to 10 percent or more
- When visitors abandon after two page views, can navigation increase it to three?
- If 5 percent of visitors post a comment, how can you encourage more to do so?
- If the average cost per activated user is $1, how can you lower it to $0.75 or $0.80?
- Can you improve e-mail open rates from 22 percent to 30 percent?

Getting more is what optimization is all about, and you'll do it from this moment until the moment you're selling off your furniture or ringing the bell at NASDAQ. This and the next two web/mobile sections provide a primer on optimization, the subject of many full-length texts. In this section, you will:

- Get a basic primer on optimization strategy
- Take a look at how optimization goes to work at a hypothetical web startup
- and learn about the key optimization tools and how they work

The next optimize "Get" web/mobile section will take what you learn from this section and show you how to put your "new" tools to work. And the third section will do the same for "keep" and "grow" customers activities.

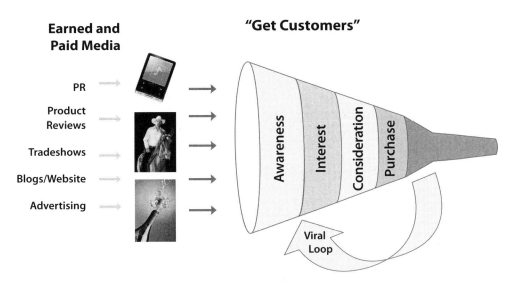

Earned and Paid Media

PR

Product Reviews

Tradeshows

Blogs/Website

Advertising

"Get Customers"

Awareness

Interest

Consideration

Purchase

Viral Loop

The "Get Customers" Funnel in Physical Channels (Figure 10.2)

Before you start

Before you start optimizing your site/app, just as a reminder that the following building blocks must be in place:

1. *A hi-fidelity MVP.* It must be live and the product should look "finished" (even if the MVP isn't fully featured). This ensures clear product feedback and the most accurate measurement of "get customers" program results.

2. *The Acquire plan and tools.* E-mails, AdWords, banners, pr efforts, viral programs and other tools that will drive consumers to engage with the product.

3. *The Activate plan and tools*. Home and landing pages encourage people to buy, engage, or activate, supported with activation tools such as follow-up e-mails, calls, or viral and promotion programs for those who don't buy or engage at once.

4. *A dashboard* to monitor customers' behavior. It should be working and the product should be instrumented to deliver real-time data on results of acquisition and activation programs.

Customer Optimization Strategy

Optimization efforts should focus on:

- *Volume*: Acquire as many visitors as possible and drive to them to the product
- *Cost*: Steadily improve the cost per activated customer
- *Conversion*: Increase the number of visitors who activate and become customers or users

The first question to address is "What do I optimize?" Different types of web business optimize for entirely different things.

The first question to address is, "What do I optimize?"

Here's how three types of web/mobile business should be thinking about their "Get" customers optimization:

- *E-commerce sites* should start by optimizing traffic and initial orders, of course, and then move on to focus on average order size, repeat orders, and customer referrals
- *Multi-sided markets* (usually ad-supported) should focus first on total traffic, then on members or subscribers, DAU (daily active users), minutes of engagement, repeat visits, and referrals. They should then move to the "other side" to maximize ad revenue, CPM, and sales pipeline
- *Marketplaces* should focus on everything an e-commerce site would optimize as well as the number of vendors, seller acquisition and retention and liquidity (how many of the items for sale actually get sold). Then they should try to optimize daily transactions and average transaction size

More Keys to Successful Optimization Strategy:

- *Know exactly why you're testing,* as in "to see if we can improve registrations" or "to see if free shipping materially increases orders."

Don't test everything, test the important things.

- *Don't overtest.* This is a major mistake made by many web startups because testing is just so easy online. Don't test everything, test the important things. Don't test more than two changes to a page at a time, to avoid confusing your visitors so you can tell which change drove which improvement. When a test "succeeds," be sure you know what made the difference

- *Run controlled tests* to guarantee randomness and validity. A strict A/B test, the most common controlled test, shows every other visitor version "A" or version "B" of a page or an offer. It rigorously controls the variables. It doesn't show "A" on Monday and "B" on Tuesday, since there's no way to determine what else might have influenced customer behavior in the test, which could be almost anything: a sale at a competitive site, a change in the weather, or even the time of day (people mostly surf at work during lunchtime)

- *Always keep lifetime value in mind.* The cost of getting a customer is nowhere near as important as the revenue that customer brings you over time, and the lifetime value math for "get customers" is pretty simple:

$$LTV => CAQ$$

LTV or *Lifetime value* (the total amount of money you'll make from this customer) must be more than the *CAQ* or *customer acquisition cost* (costs to acquire and activate the customer).

Too many companies go out of business telling themselves, "This customer will be worth 'X' over five years," forgetting the second part: "only if we're still here and they're still with us." Use a reasonable, not-too-long lifetime value. For example, how many months of subscription revenue will it take to repay my "get customers" cost?

In summary: The optimization plan will change often, perhaps as often as every day. Start by defining the specific acquisition metrics to optimize. Don't tackle too many at once, and always know what your goal is when you begin the experiment. As you're running your tests, create alternatives for the tactics that don't perform well after optimization.

Optimization is a never-ending data-driven process of "test, measure, tweak."

Optimization is a never-ending data-driven process of "test, measure, tweak" that stops only when the company closes its doors. Founders should be intimately involved with, if not leading, the process, since it's vital to your company's efficiency, scalability, and future.

A Lesson in Optimization Tactics

Let's look at how optimization works in real time in a hypothetical company selling the first in a series of downloadable $39.95 software apps for home-based businesspeople. The CEO has focused her team on two key metrics at the widest part of the funnel: the total cost of activating a customer (including the cost of acquiring him or her), and the ultimate value of each activated customer individually. Let's follow along, starting with a look at the data chief's first analysis of acquisition and activation programs. Here's how it looks in chart form:

Funnel Step	Clicks	Cost Per	Spend Total	Revenue
Acquisitions	200	$ 5.00	$1,000.00	
Activations	40	$25.00		(none yet)
Buy once	20	$25.00		$ 800.00
Valued Customers	10	$50.00		$1,000.00
TOTAL			$1,000.00	$1,800.00

Example of Optimization Tactics Chart (Table 10.2)

Walking through the example one line at a time provides a wealth of insights into the optimization process itself.

- *Acquisition* delivered 200 "lookers" at an average cost of $5 per customer click, or $1,000 (clicks can cost as little as pennies or as much as $50 or more, depending on demand for the AdWords). If we could reduce the cost per looker by 20 percent we would deliver 25 percent more prospects to the company without increasing the budget
  - *Acquisition Improvements to test*: Stop using the most expensive AdWords. Try alternative sources of traffic beyond Google. Explore alternative programs like banners and textlinks. Reduce daily AdWords budgets or hours or geography (eliminate overnight hours, Europe, or weekends for example). Increase viral marketing at low cost
- *Activation* 40 people (20 percent of the 200 who clicked to the site) activated – meaning they took a demo or provided their contact information. Therefore the cost of each activation was $25 (or $1,000 spent divided by 40 people). Yet at this point no one has bought anything
  - *Activation Improvements to test*: Intensify or enlarge calls to action or graphics. Improve or increase activation incentives. Change price or introductory offer. Reorganize the way features/benefits are prioritized and explained. Consider a free trial

- *Purchase* – half the activated customers buy an application for $39.95. In this example that's 20 people, each spending $40, for a total of $800 in sales. These customers, while apparently profitable (on a gross profit basis), are "losers" because it cost $25 to get someone to spend $40—63 percent of the sale—which can't be viable for most businesses, as it leaves very little to cover product, staff, overhead and, profit. But, if the funnel delivered just five more customers, the same $1,000 investment would deliver $200 more in sales.

- *Purchase Improvements to test*:
  - Deploy activation improvements, but also research non-buyers to understand why they're non-buyers
  - Add a demo
  - Add "click to call" contact option
  - Conduct A/B tests of price and offer
  - Consider follow-up e-mail or phone calls to close

Now take a last look at Table 10.2. Imagine that in addition to the 20 buyers of our $39.95 software package, the company acquires 10 additional Valued Customers. Instead of just buying one software product, these customers buy on average 2.5 software packages, spending $100 each to do so. That generates $1,000 in revenue from valued customers. Over time, these Valued Customers are probably worth even more, since they may also generate referrals to others and buy more packages themselves later.

In all, this test would be labeled at best a modest victory for some (where the cost of goods is very low, as it is for software downloads). Generating $1,800 in revenue as well as future prospects—activators who never bought—with $1,000 on marketing spending reflects a software company with a promising future, assuming it can further optimize its funnel for the long term.) Clearly, improvements at every step of the funnel process can deliver big incremental revenue and profit improvements.

Apply this kind of thinking and detailed analysis to every key program outlined in your "get" plan. Test a program, measure the results, and brainstorm ways to improve the results. Change some aspect of the program (the offer, the graphics, the messaging, as outlined in your plan) and test it and measure it again. Once it's measured, assess the results, develop the next improvement idea, and test it again…and again…and again. As we said at the outset, this is the lifeblood of web/mobile startups, and the process truly never ends.

Optimization Tools:

Like any good craftsperson, good tools are essential to doing a good job. Here is an overview of the key tools used most often by web and mobile marketers. In the next two web/mobile sections, we'll talk to you about where and how to use each one. In most cases, they're used in each of the three get, keep and grow optimizations, since most (but not all) customer interaction happens online.

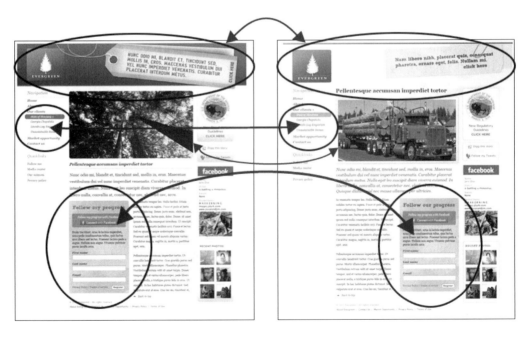

Sample A/B Tests Compare Changing Home Page Results (Figure 10.3)

A/B Testing

A/B testing is the most widely used way to optimize web and mobile "get, keep and grow" activities. It can also be used to optimize web/mobile product performance (the subject of a different book). A/B testing compares one web page version with another to see which produces the best results. It's the most used method for testing key landing-page elements. Did a big blue button get more activations than a small line of text? Which headline, picture, or product offer generated more sign-ups, sales or abandons?

Activation mantra: The more we test, the better we do.

Identify the key elements of your landing page that drive activation, and test them carefully, fairly, and sequentially. Think of the process as "try it, measure it, tweak it." The activation mantra: The more we test, the better we do. Remember to maintain a clear control group: change the presentation to half the audience, ideally alternating from one visitor to the next (in A/B, every second visitor sees "b"). Many testers drive 80% of the traffic to one alternative, and 20% to the other, which can test on high-traffic pages well.

Usability Tests

Usability testing checks whether the users of the site/app/product use it the way you intended them to. It can be as informal as inviting consumers into the conference room and watching them spend time on the website or as comprehensive as a formal focus-group testing. It can identify weaknesses in the site's explanation of the product, its benefits, and the reasons to buy. It can trace users' behavior on the site to determine ways to optimize the conversion rates, enhance online product demonstrations, or find confusing copy, diagrams, or navigation. Inexpensive tools and expensive services can both help with the testing.

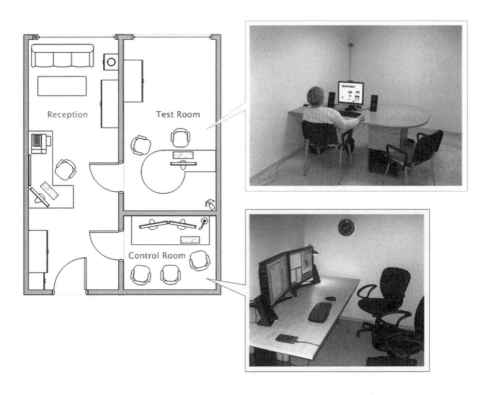

Usability Tests happen in Starbucks or test facilities *(Figure 10.4)*

Invite your target customers to the office and watch as they engage with the site or app (and use any of the online services like Userfy or Usertesting that do low-cost user testing). Watch these customers explore uninterrupted while watching over their shoulder. Make notes about where they went and where they didn't, and follow up to learn why they did what they did. Obviously, as you learn about confusing or suboptimal locations or navigation on the site, test and measure alternatives until the problem goes away. Consider conducting user testing with a laptop at Starbucks, where random customers get coffee or a gift card for spending 10 minutes with you, exploring and discussing the new product, app or site.

Heat Maps

Heat maps use eye tracking to show where most people look or click on a website or page. Software tracks a user's gaze and translates them into regions colored yellow, orange and red. The richer the color, the more eyeballs are focused on the button, headline or graphic.

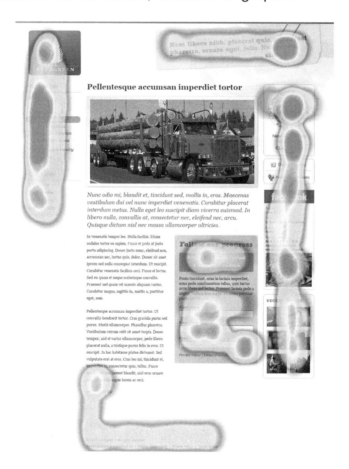

Example of Heat Mapping *(Figure 10.5)*

If too many customers are drawn to the "demo" button instead of the "try now" button, perhaps the sizes or locations or both should be changed. The heat map indicates high-traffic spots on a page, where the most important product features or offers should be located. Heat maps may even show that visitors are clicking on graphics or copy that aren't linked to anything.

Eye Tracking

Eye tracking uses heat-map technology in a different way. When people visit a website, what do they look at first, second, or third?

Example of Eye Tracking (Figure 10.6)

The "Z" pattern is considered the most common way Americans read a web page, starting across the top, from left to right, and then skimming diagonally downward across the page. Eyes move at astounding speeds, and users are known to spend as little as a few seconds scanning a page to find something of interest. It pays to put key content and invitations for user interaction in the places where the users tend to go. (Keep in mind that web pages in other languages may scan differently.)

Copy Testing

While copy isn't a tool the way a heat map or an A/B test might be, using those and other tools to test copy makes the "copy buffer" a very important tool. It's almost axiomatic that no headline is ever the best possible headline, and there's always a way to improve "sell" copy, offer copy, and the way you get people excited about your product, its features, and the reasons they should buy. Copy testing can happen on the site, in focus groups, or through web surveys. Bigger sites create alternate mirror sites to A/B-test different copy versions. This is a powerful optimization tool.

Visitors focus on headlines, highlighted words and bulleted lists but scan the text.

No matter how polished the prose or how many people edit the copy, few visitors read all or even many of the words. Tests by industry expert Jakob Nielsen suggest that most visitors focus on headlines, highlighted words and bulleted lists but scan the text. He notes that the three most effective design elements are plain text, faces, and cleavage and other body parts.

In the next web/mobile section, you'll strap on your e-toolbelt and go to work, optimizing your "get" customers activities.

Get Out of the Building and Test Sell   (Physical)

Buy a big briefcase and a pile of airplane tickets and kiss the family goodbye, since this validation phase keeps founders on the road, "test-selling" until the hypotheses are proved with real orders at or near full price. It's time to get face-to-face with more than a handful of earlyvangelists and try to get some early orders.

Test Selling

Anyone can give away or deeply discount a product to get an order, but that doesn't test true buying intentions. Earlyvangelists see the advantage of getting the new product early, ahead of competitors or envious neighbors. The earlyvangelist by definition should almost leap across the table and grab someone by the collar to get early access to the product. They *need* the product to cure a severe pain or secure a competitive advantage (and over time, they'll help make the product better). Customer enthusiasm is best-tested when the product is sold for as close to full price as you can get. In fact, you want to label access to the product as the "early access program" and have customers fight to be a part of it. No interest? Then you've gotten valuable feedback on how important the product is to people you've labeled your most valuable customers.

Anyone can give away or deeply discount a product to get an order.

There are two risks in calling on earlyvangelists. One is the request for customization. Visionary customers might ask for unique extensions or modifications to your standard product. Sometimes these requests are good news. If enough customers ask for the same set of "custom" features, they're not custom at all, since customers are suggesting the "real" product requirements. The art of being a founder lies in knowing when to incorporate those requests into the spec and declare them features. The danger and challenge is to avoid an inadvertent migration to a custom products business where all the economics change at a disadvantage to the company.

The other earlyvangelist risk is the request for an "exclusive" or a "most favored nations" clause. From the customer point of view, this is a reasonable and rational request. "I'm going to take a risk on you, so I want a competitive advantage by being the only one with your product"—an exclusive. Or, "I want the best pricing forever" for being first. Tread very carefully here. Often these are requests from big-company execs with little real-world understanding of how a startup works. Don't give up your rights to sell to other customers or you'll end as a development arm of the first company that asks you for an exclusive.

The Sales Process

Entrepreneurs, hate "process," but some basic steps are critical in any business-to-business sale. Here's a primer using enterprise software as the model:

1. *Start with research:* Know the companies and the individuals you're calling on. Use market and web research to gather data. At a minimum, you should be able to draw their org charts and understand their financial situations and latest information before making your first sales presentation.

2. *First meeting:* Use the first meeting to understand the company's problems, needs, business goals, and the potential "fit" between your solution and their problem. Try to gain a sense of how important your product might be to the company and how it would go about deploying the product.

3. *Know where to "enter":* Get "to the top" as quickly as you can but not too quickly. Meet one-on-one first with one or several midlevel people, and then get in at a high level.

4. *Visualize the "before and after:"* Understand how the company solves the problem today and how your product would better solve it. Try to deter

mine the return on investment, the ease of adoption and use, and how it will save the company time and money.

5. *Customize your presentations:* Do this as early as possible to reflect all the learning above.

6. *Create a purchase action plan:* Get the buyer visualizing his purchase and use of the product by discussing the sequence of steps, putting dates next to each, and talking about things like the launch date to help make the purchase feel inevitable.

7. *Engage senior management at every opportunity:* Introduce your senior team to theirs; wine and dine; build bonds with higher-ups who can either approve or kill the deal.

8. *Present a custom proposal and get it signed:* Need we say more (other than "celebrate," of course)? Provide attention and follow-through long after the check clears.

Collect and Record Sales Findings

As you're out test-selling, collect and collate the findings consistently, regardless of who conducts the sales call and whether it happens in a Starbucks, an office, or a conference room. If more than one of you is out trying to sell, agree on the key set of facts and feedback to gather on each call. Include objective metrics like "How many will you use?" or "How many people will use it?" as well as subjective comments like "If it works, I'll recommend it" or "I really like this product better than product X." Develop a consistent sales-call report card, similar to the one developed in customer discovery, to record responses consistently. End every report card by answering four identical "buy" questions:

- Is a purchase order in hand or on the way?
- How many units (or dollars' worth) will the customer purchase?
- What's needed to get a deal signed?
- When might the deal be signed?

For best results, record detailed notes in the parking lot, after the meeting, when details are freshest. Identify follow-up opportunities, action items, and other people to see either at the company or at others the prospect may have mentioned. Note any competitive products discussed. Then drive on to the next test-sales session. Remember to send a thank-you note confirming details and next steps.

While answers other than a purchase order are rarely binding on the buyer, you should get a good sense of the product's sales potential. Aggregate the numbers to create a "probability-adjusted sales forecast," a "best guess" of how many dollars will come in and when. In the customer validation step, many of your initial visits won't deliver short-term orders. That doesn't make the meetings unimportant. Remember, the primary goal is customer feedback, not sales.

Without a doubt, everyone (including your board!) will focus on the sales forecast. Try to uncover more about the value proposition, competitive situation, pricing and, most important, whom to call on and in what order to make a sale.

Understanding why customers said no is more important than understanding why they said yes. Understand where in the process turndowns happen…

Create a spreadsheet summary for the data, making sure to allow plenty of room for the comments, which are often most valuable of all. Weight the comments and ratings based on the customer's size or potential volume. Keep very close tabs on win/loss statistics on sales calls. Understanding why customers said no is more important in this step than understanding why they said yes. Understand where in the process turndowns happen (introduction, product presentation, organizational issues, not-invented-here issues, technical issues, pricing) to help refine the sales roadmap.

The Pivot

As optimistic as a startup may be, the most likely outcome of the first sales push is either no orders at all, or far fewer than you expected. Typically there are two root causes:

- The company hasn't found earlyvangelists and needs to keep searching in the current customer segment or abandon it and explore others
- Other parts of the business model just aren't compelling, whether it's product, features, benefits, price, issues, partners or several

Either way, you need to stop and think about why what you thought would happen *didn't* happen. This test-selling effort is still a learning exercise. This is when you go back to your business model canvas and review the hypotheses you assembled in discovery. If you can't get early orders now, clearly some were wrong. Did you pick the wrong customer segment? Did the value proposition not match this segment? Did the revenue model not fit their budget? The business model canvas provides a visual way to diagnose what went wrong and what you can change and test.

How Many Orders Do I Need to Prove Validation?

One of the first questions founders ask is, "So how many orders do I need to validate my business model?" While we'd like to tell you the number is 7, it's more complicated than that.

You and your board of directors do need to agree on a number.

If you're selling million-dollar enterprise software packages, three to five repeatable sales from the same customer segment may give you a good indication that it's time to scale a professional sales organization.

However, if you're selling new kitchenware or appliances through a consumer retail channel, you won't know if you have it right until the channel puts in a reorder.

There's no one magic number. But you and your board of directors do need to agree on a number. You and your investors always need to be in sync about what the criteria are for scaling and the cash burn rate resulting from that decision.

Get Out of the Building: Optimize Getting More Customers (Web/Mobile)

⇨ In the prior phase, you got basic lessons in web and mobile performance optimization, had some basic training in how optimization works, and reviewed the tools and techniques you'll use to create your optimization strategy. This phase takes that learning and puts it to work at the widest part of the "get customers" funnel—where customers come from—the acquire and activate steps of "get, keep and grow."

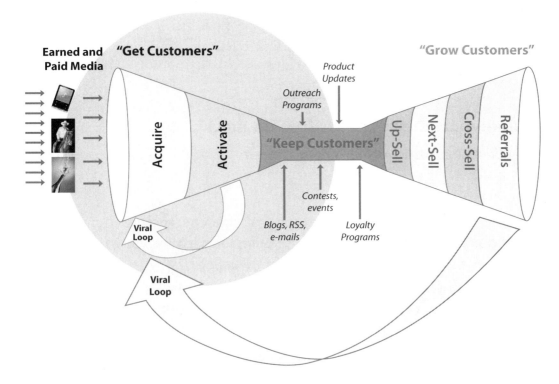

The "Get Customers" Funnel in Web/Mobile Channels *(Figure 10.7)*

For some websites 98 percent of people who visit ("acquired") never ever return. That means only two percent of acquired prospects have a chance of becoming a customer or user, even after you've spent many millions acquiring them. If that statistic doesn't call attention to the need for optimizing activation efforts, nothing will!

---

98 percent of people who visit never ever return...

How will Your Startup Optimize its "Get Customers" Efforts?

Optimization objectives vary by your business model. For example:

- *Subscription products* (e.g., software as a service) try to get customers to explore, try, or use the product any way they'll agree to do so, often with freemium or low-cost trials
- *Expensive products and services* strive to ensure that customers will be driven to, and continue to engage with, the appropriate sales channel
- *Inexpensive apps and games* often try to sell as soon as they engage customers
- *Social networks* will encourage first-timers to engage with the network, participating at least a few times to get "hooked," and then to invite friends
- *Multi-sided market* businesses try to attract users who will use the site frequently, stay a long time, and bring their friends
- *Marketplaces* (think Etsy or eBay) encourage sellers to join, list multiple items, and enjoy early success on the site

> **PROCEED WITH CAUTION:** Remember, this is an overview and a tutorial. There's no way to implement or even process this in one sitting.

How to Run the "Get" Optimization Process

Review the results of the "get" programs you've done to date, always asking your data and team, *which program*:

1. *is most important to us?* Start with the free "get" programs for because if they're working they are the easiest to scale up. Accelerate the most productive program. If you're getting tons of customers from SEO or bloggers, for example, start here to optimize that effort.

2. *is the most disappointing?* When you launched your "get" programs, you had great expectations for certain programs, whether it was an AdWords campaign, referrals to friends, natural search or a blimp flying over your city. Design pass/fail tests to improve the results.

3. *gives you the best customers?* If, for example, an e-mail campaign gets you customers who buy faster, spend more, or visit more often and stay longer, you obviously want more of those folks. So prioritize the plan to optimize that program.

4. *gives you early customers with high lifetime value* (LTV)? Get and seek more that look like them. Identify high-LTV behavior (frequent visits, purchasing, posting or referrals, for example) in specific customers and track back to their source, demography, or other common traits. Then go find more customers like them. This is hardest in the company's early days, when few customers exist and there's less time to observe them.

Test a wide range of offers, incentives, deals and discounts.

Finally, test a wide range of offers, incentives, deals and discounts. While alternatives are almost as obvious as they are endless, here are a few to try: Offer a gift with purchase instead of a discount. Consider a time limit on the offer, as in "until midnight only" or "this week's special." Create limited offers, as in "for the first 500 to sign up."

Always review the top 10 or 12 performance metrics daily, led by the data chief recruited earlier. That's a dozen metrics, not dozens—on the "get customers" program results. Prepare to be disappointed often, but the review—good or bad—always ends with the same question: "how do we improve it?"

For less experienced web marketers

If you're not an experienced web/mobile marketer, and don't know an important program from a disappointing one, try this approach instead. First, focus on increasing the number of activations, since activations matter most. (If you've acquired only a handful or a few dozen visitors, start talking about possible pivots instead.)

Find the largest single source of customers and figure out how to increase the volume. How does more spending, improved creative, different offers or greater frequency improve the result? Test each one, one at a time, and often more than once per test.

Remember, don't optimize too many programs at once, or the results will be confusing—you won't be able to tell what worked and what didn't. Recognize "getting customers" means that the acquire and activate programs work hand in hand. You need both parts to work to truly "get" a customer…not just someone who comes to your site or app, but who buys and engages.

Common Optimization Opportunities and Problems

If this book were to list every possible way to optimize getting customers, it would be impossible to carry. The balance of this section addresses the most common problems where optimization can help—getting more clicks to your site and more out of every click. Since we hear these questions from entrepreneurs so often, we've organized the approaches to optimization based on the questions we hear most.

Problem: I have a website but nobody visits...

Other than perhaps CIA.gov, we don't think there's been a web business yet that didn't want more people exposed to its product or service, or more visitors to its home page. Visitors are clearly the lifeblood of every web/mobile business.

Diagnosis: You are perilously close to extinction. There are tens of millions of websites, and just "being there" doesn't drive traffic as a rule.

You are perilously close to extinction. Use every tool we have described in the prior 383 pages.

Solution:

1. Return to the start of "Get Customers" web/mobile (page 147). Read it again and get to work.
2. Find more e-mails, Tweet more people, beg friends to invite their friends, create a funny YouTube and try to viralize it.
3. Consider changing the URL to something people will find more naturally (your site's promise, like "instantlove.com" rather than "socialdatinginc.com, for example).
4. Pay the smartest people you can find to optimize your site for natural search in a hurry.
5. Do something crazy....big events, promotions, hand out flyers on street corners, scream, set your hair on fire, but do it fast!

Tools to use: Use every tool we have described in the prior 383 pages, then go online and find dozens more. Start at www.steveblank.com for a thorough updated list.

Problem: Visitors come to my site or app, but don't stay...

This common problem presents many optimization opportunities.

Diagnosis: The most likely problem: something isn't "clicking" with your value proposition and product positioning, so start testing alternate versions. Then look at the acquisition tactics you're using and rank them based on productivity (the most acquisitions with the least money or effort). Start with the worst performing tactics and test alternatives.

Solution:

1. Start by changing your messaging, whether you're using e-mail, banner ads, or banners pulled by WWII biplanes.

2. If it's AdWords, for example, pause all programs and start over. Spend more per click, change the geography or hours your keywords are active and for sure experiment by buying different AdWords and testing alternate ad copy.

3. Test alternative calls to action. Offer something for free, whether it's a trial or a prize for visiting the site. And keep running this optimization process *forever.*

4. Change the offer. If you're offering annual signups, test monthly or "first 30 days free." Develop other reasons why people should come visit your site.

5. Interview lots of customers face-to-face. Find out what they like and, more important, what they don't.

6. Be sure you have multiple calls to action on the home page (like "take a tour," "try now for free," "learn more" *and* "get more info").

Tools to Use: Copy testing, A/B testing, and another look at your value proposition messaging (unique selling proposition, features you're promoting, introductory offer, to name a few).

Problem: People Visit the Site, but don't Click (no Activation)...

Diagnosis: This deadly problem is often masked by "vanity metrics," where the team high-fives and celebrates because unique visitors and page views are increasing every day. So what!! If people come to the site or app and don't engage, try it, do something, sign up or pay up, your business is simply dead. Period.

If we just described your site, ring the alarm bell and if your "data chief" and marketing person aren't sure what to do or test, it may be time to call in (preferably smart freelance) consultants, buy the tons of other books on optimization, and call home and tell'em you won't be home for a while...your business is at serious risk of implosion.

Solution: Pull out all the stops, remembering not to test too many things all at once. Start by talking to customers who've been acquired but not activated (hopefully you have some of their e-mails, but *call* or ask them to call you— don't just e-mail) and find out what was uninteresting or unappealing to them (that's why it's called Customer Development).

Then start to implement some optimization tactics.

1. Find the page where most users abandon ship. Start testing stronger calls to action and improved navigation on this page *fast*

2. Test a variety of calls to action...click here to do this, sign up and get a free...

3. Do some heat mapping studies to see what people are looking at on the page, and move calls to action closer to where their eyeballs go

4. Test bigger, smaller, or different calls to action: louder copy, bigger buttons, maybe a blinking or brightly-colored "try now," for example

5. Be sure your "no spam" guarantee/promise is visible in every communication

6. Conduct usability testing where you watch actual customers as they review your home page. What questions do they ask, what do

they click on, do they get confused? Then ask them flat-out: "what don't you like about my site, product, or offer?"

7. Buttons: Do more people click on a big ugly button or a small pink one? Do they like round or square, a midpage location or lower left?

8. "Sell" and body copy: constantly test new copy versions to see which gets more response

9. Graphics: Test alternative product pictures, illustrations, how-to graphics and other elements to see better activations

Tools to Use: Every tool in the toolbox works overtime on this crisis. A/B test everything. Spend money on usability testing and one-on-one customer interviews. Use heat maps, magic tricks, anything you can find, as your business is clearly threatened with extinction *right now.*

Problem: We're Getting Some Customers, but they don't refer others...

Diagnosis: While this is certainly a "get" customers problem, we consider it a "grow" problem and address it in the next section. After all, to be technical, first you have to acquire and activate a customer to "grow" him or her. There are two ways to "grow" a customer: get them to spend more, or to refer others. Both are addressed in the next web/mobile section.

Problem: People are engaging, but not doing what you want …

Diagnosis: You're getting good traffic, and people are clicking or at least viewing multiple pages. But nobody's signing up, posting comments, playing the game, adding pictures, spending money, or doing whatever you want them to do.

Solution: Once again, you need to put almost the entire optimization toolbox to work.

1. Start with heat maps and eye tracking to see what people are actually doing when they're on the site
2. Start A/B testing by first testing your calls to action. Make the graphics different or bigger; consider adding demos or animation; Simplify the messaging to make it clearer, and A/B test it both onsite and in person
3. Develop more "pathways" through the site—make the navigation bigger and test providing at least a few more options ("read more," "free trial," and so forth)
4. Can users easily sign up, post a comment, upload a picture, or buy something on the site? If not, fix it.
5. Do users make lots of errors downloading the app, a pdf or a picture? If so, improve the process by rewriting the copy, adding graphics, shortening the instructions or adding a video.
6. Does anybody remember your headline or "sell points" five minutes after visiting? If not, test alternatives
7. Be sure your company's positioning and promise, plus endorsements or happy user quotes are prominent on the site to give users comfort

Tools to use: Use the entire toolbox: heat maps, eye tracking, A/B testing, customer interviews, usability testing and a magic wand will all help.

Get Out of the Building: Refine the Sales Roadmap (Physical)

You developed your Sales Roadmap back on page 344. In this section you'll continue to refine it. Only when a team follows the same path through a company and it results in sales over and over again does the road-map hypothesis become fact.

Company and Consumer Organization

Startups making sales calls on corporations find that a pattern emerges. Companies don't have hundreds of types of org charts but tend to be organized in one of four ways: by product in operating divisions; functionally (engineering, marketing, sales, etc.); as a matrix organization by both function and product; or as a distributed franchise. This makes finding the repeatable path, and cracking the corporate sales roadmap much easier for an entrepreneur. So first figure out which of the four types you're calling on.

The approach is different for consumer products. Consumers may be organized by archetype, demographics, phychographics or "jobs they want done." When trying to reach twentysomethings with a new product, for example, questions might include:

- Is access to a specific demographic segment required? Should the focus be college students? Parents? Families? Athletes?
- How many people have to say yes to close a sale? Is this an individual or family decision?
- If this sale requires that multiple members of a family or group agree, is there a logical or helpful sequence to use? What's the script for each?
- What steps can derail the entire sale?

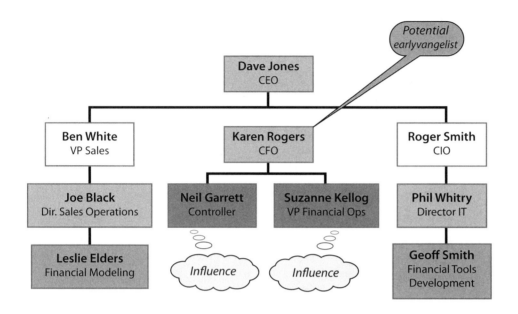

- Assume we are selling a new financial tool to finance
- We've found our visionary in the VP of Financial

[grey box] in house competition   [white box] issues to be addressed before a sale

Typical Influence Map in a Company Organized by Function *(Figure 10.8)*

Using the Organization Chart to Build an Influence Map

First, get a copy of the company's organization chart. If you can't get one, figure it out by talking to multiple low-level employees. Then map the org chart into an "influence map," a map that let you diagram and navigate friends and foes within a corporation. An influence map starts with the org chart. Next, locate your earlyvangelist on the chart—the person whose problem your product solves. Then use the information you've gathered in multiple sales calls to figure out who the influencers, recommenders, saboteurs and economic buyers are (see Chapter 3). In the example in Figure 10.8, the company is organized functionally. CFO Karen Rogers is the earlyvangelist. It's her decision to buy your early, buggy unfinished enterprise financial software. Her two direct reports, Neil and Suzanne, will influence her. But before Karen will buy, two in-house competitors must be at least neutralized if not won over: the financial-modeling and tools-development staffers in the sales and IT departments. In addition, their bosses—the CIO and the sales VP—will weigh in before Karen can get her CEO to sign off on the purchase.

Draw the influence map of each earlyvangelist you call on, looking for common patterns. As repeatable patterns emerge, sales will come quicker and easier.

Your customers will teach you how to sell to them.

Refine the Core Strategy

On page 347 you developed Figure 10.9, and learned that you needed to win the support of four groups to get a deal done. Winning a high-level executive sponsor and buy-in was the top priority (in this case it was the CFO as the earlyvangelist with a budget), followed by using that enthusiasm to generate support from the CIO. With those approvals in hand, next came support from end users (who work for the CFO) and finally support from the IT staff who work for the CIO.

	Operational	**Technical**
High	Executive	CIO or Division IT Executive
Low	End Users	Corp. IT Staff or Division IT Staff

Core Strategy (Figure 10.9)

Refine the Access Map

How do you get into a potential corporate account? Whom should you call on first? The most senior executive? While entrepreneurs' instinct is to get to the most important and highest-level executives they can find, keep in mind that you usually don't get multiple meetings with "C-level" executives. Practice by calling on lower-level employees until you're certain you understand you have a product/market fit.

After multiple sales calls on a variety of companies, your startup should have learned which department or departments it should call on first to gain interest and entry. Once inside the account, summarize the company's needs, assemble a sales strategy, present a solution, and work to sell the account. Figure 10.10 is an example of an Access Strategy Map.

Key patterns to watch for:

- Who should you call on first at a prospect to make a sale fastest?
- Who else at the prospect needs to be called on, and in what sequence?
- Who will need to approve the sale, and how long will the process take?
- Who influences the decision, positively or negatively, and how do you approach them?

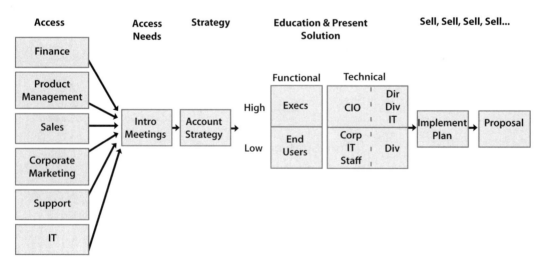

Example of an Access Strategy Map *(Figure 10.10)*

Use the selling-strategy map to answer a wide range of questions, including:

- At what level do we enter the account? High-level executives or operational staff?

- How many people on the organizational map need to say yes in order to make a sale?

- Does each department perceive and care about the customer problem the same way?

- Which executives can influence or sabotage the sale?

- In what order should people be called on? How do the scripts vary for each?

- How much purchasing authority does each level you're dealing with have? Are they authorized to sign for $1,000? For $100,000? Do they need anyone else's approval to deploy a product across their departments or divisions or to their customers?

Diagram the people involved in a business-to-business sale to identify the buyer, influencers, in-house competitors and issues that need to be addressed before a sale is made. See the example of an organizational map and a selling-strategy map below. Use the tools that make the most sense for the situation.

Keep refining the access strategy map by making sales calls until a predictable, repeatable pattern emerges that will work equally well when the company has 20 or 30 field salespeople instead of two or three. As the pattern emerges, the selling strategy will, too. You're not done until clear common threads have been found. If there aren't any common threads, get back out into the field and make even more test-sales calls until a series of purchase orders and patterns emerge. Keep a keen eye out for "danger" patterns that may include:

- testing or demo requirements before a sale is considered

- formal RFP, bidding processes or timetables affecting new-product consideration

- companies requiring that all initial presentations be made only to the purchasing department

- companies that refuse to buy from startups (sometimes the case in enterprise software)

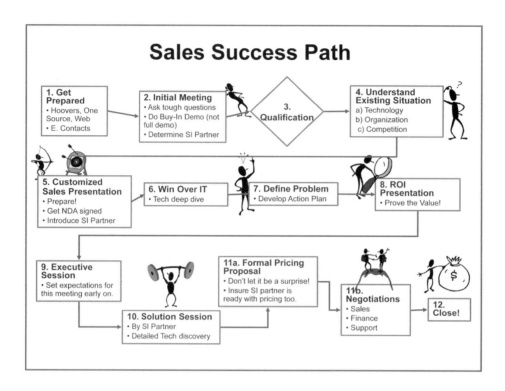

Example of a Sales Roadmap *(Figure 10.11)*

Develop a Sales Roadmap

The ultimate goal of this exercise is to develop a sales roadmap. This is a detailed diagram of how to get repeatable orders that you, the founder, hand to a professional sales VP. It's the playbook for the repeatable, scalable sales process. It details every step, every presentation, every e-mail and price, and every move you've learned for getting an order. You write it up as a flow chart and document each step. Your hiring test of the competence of prospective sales VPs will be whether they discard it and go back to their old rolodex or if they use it and refine it.

It's not sold until the check clears.

The selling process seldom ends when the visionary customer says, "Thumbs up, I'll buy." Particularly in business-to-business sales (as well as sales where husband and wife must agree), much can happen between the agreement to buy and the arrival of the check. Recognize and identify any steps required before the sale is completed and the product is delivered and paid for. Determine who follows up to manage the process.

For example:

- Do the CFO and/or CEO need to approve?
- Does the board or procurement group need to approve?
- Does Mom or Dad need to weigh in?
- Is there a budget cycle, lease or loan requirement in the cycle?
- Must the company be an approved vendor?
- Are there other systems/components from other vendors? Or other dependencies like rewiring, adequate power supply, or a renovation that have to happen first?

Get Out of the Building: Optimize "Keep" and "Grow" (Web/Mobile)

⇨ The common wisdom is that it cost 10 times more to get a new customer than to keep and grow an existing one. Now that your company has users or customers, this step optimizes how you "keep" and "grow" them. In the first "optimize" phase, you chose a set of optimization tools and a plan for deploying them to improve the results of your "keep" and "grow" efforts. Now it's time to put those plans into action. Believe us, this process is never-ending.

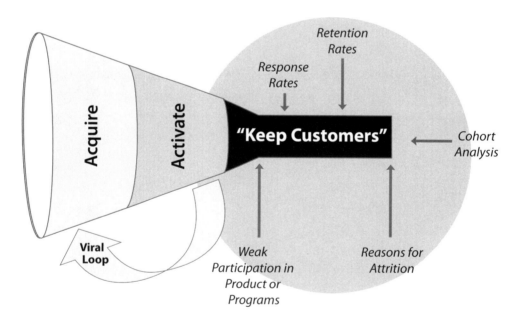

The "Keep Customers" Funnel in Web/Mobile Channels (Figure 10.12)

PROCEED WITH CAUTION: Remember, this is an overview and a tutorial. There's no way to implement or even process this in one sitting.

Optimizing "Keep" (or Customer Retention) Programs

Launch at least some basic customer retention and growth programs, you developed in the customer-relationship hypotheses: loyalty programs, customer check-in calls, customer-satisfaction surveys, product updates and upgrades, and close monitoring of customer complaints. Where possible (recognizing that it's early and there aren't many customers yet), monitor the costs and return on investment for the programs individually to be sure they're incrementally profitable. Do customers in the "points" program spend more and stay longer, for example?

Remember that customer retention, or "keep" customers, begins with great products and customer service. Your customer-relationships hypothesis should include a plan for testing at least a few of these programs now, during customer validation.

Here are some things to watch for in the most common customer retention programs, and ways to optimize the program results:

- *User outreach programs:* What do customers say when you e-mail, Tweet, or call them about their use of and satisfaction with the product? Do they even take your calls or answer your e-mails? If not, consider calling instead of e-mailing, or testing more urgent/ambitious subject lines on your e-mails

- *If customers are responding in small numbers,* add an incentive to stimulate response, such as "Tell us your opinion and get a free month's service just for speaking up." When you get negative feedback, first respond, and then tell all your customers, not just the complainers, that you've listened and made the improvements your customers suggested

- *Loyalty programs:* First, are customers participating in the loyalty program? If not, are you marketing it ambitiously enough? A/B-test some special sign-up offers, like "5,000 bonus points just for joining to get you started." If you're getting sign-ups, the next question is whether the program creates incentive for the behavior you want, whether it's more active site use or more frequent purchasing. A/B-test different messages, incentives, and promotions to get the most out of your loyalty-program participants

- *Contests and events:* These can only help retention if people partici-pate, so A/B-test, copy-test, and constantly refresh promotional campaigns both on the site and through e-mail to users. Do your changes get more people to participate? If not, keep testing. Over time (at least three weeks, maybe longer), monitor whether the use of these promotions and contests is driving the behavior you want, be it more clicks, uploads, downloads, or purchases. Keep A/B-testing new options forever!

- *Information feeds:* Whether you're using a blog, an RSS feed, e-mail or smoke signals to keep your customers updated on product enhancements, how-to tips, or other helpful information, they're of little help if nobody reads them. A/B-test a variety of ways of deliver-ing the same message, using different headlines and headline sizes, videos, cartoons, or diagrams. Consider making offers like "get bonus points for reading (or forwarding) our latest bulletins." This exercise, like most customer-loyalty efforts, continues forever as well

Watch the initial results of each program for perhaps a week or 10 days, at least at first (in reality, you'll be watching and optimizing them indefinitely). Never look at the programs as a whole, since each keep activity will operate independently.

Cohort Analysis Should Guide your "Keep" Efforts

Cohort analysis should guide retention efforts. A cohort is a group of customers with common attributes, and in the web/mobile channels, the key cohort to watch is the customer activation date. Why? New customers may stay for months, while older customers may tire after perhaps three or four months. New customers may visit 10 times a week, staying 20 minutes per visit, while older customers visit twice a week for 10 minutes each time.

Measuring retention based on averages can be extremely deceptive, suggesting, say, that retention is OK since we lose only 8 percent of our customers every month. But if those customers were all heavy users or spenders or all disappear in two months or five months, the company obviously has a problem. Studying users in terms of cohorts rather than in aggregate makes it much easier to spot danger signs.

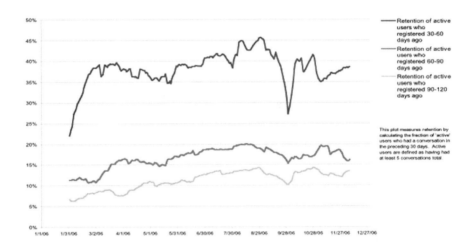

Cohort Analysis of a Sales Funnel (Figure 10.13)

Another important cohort to consider (usually when there are at least many thousands of customers) is users by source: do customers referred by Google stay longer than or not as long as those referred by Bing or Yahoo? Do customers who first accept a free trial leave more quickly than those who pay from Day One? Each cohort analysis delivers a strategy for improving retention.

Optimize "Grow" Customers

There are two ways to grow customers: get customers to buy more, or get them to refer other customers to the company.

The optimization principles for growing new revenue are described in Chapter 3 (page 180) and can be helped by cohort analysis, described above.

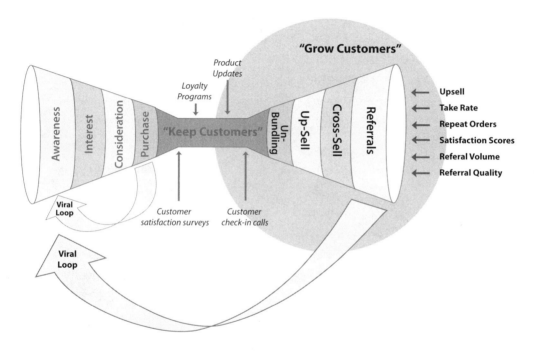

"Grow Customers" Activation Activities in Web/Mobile Channels *(Figure 10.14)*

Get Customers to Buy More

Here are key metrics to optimize when trying to grow revenues and customers:

- *Incremental dollars* (above initial order) sold, on average, to all customers: if you're not getting at least 15 percent larger orders from repeat customers, you're not working hard enough. Experiment with more and different offers, add more generous offers, and find additional places to make the offers

- The *"take rate:"* This is the percentage of customers reviewing (and taking) an upsell/next-sell offer. It tells you how well the upsell is working. Aim for a double-digit take rate even though it may not always be achievable. A/B-test more generous offers and spontaneous offers that seem urgent ("24-hour sale" or "today only"), and (see above) find other innovative places, media, and ideas for promoting upsells

- *Average order size:* Also called "market basket" (a century-old term borrowed from the physical channel). Make the order bigger by A/B-testing a variety of offers, such as longer-term subscriptions, "bonus" products for people taking the upsell offer, and deeper discounts on the upsell. Remember you've already spent the "big" money acquiring this customer, so accept a more narrow margin on these incremental revenues

- *Number of opt-outs* or closed accounts resulting from additional offers: This is an important "watch out" number that'll quickly tell you if you're being too pushy. Look at your overall opt-out rate, and if these grow offers increase that rate by 25 percent or more (it should be around 2 percent or 3 percent), either slow down your efforts, tone down your copy, or call some customers and find out what they liked and didn't like and adjust accordingly

---

You'll be amazed how delighted many customers will be to receive an e-mail or, better yet, a phone call.

- *Customer Satisfaction:* Getting existing customers to buy more starts by ensuring that they're satisfied with the product, its performance and the price. Unhappy customers won't be buying from you again. Stay in touch with your customers through regular satisfaction surveys, outreach phone calls, and the like

You'll be amazed how delighted many customers will be to receive an e-mail or, better yet, a phone call saying, "Hi, we just want to thank you for your business and find out how you're liking our product." You can usually gently slide in a special offer or a discount on more purchases toward the end of the call or e-mail. These basic customer-growth strategies work in consumer goods as well as business-to-business.

Get Customers to Refer Other Customers

Customer referrals are by far the most powerful, leverageable opportunities to get more customers and thus increase revenue. Why? Because invitations from one friend to another saying "try this" are highly credible and often free. Referral metrics to optimize include:

- percentage and number of customers sending e-mails, Tweets, messages to friends
- average number of referrals per customer
- conversion (or acceptance) rate of customer referral offers
- purchases, activations, or sign-ups per user and per member referred by other members or customers

Many of the viral marketing techniques discussed earlier, such as getting users to "like" the company on Facebook or re-Tweet news of a new game or app, adds the friend's credibility and endorsement to your marketing message. Most consumers prefer to get messages from friends rather than marketers, knowing their friends wouldn't tout something of little interest.

Start with Two "Grow" Metrics

Two metrics guide the monitoring of "Grow" efforts: viral growth factor and customer lifetime value.

The viral growth factor, or *viral coefficient*, helps measure the number of activated users referred by your current users. If a user invites five friends but only one actually activates and buys from or signs up for your site, your viral coefficient is 1.0 (one user refers one activated new user, or 1 for 1), the minimum for real viral growth. Think about it—you'd actually double your audience if every customer got you one more activated customer!!

How do you calculate your viral coefficient?

Here's an example. Imagine 100 users of your site each refer 10 friends who come to your site or app delivering 1,000 "acquired" users lucky you). Now imagine if 15 percent of those invited friends (150) actually sign up, buy, or engage (making them activated users).

Calculations:

1. Start with the number of users (100)
2. Multiply users by the average number they referred (100x10)
3. Then compute the average conversion to "activated" users (15%)
4. You now have 150 new users (15% of 1,000 have activated)
5. The result = 150 new users divided by 100 "old" users equal a viral coefficient of 1.5

Work to achieve a viral coefficient greater than 1.2 or 1.3, which is closer to linear or modest growth and not dramatic. Ideally, you'll experience the kind of explosive growth seen from a top YouTube video, a hilarious joke, or a scam e-mail like "get a free iPad." Many people forward hilarious YouTube videos or jokes to dozens of people or more, many of whom watch the video or read the joke. This can deliver superb viral coefficients of 12, 20, or even more. The higher the coefficient, the faster the resulting viral growth and the more customers you're adding at any given time. With any viral coefficient below 1, you're stagnant at best.

A top YouTube video or a hilarious joke can deliver superb viral coefficients.

Be careful to measure activated users, not just gross referrals, which can deceive you. What good is it if a customer brings 10 people to a store, for example, and they sure do like the fashion, but none spend a dime?

The work to increase a viral coefficient is hard—very hard—because it's the greatest single source of new customers at the lowest possible cost. Use all the tactics we've already described, including:

- A/B test the offer, the copy, the calls to action
- Create and test incentives, promotions, deals and discounts
- Test a variety of incentives to encourage people to refer their friends… be sure to incentivize both the current and the potential customer
- Apply the core "get customers" tactics to every step in this process, since while this is a referral, it's all about getting a new customer

Recognize, too, that nothing creates great virality better than a great product! Few people go out of their way to tell any of their friends about a boring company with mediocre products and service. Monitor the viral growth factor at least weekly, constantly brainstorming ways to improve the score.

Optimization **never** ends.

Keep in mind that not all products on the web are viral. Social media is viral. Multiplayer games are viral. But there are sites in some categories that you definitely don't invite lots of friends to (dating sites, spouse-cheating sites, legal and illegal drug sites, etc.). YouTube is perhaps the canonical example of a high-coefficient site. Think about the last hilarious YouTube video you viewed. How many friends did you forward it to?

Customer lifetime value (LTV), or how much the customer is worth to the company, can grow in several different ways: a customer buys more, refers more new customers or, in the case of multi-sided markets, become more active on the site and generate greater revenue for the company. "Grow customers" programs are the primary driver of lifetime value growth.

Monitor LTV growth over time, and use new programs and offers and improve efficiency.

Multi-sided Markets Must Optimize the "Other Side"

As discussed earlier, startups operating multi-sided markets need to optimize the "other side" of their market, the side that generates cash. It's time to get out of the building and verify the hypothesis that certain advertisers find the audience attractive and will pay the CPM ad rates that the hypothesis indicates will drive a profitable business model.

While orders would be lovely at this point, the primary objective is validation of the potential revenue so glowingly described in the hypothesis and your pitch to investors.

Follow the "get customers" processes outlined earlier (you are getting customers, after all), recognizing that you basically have to do most of the work a second time. Why? The acquisition activities and sales pitch to the payer side of a market are totally different from the materials, positioning, and value proposition that attracts free users to the site or app. Don't expect orders or revenue yet, since traffic will be negligible, but:

- Learn the rules of the game: Does the site need to have a million page views a week or a month in order to be considered? Are certain ad units or features required? Is the audience distinctive enough to command an ad-rate premium? Are there any other rules about content, longevity, or anything else that might prevent a deal?

- Determine the sales roadmap: How long does it take to get an order, and how many steps does the approval process involve? Does the advertiser make its buys once or twice a year or on an ongoing basis? How big are typical initial insertion orders? Who needs to approve the site, the price, the content? How might you get an order sooner?

Summary: Optimization never ends!

Get Out of the Building: Test Sell Channel Partners
(Physical)

If you sell through an indirect sales channel, now is the time to validate the channel strategy you assembled in Phase 1. Validation means an order or at least a firm commitment from prospective partners in your sales channel.

(Trying to get orders from channel partners earlier, without enthusiastic end users, would have been counterproductive. The typical channel partner response: "That sounds interesting, but will there be any demand for this product? What do potential customers think?" What the prospective channel partner was really asking: "Can I make money from this product? If so, how much?" With actual sales and reports of enthusiasm from their customers, the answers are far more credible.)

At each meeting, try to learn as much as possible about the potential channel partner:

- Will the channel partner buy and sell the product, based on its value proposition, proposed pricing, and terms?
- What percentage of the product's retail price will the channel require? Are there other costs such as freight, advertising, or promotion? What's the return policy?
- Does the channel partner have any sense of potential sales volume? Where and how will the partner promote or merchandise the product?
- How can the channel be influenced to sell more: bonuses, training for salespeople, sales meetings or product demonstrations, a golf tournament? What means of encouraging more sales through the channel are acceptable and affordable?
- Will the channel target buy and sell the product, based on its value proposition, proposed pricing, and terms?

- What percentage of the product's retail price will the channel require? Are there other costs, such as freight, advertising, or promotion? What's the return policy?

- Does the partner have any sense of potential sales volume? Where and how will the partner promote or merchandise the product?

- And the most important…does the channel partner create demand or just fulfill it, when customers seek out the product.

Sometimes these discussions lead to an early channel stocking order. If so, congratulations. Make it happen. The initial order may be a test market in a few stores or a region, or a small quantity "to see how it sells." Seize this opportunity, knowing that your primary mission is to learn as much as possible about the channel, assuring everyone that when the product is ready, it can actually get to market.

Identify the Channel Targets

Test prospective channel partners of varying sizes and types. Just like listening to customers, founders should lead the charge in each channel so that they hear reactions firsthand.

Begin by making lists of the key people to see in each targeted channel, including contact information and everything known about the target (drawn from customer discovery research). Getting that first appointment with a national chain is a hard, low-percentage game, so prepare to be disappointed, persistent, and tenacious.

Position the meetings as informational in nature, and be prepared to fly halfway across the country for 20-minute meetings on regular basis. (One national chain buyer is known to turn over a three-minute egg timer at the start of sales pitches.)

Where the channel involves retailers, validation is a bit tricky. When will the product be available in sufficient volume for the retailer to actually buy it? Will the partner agree to a limited test market sooner, hoping test-market success leads to far larger, chain-wide orders?

Channel validation also includes meetings with independent sales reps and distributors. Independent reps have a keen sense of their markets and usually have a handful of key retail or chain customers whose buying preferences and patterns they know well, largely because their income depends on it. Talk with these folks in multiple markets. Will the industry's No. 1 or 2 rep firm in the region take the product on and sell it once it becomes available? This is hardly a given, since reps can rarely carry competitive products. What's the rep's sense of his key customers' potential for buying and marketing the product? How long will it take to get distribution, and what kind of volume might the startup expect? Meet with distributors to discuss the same issues.

A Channel Is Just a Grocery Shelf

One caveat in channel discussions: *never confuse channel partners with customers.* Persuading a partner to carry the product, or a big system integrator to work with your company, is decidedly not the same as getting a customer to buy. While channel partners may place product orders, they order only when customer demand pulls the product through their channel. End users pay the bills; channel partners take your company seriously only when you drive their revenue.

Never confuse channel partners with customers.

The best introduction to a channel partner begins with "we may have customers for you." While this seems blindingly obvious, lots of startups fall into the trap of thinking their sales problems are over once a channel partner signs up, or they pop the Champagne corks when the first "stocking" order arrives from an indirect-channel partner. Wrong. Think of all indirect channels as nothing more than shelves in a grocery store. Until customers become familiar with the brand, they'll never search for the product. Until they pick it up, it isn't sold. And just like retailers, channel partners are notoriously slow to pay their bills.

Keeping all this in mind, update the channel/service partner presentation with information about early customer orders. Then hit the street and present to them. The goal is to come back with a committed relationship (usually evidenced by an order). Create a channel sales-call "report card" similar to the sales report card, and use it to estimate sales that might eventually come from the channel. At this stage, channel-volume estimates will be difficult, but you have to start somewhere!

Get Out of the Building: Test Sell Traffic Partners (Web/Mobile)

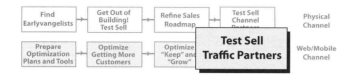

⇨ It's not uncommon to hear, "Well, I built a website, but nobody came to it." This is the death knell for a startup in the web/mobile channel. You need partners to drive traffic to your site, whether they run textlinks to you, post banner ads encouraging their visitors to visit you, or highlight some of your content or even your features on their site with links to yours. A wide variety of partnerships can be used to increase traffic. In web companies, the function is often called "business development."

A few examples of the types of partnerships:

- A social network might get traffic from other related commerce or content websites

- A kid-game company might offer a free trial version on kid-oriented websites

- A computer parts e-tailer might get traffic from computer-news sites

Meet prospective partners and try to sign the traffic deals you envisioned in the traffic-partners hypothesis. If you do, how much revenue or traffic will they actually deliver, and at what cost? Set up meetings with sites that reach the same types of customers you want to reach and start making deals like these:

- Feature content from each other's sites with links to the partner's site.

- Swap e-mail lists so each partner can introduce its users or customers to the other

- Trade ads and textlinks on your partner's site for those on your own, using unsold inventory at each site

- Highlight the partner as a "content partner" or otherwise promote each other on site
- Create microsites with noncompetitive content or offers on each other's sites
- Offer one site's features (social networking or free games, for example) on the other

The list of traffic opportunities is virtually endless and provides a great creative challenge that can deliver massive incremental traffic to one partner or both. When one partner benefits more than the other, cash often brings the trade back into balance. Cash offers are the best way to get a prospective partner's attention. Use your initial conversations to compare the potential volume and cost of partner-delivered revenue or traffic with the traffic your company generates on its own. Get some traffic partnerships going as fast as you can, and monitor and evaluate the results.

Partnership opportunities are viewed as a dime a dozen.

Identify your target partners from lists developed in the traffic-partner hypothesis. Recognize that these meetings are largely exploratory in nature, since the first question a prospective partner is likely to ask is "How much traffic do you have now?" and the answer is probably very close to zero at this stage of the validation process. After all, most partnerships are mutually beneficial, and before scheduling a meeting, the partner candidate is likely to want to understand what's in it for him or her.

These meetings are hard to get. Partnership opportunities are viewed as a dime a dozen, and companies are reluctant to spend time on all but the biggest opportunities. Some tips for breaking through the barrier:

- Use personal referrals and aggressive follow-up as described in the "customer contacts" section of customer discovery

- Focus the introductory e-mail on what's in it for the potential partner. This might include traffic, money, or new customers, depending on how the partnership works

- Explain your startup's vision and why partnering with your new company is important

- Network at appropriate conferences and trade shows to meet partners face-to-face

- Not every deal needs to be signed in these initial meetings, especially since these commitments are hard to come by

Create a post-meeting report card that assesses and estimates the size of the opportunity: how much traffic, and how much cost. Use a report card similar to the one described on page 241 to track and quantify results.

| Product Positioning | → | Match Positioning To Market Type | → | Company Positioning | → | Validate Positioning | | All Channels |

CHAPTER 11

Customer Validation, Phase Three: Develop Product and Company Positioning

In this phase of customer validation, you'll use all the test results from your experiments about customers, their reactions to the initial value proposition, and why they buy. The result is two positioning statements: one for the company and one for the product. In this phase, you'll:

- develop product positioning
- match product positioning to market type
- develop a company positioning
- make presentations to analysts and industry influencers to validate the positioning

Positioning is the attempt to control the public's perception of a product or service as it relates to competitive products. In Phase 1 of validation, you crafted initial positioning for product and company, but formal positioning at that time would have involved too much guesswork. Now, with 50 or 250 face-to-face customer interviews and thousands of online customer interactions under your belt, the company has real facts about why customers buy and real customers to help further test and refine your positioning.

Thus far, even through the validation stage, spending on customer acquisition has been modest and the risks relatively low. But now, as the company prepares to scale from dozens or hundreds of customers to thousands or even millions, it needs to be able to communicate what the product is and does, and why the customer should buy or use it.

No PR Agency

Most technology-driven startups believe they need professional "marketing people" from a public relations agency to execute this positioning phase. In reality, the first pass is best-done (and far more affordably) by the Customer Development team with feedback from Product Development. At this moment, no one is closer to the customer or better understands what problems customers say the product solves. No one else has struggled to learn customers needs, get an order, and find a repeatable sales process. The Customer Development team is clearly best-qualified to develop a first pass at describing what makes the company and the product unique. Later, during customer creation, it'll be time to bring in the "experts" and their monthly retainers and invoices. By then you'll be able to hand them facts explaining why customers bought.

The Positioning Audit

Before the company spends time on positioning, it's a good idea to air out the conference room and get some facts. The best way to do this is with a positioning audit. An audit is an unbiased way to learn how others perceive your company and products. An *external audit* interviews a representative sample of people from a variety of categories, including customers who know or have heard of your company and those who don't; others who will carry your message for you (industry analysts and influencers, bloggers, members of the press, and others); competitors and others who are knowledgeable about the industry or market.

External Audit Questionnaire

Recognition
- ❑ Have you heard of the company? Do you know what they do?

Market Focus
- ❑ Are there other products in the market similar to the company's?
- ❑ If so, how are the company's products different?
- ❑ Which do you like the best? Why?
- ❑ If not, how would you describe the space the company is in?

Customer Focus
- ❑ Are you familiar with the types of customers the company is calling on?
- ❑ Are you familiar with the kinds of problems these customers have?
- ❑ Do you believe company's product will solve these problems? How?

Product Focus
- ❑ Do you know what the top three features of the company's product are?
- ❑ Are these "must have" features?
- ❑ What features must the company get to market in the next release? The next release?
- ❑ What do you think of the company's core technology? Is it unique? Defensible? How does it compare to others coming into the market?

Positioning
- ❑ Have you heard the company describe its positioning? Do you believe it? Is it credible?
- ❑ Have you heard the company describe its mission? Do you believe it?

Competition
- ❑ Who do you think the company will compete with in its first year?
- ❑ Who do you think are the company's ultimate competitors?
- ❑ What does the company need to do to win against these competitors?

Sales/Distribution
- ❑ Is the company's distribution strategy the right way to reach customers?
- ❑ Is the company's sales strategy effective?
- ❑ Does the company have the right pricing? Is it charging too much? Too little?

Strengths/ Weaknesses
- ❑ What are the strengths of the company? (Product, distribution, positioning, partners, etc.)
- ❑ What are its weaknesses? (Lack of "whole product," sales, product features, etc.)

Trends
- ❑ What technology/product trends should the company worry about?
- ❑ Who are the key opinion leaders in this technology? Who do you respect?
- ❑ What business trends should the company worry about?
- ❑ Who are the key opinion leaders in these business trends? Who do you respect?

Acquisition Information
- ❑ What do they think is the best way for the company to get product information to its customers? What do you think influences customers' opinions?
- ❑ What is the best way for the company to get you to be interested in its products? Can the company call you?

Example of an External Audit Questionnaire *(Figure 11.1)*

Each interview asks these groups a series of questions about how they perceive your company and its key competitors: Do they know and respect your product, your reputation, and your leadership? Do they think your company is a credible, trustworthy provider of the product or service it's selling, and where do they think it fits in the competitive set? The results form a baseline of the perceptions others have about your company.

Form a baseline of the perceptions others have about your company.

Once you understand what others think (usually a surprise to most startups breathing the rarefied air of their own conference rooms), the company can work on changing and shaping those opinions. An example of an external audit questionnaire for customers, press, influencers, and analysts is shown in Figure 11.1.

While conducting an audit is the kind of activity pr agencies excel at, handing this function off completely is a serious mistake in a startup. Just as your early sales calls were too important to be handled by salespeople, your early audits are too important to be handed off to a pr agency. The members of the founding team should at least perform the first five or ten calls themselves.

Listening to external perceptions of the company is half of this audit step. Listening inside the company is the other half. An *internal audit* directs the same questions to the founding team executive staff and board members. Most startups assume they have complete internal unanimity on the all the issues in the external audit. An internal audit will probably reveal that you have a cacophony of voices (and you most definitely don't want to be out of sync with your investors.) The internal audit should unearth those differences and extract new ideas. When the company has agreed on a final positioning at the end of this phase, you communicate those ideas back to the entire organization so it speaks with one voice.

Develop Positioning: Product Positioning

In this step you'll put a stake in the ground and formalize the product's positioning. The positioning doesn't have to be perfect, since it will be refined further during customer creation. The result of this product-positioning step is a one-page "product positioning brief" that updates the positioning briefs developed earlier. As sales literature (data sheets, sales presentations, website and copy) and marketing campaigns are created, this brief should be used to keep all the messages "on point."

Feedback from customers and channel partners in customer discovery and customer validation has continually refined or affirmed the answer to what your positioning is. You wrote your first version of a positioning statement when you created the sales presentation, answering the question of why an early customer should buy the product. Think about customers' reaction to that description. Did it generate excitement? Was it credible? If customers couldn't or didn't explain why the product was interesting to them—or not—do you understand why? If not, re-contact them and find out the reasons. There's no better input into product positioning than feedback from folks who were exposed to the product itself.

The Product Positioning Brief

Return to the simple, single-phrase positioning statement you developed at the outset of customer validation (remember "Absolutely positively overnight" from FedEx?). Did it resonate with the customers encountered during the validation process? Did they find think it explained why they should buy the product or what it did, and did they find it credible and effective? If not, back to the drawing board.

To refresh your memory, review product-positioning example developed early in Chapter 9 (which may have been several months ago by now):

PRODUCT POSITIONING STATEMENT EXAMPLE
• *Mobiledough* is **FOR** busy executives who travel a lot
• **WHO WANT/NEED** to do expense reports accurately in the least possible time
• And Mobiledough **IS AN** easy-to-use tool for receipt tracking and expense tabulation
• **THAT PROVIDES** a detailed weekly expense report in under 10 minutes
• **UNLIKE** expense report packages, Mobiledough scans, sorts and totals receipts and presents a near-final report draft for review in 11 popular expense reporting formats

Example of Product Positioning *(Figure 11.1)*

A thorough positioning effort made soon after customer-validation interviews will often save the company time and money at the start of customer creation. If it already knows how to position the new product against competition in a way that resonates with customers, it can hire a pr or marketing communications agency and have it get right to work creating buzz or promotional materials or both. Neither time nor dollars are wasted on ponderous, costly positioning studies and analyses. Instead, the agency is told "here's the positioning. Run with it unless you have a significantly better idea." The agency will know how to package the product, the pr messages, and other marketing communications tools and can get right to work generating results. (Agencies hate this, because thinking and "strategizing" are far more lucrative and less accountable activities.)

	Existing Market	New Market	Resegmented Market	Clone Market
Company Positioning Statements	Compare the product to its competitors. Describe how some feature or attribute of the product is better, faster – *an incremental improvement.*	It's too early for customers to understand what the product's features will do for them. Instead, describe the problem the product will solve and the benefits the customers will get from solving it – *a transformational improvement.*	Compare the product to its competitors. If it's low cost, describe price and feature set. If a niche, describe how some feature or attribute of the product solves the problem customers have in a way comparable products do not. Describe the benefits the customers will get from solving their problem this new way.	If users are familiar with foreign sites, compare to them. If not, treat as a new market.

Product Positioning by Market Type *(Table 11.2)*

Develop Positioning: Match Positioning to Market Type

Market type dramatically changes the messages your company wants to send about itself and its products. So now it's time to match the positioning to the market type you've selected.

For an Existing Market

If you're entering an existing market, company positioning is about creating the notion that your company is both different and credible. And solves a problem that customers believe is important. When Apple entered the smartphone market, people understood that the company was a manufacturer of iPods but was now going to offer a phone and a web browser, too.

Once your company positioning is chosen, product positioning follows. Since in an existing market comparable products exist, product positioning typically describes how and why your product is different along an existing axis/basis of competition. Differentiation in an existing market can take one of three forms: you can describe differences in product attributes (faster, cheaper, less filling, 30 percent more), in distribution channel (pizza in 30 minutes, home delivery, see your nearest dealer, build it yourself on the web), or in service (five-year, 50,000-mile automobile warranty, 90-day money-back guarantee, lifetime warranty). Or it can take the form of how the product fills a need or solves a problem the customer was searching for.

For a New Market

If you're creating a new market, company positioning can't be about how different your company is, since by definition there are no other companies to compare it with in a new market. So in a new market, company positioning is about communicating a vision of and passion for what could be. It answers the questions "What's wrong with the world that you want to make right?" and "What is it that your company is trying to change?" When Airbnb reinvented hotel/motel/bed and breakfasts with "peer-to-peer" accommodations, they first had to communicate a radical idea: people would want to rent out their homes to strangers who would want to stay in other strangers' homes.

After positioning the company, positioning the product in a new market becomes pretty simple. Touting a new product's features is unproductive, since there's no context for understanding them—no comparable products exist—and customers have no idea what you're talking about. If Airbnb had positioned its service as "rooms for $89" or "sleep in a stranger's bed" no one would have had a clue what it was talking about. Instead, Airbnb positioning talked about a "sharing economy" and emphasized the economic benefits for both parties.

In a Clone Market

Cloning a business model from the U.S. that hasn't made it to your country (due to language, cultural or legal barriers) is a viable business strategy. Clones are typically found in countries such as China, Russia, Brazil, India and Indonesia that are large enough to grow companies to substantial size (greater than 100 million people).

Company positioning can't be about how different your company is, as there are no other companies in your country to compare it with, but you can act as if you can predict the future. You know how the equivalent companies are positioned in the U.S. Clone their positioning.

The same is true for product positioning. Touting a new product's features is unproductive at first, as there's no immediate context for understanding the features—no comparable products exist—and customers have no idea what you're talking about. But here again you can pretend to be psychic. You know how the equivalent companies are positioned in the U.S. As soon as the market is educated, clone their positioning.

For Re-Segmenting a Market

If you're re-segmenting an existing market, company positioning depends on market segmentation. Segmentation means you've picked a clear and distinct spot in customers' minds that's unique and understandable. Most important, concerns something they value and want and need now. Company positioning for this market type communicates your deep understanding of customer problems/needs for un- or underserved markets. And your astute understanding of how to uniquely solve it.

There are two types of market re-segmentation; a segmented niche and a low-cost provider. Two examples of low-cost re-segmentation are Jetblue and Southwest Airlines. Both offer cheap fares matched by minimal frills, they entered the airline business low-cost passenger airlines that provide high-quality customer service on point-to-point routes.

There are two types of market re-segmentation; a segmented niche and a low-cost provider.

The rise of Walmart was another example of an entrepreneur's recognition that an existing market was ripe for a niche re-segmentation. In the 1960s and '70s, Sears and Kmart dominated big-box discount retailing, opening large stores where there was sufficient population to sustain them. Smaller communities got catalog stores (Sears) or were simply ignored (Kmart). Sam Walton saw towns dismissed as "too small" as an opportunity. "Small towns first" was his unique niche re-segmentation. Once established, Walmart proudly positioned itself as a "discounter"—a sobriquet the large retailers avoided like the plague. They sold name-brand health and beauty aids at cost. This strategy, supported by heavy advertising, pulled in customers who then bought other products which, while priced low, carried high gross margins. Equally important, Walmart adoption of cutting-edge technology to track how people shop and to buy, and its ability to deliver goods more efficiently and cheaply reduced its cost of sales to a small fraction of competitors'. By 2002, Kmart was bankrupt and Walmart was the largest company in the world.

When you're re-segmenting a market, product positioning is a hybrid of market and existing market positionings. Since your segmentation has moved your product into a space adjacent to your competitors, product positioning describes how and why your new segment is different and important to your customers.

Develop Positioning: Company Positioning

With the product positioned in one of the four market types, articulate company positioning the same way. What's the difference between product positioning and company positioning? Product positioning focused on the specific product attributes within a market type, while company positioning answers the questions "What does this company do for me?" and "Why do I want to do business with them?" and "Why does this company exist and how is it different?"

Write the first version of a company positioning statement as simply as possible, always keeping customers in mind. Describe the company to encourage potential customers to say, "Tell me more. It sounds like you're solving a problem I have."

Here's a great but verbose example from Amazon.com: "We seek to be Earth's most customer-centric company for three primary customer sets: consumer customers, seller customers, and developer customers." UPS points to its breadth: "As the world's largest package delivery company and a leading global provider of specialized transportation and logistics services, UPS continues to develop the frontiers of logistics, supply chain management, and e-Commerce, ...combining the flows of goods, information, and funds." One more, from the simpler, more narrowly focused Zappos, speaks volumes about why you'd want to do business with the company: "We've aligned the entire organization around one mission: to provide the best customer service possible. Internally, we call this our WOW philosophy." Notice, that company positioning is not about product or features.

Sometimes, founders creating a new market are tempted to name the new market. This can be helpful or, more often, dangerous and expensive. Generally it's helpful only if it helps explain the product's attributes, with terms like *handheld video game* or *instant photography*. If the new market name is cute or esoteric, prepare to spend lots of money explaining the market and why it's important to customers, who need a frame of reference to understand the company positioning.

No-frills airlines and *movies on demand* explain markets and position new companies within them. Tivo spent hundreds of millions convincing customers it wasn't a digital VCR.

Table 11.2 illustrates company positioning by market type. Like product positioning, company positioning doesn't have to be perfect yet, since it will be refined further during customer creation.

	Existing Market	New Market	Resegmented Market	Clone Market
Company Positioning Statements	Compare the company to its competitors. Describe how the company is both different and credible.	It's too early for customers to understand how different the company is, since in a new market there are no other companies to compare it to. Therefore, company positioning is about communicating its vision and passion for what could be.	Company positioning for this Market Type communicates the value of the market segment chosen and the innovation the new company brings to it. What do customers value, want and need now?	Borrow positioning from existing country. Translate into local needs.

Company Positioning by Market Type (Table 11.2)

As with product positioning, the result of this exercise should be a "company positioning brief," *brief* being the operative word. As marketing literature (press backgrounder, sales presentations, website) unfolds, this brief will be used in conjunction with the product brief for consistency's sake.

As a consistency check for company positioning, revisit the mission statement written during customer discovery. How did customers react to it during validation interviews? Did they find that explained why the company is different or special and encourage them to do business with the company? In addition, compare the company's description and mission statement with those of its competitors. What are their company positionings, and is the new company's positioning distinct or differentiated, particularly as buyers are concerned. Is it simple? Beware: unsubstantiated superlatives like *easiest, best* and *greatest* are meaningless. Demonstrable, provable claims like *fastest* and *cheapest* are stronger, although cheapest is a high-risk strategy as a rule, since competition can quickly respond.

Unsubstantiated superlatives like *easiest, best* and *greatest* are meaningless. Demonstrable, provable claims like *fastest* and *cheapest* are stronger.

Develop Positioning: Validate Positioning

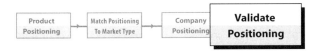

Industry analysts and influencers help deliver the foundation of credibility that a startup needs. What's an industry analyst? In the technology arena, many firms charge customers to provide an "independent" and dispassionate analysis of markets, trends, or specific products and their fit in those markets. These firms vary in size and influence. In some technical markets (enterprise software, for example) sales to large companies are very difficult until one of the large analyst firms (Gartner, Forrester, Yankee) has blessed the product, particularly if it's new. In the entertainment business it might be Kagan, in consumer products the NPD group.

Unlike analysts, industry influencers are a less formal category. Every industry has a handful of pundits who publish articles, write blogs or hold conferences, and their prominence in the field influences what gets talked about. Sometimes these influentials work at industry-leading companies but speak at lots of conferences. Other influentials include writers at general, business, or trade publications. Sometimes they teach at universities.

Test to see if they'll sing your company song.

Identification of key analysts and industry influencers began in customer discovery. Meet them and get their insights and feedback on the initial positioning (market, product, and company) just created and their thoughts about product features. Test to see if they'll sing your company song (and if not, figure out why). Even though early adopters will be evangelizing the product inside their company or to their friends and family, it helps to have other "outsiders" who will say, "Yes, we've heard of them, and while it's too early to say how good their product is, we think their idea is quite valuable." It's also important to line up industry analysts and influencers as references for press interactions in the customer creation step.

All this would have been difficult without real customer contacts, feedback, and orders, but now it's appropriate to contact the analysts and influencers who have been tracked since early on in customer discovery. Hopefully, their names were recorded in a database after the company met them at conferences, seminars, and trade shows. Before any meeting, the team should spend time understanding their opinions on the market and product space (if not, don't use the meetings in this phase to get up to speed; do the homework first).

Before contacting analysts and influencers, be sure to understand what companies and industries their firms cover and what particular area or companies the individual analysts cover. (There's nothing worse than seeing the wrong person or even the wrong company. It tells everyone that nobody did their homework.) Develop a short script explaining why they should meet. Understand what they cover and explain why the new company will shake up their market and why the product and company are important. With this accomplished, the "what's in it for them" is obvious; they won't want to miss an influential and important company. (They'll almost certainly also try to sell their consulting services, which at least theoretically have no bearing on their opinion about the new client's product.) Make sure to reference early customers and the problem/pain points that the product solves for them. When they agree to meet, ask how much time they'll allocate, what presentation format they like (formal slides, demo, whiteboard talk, etc.) and whether the presentation should focus on technology, markets, customers, problems, or all the above.

Each analyst organization or influencer has a view of the market or products it covers.

Assemble the presentation, keeping in mind this isn't a sales pitch. Focus on market and product positioning as well as details of product features. The objective is to validate the product and company positions and, wherever possible, to influence analysts' thinking, not to sell them. Each analyst organization or influencer has a view of the market or products it covers—understand that view upfront (know it well enough to draw it on the board). If creating a new market, get the slides describing its view of the adjacent markets it will affect.

Meeting an industry influencer may require the same formal preparation as meeting an analyst, or it may be a lunch at a nearby pub. Do the homework to understand how the influencers acquire and disseminate information upfront, and adjust presentation length and style accordingly.

When meeting influencers and analysts, remember that the goal is to gather feedback (and hope for wild enthusiasm). Also use the interaction to gather intelligence about the marketplace. Make a mental checklist of critical learning objectives. For example:

- What other companies are doing anything similar?
- How does the new company's vision fit with market needs?
- With customer needs?
- How can the company best position its product, its place in the market, and the company itself?
- Is the product pricing right?
- How does it compare with competitors' pricing?

The analysts can often clarify who in a company the sale should be made to and the kinds of obstacles that will be faced. With feedback from analysts and influencers as well several real customers, continue to the next and final phase of customer validation.

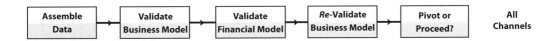

| Assemble Data | → | Validate Business Model | → | Validate Financial Model | → | *Re*-Validate Business Model | → | Pivot or Proceed? | All Channels |

CHAPTER 12

Customer Validation, Phase Four:
The Toughest Question of All:
Pivot or Proceed?

THIS IS THE MOST CRITICAL, MOST GUT-WRENCHING phase of customer validation: honestly determining whether there's a scalable, profitable business model ahead. Is the company ready to go forward to the customer creation step, when millions of dollars are often spent to fuel rapid customer growth? This step literally "calls the question" about the company's future directions. It's time to study all the test results, all the customer learning and all the insights you've had from the facts you've gathered. Its time to see if the company is ready to start spending money to scale, and that the result will be a great, profitable company.

There are three steps to answering the crucial "pivot or proceed" question:

- Assemble and review all key discovery and validation findings
- Review the business model hypotheses and their interactions with one another
- Focus on the "metrics that matter" in the financial model

Pivot or Proceed: Assemble Data Findings

By this point, the team has assembled a massive amount of hard data: industry research, customer segments, customer feedback, marketing program results, channel and cost input and much more. The data needs to be verified, with any gaps, discrepancies, or anomalies filled in along the way. A few examples:

- The company needs 10,000 customers in order to be profitable, but the market isn't that large
- Customer acquisition or channel costs are too high, rendering the company unprofitable
- The sales roadmap is too long and complex, making the cost of sales way too high
- Despite best efforts, referrals just aren't delivering additional customers

These anomalies are relatively easy to spot when all the data is collected in one room. They often call for further customer, channel, or product development discussions. At times, they drive a business model pivot.

The best way to "translate" piles of data, is to make it as visual as possible.

Build a War Room

The best way to "translate" piles of data, reports and questionnaires is to make it as visual as possible. For best results, lock the founding team in a room for a day or two to walk step by step through each hypothesis. Cover one wall with a blown up "final" business model canvas. Cover the other wall with the hypotheses themselves, sorted to keep the pieces of each hypothesis together (remember, many hypotheses have multiple parts). Use another wall for supporting diagrams, and allow space for the most recent canvas and perhaps one or two earlier iterations. Leave a large white-board available for keeping score of questions and changes and for the key "metrics that matter" numbers that emerge (discussed in detail in Step 3). While not every diagram is appropriate for your startup, review:

- a *work-flow map* of the prototypical customer that diagrams how customers do their jobs or live their lives both with and without the new product
- an *organizational/influence map* showing whom consumers or businesspeople interact with, how often, and how those people influence buying decisions.
- *customer archetypes*: how they earn and spend their money and use their time
- *a market map* showing where your customers will come from
- *a channel or sales roadmap* diagramming how sales will happen
- *a fully updated business model canvas* (along with a few earlier versions)

Review the Data

The most important hard data to review includes:

- customer feedback, particularly from sales report cards evaluating customer enthusiasm for the product and its potential sales revenue over time
- market size and market share estimates
- channel feedback and revenue potential summaries
- pricing, customer acquisition costs, and any major product cost changes
- detailed information about the industry, the customers, and their behavior
- competitive product and pricing information

- results of your web "get, keep and grow" tests
- details of your customer acquisition costs and viral coefficient and the latest stats on page views per visit, visit frequency, user growth, and retention optimization
- user-testing results, showing the rate of improvement for activation, conversion, retention and growth activities

The team, often including investors, should review all the materials to ensure that all the learning from discovery and validation has been integrated into the latest versions of the hypothesis documents and into an updated version of the business model canvas that will be discussed in the next step. The key activity at this stage is to look at the intersections of, or interactions among, the business model components, since no doubt many components have changed along the way. The process is a healthy one, and the results fuel the next steps of the pivot-or-proceed process.

Look at the intersections of, or interactions among the business model components.

The Business Model Checklist (Figure 12.2) gives you and your management team the questions you should be asking and worrying about. Print them out. Keep them handy. And worry "Am I going to bet my company that I got them right?"

Pivot or Proceed: Validate Your Business Model

It's been a long road but you've converted most of your business model hypotheses from customer discovery into facts. You've done so by extensive testing through face-to-face customer interactions. So, if the customer-relationships hypothesis said one of every five acquired customers will activate and pay for the service or app, this actually happened in validation, with hundreds if not thousands of customers. Or you've proven that people return to the product or app three times a week for an average of 20 minutes per visit or spend $100 a month visiting once.

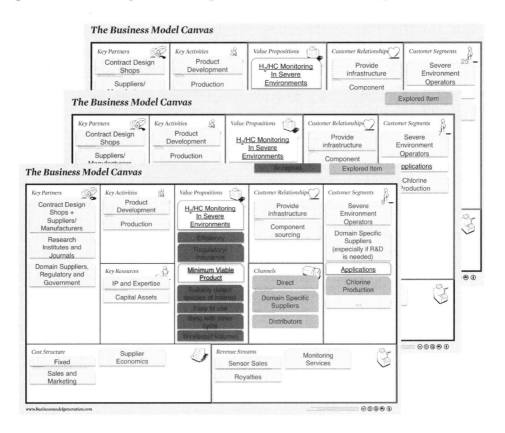

Review Business Model Hypotheses (Figure 12.1)

The team should assemble data collected in the last phase in its "war room" use the checklist to walk through the business model hypotheses, box by box, and ascertain that there are factual, definitive answers to at least every question on the checklist.

In this final phase of customer validation the company asks itself the same questions it asked in Phase 4 of customer discovery. But at this point, it should have much more quantitative, irrefutable proof of the answers, since you've spoken to far more customers and conducted many more tests.

⇨ Web/mobile startups have a unique set of business model hypotheses that they need to validate, particularly in the "Get/Keep/Grow" Customer Relationships area. These questions include:

- Has the company proven it can acquire and activate a steadily-increasing number of customers at a cost in line with the cost structure?
- Are the customers being acquired demonstrating that they will spend and "stick" with the company at rates that will deliver the revenue plan?
- And are customers referring other good quality customers in sufficient numbers to deliver these often-free new customers, reducing the average acquisition cost?
- In multi-sided markets, are customers visiting often enough, participating actively enough, and staying active long enough to help the company generate the revenues it needs to succeed?

The Business Model Canvas as a Scorecard

Hopefully you've been taking regular snapshots of your business model canvas — either week-by-week snapshots, or at least at each major pivot. If you've done it this way you now essentially have a film strip of the entrepreneurial process.

As you can see from Figure 12.1, each stage of discovery and validation refined the canvas. Experiments were run, learning caused iterations and a few pivots, and all were documented in a new canvas (reread page 63 for tips).

Now that you have your canvases up on the wall use them as a point of discussion.

The answers to "Is this a business?" can be found in the results of the multitude of tests you've conducted throughout the validation process.

The answers to "Is this a business?" can be found in the results of the multitude of tests you've conducted throughout the validation process. As is often the case, when the results aren't convincing enough, or when they don't deliver the traffic or financial targets of the business model, it's time to iterate or pivot, and retest to see if the new approach improves the results. After all, the company will very shortly be spending millions of dollars in the customer creation phase, where results are expected to be far more predictable, and much more is at risk. While this may seem ambitious and unreasonable, the closer a company is to this "fact-based plan," the greater its chances for business and fund-raising success.

Business Model Checklist

√ **Value Proposition:**
- Are customers passionate about long-term product vision? Cannot be translated to be quantified revenue projections?
- Do the product features and benefits still make sense? Can they be built within the development budget and timetable?
- Did Customer Validation interviews validate the Value Proposition components?

√ **Customer Segments:**
- Are the Customer Segments tested and proven can they map?
- Are customer needs active or urgent? Can they drive forecasted revenues?
- Does the product improve a "day in the life"?
- Does the company understand the customer purchase influences and associated costs?

√ **Value Proposition 2: Market Type**
- Did customer feedback confirm the Market Type hypothesis?
- Are the cost impacts of the Market Type selection factored in where appropriate?
- Is the team confident its Market Type selection will deliver the forecasted customers?

√ **Channels:**
- Does the company fully understand the food chain, its responsibilities and costs?
- Does the team have confidence in its channel revenue forecasts roadmap?
- Are there any important indirect channel costs such as sales reps or promotional fees?
- Are the channel partners willing to buy?

√ **Customer Relationships:**
- Are "get" plan elements aligned with schedules?
- Are the test plans for Get/Keep/Grow complete with schedules and budgets?
- Are "get" customers costs affordable?
- If a multi-sided markets, have the "get" costs been computed for both sets of customers?

√ **Cost Structure:**
- Are all the core company operating and overhead costs (payroll, benefits, rent, legal, overhead) clearly identified?
- Are all the product development and manufacturing costs calculated?
- What "corporate" costs (legal, accounting, pr, taxes) are forecast?

√ **Revenue Stream:**
- Has the company sized its market opportunity?
- Has the pricing model volume, demand, purchase frequency and other revenue variables been confirmed?
- Does the forecast indicate an increasingly scalable, increasingly profitable business?
- Has the team considered the revenue impact of competitive response to the product?

Business Model Checklist *(Figure 12.2)*

Pivot or Proceed: Validate the Financial Model

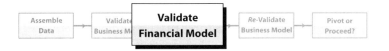

This step answers one key question: do all the tests point to a scalable, sizable business? And can it happen before the company runs out of money?

In this step, you'll figure out whether you have a potentially thriving business, a hobby, or a tax loss.

Answering the question doesn't require pounds of Excel spreadsheets or 50-item budgets. It relies more on the facts you've developed by testing your original hypotheses with the only people who have the answers, your customers, and with a short list of numbers, the *metrics that matter*.

A mere handful of numbers define the difference between a scalable, profitable business and a failure.

A mere handful of numbers define the difference between a scalable, profitable business and a failure. Successful entrepreneurs will be able to recite, adjust, and recompute this handful or so of key numbers about customers, product costs, and revenue growth while they sleep. Meanwhile, they're always focused on the two metrics that matter most: how many months' worth of cash remain in the bank? And how fast are we burning through what's left?

We guarantee that this different approach to finance will get you thrown out of just about every business school in the country, but it's all that's needed at this stage to determine whether your business model passes the validation test and is ready to move on from validation to scale in customer creation.

Metrics that Matter

Since page 1 of this book you've been using the business model canvas to organize your testing. In this section we're going to use the canvas to organize your financial model. This is a radically different approach compared to more typical use of 5-year revenue forecast spreadsheets. Think of it as bringing your "report card" home to Mom and Dad—hopefully, a report card full of A's and A+'s, since B and C responses do not a great company make. Some elements of the business model represent revenue or costs, while others fuel growth. Physical and web/mobile channel costs vary widely, as do rates of sale and growth, so one last time we'll examine the metrics three different ways:

In a physical channel, less than a dozen numbers usually tell the entire story:

- *Value proposition*: What are product cost, market size, attainable market share, and customer impact of network effects?
- *Customer Relationships*: What are customer acquisition costs, prospect conversion rates, customer lifetime value, and customer switching costs that the company may have to pay?
- *Market Type:* As discussed in Chapter 3 (page 39), different market types drive different revenue curves to consider in longer-term revenue predictions
- *Cost Structure*: What are the basic operating costs of the business?
- *Channel*: What are the costs of selling through the channel? Channel margin, promotion, shelf-space charges?
- *Revenue Streams*: What are the average selling price, total achievable revenue, and number of customers a year?
- *Burn Rate* (derived from the above): How much cash is the company "burning" (spending) a month? When will the company run out of cash? There's no precise formula for what a burn rate should be, but since it's the issue over which boards most often fire their founders, the founders and investors must agree on what the burn rate should be and how many more pivots the startup can afford in its search for the scalable, profitable business model

⇨ In the web/mobile channel, less than a dozen numbers tell the entire story:

- *Value proposition*: What is the estimated per-user cost of a user, and are there any incremental costs when one's added. Estimate the market size, attainable market share, and the customer impact of referrals or network effects

- *Customer Relationships*: What are customer acquisition costs, prospect conversion and retention rates, and how many new customers or users will your current customers get you virally, for free?

- *Market Type:* As discussed in Chapter 3 (page 39), different market types drive different revenue curves to consider in longer-term revenue predictions

- *Cost Structure*: What are the basic operating costs of the business? (Be sure not to mingle or double-count these costs with your value proposition costs)

- *Channel*: What are the costs of selling through the channel: payments to app stores, marketplace sites like Amazon.com, or related sites referring customers to you?

- *Revenue Streams*: What are the average selling price, total achievable revenue, and number of customers a year, and how long or how often will customers spend?

- *Burn Rate* (derived from the above): How much cash is the company "burning" (spending) a month? When will the company run out of cash?

A Few Words about Burn Rate

Venture capitalist Fred Wilson suggests some burn-rate guidelines for venture funded web/mobile businesses that may be helpful to entrepreneurs of all stripes. Wilson's advice looks at burn rate based on the company's growth stage.

- *Customer discovery,* which he calls the "building product" stage, should keep the burn rate between $50,000 and $75,000 a month, which should fund a team of three or four engineers building the MVP as well as the founding team, rent, operating costs and the like
- *Customer validation,* Wilson's "building usage" stage, shouldn't exceed a burn rate of $100,000 a month. This stage begins when product/market fit is achieved and fuels the "get customers" and MVP iteration discussed in this chapter
- *Customer creation,* Wilson's "building the business" stage, should ideally hold the burn rate to $250,000 a month as the company builds a team, expands marketing activities, and starts generating material revenues

These are guidelines, and there are zillions of exceptions.

Assemble all your test results to provide a forecast for the coming year, which begins on Day One of Step 3 of Customer Development, the customer creation process.

We doubt there have been many startups where the year-one financial results of customer creation matched the "metrics that matter." But any VC, uncle or rich neighbor is going to want to know why you think an investment in your startup will deliver startup-size returns. If at the end of this step the numbers are ugly—yup, you guessed it—turn back to the beginning of discovery, or at least customer validation, and start revising and retesting your hypotheses.

Three things to consider before you dive into Metrics That Matter:

- Use the time frames that make the most sense for your startup. Generally, the longer the physical-channel sales cycle (think enterprise software), the longer the "space" between calculations should be. Here we used a quarter-by-quarter forecast

- An analysis like this can—and should—often stop the pivot–or-proceed process in its tracks if the computation forecasts that the company will either run out of money within the year or won't be able to raise enough funds to survive the first year of customer creation

- Don't be in a hurry at this critical step. As an entrepreneur, if you take a pile of money to move forward here and fail, it will at least cost you a significant portion of your founders' equity, and it will often cost you your job

Metrics that Matter Scenarios

Metrics matters are a radically new approach to startup math. They're best illustrated with a series of examples. The three spreadsheet scenarios on the next pages illustrate how you can use "Metrics that Matter" to evaluate your business. The three examples are:

- a physical product sold in a physical channel
- a web/mobile product sold in the web/mobile channel
- and a multisided web/mobile market

Metrics that Matter: Example 1
"EZ Gardener" in a Physical Channel

Let's take a look at Table 12.1 what the metrics that matter for a physical channel would look like in spreadsheet form.

Here's a simple example of a rough quarter-by-quarter cash-burn computation for our hypothetical $30 (suggested retail) EZ Gardener all-in-one gardening-tool set, sold in garden stores and by mass merchants. Our timing is the coming year. (The spreadsheet starts Day One of the customer creation process.)

EZ Gardner (Physical Channel) MARKET TYPE: Resegmenting Existing Market/Niche						
Category	q1	q2	q3	q4	TOTAL	YEAR TWO
1 total number units sold	15,000	18,000	27,000	48,000	108,000	180,000
2 average retail selling price	30	30	30	30		25
3 GROSS SALES: chain/ garden/distributors	450,000	540,000	810,000	1,440,000	3,240,000	4,500,000
4 (less) channel discount (40%)	-180,000	-216,000	-324,000	-576,000	-1,296,000	-1,800,000
5 (less) other channel costs	-90,000	-90,000	-120,000	-150,000	-450,000	-300,000
6 NET COMPANY REVENUE STREAM	180,000	234,000	366,000	714,000	1,494,000	2,400,000
7 (less) sales costs: reps, tradeshows	-120,000	-120,000	-150,000	-180,000	-570,000	-600,000
8 (less) product costs (COGS)	-52,000	-63,000	-94,500	-168,000	-378,000	-540,000
9 (less) current operating costs	-120,000	-120,000	-120,000	-180,000	-540,000	-720,000
10 CASH BURN for period	-112,000	-69,000	1,500	186,000	6,500	540,000
11 cash remaining/ end of quarter	388,000	319,000	330,500	516,500	516,500	1,056,500

"Metrics That Matter": Physical Channel Model *(Table 12.1)*

Note: the leftmost numbers refer to commentary in descriptive text that follows.

A few things about the hypothetical business factored into the numbers above:

- This "friends and family" funded venture begins customer creation with $500,000 in the bank. Like most physical-channel marketers, EZ Gardener also promotes online. But they read this book, followed directions, and are "getting the most important channel right first," so they're not selling product online yet

- In year two, as the product's newness wears off, the price drops.

- Product development was completed earlier offshore, so there are no more development costs until we see how this product sells

- Revenue never scales dramatically, since the market type is "re-segmenting/ niche market"

What Metrics Matter?

There are 11 metrics that matter in this spreadsheet. Following the left-hand column of the spreadsheet, let's explore the origin of each number as well as its source a little more closely:

1. **Total number of units sold:** This number is estimated (ideally by quarter) from customer validation report cards used with buyers and channel partners. Compare these numbers with your estimates of total addressable (or if known, serviceable) market and your market share estimates (see page 71). Use the two sets of numbers to estimate the number of units to be sold in each quarter. If customers make multiple purchases within a year, factor it in.

2. **Average retail selling price:** How much the consumer will pay, on average, for the product. This number, developed in the value proposition hypothesis, should be validated in the competitive analysis and throughout customer and channel validation conversations. It's shown here as the price per unit and is often the average selling price, since retail pricing may vary by channel.

3. **Gross sales across all channels:** Total retail-dollar sales for the product per quarter. Relatively straightforward to compute, since the company is using only one sales channel. Remember to consider "guaranteed sale" situations where retailers can return unsold merchandise for full credit.

4. **(Less) channel discount (40%):** What percentage of the product's retail price will the channel take as its cost of sales? Deduct it from the retail price and apply it to all channel revenue as computed in No. 3. We've assumed a fairly typical chain-store margin here. This revenue will never reach the company's coffers, so deduct it now to get to net company revenue.

Channels are notorious for charging suppliers for advertising, promotion, and shelf space.

5. **(Less) other channel costs:** Channels are notorious for charging suppliers for advertising, promotion, and even shelf space. There may also be costs of independent sales reps or brokers who "sell in" merchandise to the channel. In the first year, the company may want to, or be forced to, purchase special promotions in order to get shelf space in an important retail channel. Estimate these costs based on channel-partner discussions.

6. **NET COMPANY REVENUE:** The net channel revenue (No. 6) is the Gross Sales (No. 3) minus the channel discount (No. 4) and other channel cost (No.5).

7. **(Less) sales costs (reps, trade shows):** How much does it cost the team to reach the garden product channel cost? In addition to specific customer acquisition costs, the company will spend money on a sales force, sales and marketing materials, attendance at trade shows and more. These costs should be identified in the customer-relationships box and perhaps also in the cost structure box.

8. **(Less) product costs:** What does it cost to build and make the product? Developed primarily from the value proposition and cost structure boxes, this is an estimate combining two sets of costs:

    - in this example the cost of developing the product is fully paid for
    - the manufacturing cost of the physical product itself

9. **(Less) current operating costs:** Compute the costs of "turning on the lights" at the company every day, which should be a relatively static number: meager founder salaries, other payroll, rent, equipment, utilities, legal, and the like. This number usually shifts the least, so worry about it less than others. The spreadsheet increases it modestly late in the year and in the second year, as is typical.

10. **CASH BURN FOR PERIOD:** Did we make or lose money this quarter? How much? Start with the net company revenue (No. 6) and subtract all the costs beneath it, Nos. 7, 8, and 9. The result of that equation is the "cash burn," or the reduction in the company's bank account each quarter. In the example above, the company is losing money, or "burning cash," until the fourth quarter, when customer growth and reduced product-development costs improve the company's cash flow quite dramatically.

11. **CASH REMAINING:** Start by counting the money in the bank on Day One of the quarter. Our hypothetical company began its first year of customer creation with $500,000 in the bank. Reduce it by the quarter's cash burn to determine how much will be left at quarter's end.

If These Were Your Numbers, What's a Founder to Do?

This is a "nice little business," and while it will make a lovely living for its founders and a nice return for its investors, it's hardly a scalable business like the many heroes of Silicon Valley. But even though this company is returning as much pretax profit in year two as it had in the bank on day one of year one, it's basically going nowhere fast. It's a one-product company, and the only way it got strong revenue growth was by reducing its retail price—never a good sign.

Some things the founders and board should really be discussing:

- Are there any potential dramatic changes to the business model that can have significant impact on the company's future growth prospects?
- What about overseas markets? Are they a growth opportunity?
- How can the company capitalize on its one modest success. Are they building a brand enough, and creative enough, to perhaps launch other products

both in and beyond the garden area. They might start with "EZWeeder" and "EZhoe" first, and perhaps expand to "EZgrass" or "EZflowers" to take maximum advantage of their brand, credibility and channel relationships to scale the company broader and faster?

- Can they extend beyond the garden, maybe adding "EZcooker" or "EZcleaner" or "EZcleanup" perhaps? Regardless of the new products, the company would need to spend some serious product development dollars and spend heavily on marketing (especially if moving beyond the garden) with no assurances of further success. (They actually need to develop a whole new set of hypotheses)

- Unless the company invests in new product development, this business is more of a hobby than a scalable business

Hold these thoughts—and others—for the final section of this phase, the pivot-or-proceed discussion. Next, look at the second of three business models for a software product sold in the web and mobile channels.

Metrics that Matter: Example 2

Expense Reporter Sold via Web/mobile Channels

⇨ Let's take a look at Table 12.2, another $30 retail product, downloadable XpensePro software, sold through the web/mobile channels only.

Expense Reporter (Web/Mobile) MARKET TYPE: Resegmenting Existing Market/Niche						
Category	q1	q2	q3	q4	TOTAL	YEAR TWO
1 DIRECT unit sales (web)	4,000	5,000	6,000	8,000	23,000	28,750
2 gross direct revenue (@ $30 each)	120,000	150,000	180,000	240,000	690,000	862,500
3 (less) customer acquisition cost $6	-24,000	-30,000	-36,000	-48,000	-138,000	-172,500
4 NET Web Revenue Total	96,000	120,000	144,000	192,000	552,000	690,000
5 DIRECT sales/ mobile (units)	2,000	2,500	3,000	3,500	11,000	13,000
6 gross revenue mobile unit sales	60,000	75,000	90,000	105,000	330,000	390,000
7 (less) referral incentive @ $4 each	-8,000	-10,000	-12,000	-14,000	-44,000	-52,000
8 NET direct mobile revenue total	52,000	65,000	78,000	91,000	286,000	338,000
9 CHANNEL appstore sales (units)	8,000	12,000	16,000	24,000	60,000	90,000
10 gross revenue (@ $30 each)	240,000	360,000	480,000	720,000	1,800,000	2,700,000
11 (less) market/ appstore 30% fee $9	-72,000	-108,000	-144,000	-216,000	-540,000	-810,000
12 Total NET APPSTORE revenue	168,000	252,000	336,000	504,000	1,260,000	1,890,000
13 TOTAL revenue all channels	316,000	437,000	558,000	787,000	2,098,000	2,918,000
14 (less) product/ prod dev costs	-400,000	-300,000	-200,000	-150,000	-1,050,000	-480,000
15 (less) current operating costs	-150,000	-150,000	-150,000	-150,000	-600,000	-720,000
16 CASH BURN for period	-234,000	-13,000	208,000	487,000	448,000	1,718,000
17 cash remaining/ end of quarter	64,000	51,000*	259,000	746,000	746,000	2,464,000

*dangerously low!

"Metrics That Matter": Web/Mobile Sales Model (Table 12.2)

Note: the leftmost numbers refer to commentary in descriptive text that follows.

In this scenario, our hypothetical company is selling XpensePro only as a web or mobile app download directly from its website and via app stores. As in the previous example, things are factored into the numbers above:

- Product-development cost is heavy at first and then declines.
- Incremental product unit costs are practically zero, since the product is a download
- Revenue never scales dramatically, since the market type is "re-segmenting/niche market," but the year-to-year revenue increases are significant enough to promise downstream success
- This angel-funded business starts with $300,000 cash remaining. More money will be hard to get

What Metrics Matter?

There are five metrics that matter in this spreadsheet:

- Revenue comes from three channels
    - Direct revenue from web sales, net of acquisition cost
    - Direct mobile sales revenues, after subtracting referral incentives
    - Revenue from the appstore channel, after subtracting channel fees and marketing costs
- Cash burned or made during the period
- Cash remaining at the end of the quarter

Because the business is operating in three distinct channels, each of which operates differently, it takes 17 different numbers to create the above five metrics, but the board just needs to focus on five rather than 17. If one's ever out of whack or way off budget, drill down into the supporting details numbers that make that number up: unit sales, gross direct revenue, cost of customers or sales, and net revenue from the channel.

Following the left-hand column of the spreadsheet, let's explore the origin of each number and its source:

Web Sales:

1. **Direct web unit sales:** How many web apps are downloaded from the company's site. Customers are unlikely to make multiple purchases within a year.

2. **Gross direct revenue:** Multiply the number of units (No. 1) by the average selling price of $30.

3. **(Less) customer acquisition cost:** The cost to make a sale over the web On average, $6 worth of AdWords, incentives, e-mail and the like to acquire one customer. Multiply $6 by the number of solid units (No. 1).

4. **Net web revenue total:** Subtract the customer acquisition cost (No. 3) from the gross direct revenue from website sales (No. 2).

5. **Direct mobile unit sales:** A few customers will find and download the app's mobile version at the company website (most will find it at the app stores). Calculate the quarterly units using the process described in EZ Gardner metric #1 on page 443.

On the surface, this looks like a really lovely business.

---

6. **Gross revenue/direct mobile units:** Multiply the number of mobile units sold directly to customers (No. 5) by $30, the average selling price.

7. **(Less) referral incentive:** The customer-relationships hypothesis indicates that a third of the company's direct sales will come from referrals by happy customers encouraged by a $4 incentive. Take 1/3 of the direct-sales web (No. 1) and mobile (No. 5) units and multiply by $4.

8. **DIRECT mobile revenue total:** How much cash winds up in the company's bank from this channel? Multiply units (No. 5) by revenue/unit (No. 6) and then subtract the referral incentive (No. 7) to find the answer.

9. **CHANNEL app-store sales (units):** Calculate units using the channel method outlined in EZ Gardner unit sales #3, page 442.

10. **CHANNEL gross revenue:** multiply the channel units sold (No. 9) by the retail price of $30.

11. **(Less) market/app-store 30% fee:** Every download sold will cost the company an app store fee of 30 percent, or $9. Multiply units (No. 9) by $9.00 and subtract it from channel revenue (No. 10).

12. **TOTAL NET APPSTORE revenue:** Subtract the app-store fee (No. 11) from channel revenue (No. 10) to find the amount of cash that will wind up in the company's bank from app-store sales.

13. **TOTAL NET revenue (all channels):** Add three revenue numbers— No. 4 (direct web revenue), No. 8 (direct mobile revenue), and No. 12 (net channel revenue)—to compute the company's net sales.

14. **(Less) product/product-development costs:** What does it cost to build and make the product? Compute your ongoing product development costs, plus download and bandwidth charges. There's no physical cost of the product itself.

15. **(Less) current operating costs:** Compute the costs of turning on the lights at the company every day, as in Example 1, line 9, page 444.

16. **CASH BURN FOR PERIOD:** Did we make or lose money this quarter? How much? Follow the process for calculating cash burn outlined in Spreadsheet 1, line 10.

17. **CASH REMAINING:** Follow the process in Spreadsheet 1, No. 11.

If These Were Your Numbers, What's a Founder to Do?

On the surface, this looks like a really lovely business. It plans to generate $746,000 in positive cash flow in its first year of customer creation, and to roughly triple that cashflow in its second year. But can a business doing

$2.5-million in revenue after four years really make investors and founders happy? That's not for us to decide, and the numbers don't tell us whether they spent $500,000 and a year—or $5,000,000 and five years—to get to the start of the spreadsheet, so it's hard to applaud or bash the outcome.

Seems like the next board meeting should pull out the latest business model canvas and look for some game-changing growth opportunities, almost no matter what. The company isn't spending all that much money on product development or staff costs (those numbers are relatively flat), and it's almost turning into a cash cow long before it should be turned out to pasture.

After all, almost any business that can get almost 100,000 new customers in a year should be trying to figure out how to either add a zero to that number in a year or two, or at least double it, perhaps, in the second year. The company's year two plan seems unambitious at first glance, even though the profits double.

Meanwhile, on the downside:

- The $4 incentive (No. 7) might deliver too few sales and need to be beefed up, changing net revenues adversely
- App-store (No.12) approval process could delay launch in the biggest channel, hurting revenues
- More staff (No. 15) might be needed for support, channel relations, or who-knows-what
- Mobile sales direct to consumers (No. 5) could be a total flop, hurting that revenue

Even though the numbers look pretty good in the spreadsheet, hold the high-fives and look at ways to improve them anyway. After all, they're still estimates based on customer validation proof—they're not money in the bank by any means. Review the "what's a founder to do" section under Spreadsheet 1 to explore ways to reduce the cash burn where it makes sense. Hold all these thoughts—and others—for the final section of this phase, the pivot-or-proceed discussion.

Expense Reporter (Web/Mobile) MARKET TYPE: Resegmenting Existing Market/Niche						
Category	q1	q2	q3	q4	TOTAL	YEAR TWO
1 New activated users	300,000	400,000	600,000	750,000	2,050,000	3,000,000
2 New user acquisition cost @ $3 each*	900,000	1,200,000	1,800,000	2,250,000	6,150,000	6,000,000
3 Total active users**	300,000	700,000	1,300,000	2,050,000	2,050,000	5,000,000
4 Average page views /user/quarter	60	66	72	80		100
5 TOTAL PAGE VIEWS per quarter	18 million	46 million	93 million	164 million	321.8 million	500 million
6 (less) page view attrition @ <+/- 7%/quarter	n/a	-3,260,000	-6,420,000	-12.3 million	-22,780,000	-60,000,000
7 **TOTAL CPM's (000's of pages) to sell**	**18,000**	**42,740**	**86,580**	**151,700**	**299,020**	**440,000**
8 Average $2.50 CPM x4 ads per page	10	20	24	30		36
9 **TOTAL advertising revenue**	**180,000**	**854,700**	**2,077,920**	**4,551,000**	**7,663,620**	**15,840,000**
10 email list rental revenue	0	14,000	78,000	164,000	256,000	2,000,000
11 **TOTAL revenue**	**180,000**	**868,700**	**2,155,920**	**4,715,000**	**7,919,620**	**17,840,000**
12 (less) user acquisition cost	-900,000	-1,200,000	-1,800,000	-2,250,000	-6,150,000	-6,000,000
13 (less) product /prod dev costs	-2,000,000	-1,500,000	-1,20,0000	-600,000	-5,300,000	-3,600,000
14 (less) current operating costs	-1,200,000	-1,200,000	-1,200,000	-1,500,000	-5,100,000	-6,000,000
15 **CASH BURN for period**	**-3,920,000**	**-3,031,300**	**-2,044,080**	**365,000**	**-8,630,380**	**2,240,000**
16 cash remaining /end of quarter	6,080,000	3,048,700	1,004,620	1,369,620	1,369,620	**$3,609,620!**
*acquisition cost declines $1.00 in year two ** some users have departed						

"Metrics That Matter": Multi-sided/Ad-Supported Model *(Table 12.3)*
Note: the leftmost numbers refer to commentary in descriptive text that follows.

Metrics that Matter: Example 3

A Multi-sided Market Example

Here's a third way to look at a totally different business model *for the exact same product,* XPensePro software. Let's explore a multi-sided market, where the product is identical but it's *absolutely free to users.* Advertisers eager to reach businesspeople with active expense accounts will pay to reach the audience, and company revenues come from advertising and sales of e-mail lists, the other "side" in this multi-sided market example.

A multi-sided market, where the product is identical but it's absolutely free to users.

In this scenario, our venture-backed multi-sided market company is offering its products to users for free, provided that they agree to receive two e-mails per week from advertisers. The product is a digital download, but considerable resources are expended selling ads to the other side of the market. (It's interesting to note how dissimilar these metrics that matter are when compared with the other two business models.) As in the previous example, several things are factored into the numbers above:

- Our VC-backed example has a $10-million war chest
- Product-development cost is heavy at first and then declines
- Product costs are practically zero, since the "product" is a download.
- Revenue never scales dramatically, since the market type is "re-segmenting/niche market," but the year-to-year revenue increases are significant enough to promise downstream success
- Much of the cost of advertising and e-mail sales is factored into the revenue numbers, which are net of network or rep commission costs
- It still costs real money to acquire users through PR, e-mail, and other activities, even for a free product. As the company iterates and becomes smarter, its acquisition cost declines in the second year

Metrics that Matter/Add It All Up

There are 16 "metrics that matter" in this spreadsheet because we need to monitor revenue and costs on both sides of the multi-sided market. (The company pivoted and eliminated cash sales of its product in this scenario.) Following the left-hand column of the spreadsheet, let's explore the origin of each number as well as its source a little more closely:

1. **New activated users :** How many people will download the free app and begin actively using it. *Active* is defined as generating at least the average number of page views (No. 4).

2. **New user acquisition cost @ $3:** On average, the customer acquisition costs to generate one active user (No. 1). Some will come virally for free, others will cost $6 or more.

3. **Total active users:** Average active monthly users during the quarter.

4. **Average page views per user per quarter:** Actual user clicks on the site will generate this number by dividing the number of active users (No. 3) into total page views (No. 5). This is an important measure of the business health and growth.

5. **Total page views per quarter:** Multiply the total users (No. 3) by the average page views per user (No. 4) to begin to understand available advertising-sales opportunities for the period.

6. **Less attrition:** Lots of users abandon things they download but don't have to pay for, so watching this number (generated by instrumentation) is important. We've defined attrition as a user who hasn't generated a page view a week for two consecutive months.

7. **TOTAL CPMs to sell:** subtract attrition (No. 6) from total page views (No. 5) and divide by 1,000 for the "salable CPMs" needed (ad sales are based on cost per thousand, or CPM). The +/- 7% average gets worse in year two as more competitors emerge.

8. **Average CPM x 4 ads/page:** Competitive analysis and "buy-side" customer validation research will determine what CPM advertisers are willing to pay to reach this audience. Assuming four ads on each page, multiply the average CPM by 4 to compute the average revenue per 1,000 pages viewed. In this example, we've already deducted the cost of sales, whether it's commissions for sales reps or network ad sales. *The CPM increases (Q3-4) as the site gets more attractive to advertisers.*

9. **TOTAL ADVERTISING REVENUE:** multiply the number of M's (No. 7) or total CPMs available for sale by the 4x average CPM (No. 8) to compute advertising revenue. The figure grows dramatically as the number of users and their site traffic rise.

The business model looks so strong and compelling...

---

10. **E-mail-list rental revenue:** An estimate based on competitive analysis and buy-side customer validation research. This starts out small and at very low rates (per thousand) and, both CPM and volume build as the audience becomes large enough to be attractive to advertisers.

11. **TOTAL REVENUE:** This ad-supported multi-sided marketer has only two sources of revenue. Add the advertising revenue (No. 9) to the e-mail-list rental revenue (No. 10).

12. **(Less) user acquisition cost:** Subtract the number from Line 2 here.

13. **(Less) product/product-development cost:** Computed from customer validation and cost structure boxes of the business model. While this declines later in the first year as the initial product matures, the budget increases in the second year to add features that will help the company continue attracting new customers.

14. **(Less) current operating costs:** Compute the costs of turning on the lights at the company every day, as the EZ Gardner example, line 9 on page 442.

15. **CASH BURN per period:** Subtract the three cost centers (Nos. 12, 13 and 14) from the total revenue (No. 11) to compute the quarterly cash burn.

16. **Cash remaining/end of quarter:** Subtract the cash burned (or collected) during the quarter from the checkbook balance as of the first day of the quarter to calculate the cash remaining at quarter's end. This number becomes attractive rather quickly in this model.

If These Were Your Numbers, What's a founder to do?

There's an old rule in startups that a spreadsheet is worth 48.5x the paper it's printed on. But if this spreadsheet set of "metrics that matter," is anywhere close to accurate, our founders and investors at Expensereporter may indeed have a homerun on their hands.

In this case, the business model looks so strong and compelling that the founders have two clear priorities. Job #1 is to play strong defense, and make certain that they deliver on all the key numbers in the plan (which, as you recall, are already turned into immutable facts through two grueling stages of Customer Development). That process starts with a step-by-step revalidation of every single number on the page, to be sure there are no mistakes. Next step: a detailed "worst case" analysis.

As every business should, the founding team here should expand this one set of metrics into three: a worst case and a high case, on both sides of the hypothetical set of metrics shown here. And since the business is totally dependent on advertising revenue, they should quickly return to their channel validation efforts and probe further to make sure they're as valid as everyone believes. They should also focus on reducing user attrition.

With all that accomplished, review the analyses from Spreadsheets 1 and 2 about reducing costs and optimizing activation and revenue. Then, just in case, put a case of great French Champagne in the office fridge!

Some Final Thoughts About the Financial Model

Market Type Affects Revenue Streams. Each of the four market types has a distinctive sales-growth curve shaped by the degree of difficulty involved in transitioning from sales to the earlyvangelists to sales to mainstream customers. Obviously in new markets, it typically takes considerable time for the product to catch on beyond earlyvangelists, who aren't typically high-volume mainstream buyers. So success with early sales doesn't guarantee fast revenue scaling.

The sales-growth curves for a new market and an existing market graphically illustrate the difference. Even after finding and successfully selling to earlyvangelists, the rate of sales differs in later years because of the different adoption rates of mainstream customers.

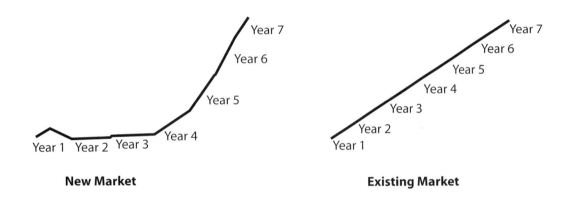

New Market   **Existing Market**

Revenue Growth in New and Existing Markets (Figure 12.3)

Estimating revenue in an existing market is relatively simple: Look at the incumbents and calculate the increasing percentage of market share the startup will grab each year.

Estimating a new market's size might seem impossible, since it doesn't exist yet. What to do? Estimate the opportunity based on proxies and adjacent markets. See if there are any comparable companies. Have others grown as fast as the estimate? Why will this startup perform similarly?

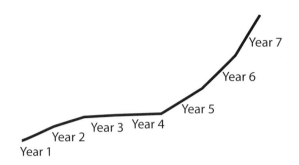

Revenue Growth in a Resegmented Market *(Figure 12.4)*

The sales curve in a re-segmented market is somewhat easier to estimate. It's generally similar to that of a new market in that it takes time to gather a head of steam. There are three steps to assessing a re-segmented market: assess the size of the existing market, figure out how large your startup's "segment" is, and calculate the adoption rate, or the time it will take for that segment to recognize the new product as the solution of choice. Count only the segment that will switch, and beware of long-term contracts, service contracts, and "sunk costs" such as training and installation, all of which are often "lock-ins" or hidden barriers to switching.

Revenue growth curves depend on Market Type!

Demand Curve Affects Revenue: The "demand curve" seeks the optimum intersection between sales volume and net profit. For example, if a physical product is most efficiently manufactured in lot sizes of 5,000, can that inventory be sold in a reasonable time when current unit sales are 50 a month? A startup selling new electric cars for $29,000 will generate massive demand. But if they cost $45,000 to manufacture, the company will go bankrupt very quickly. Consider:

- the actual price per unit, for multiples, and for subscriptions
- how pricing can be used to attract more users

- how pricing can create larger or more frequent purchases by the same user; volume discounts, free shipping, loyalty points and similar pricing mechanisms are used for what's typically called "market basket" optimization
- how pricing can be used to enhance profitability or volume
- how the company can forward-price the product to intersect the economies-of-scale curve (as in, "If we could build 10,000 at a time, our production cost drops 32 percent")

When to Bring in the Accountants

Eventually, prospective investors, banks, and others will want to see the traditional P&L, forecast, and more, and that's fine. Once the metrics that matter are firmly understood to make sound business sense *and are validated,* almost any finance type (or high school math student) can convert them into a VC-ready multiyear P&L spreadsheet, balance sheet, and cash-flow statement (the "usual stuff" everyone is accustomed to seeing) with ease.

On rare and welcome occasions, metrics that matter actually don't matter at all. If customer acquisition and activation are proceeding at warp speed month after month or the economy is hot, investors may ignore most of the other metrics, throw caution to the wind, and vote to scale the company rapidly. This seldom happens, but we hope it happens to you. It can happen more often in frothy vertical markets, as it did in social networking and other multi-sided markets or strong IPO markets. But nine times out of 10, the metrics that matter do matter quite a bit when it comes time to spend serious investor dollars.

Adding it all up

This phase is a vital make-or-break analysis of how well the business model should work. But remember that the numbers are still only educated guesses, validated—we hope—through extensive customer discovery and validation effort with scores if not hundreds of customers.

Pivot or Proceed: *Re*-Validate the Business Model

It's the perfect time to take one last look at the key business model components, for several reasons. In a few days, a great deal will change if the vote is "go forward" to the customer creation step. Customer creation is a radically different stage during which the company suddenly shifts from "searching for a business model" to "executing one." It's no longer celebrating mistakes and wrong turns. It shifts full-throttle into "execute" mode, with revenue targets and timetables to hit, product and plans to deliver, and more granular and precise accountability to investors and board members.

The company is about to spend a great deal of money far faster, and irrevocably, as it works ambitiously to deliver its chosen business model. With that comes the typical "career risk" for founders, which always prompts investors to ask if the seemingly manic "founder type" should be replaced by a "seasoned" leader with proven execution skills. Massive amounts of money are about to be spent on a single, focused bet that the business model, as developed, has a high likelihood of scaling to profit and success. Boards and investors are suddenly less forgiving and typically far less welcoming of reports like "That idea was wrong" and "That didn't work as we hoped" than they were during the earlier "search" phases.

Long story short, it's time to revisit the core business model elements one last time.

Best Bets

You're almost done. You've run the numbers in the last section and are still feeling like your business is a winner. But have you picked the best value proposition? Is your product delivery schedule right? Are you confident you've gotten the optimum revenue model and costs? And have you missed any best moves on the overall business model? Here are a few last things to check.

Make Sure the Value Proposition is Right

After going through the "metrics that matter" in the last section, are you absolutely convinced you have the right value proposition? You're about to live with it for awhile. If you don't feel that it's going to win the marketplace now, it doesn't get better over time. It may be time to reconfigure, repackage or unbundle the product. This requires a loop all the way back to customer discovery. Once there, use the core technology to develop another product, configuration, distribution method or price and then modify product presentations and return to Phase 3 (product presentation) and do it again. Yes, it hurts, but it hurts far less than failure.

Make Sure the Product Delivery is Right

Even with selling success, check the product delivery timing with the product-development team. Schedules inevitably change, seldom for the better. Can the company still deliver what was just sold and do so as promised, or was the sale actually vaporware? If vaporware, at best the company secured a few pilot projects. Continuing to sell as if nothing has changed is a bad idea. As schedules slip, hard-won earlyvangelists weaken, and references evaporate quickly. The good news is, if this happens (it happens often), the situation is still recoverable. There aren't many people to fire, and the burn rate is low. (As discussed earlier, it's always important to have enough cash to get this phase wrong at least once.) The solution is to shut down any additional selling for a while, admit mistakes, and turn pilot projects into something useful—first for the customer and then as a marketable product.

Make Sure the Revenue is High and Costs are Low

There's nothing worse than leaving money on the table or spending more than you needed to. The best way to answer these questions and more is to "walk" slowly through the business model one more time.

- Start with the value proposition. Are there too many features or not enough variety? Would a lower price sell far more units or sell the same number at a lower acquisition cost? What if the product were free, or free to those bringing three or five or 10 other customers along?

- In the customer-relationships hypothesis, is there rock-solid confidence in the plan, or might a freemium or multi-sided alternative deliver bolder, faster growth? Will that costly AdWords effort deliver the planned result?
- Can a different channel deliver fewer sales and more profit?
- Will partners deliver the revenue growth you need and expect?
- Are there higher level business model patterns you may have missed?

Make Sure Your Business Model is Right

Grab a fresh business model canvas and a pack of Post-it notes. Explore alternatives seriously. The team is about to put a big pile of chips, probably millions, on "red" or "black," as in "pass" or "fail." Is everyone confident the choice is the right one?

Changing direction at this juncture is a bold move indeed. It's not what the investors expected, especially after a long, grueling process of customer discovery and validation. Then again, bold moves are the work of great entrepreneurs. And even though a pivot at this point leads to more customer validation and more time, it's far better to pivot now than to forge ahead at full speed and full spend if it's possible that there's a better idea out there somewhere.

Further validate the business model, not just looking for enhancements in revenue opportunity and places to reduce cost, but looking for "game changers." Can you change a product sold by features into a branded-experience that becomes a "got-to-have-it" fashion? Can you change a revenue model from a unit sale into a network effects model? Look for the non-obvious business patterns. Even if the team is certain the current model is the best way forward, now's the time to bring in your advisory board and have them throw stones (painful as it is) at your canvas. Do they see a huge move that you missed? No doubt the financial model review just completed raised at least a handful of questions and perhaps pointed to some opportunities. Revisit the business model checklist questions. Are any of the answers different? Does the team want to have more money in the bank or spend less? Where can savings be effected or additional dollars efficiently put to good use?

If the team has turned over every possibility in its review, looking both at radical changes and modest improvements in the business model, and confidence still carries the day, it's time to move on to the ultimate question: pivot or proceed?

The Toughest Startup Question: Pivot or Proceed?

This is the moment of truth when the team and the investors will vote on whether to begin spending massive amounts of money to execute the business model. To vote honestly, the team needs to take a hard, honest look at the pivot-or-proceed analyses developed in this phase.

As grueling as the customer validation process is, it's quite likely that the company will require another turn of the wheel before everyone can enthusiastically vote to move forward. Don't despair—this need to pivot arises almost every time, and often calls for a return all the way to customer discovery.

Hubris is the evil twin of a passionate entrepreneur.

The alternative is even more painful. In the past, investors magically assumed flawless execution and fired executives who failed. It's time to reflect, thinking seriously about the company's genuine chances for scalable, profitable success. It's a hard decision, particularly for self-confident entrepreneurs who pride themselves on their tenacity, and problem-solving abilities. "I'm an entrepreneur. I make things happen against all odds" just doesn't cut it when staring at the hard facts and statistics. Don't confuse hubris with passion or facts.

Did validation really convert opinions to facts, or is everyone just moving the goalposts to reach customer creation? The next step seriously cranks up the company's cash burn rate, sharply diminishing if not extinguishing available cash or runway.

Did the product sell well and easily? Is it absolutely, unequivocally clear that when more money is spent to acquire customers, they'll arrive at a steady, predictable, profitable pace? This question in particular probably sends 90 percent of startups back into the depths of Customer Development to refine and retest components of the business model.

If the "ramp" to more customers, revenue and profits isn't proved to be predictable in test results, it's also a reason to pivot. Using everything you learned in customer validation, go back to Phase 1 of this step (get ready to sell) and try it again. Sorry. This isn't easy to do.

If everything checks out (again, it seldom does the first time around), the end of customer validation is a major milestone. Customer problems are understood, a set of earlyvangelists has been found, and the company has delivered a product its customers want to buy, developed a repeatable and scalable sales process, and demonstrated a profitable business model. Hopefully, all the learning is captured in writing and the business model diagram is updated. Fund-raising, while never easy, will be far easier than at this point than it was before.

When you've answered "yes" to that taxing list of questions, you deserve a night off, if not a week. Congratulations! The company is prepared to move full speed ahead to the customer creation process.

⇨ What's Next?

The first two steps of Customer Development are where entrepreneurs live or die in the search for a repeatable and scalable business model. When a company has successfully exited Customer Validation, there's a library full of business-building texts available to help execute the business model. So, at least for now, if you're eager to execute the next two steps—Customer Creation and Company Building—return to the original Four Steps to the Epiphany, or turn to a more targeted text for fine-tuned support.

Whatever you do next, the successful completion of Customer Validation is a momentous step in the life of your startup. You have completed an arduous, challenging journey. Our warmest, most sincere congratulations. We look forward to learning about your success!

The Startup Owner's Manual "Site" Map

STEP ONE: Customer Discovery

Chapter 5:

Chapter 6:

Chapter 7:

STEP TWO: Customer Validation

Checklists

Use these checklists at the completion of each step. They'll help assure that you've completed each of the tasks outlined in each section. Adjust the "to do" lists and tasks as appropriate to your startup's type, goals, and situation.

Board And Management Buy-In All Channels

Goal: Agreement among investors, founders, and team on commitment to the Customer Development process.

Reference: Chapter 2, Manifesto Rule #14
- ☐ Commit to use of Business Model and Market Type.
- ☐ Understand the difference between "search" for a business model and "execute" a business plan
- ☐ Learn differences between Product Development and Customer Development
- ☐ Discuss number of "funded Pivots" available and how board and team will measure company progress

Customer Development process emphasizes learning and discovery
- ☐ Is there board and founding team buy-in for this process?
- ☐ Is there is enough funding for 2 to 3 Pivots in Discovery and Validation?

Discuss Market Type (initial decision)
- ☐ Existing, Resegmented, New or Clone?
- ☐ First pass with board on initial agreement of Market Type
- ☐ First pass with board on different funding needs by Market Type

Agree on Customer Development Time Frame
- ☐ Approximate time for Discovery and Validation
- ☐ Discovery exit criteria determined
- ☐ Validation exit criteria determined

Exit Criteria:
- ☐ Buy-in of the team and board for Customer Development process
- ☐ Market Type and exit criteria for each step

Checklist 1

The Customer Development Team   All Channels

Goal: Set up the Customer Development Team.

Reference: Chapter 2, Manifesto Rule #1

Review the organizational differences between Customer Development and the traditional product introduction process
- ☐ Founders spend time outside the building
- ☐ No VP of Sales or Marketing
- ☐ Initial team responsibilities

Team Setup and Goals
- ☐ Agree on who leads the team
- ☐ Agree on the "getting out of the building" methodology
- ☐ Agree on % of customer feedback online versus eyeball
- ☐ Agree on the team roles for each of the four Customer Development Steps

Enumerate 3 to 5 Core Values of the Founding Team
- ☐ Not a mission statement
- ☐ Not about profit or products
- ☐ Core ideology is about what the company believes in

Exit Criteria:
- ☐ Buy-in of the team and board for a customer development team
- ☐ Are the right people in those jobs?

Checklist 2

Market Size   All Channels

Goal: Estimate the total market opportunity for the company

Reference: Chapter 4, Market Size Hypothesis

Estimated market size:
- [ ] TAM or Total Available Market
- [ ] SAM or Served Available Market
- [ ] Target Market

Estimate current product and follow-on products
- [ ] Appropriate metric for measuring determined
    - [ ] Units/dollars/page views/other measures?
    - [ ] Per member for subscription services/per page view for advertising-supported businesses?
- [ ] Research conducted to "size" the overall market
    - [ ] Read industry analyst reports, market research reports, competitors' press releases, etc.
    - [ ] Talk with investors and customers
- [ ] If assessing an existing or resegmented market, adjacent markets that customers might switch from are considered
    - [ ] Will the startup's product encourage switching?
    - [ ] Only the switchable subset counted (Beware of long-term lock-ins from incumbents)
    - [ ] Growth computed for all customer sources over 3-5 years
- [ ] If assessing a new market, the opportunities are estimated based on proxies and adjacent markets
    - [ ] Are there comparable companies?
    - [ ] Have others grown as fast as the estimate?
    - [ ] Why will this company perform similarly?

Exit criteria:
- [ ] Written sense of market size, estimate of how much the company can capture
- [ ] **Pass/Fail tests identified**   Checklist 3

Product Vision   All Channels

Goal: Team agreement on the long-term vision and 18-month schedule

Reference: Chapter 4, Value Proposition Hypotheses/Product Vision

Vision
- ☐ What's your long-term vision for your company?
- ☐ What do you ultimately want to change or solve?
- ☐ Are you going to do it with a series of products?
- ☐ How do you expand into adjacent markets?
- ☐ Do you need to get people to change their behavior?
- ☐ What will the world look like 3 years after you arrive on the scene? Five years?

☐ **Put together a short narrative in bullets about your strategy**

Delivery Dates
- ☐ MVP Delivery Date and features
- ☐ 18-month product vision and delivery dates

Long Term Product Strategy
- ☐ Will your product create network effects?
- ☐ Can you price it with a predicable model?
- ☐ Can you create customer lock-in/high switching costs?
- ☐ Can you have high gross margins?
- ☐ Does it have organic demand versus requiring marketing spend?
- ☐ List product enhancements anticipated up to 18 months
- ☐ List key follow-on product enhancements

Exit criteria:
- ☐ Vision
- ☐ Narrative
- ☐ Long-term product strategy
- ☐ Update your business model canvas

☐ **Pass/Fail tests identified**   Checklist 4

Product Features And Benefits   All Channels

Goal: Explain what the product is and why people will buy and use it

Reference: Chapter 4, Product Features/Benefits Hypothesis and **Low-Fidelity MVP Hypothesis**

What problem or need are you solving?
- ☐ What do you think the biggest *pain* is in how customers work/play?
- ☐ If they could wave a magic wand and change anything what would it be?
- ☐ How does the product solve those problems or needs?
- ☐ What do people do today to solve their problem?

Product Feature List
- ☐ 10 one- or two-sentence descriptions of product features
- ☐ Explain the general goal of the product
- ☐ Does it address a market niche or segment?
- ☐ Does it solve a problem or address a need in a new, different, faster or cheaper way?

Product Benefits List
- ☐ List the benefits through the customer's eyes
- ☐ Something new? Better? More? Faster? Cheaper? Etc.
- ☐ Underneath the features above, summary benefits for each
- ☐ Will these Benefits be accepted as such or do they need explanation?

Describe the Minimum Viable Product (MVP)
- ☐ What do you want to learn?
- ☐ From who?
- ☐ What is the smallest feature set?

Create a One-Page User Story
- ☐ Include product vision, features, benefits

Exit criteria:

- ☐ Describe the product's features and benefits
- ☐ Describe the MVP
- ☐ **Create a User Story describing what job the product will do**
- ☐ Update your business model canvas

☐ **Pass/Fail tests identified**

Checklist 5

Customer Segments   All Channels

Goal: Develop a hypothesis of who your customers are and what problems they have that will drive them to use your product
Reference: Chapter 4, Customer Segments and **Source Hypotheses**

Define the Customer Problem
- ☐ Does the customer have a latent, passive, active or vision problem/need?

Define the Customer type
- ☐ Define the distinctly different types of "customer"
- ☐ Who will be the actual day-to-day users of the product?
- ☐ Who are the influencers and recommenders?
- ☐ Who is the "Economic Buyer"? (i.e. whose budget will pay for it?)
- ☐ Do you think the Economic Buyer has an existing budget for this product or do they need to get one approved?
- ☐ Who are the "Decision Makers?"
- ☐ Who else needs to approve the purchase? And who can kill it?

What are the Customer's wants and needs?
- ☐ Rated on a "problem recognition scale"
- ☐ Does product solve a mission-critical company problem or satisfy a must-have customer need?
- ☐ How painful is this problem?

☐ **Draw the Customer Archetypes**
☐ **Draw the Day in the life of a customer – before and after your product**

Draw the Organizational and customer influence maps
- ☐ List those who could influence a customer's buying decision
- ☐ Consider the product's influence on his daily life

Exit criteria:
- ☐ Customer types and problem or need
- ☐ Customer archetypes
- ☐ Depict a day in the life of a customer
- ☐ Organizational and customer influence maps
- ☐ Update your business model canvas

☐ **Pass/Fail tests identified**

Checklist 6

Channels   All Channels

Goal: Develop a hypothesis of your distribution channel

Reference: Chapter 4, Physical and **Web/Mobile** Channel Hypotheses

☐ **What channel will your users use to buy from you?**

Draw the Distribution Channel Diagram
☐ How much will the channel cost (direct expenses or channel discounts)
☐ Are there indirect channel costs (presales support, promotional dollars…)
☐ What else is needed for customers to use/buy the product?
☐ How do they acquire those pieces?
☐ What is the net revenue after channel costs?

Is this a Multi-sided Market?
☐ How will you address each side of the market?

Exit criteria:
☐ Distribution channel selected
☐ Update your business model canvas

☐ **Pass/Fail tests identified**

Checklist 7

Market Type

All Channels

Goal: Select an initial Market Type

Reference: Chapter 4, Market Type

- [ ] **Do you have a new product in an existing market?**
- [ ] **Do you want to clone an existing market?**
- [ ] **Do you need to redefine/reframe a market?**

- [ ] **Or do you want to create an entirely new market?**
  - [ ] Is your product/service a substitute for something customers already have?
  - [ ] Is it a replacement?
  - [ ] Is it a variant on something already out there, but can be "respun" into something new?
  - [ ] Is it something totally new?

Positioning in An Existing Market
- [ ] Define the basis of competition
- [ ] Who is driving the existing market?
- [ ] Do you have some advantage or appeal among any vertical or horizontal market segment?

Positioning in An Existing Market you Want to Resegment
- [ ] Define the basis of the how you want to change the market
- [ ] Who is driving the existing market you want to resegment?

Positioning in a New Market
- [ ] How will you create the market
- [ ] Estimate of market creation costs

Exit criteria:
- [ ] A preliminary first hypothesis of the type of market
- [ ] Update your business model canvas

- [ ] **Pass/Fail tests identified**

Checklist 8

Customer Relationships   Physical

Goal: How you will "Get, Keep and Grow Customers" in a physical channel

Reference: Chapter 4, Customer Relationships

- [ ] **Draw Your "Get/Keep/Grow" Funnel**

- [ ] **Describe your "Get Customers" Strategy**
  - [ ] Awareness
  - [ ] Interest
  - [ ] Consideration
  - [ ] Purchase
- [ ] **What are your "Get Customers" Tactics?**
  - [ ] Earned Media?
  - [ ] Paid Media?
- [ ] **Describe your "Keep Customers" Strategy**
  - [ ] Interact
  - [ ] Retain
- [ ] **What are your "Keep Customers" Tactics?**
  - [ ] Loyalty programs?
  - [ ] Product updates?
  - [ ] Customer Surveys?
- [ ] **Describe your "Grow Customers" Strategy**
  - [ ] New Revenue from existing customers
  - [ ] Customer referrals
- [ ] **What are your "Grow Customers" Tactics?**\Up-sell/Cross-sell/other tactics
  - [ ] Referral generation programs to test

Exit criteria:
  - [ ] A preliminary first hypothesis of all Get/Keep Grow activities
  - [ ] Update your business model canvas

- [ ] **Pass/Fail tests identified**

Checklist 9 Physical

Customer Relationships   Web/Mobile

Goal: How you'll "Get, Keep and Grow" Customers in a web/mobile channel

Reference: Chapter 4, Customer Relationships

- ☐ **Draw Your "Get/Keep/Grow" Funnel**

- ☐ **Describe your "Get Customers" Strategy**
  - ☐ Acquire
  - ☐ Activate

- ☐ **What are your "Get Customers" Tactics?**
  - ☐ Search (SEM/SEO)
  - ☐ Viral
  - ☐ PR
  - ☐ Trials

- ☐ **Describe your "Keep Customers" Strategy**
  - ☐ Interact
  - ☐ Retain

- ☐ **What are your "Keep Customers" Tactics?**
  - ☐ Customization?
  - ☐ User groups? Blogs?
  - ☐ Loyalty or other physical channel programs

- ☐ **Describe your "Grow Customers" Strategy**
  - ☐ Incremental customer revenue
  - ☐ Referrals

- ☐ **What are your "Grow Customers" Tactics?**
  - ☐ Upgrades
  - ☐ Contests
  - ☐ Up-sell/Cross-sell
  - ☐ Viral

Exit criteria:
- [ ] A preliminary first hypothesis of all Get/Keep Grow activities
- [ ] Update your business model canvas

- [ ] **Pass/Fail tests identified**

Checklist 9 Web/Mobile

Key Resources Hypothesis   All Channels

Goal: Identify external resources critical to the company's success, and how the company will find and secure them

Reference: Chapter 4, Key Resources

Describe the all key resources costs, and how they will be acquired
- ☐ Physical resources
- ☐ Financial resources
- ☐ Human resources
- ☐ Intellectual property
- ☐ Other key resources
- ☐ Dependency analysis

Exit criteria:
- ☐ Physical, financial, human, intellectual property resources required
- ☐ What they will cost
- ☐ Where they'll be found
- ☐ How they will be secured
- ☐ Update your business model canvas

☐ **Pass/Fail tests identified**

Checklist 10

Partners Hypothesis   All Channels

Goal: Identify essential partners and the company's "value exchange" with each

Reference: Chapter 4, Partners and **Traffic Partners**

Understand Potential Partner Types

- ☐ Strategic Alliances
- ☐ Joint new business efforts
- ☐ Coopetition
- ☐ Key suppliers
- ☐ **Traffic Partners**

List your target partners

- ☐ Necessary partners
- ☐ What they will provide
- ☐ How the Company will reciprocate

Exit criteria:

- ☐ Understand potential partner types
- ☐ List target partners, their contributions and what the company will offer in return
- ☐ Update your business model canvas

- ☐ **Pass/Fail tests identified**

Checklist 11

Revenue And Pricing Hypothesis   All Channels

Goal: See if the business model makes financial sense

Reference: Chapter 4, Revenue and Pricing Hypothesis

How many will we sell?
- ☐ Market Size & Market share hypotheses
- ☐ Channel hypothesis

What's the Revenue Model
- ☐ Sales?
- ☐ Subscriptions?
- ☐ Pay-per-use?
- ☐ Referral?
- ☐ Affiliate?

What Are the Pricing Tactics
- ☐ Value pricing
- ☐ Competitive pricing
- ☐ Volume pricing
- ☐ Portfolio pricing
- ☐ Razor/razor blade model
- ☐ Subscription
- ☐ Leasing
- ☐ Freemium
- ☐ Etc.
- ☐ Does it Add up to a Business Worth Doing?

Exit criteria:
- ☐ The units/users, revenue model and pricing add up to a business worth doing

☐ **Pass/Fail tests identified**

Checklist 12

Design Tests   All Channels

Goal: Devise experiments for testing the Business Model Hypotheses

Reference: Chapter 5, Design Tests and Pass/Fail Experiments

- ☐ List key areas to learn
- ☐ Design simplest pass/fail tests
- ☐ Run Tests
- ☐ Process for tracking learning and insights from test results

Exit criteria:

- ☐ Objective pass/fail tests for testing Business Model Hypotheses
- ☐ Process for tracking results

☐ **Pass/Fail tests identified**

Checklist 13

Prepare For Customer Contacts   Physical

Goal: Get meetings scheduled with potential customers to understand the customer problem and whether the company's proposed solution solves it

Reference: Chapter 5, Prepare for Customer Contacts

- ☐ List of 50 initial target customers
- ☐ Develop a Reference story
- ☐ Craft an Introductory email
- ☐ Contact initiated
- ☐ Build a master calendar of booked appointments
- ☐ Expand the list of contacts
- ☐ Create the innovators' list
- ☐ Create the initial list of advisory board candidates

Exit criteria:

- ☐ Meetings arranged targeted number of potential customers

☐ **Pass/Fail tests identified**

Checklist 14 Physical

Build A Low Fidelity MVP   Web/Mobile

Goal: Develop a low fidelity MVP to test and assure problem customers care about the problem

Reference: Chapter 5, Build Your Low Fidelity MVP

Build a low fidelity website
- ☐ Splash or landing page with value proposition
- ☐ Benefits summary
- ☐ Call to action (learn more, survey, preorder)
- ☐ Multiple MVPs considered?

Exit Criteria:
- ☐ A simple live website or prototype for testing whether customers care about the app or site being developed

☐ **Pass/Fail tests identified**

Checklist 14 Web/Mobile

Test The Problem And Assess Its Importance   Physical

Goal: Measure seriousness and importance of the customer problem or need as the customer sees it

Reference: Chapter 5, Test Understand the Problem and Assess its Importance

Develop the "Problem" presentation
- ☐ Perceived Problem
- ☐ Current Solution
- ☐ Startup's proposed solution
- ☐ Top 3 things to learn at each customer call
- ☐ Two presentations for multi-sided markets
- ☐ Presentation rehearsed?

Create a Report card for collecting data
- ☐ Perceived problems, ranked by customer
- ☐ Cost
- ☐ Current solution
- ☐ Startup's solution
- ☐ Referrals

Create a Scorecard for results

Exit criteria:
- ☐ Problem presentation developed and rehearsed
- ☐ Report card for collecting data at each call
- ☐ Scorecard for results

☐ **Pass/Fail tests identified**

Checklist 15 Physical

Low Fidelity MVP Problem Test   Web/Mobile

Goal: Determine whether enough people care about the problem the startup is solving or need it is fulfilling

Reference: Chapter 5, Low Fidelity MVP Problem Test

- [ ] **Invite customers to the Low Fidelity MVP**
  - [ ] Push tactics
  - [ ] Pull tactics
  - [ ] Paid tactics

- [ ] **Collect e-mails for future contact**

- [ ] **Measure response**
  - [ ] Raw web hits
  - [ ] Conversion rates
  - [ ] Time spent on site
  - [ ] Source of users

- [ ] **In-person interviews in addition to online responses**
- [ ] **Process for analyzing feedback, determining scalability**

Exit criteria:
  - [ ] Robust customer interest in the problem or need
  - [ ] High response rate to startup's proposed solution

- [ ] **Pass/Fail tests identified**

Checklist 15 Web/Mobile

Gain Customer Understanding   All Channels

Goal: In-depth understanding of potential customers

Reference: Chapter 5, Customer Discovery, Get Out of the Building to Test the Problem. Do People Care?

- [ ] **Research and Customer interviews**
  - [ ] How customers' money and time are spent
  - [ ] Current workflow
  - [ ] Pain or need
  - [ ] Current solution and cost
  - [ ] How workflow would change with startup's product
  - [ ] Customer publications
  - [ ] Customer influencers

- [ ] **Spend a day doing what customers do**
- [ ] **Attend customer events**

- [ ] **Become a customer**
  - [ ] Their websites and publications
  - [ ] Online experiences
  - [ ] How and where they spend time
  - [ ] How and where they discover new ways to spend time

- [ ] **Report card for recording information learned**
- [ ] **Process for analyzing data collected**

Exit criteria:
  - [ ] In-depth understanding of customers, what they read, who they listen to, how they work, spend leisure time and money

- [ ] **Pass/Fail tests identified**

Checklist 16

Capture Market Knowledge, Traffic/Competitive   All Channels

Goal: Gain understanding of overall market

Reference: Chapter 5, Capture Market Knowledge and **Traffic/Competitive Analysis**

Meet with peers in adjacent markets, industry analysts, journalists, other key influencers
- ☐ Industry trends
- ☐ Key unresolved customer needs
- ☐ Key players
- ☐ Must-read/Must-ask/Must-meet
- ☐ Potential competitors/Innovators in the space

☐ **Research!**
- ☐ Trends
- ☐ Key players/Influencers
- ☐ Business models
- ☐ Key metrics
- ☐ **Traffic measurement, comparison tools**
- ☐ **App stores**
- ☐ **Quora.com**

☐ **Construct a Competitive grid**

☐ **Construct a Market map**

☐ **Attend Industry events**
- ☐ Demos
- ☐ Hands-on time with competitive and adjacent products
- ☐ Spot talent, trends

Exit criteria:

☐ In-depth understanding of the overall market, its trends, players, current products and vision for growth

☐ **Pass/Fail tests identified**

Checklist 17

Update The Business Model And Team   All Channels

Goal: Prepare to assess whether to move ahead or pivot

Reference: Chapters 4,5, 6, Customer Discovery

- [ ] **Assemble the Customer Data**
    - [ ] Build a Workflow map of prototypical customer
    - [ ] Customer workflow with and without new product or app

- [ ] **Detailed findings from customer interviews**
    - [ ] Problems customers have
    - [ ] Pain level
    - [ ] How the problems are being solved
    - [ ] What was learned
    - [ ] Biggest surprises/Biggest disappointments

- [ ] **Assessment of data**
    - [ ] How well preliminary product specs solve customers' problem
    - [ ] Product/market fit
    - [ ] Review and prioritize features list
    - [ ] Features matched to customer problem
    - [ ] Customer interest/enthusiasm quantified

- [ ] **Review the Phase 1 hypotheses**
    - [ ] Update the Business Model Canvas
    - [ ] Update the 18-month delivery schedule

- [ ] **Pivot-or-proceed discussion**

Exit criteria
- [ ] Determine whether the company has uncovered a problem that many customers are eager to solve, or if the Value Proposition works
- [ ] Update the Business Model Canvas

- [ ] **Pass/Fail tests identified**

Checklist 18

The Product/ "Solution" Presentation   Physical

Goal: Develop a solution presentation for use with customers to confirm the product solves a serious customer problem or fills an important need

Reference: Chapter 6, Create the Product/Solution Presentation

☐ **Develop a Solution-oriented presentation**
 ☐ Review problem
 ☐ Describe product (five key features)
 ☐ Insert multiple prompts for customer feedback
 ☐ No marketing or positioning information

☐ **Draw the Customer workflow diagram**
 ☐ Before the product
 ☐ After the product
 ☐ Product future 18 months out

☐ **Develop a Demo or Prototype where possible**
☐ **Keep a Scorecard to track customers' reaction**

Exit criteria:
☐ Detailed presentation that sets out the customer program,
   shows the startup's solution and invites additional customer feedback

☐ **Pass/Fail tests identified**

Checklist 19 Physical

High Fidelity MVP Test   Web/Mobile

Goal: Identify a test that gauges the intensity of customers' enthusiasm for the product

Reference: Chapter 6, High Fidelity MVP Test

- ☐ **Run the High Fidelity "Solution" test**
  - ☐ Invite a limited number of customers
  - ☐ Not a live launch; small scale test – by invitation only
  - ☐ Includes a call to action – "buy now," "sign up," "learn more"

- ☐ **Measuring Customer response**
  - ☐ Number of visits before someone activates
  - ☐ Number of people who tell friends
  - ☐ Speed with which those people activate
  - ☐ Rate of customer return to site

Exit criteria
  - ☐ Simple test for assessing customer interest in the app or site
  - ☐ Tactics for measuring response

- ☐ **Pass/Fail tests identified**

Checklist 19 Web/Mobile

Test The Product Solution With The Customer   Physical

Goal: Gauge whether customers believe the product is a strong solution to an important problem and if they'll buy it

Reference: Chapter 6, Test the Product Solution with the Customer

- [ ] **Prepare for the Meetings**
  - [ ] Introductory e-mail
  - [ ] Reference story
  - [ ] Script

- [ ] **Conduct Customer Interviews**
  - [ ] Customers who heard first "problem" presentation
  - [ ] Targets on expanded set of contacts
  - [ ] Several of each customer type
  - [ ] Use demo, prototype or MVP to describe product
  - [ ] Indirect sales – potential channel partners

- [ ] **Develop a Customer report card to record feedback**
  - [ ] Product and features
  - [ ] Intended market
  - [ ] Pricing
  - [ ] Distribution
  - [ ] Referrals

- [ ] **Thank-you notes**

Exit criteria
  - [ ] Solid understanding of customers' problems
  - [ ] Robust customer interest in product
  - [ ] For indirect sales, be able to draw each channel partner's business model

- [ ] **Pass/Fail tests identified**

Checklist 20 physical

Measure Customer Behavior   Web/Mobile

Goal: Determine customer enthusiasm for MVP

Reference: Chapter 6, Measure Customer Behavior

☐ **Identify Critical Customer Metrics**
- ☐ Purchase
- ☐ Engagement
- ☐ Retention
- ☐ Referral
- ☐ Cohorts

☐ **Mine the Data**
- ☐ Traffic sources
- ☐ Acquisition, activation rates
- ☐ Customer engagement (time on site, number of visits before registration, etc.)
- ☐ Number of referrals

Exit criteria:
- ☐ Robust customer interest, excitement — enough to warrant moving forward

☐ **Pass/Fail tests identified**

Checklist 20 Web/Mobile

Identify First Advisory Board Members   All Channels

Goal: Begin to identify first advisory board members

Reference: Chapter 6, Identify First Advisory Board Members

- [ ] **Potential advisors approached**
    - [ ] Technical problems
    - [ ] Key customer introductions
    - [ ] Domain-specific knowledge
    - [ ] Product development

- [ ] **Potential advisors approached**

Exit criteria
- [ ] Initial list of advisory board prospects

- [ ] **Pass/Fail tests identified**

Checklist 21

Verify Product/Market Fit   All Channels

Goal: Verify that the company has identified a serious problem, has a product that will address that problem and that there are enough customers willing to pay for that product.

Reference: Chapter 7, Verify Product/Market Fit

- [ ] **Assessment: Serious problem or important need?**
  - [ ] Number of customers with the problem
  - [ ] How customers rated problem
  - [ ] Whether customers attempted home-grown solutions
  - [ ] Workflow diagram with and without new product

- [ ] **Assessment: Does product addresses product or need?**
  - [ ] Customer feedback reviewed
  - [ ] Amount of customer enthusiasm for product
  - [ ] Referral rate
  - [ ] Activation/acquisition rates
  - [ ] Review feedback
  - [ ] Review product messaging

- [ ] **Assessment: Are there enough customers?**
  - [ ] Market size, now and anticipated
  - [ ] Customer feedback
  - [ ] Competitive threats

Exit criteria:
  - [ ] Verify sizeable demand for solving the problem
  - [ ] Verify that the product fills the demand well in the customers' eyes
  - [ ] Update the Business Model Canvas

- [ ] **Pass/Fail tests identified**

Checklist 22

Verify Who Customers Are and How to Reach Them
All Channels

Goal: Verify that company knows its customers and how to reach them

Reference: Chapter 7, Verify Who Customers Are

- ☐ Customer archetypes
- ☐ Day in a Life of a Customer
- ☐ Customer responses assessed
- ☐ Customer behaviors, influencers assessed
- ☐ Channel map
- ☐ Costs assessed for each step of moving product
- ☐ Updated business model reflecting changes in customer acquisition costs

Exit criteria:
- ☐ Detailed understanding of who the customers are, how to reach them and what it costs to get them
- ☐ Update the Business Model Canvas

☐ **Pass/Fail tests identified**

Checklist 23

Verify Can We Make Money   All Channels

Goal: Determine whether the company can be profitable

Reference: Chapter 7, Customer Discovery, Verify Business Model/Pivot or Proceed

☐ **Revenue Model Data**
  ☐ Summary of customer report cards, indicating potential sales revenue over time
  ☐ Market size estimates
  ☐ Detailed information about the industry, customers, their behavior
  ☐ Competitive product and pricing information
  ☐ Channel cost and revenue potential summaries
  ☐ Pricing plan
  ☐ Customer acquisition costs

☐ **Accurate net revenue forecast for the next 4-8 quarters done three ways (good/better/best)**
  ☐ Direct revenue
  ☐ Net channel revenue
  ☐ Total revenue
  ☐ Acquisition costs
  ☐ Basic operating costs
  ☐ Cash burn
  ☐ Cash at quarter end, by quarter

Exit criteria:
  ☐ Reasonable rough estimate of the company's revenue expectations across next four-eight quarters
  ☐ Update your business model canvas

Checklist 24

Verify Business Model – Pivot or Proceed   All Channels

Goal: Assess whether the modified hypotheses provide a solid foundation for moving forward to larger-scale testing in Customer Validation

Reference: Chapter 7, Customer Discovery, Verify Business Model/Pivot or Proceed

☐ **Modified hypotheses assessed**
    ☐ Problem/need identified
    ☐ Product solves product/need
    ☐ Sizeable market
    ☐ Viable, scalable, profitable business model
    ☐ Day in the Life of the Customer, with and without product
    ☐ Organizational chart of users, buyers and channels

☐ **Clear, measurable Validation Checkpoints identified**

Exit criteria: Full, honest assessment of Customer Discovery effort:
    ☐ Is there a big enough market that's hungry for the product?

Checklist 25

Craft Company Positioning   All Channels

Goal: Create a clear, compelling message explaining why **your company** is different and the product is worth buying

Reference: Chapter 9, Customer Validation Phase 1: "Get Ready to Sell"

- [ ] **Message statement**
    - [ ] Condenses Value Proposition into single phrase or sentence
    - [ ] Emotionally compelling
    - [ ] Credible
    - [ ] Takes Market Type into account

Exit criteria:
- [ ] A short, pithy message that explains what the company stands for, what the product does and why customers should buy from it, trust it, and care

Checklist 26

Get Ready To Sell: Sales and Marketing Materials   Physical

Goal: Create a first version of the marking collateral toolset that will help close a sale

Reference: Chapter 9, Customer Validation Phase 1: "Get Ready to Sell"

- ☐ **Online tools**
  - ☐ Website
  - ☐ Social marketing tools
  - ☐ Email messages and emailable marketing tools

- ☐ **Physical Sales Collateral and Materials**
  - ☐ PowerPoint sales presentation
  - ☐ Presentation leave-behind folder or brochure
  - ☐ White paper or other executive summary
  - ☐ Product feature spec sheet
  - ☐ Product problem/solution overview
  - ☐ Customer testimonials
  - ☐ Business cards, order pads, etc.

- ☐ **Sales Presentations**
  - ☐ Updated Problem Presentation
  - ☐ Updated Solution Presentation
  - ☐ Updated Product Presentation

- ☐ **Demos/Prototypes**
  - ☐ How product works
  - ☐ Key selling points
  - ☐ Old way vs. new way of solving the problem

- ☐ **Data Sheets**
  - ☐ Product data sheet for Existing Market
  - ☐ Solution data sheet for New or Clone Market
  - ☐ Product and Solution data sheets for Resegmented Market

- ☐ **Other materials**
  - ☐ Price lists
  - ☐ Contracts
  - ☐ Billing system

- ☐ **For B-to-B companies, three versions of collateral materials**
  - ☐ For earlyvangelists
  - ☐ For technology gatekeepers
  - ☐ For mainstream buyers

- ☐ **For B-to-C companies**
  - ☐ Shelf talkers
  - ☐ Retail packaging
  - ☐ Coupons
  - ☐ Ad slicks
  - ☐ A plan that distinguishes the objectives, targets for and timing of each of the above

Exit criteria:
  - ☐ Full complement of initial versions of sales and marketing materials

- ☐ **Pass/Fail tests identified**

Checklist 27 Physical

Get Ready To Sell — Acquire/Activate Customers   Web/Mobile

Goal: Devise plans for getting customers to the app or site to sign up or buy

Reference: Chapter 9, Customer Validation Phase 1: Get Ready to Sell

☐ **Acquire plan and tools**
- ☐ Who is responsible for driving the program
- ☐ Tactic
- ☐ Budget
- ☐ Timing
- ☐ Acquisition goals
- ☐ Multisided or not
- ☐ Social, network and viral components
- ☐ 4 weeks' worth of initial activities to test

☐ **Activation plan and tools**
- ☐ On landing page
- ☐ How customer arrived at site
- ☐ Reinforce language/tone of invitation
- ☐ Issue multiple clear calls to action
- ☐ Explain what problem the product solves
- ☐ Off landing page tactics to test
- ☐ A/B tests

Exit criteria:
- ☐ Initial "acquire" and "activate" plans for the first four weeks

☐ **Pass/Fail tests identified**

Checklist 27 Web/Mobile

Get Ready To Sell: Hire A Sales Closer   Physical

Goal: Identify someone with the necessary skills and experience to close deals

Reference: Chapter 9, Customer Validation Phase 1: Get Ready to Sell

- ☐ Experienced startup salesperson
- ☐ Good contacts in the target market
- ☐ Stellar listening, pattern recognition and collaboration skills
- ☐ Understand difference: closer vs. VP of sales
- ☐ Does not replace founders getting out in front of customers personally

Exit criteria:

- ☐ Experienced sales closer is hired

Checklist 28 Physical

Create a High Fidelity MVP   Web-Mobile

Goal: Develop a polished, functional MVP

Reference: Chapter 9, Customer Validation Phase 1: Get Ready to Sell

- ☐ Refined, more "complete" or polished version of the low-fidelity MVP used in Customer Discover to elicit customer feedback
- ☐ Part of the product – incomplete but polished rendering of product vision
- ☐ Limited features, but not second-class
- ☐ Invites more users to the product to test the acquisition and activation tactics
- ☐ Architected to deliver customer and product behavior data

Exit criteria:
- ☐ A High Fidelity MVP, which will be used to generate a steady stream of customer and product behavior data to refine the business model and product

Checklist 28 Web/Mobile

Sales Action Channel Plan   Physical

Goal: Develop a preliminary Sales Channel Action Plan to test the channel hypothesis developed in Customer Discovery.

Reference: Chapter 9, Customer Validation Phase 1: Get Ready to Sell

- [ ] **Refined distribution channel plan**

- [ ] **"Food chain" drawing**
  - [ ] All organizations between company and end-user customers identified
  - [ ] Each organization and its relationships with the company and with one another identified

- [ ] **Channel Responsibility Map**
  - [ ] Relationships in the Company's distribution channel diagrammed
  - [ ] Written descriptions of all responsibilities

- [ ] **Financial relationships between channel tiers mapped out**
- [ ] **Channel management plan devised**
- [ ] **Process identified for monitoring channel management plan**

Exit criteria: Preliminary sales action plan that
  - [ ] Describes the channel "food chain" and attendant responsibilities
  - [ ] Figures out the costs associated with each tier of the channel
  - [ ] Addresses management of the sales channel

- [ ] **Pass/Fail tests identified as appropriate**

Build Metrics Toolset　　　　　　　　　　　　Web/Mobile

Goal: Determine which key business metrics to measure and develop a system or dashboard for collecting and monitoring data

Reference: Chapter 9, Customer Validation Phase 1: Get Ready to Sell

- [ ] **12 key metrics identified: Basic visit metrics (page views, unique visitors, pages/visit)**
  - [ ] Acquisition activities and behaviors
  - [ ] Activation activities and behaviors
  - [ ] Referral activities and behaviors

- [ ] **Dashboard created or purchased to collect and monitor data**
  - [ ] Focused on key metrics, not all metrics
  - [ ] Easy, at-a-glance format
  - [ ] Able to accommodate metrics needed later to monitor retention and referral, including user cohorts

Exit criteria:
  - [ ] List of key metrics to measure for customer acquisition, activation and referral efforts
  - [ ] System for monitoring metrics near real-time

Checklist 29 Web/Mobile

Develop/Refine The Sales Roadmap   Physical

Goal: Who are the company's customers and how will they purchase your product?

Reference: Chapter 9, Customer Validation Phase 1: Get Ready to Sell

- ☐ Sales roadmap developed
- ☐ Organization and influence maps refined
- ☐ Customer Access Map refined
- ☐ Sales strategy developed
- ☐ Implementation plan devised
- ☐ Team members identified to manage each facet of the plan

Exit criteria:
- ☐ A thorough plan for getting a foot in the door, making the sale, and seeing it through

Checklist 30 Physical

Hire a Data Analytics Sales Chief   Web/Mobile

Goal: Have a dedicated analytics expert on the senior management team

Reference: Chapter 9, Customer Validation Phase 1: Get Ready to Sell

- ☐ **Analytics chief identified**
  - ☐ Agility with numbers and analytics tools
  - ☐ Innate curiosity
  - ☐ Highly creative
  - ☐ Good collaborator
  - ☐ Easy to work with
  - ☐ Clout to make things happen when a pivot is required

- ☐ **Reporting schedule devised**

Exit criteria:
  - ☐ Data Analytics expert hired to drive continuous improvement for the company

Checklist 30 Web/Mobile

Formalize Advisory Board   All Channels

Goal: Formally engage advisors who can facilitate high-level introductions and are top-notch "out of the box" thinkers

Reference: Chapter 9, Customer Validation Phase 1: Get Ready to Sell

☐ **Advisory board roadmap assembled**
    ☐ Size – quality vs. quantity
    ☐ Ability to make high-level introductions
    ☐ Technical expertise
    ☐ Meetings or no meetings?
    ☐ Key potential customers
    ☐ Domain experts
    ☐ A seasoned CEO type
    ☐ Decide about compensation

Exit criteria:
    ☐ Formal depiction of the size, makeup and operation of the company's advisory board(s)

Checklist 31

Find Earlyvangelists   Physical

Goal: Identify passionate early visionaries to try to sell

Reference: Chapter 10, Customer Validation Phase 2: Get Out of the Building and Sell!

- [ ] **Earlyvangelists identified**
- [ ] **Appointments made**
  - [ ] Introductory email
  - [ ] Reference story
  - [ ] Script
- [ ] **Hit-rate results tracked**
- [ ] **List of contacts expanded**

Exit criteria:
- [ ] Sales appointments with earlyvangelists

Checklist 32 Physical

Prepare Optimization Plans And Tools   Web/Mobile

Goal: Prepare tools for testing the business model

Reference: Chapter 10, Customer Validation Phase 2: Get Out of the Building and Sell!

☐ **Optimization metrics identified**
☐ **Optimization priorities set**

☐ **Testing tools in place**
    ☐ Dashboard for monitoring results
    ☐ High-Fidelity MVP
    ☐ Acquire plan, tools
    ☐ Activation plan, tools

Exit criteria:
    ☐ Plan that defines acquisition metrics to optimize
    ☐ Plan for how customer behavior will be monitored/optimized

☐ **Pass/Fail tests identified**

Checklist 32 Web/Mobile

Get Out of the Building and Sell!   Physical

Goal: Test sell the product

Reference: Chapter 10, Customer Validation Part 2: Get Out of the Building and Sell!

☐ Report card for collecting sales findings
☐ First meeting understanding: agenda, goals
☐ Agree on plan to enter at the right level
☐ "Before" and "after" visualized
☐ Customized presentations
☐ Purchase action plan (after positive meeting)
☐ Senior management engaged
☐ Thank-you note with next steps
☐ Custom proposal (signed)
☐ Spreadsheet of win/loss statistics, summarized data
☐ Agreed-upon number of orders to prove validation

Exit criteria: A realistic sense of the product's sales potential

☐ **Pass/Fail tests identified** (orders to prove validation)

Checklist 33 Physical

Optimize Getting Customers   Web/Mobile

Goal: Optimize "get customers" effort

Reference: Chapter 10, Customer Validation Part 2: Get Out of the Building and Sell!

- ☐ Customer Relationship hypotheses reviewed
- ☐ Dozen metrics identified for testing, daily monitoring
- ☐ Sequential plan for optimizing "get" funnel
- ☐ Optimization plan under way
- ☐ Spreadsheet for monitoring daily progress, next steps
- ☐ Test
- ☐ Retest
- ☐ Test again

Exit criteria: Quick, cost-effective, proven means for getting customers

☐ **Pass/Fail tests identified**

Checklist 33 Web/Mobile

Refine the Sales Roadmap   Physical

Goal: Develop an effective sales process

Reference: Chapter 10, Customer Validation Part 2: Get Out of the Building and Sell!

- ☐ **Corporate organization and influence maps**
  - ☐ Influencers, recommenders, saboteurs, economic buyers ID'd

- ☐ **Selling strategy map**
  - ☐ How account is entered
  - ☐ Who is called on
  - ☐ Order of calls
  - ☐ Presentation

- ☐ **Flowchart depicting sales process**
- ☐ **Steps identified to completing sale, delivering product**

Exit criteria: Playbook for a repeatable and scalable sales process

- ☐ **Pass/Fail tests identified**

Checklist 34 Physical

Optimize "Keep" And "Grow" Results   Web/Mobile

Goal: Improve methods for retaining and "growing" customers

Reference: Chapter 10, Customer Validation Part 2: Get Out of the Building and Sell!

- [ ] **Basic customer retention and growth programs launched**
  - [ ] Costs, ROI monitored for each
- [ ] **Cohort analysis under way**
- [ ] **Two "Grow" metrics**
  - [ ] Viral Growth Factor
  - [ ] Customer Lifetime Value
- [ ] **"Other side" of multi-sided market also optimized**
  - [ ] Learn how "other side" works, buys
  - [ ] Determine sales roadmap for "other side"
- [ ] **Revenue model refined based on learning from optimization efforts**

Exit criteria:
  - [ ] Optimized "keep" and "grow" processes
  - [ ] Validated sales potential of app or site
- [ ] **Pass/Fail tests identified**

Checklist 34 Web/Mobile

Test Sell Channel Partners   Physical

Goal: Validate your channel strategy

Reference: Chapter 10, Customer Validation Part 2: Get Out of the Building and Sell!

- [ ] **Channel targets identified and researched**
- [ ] **Meetings scheduled**
  - [ ] Introductory e-mail
  - [ ] Reference story and script
- [ ] **Channel/service partner presentation updated with early channel orders**
- [ ] **Report card for estimating sales from each channel**
- [ ] **Spreadsheet for summarizing data**

Exit criteria
  - [ ] Orders or firm commitments from prospective channel partners
  - [ ] Sales estimates from each channel

- [ ] **Pass/Fail tests identified**

Checklist 35 Physical

Test Sell Traffic Partners   Web/Mobile

Goal: Validate your traffic partner strategy

Reference: Chapter 10, Customer Validation Part 2: Get Out of the Building and Sell!

- ☐ **Traffic partner targets identified and researched**

- ☐ **Meetings scheduled**
    - ☐ Introductory e-mail
    - ☐ Reference story and script

- ☐ **Report card for estimating sales from each channel**
- ☐ **Spreadsheet for summarizing data**

Exit criteria
    - ☐ Deals or firm commitments from prospective traffic partners

- ☐ **Pass/Fail tests identified**

Checklist 35 Web/Mobile

Develop Product Positioning   All Channels

Goal: Formalize your *product's* positioning by Market Type

Reference: Chapter 11, Customer Validation, Phase 3: Product Development and Company Positioning

- ☐ Initial product positioning brief reviewed
- ☐ Customer feedback factored in
- ☐ Product positioning updated and refined

Exit criteria:
- ☐ Revised product positioning brief

Checklist 36

Match Positioning To Market Type   All Channels

Goal: Ensure product positioning matches company's market type

Reference: Chapter 11, Customer Validation, Phase 3: Product Development and Company Positioning

☐ **Existing and Re-segmented Markets**: Product compared
to its competitors'

☐ **New Market**: Vision and passion of what could be communicated

☐ **Clone Market**: Knowledge of comparative firms
used to "predict the future"

Exit criteria:
  ☐ Ensure product position matches market type
  ☐ Validate positioning with customers

Checklist 37

Develop Company Positioning   All Channels

Goal: Articulate Company Positioning

Reference: Chapter 11, Customer Validation, Phase 3: Product Development and Company Positioning

- [ ] **Mission statement developed in Customer Discovery revisited**
- [ ] **Company description, mission statement compared to competitors'**

- [ ] **Company positioning statement drafted**
  - [ ] Simple
  - [ ] Keeps customers in mind
  - [ ] What Company does for me
  - [ ] Why do I want to do business with them?
  - [ ] Why does this company exist and how is it different?
  - [ ] Matched to Market Type

Exit criteria:
  - [ ] Statement that fully articulates the Company's vision and mission

Checklist 38

Validate Positioning

All Channels

Goal: Validate product and company positioning, and product features

Reference: Chapter 11, Customer Validation, Phase 3: Product Development and Company Positioning

- [ ] **Meetings arranged with key analysts, industry influencers**
  - [ ] Targets tracked and monitored since Customer Discovery
  - [ ] Analysts' reports, press clippings, websites, etc., researched
  - [ ] Script developed

- [ ] **Analyst presentation assembled**
  - [ ] Market and product positioning
  - [ ] Product feature details

- [ ] **Report card for gathering intelligence, tracking feedback**

Exit criteria:
  - [ ] Detailed feedback about the marketplace and product from key analysts and influencers

Checklist 39

Assemble Data   All Channels

Goal: Assemble all data, reports, questionnaires, map, diagrams, etc., for full review

Reference: Chapter 12, Customer Validation, Phase 4: The Toughest Question of All: Pivot or Proceed?

- ☐ Workflow map of the prototypical customer
- ☐ An organizational/influence map
- ☐ Customer archetypes
- ☐ Fully updated business model diagram (plus a few prior versions)
- ☐ Customer feedback from sales report cards
- ☐ Market size and market share estimates
- ☐ Channel feedback and revenue potential summaries
- ☐ Pricing, customer acquisition costs, and any major product cost changes
- ☐ Detailed information about the industry, customers and their behavior
- ☐ Competitive product and pricing information

Exit criteria:
- ☐ All key feedback, hard data, diagrams and the most recent business model canvas assembled for review
- ☐ Learning from Discovery and Validation incorporated into latest versions of the hypotheses documents and updated Business Model Canvas
- ☐ Intersections of/interactions among business model components reviewed

☐ **Pass/Fail tests identified**

Checklist 40

Validate Business Model   All Channels

Goal: Use facts gathered to validate the business model

Reference: Chapter 12, Customer Validation, Phase 4: The Toughest Question of All: Pivot or Proceed?

☐ **Business Model Checklist**

  ☐ Value Proposition
  ☐ Customer Segments
  ☐ Value Proposition 2: Market Type
  ☐ Channels
  ☐ Customer Relationships
  ☐ Cost Structure
  ☐ Revenue Stream

Exit criteria:
  ☐ Ensure all business model hypotheses have been converted into facts

☐ **Pass/Fail tests identified**

Checklist 41

Validate Financial Model   All Channels

Goal: Ensure the startup can become a profitable, scalable business before it runs out of money

Reference: Chapter 12, Customer Validation, Phase 4: The Toughest Question of All: Pivot or Proceed?

- ☐ **Value Proposition**
  - ☐ Product cost
  - ☐ Market size
  - ☐ Attainable market share
  - ☐ Customer impact of network effects

- ☐ **Customer Relationships**
  - ☐ Customer acquisition costs
  - ☐ Prospect conversion rates
  - ☐ Customer Lifetime Value
  - ☐ Customer switching costs

- ☐ **Market Type considerations**
- ☐ **Basic operating costs**

Channel costs
  - ☐ Channel margin, promotion and shelf space fees

- ☐ **Revenue streams**
  - ☐ Average selling price
  - ☐ Total achievable revenue
  - ☐ Number of customers/year

- ☐ **Cash balance**
- ☐ **Do the Math**

Exit criteria:
  - ☐ A full financial picture of the company's ability to succeed

- ☐ **Pass/Fail tests identified**   Checklist 42

Re-Validate The Business Model   All Channels

Goal: Further validate the business model

Reference: Chapter 12, Customer Validation, Phase 4: The Toughest Question of All: Pivot or Proceed? Revalidate the Financial Model

- [ ] **Business Model Canvas revisited**

- [ ] **Business Model Checklist revisited**
    - [ ] Value Proposition
    - [ ] Customer Segments
    - [ ] Value Proposition 2: Market Type
    - [ ] Channels
    - [ ] Customer Relationships
    - [ ] Cost Structure
    - [ ] Revenue Stream

Exit criteria:
- [ ] Determine if the company is making the best bet possible
- [ ] Assess if revenue is as high and costs as low as they can realistically be

- [ ] **Pass/Fail tests identified**

Checklist 43

Pivot or Proceed?   All Channels

Goal: Decide whether to execute the business model

Reference: Chapter 12, Customer Validation, Phase 4: The Toughest Question of All: Pivot or Proceed?

- ☐ Did the Validation effort really convert opinions to facts?
- ☐ Business model diagram is updated
- ☐ Did the product sell well and easily?
- ☐ Is it clear that customers will continue to arrive at a steady, predictable, profitable pace?
- ☐ Repeatable and scalable sales process developed
- ☐ Product delivery timing checked
- ☐ Confirmation that company can deliver on what was sold, do as promised
- ☐ Profitable business model demonstrated
- ☐ Move forward or pivot?

Exit criteria:
- ☐ An informed decision about whether to move forward

☐ **Pass/Fail tests identified**

Checklist 44

Glossary

A/B Testing compares one version of a web page with another and sees which produces the best results.

Acquisition is the first step in the web/mobile "get/keep/grow" sales funnel. It gets people to visit your website, where you can then *activate* them by getting them to engage, purchase, or at least register for future sales efforts. Specific customer acquisition categories include *earned* and *paid media*, and tactics include search (SEM/SEO), e-mail, PR/blogs, viral, social nets.

Activation is the second step in the web/mobile "get/keep/grow" sales funnel. After you *acquire customers* you get them to register, participate or purchase on the website. Specific customer activation tactics include free trials, home/landing page.

Agile Development is the engineering method used to develop products (hardware, software or services) iteratively and incrementally with flexibility to react to customer feedback. It recognizes that customer needs and the final product spec cannot be fully defined a priori. Agile is the antithesis of *Waterfall Development*.

ARPU, or Average Revenue Per User, is a measurement of revenue typically applied by subscription services like cellphone or data plans to measure average long-term spending.

Awareness. In the physical channel, it is the first step in the "get customers" sales funnel. Tactics include earned media (pr, blogs, brochures, reviews), paid media (ads, promotions), online tools

Business Model is the description of how an organization creates, delivers and captures value. In this book it specifically refers to Alexander Osterwalder's 9-box *Business Model Canvas*.

Business Plan is a document written by existing companies to describe and launch follow-on or adjacent market products. It was mistakenly used for startups for decades until it was realized that no business plan survives first contact with customers. Typically has sections labeled: opportunity, industry background, competitive analysis, marketing plan, operations plan, management summary and financial plan.

Canvas refers to Alexander Osterwalder's 9-box *Business Model Canvas.* In this book we use the canvas to capture our business model hypotheses and as a scorecard over time.

Channel is the sales and/or distribution channel. How the product gets from your company to the customer. This book talks about "physical channels" and "web/mobile channels."

Channel Stuffing fills your sales channel with more product than the channel has end-user demand for. Used as an often-illegal tactic to inflate company revenue (when revenue is recognized as shipped to the channel, rather than shipped from the channel to the end customer).

Churn (sometimes called Attrition) is the number of customers or subscribers who leave a service in a period of time. Usually measured in monthly percentages. If 1 of 10 customers leave, the churn rate is 10%.

Cohort analysis is the measurement of a specific unchanging group of customers over time.

Collateral materials are the brochures, data sheets, white papers, sell sheets and other literature companies generally in physical channels develop to market their products or services.

Consideration The third step in the physical purchase decision cycle or "sales funnel." The sales funnel includes awareness, interest, consideration and purchase.

Company Building is the fourth of four steps in the Customer Development process. Founders reorganize the company from one focused on *searching* for a business model into building an organization that can *execute.*

CPA (cost per acquisition) The price web businesses pay to purchase referrals or customers from partners or other web businesses.

CPM (cost per thousand) is an advertising industry measure for purchasing media, whether it be magazine ad space or banners on websites. Ad pricing is based on CPM. A magazine selling 6,000,000 copies has 6,000 "M's" to sell.

Cross-Sell is a tactic to grow existing customers by encouraging them to buy complementary products, increasing their average order size. "Buy this other book and get 10% off." Or "buy this suitcase and add the toiletry kit." See *Up-Sell*.

Customer Archetypes are detailed descriptions of customer traits, including hard (demographics, psychographics, etc.) and soft (interviews, anecdotal material) customer data to form a descriptive profile *and an entire story about* a typical type or group of the company's customer(s). (Most startups typically have more than one archetypical customer.) Archetypes are used by both product and customer development to better focus on the target customer.

Customer Development first described in the Four Steps to the Epiphany, is the four-step process to organize the search for a repeatable and scalable business model. Executed by the *Customer Development Team.*

Customer Development Team replaces the traditional Sales, Marketing and Business Development in the discovery and validation steps of startups. The team is responsible for validating the business model hypotheses in front of customers. The team must have at least one founder with the authority to change the company's strategy.

Customer Discovery is the first of the four steps of Customer Development. In Discovery, founders articulate their hypotheses about the business model and then run experiments to test problem and solution in front of customers.

Customer Relationships are the strategies used by companies to *get* customers into its sales channel, *keep* them as customers, and over time *grow* their value to the company through additional revenue and customer referrals from them.

Customer Segment defines a single subset of a startup's customer universe and how they differ from others, as in "50+ golfers who play more than twice a month," often including the a problems/needs they have. Companies define specific *value propositions* for each segment.

Customer Validation is the second of the four steps of Customer Development. In validation, founders take their tested hypotheses and try to get initial orders/users/ customers.

Customer Creation is the third of four Customer Development steps. In creation, once founders validate their business model, they expand sales and marketing activities to grow.

Data Chief is the senior executive at mobile/web companies who monitors and continually optimizes the results of customer acquisition, activation and retention efforts. Sometimes known as the CMO, VP-Marketing or database marketer.

Demand Creation is the specific set of acquisition activities to drive customers into a startup's chosen sales channel(s). It's the "get" customers portion of the "Get/Keep/Grow" process of creating Customer Relationships.

Earlyvangelist is a concatenation of "early adopter" and "evangelist." In a startup earlyvangelists are the company's first customers, who buy the product very early because it solves a problem or fills an urgent need for them.

Earned Media is the free exposure a company generates. It includes a wide range of exposure tools including SEO or natural search, press releases, product reviews, editorial features. Earned media are part of a company's *"Get customers"* programs.

"Executing" a Business Model is what companies do *after they have found* a repeatable and scalable *business model*. It is how companies grow revenue once they have refined and proven their plan to do so. It requires significant organizational changes. See *Search*.

Experiments are what startups conduct to test hypotheses. Experiments are designed as objective pass/fail tests. For example: "We believe we can acquire users with Google Adwords at a cost of 20 cents per click."

External Audit: is a survey of outsiders' perception of the company and/or its product, gleaned from interviews with consumers.

Eye Tracking is a tool that tells you the path users' eyes follow on a web page. Extremely useful for eliminating guess work in web page design. See *heat maps.*

Get, Keep and Grow activities are the steps companies take to acquire, retain and grow their customers. *Getting* customers, sometimes called demand creation, drives customers into a chosen sales channel(s); *Keeping* customers, or retention, gives customers reasons to stick with the company and product; and *Growing* customers involves selling them more and encouraging them to refer new customers.

"Get out of the building" is a key tenet of Customer Development. It observes that unlike an existing company, in a startup there are no facts inside the building, so founders need to get outside to talk to customers. It's the customers who can turn the startup's many guesses about its business model into facts.

Heat Maps are tools that tell you where users' eyes focus first, second and third on a web page page. It is based on *eye tracking,* which literally observes where users' eyes go on a web page.

High-fidelity MVP is the simplest minimum viable product (i.e. a website with the core features implemented, a demo of the physical product) and is often quite rudimentary or "rough and dirty." It is used to gather feedback about the validity of the customer *solution.* See *low-fidelity MVP.*

Home Page (sometimes called the "landing" page) is the initial or principal web page of a company's product or website. See *landing page and splash page.*

Hypotheses are the educated guesses a startup's founders have about their Business Model Hypotheses. Hypotheses are drawn on the Business Model Canvas, and tested and refined throughout the Customer Development process.

Internal Audit is a survey of what employees understand, perceive, or believe about the company, and its product, and their positioning. *See external audit.*

Iteration is a minor change to one or more of the nine boxes of the business model canvas. (For example, a pricing change from $39.99 to $79.99 or customer segment from boys 12-15 years old to boys 15-19.) See *Pivot.*

Interest. In the physical channel, Interest is one of four steps in the "get customers" sales funnel. *See awareness.*

Landing Page (sometimes called the "splash" page) is the web page that appears when a customer clicks on a link, ad, or e-mail. It can sometimes be a company's home page. The landing page displays sales copy that is connected to the ad or link. See *home page.*

Lean Startup is a combination of Customer Development and Agile Development popularized by Eric Ries.

Local/Global Maximum are the results of hypotheses tests, that may show a short-term low-level response (the local maximum). This contrasts with the global maximum – the best possible test result, sometimes overlooked in short-term market testing.

Low-fidelity MVP is the simplest minimum viable product (i.e. a landing page with a sign-up to get more information, a cardboard mockup of a physical product) used to gather feedback about the validity of the customer *problem. See High-fidelity MVP.*

Loyalty Programs are tactics such as "points" and "frequent shopper programs" used to "keep" existing customers and reduce churn. See *churn.*

LTV (LifeTime Value), usually calculated in dollars, reflects the total revenue a customer is worth over the lifetime of his relationship with the company. (This book arbitrarily picks three years.) LTV helps calculate how much a company can afford to spend to acquire a customer.

Market Type refers to the four startup market entry strategies:
1) entering an *existing* market with a higher performance product
2) *resegmenting* an existing market (via a niche or low-cost strategy)
3) creating a *new* market where one never existed before
4) creating a *clone* market – copying a business model from another country

Microsites are small sub-websites within a larger site dedicated to a single purpose (like a retirement planning site with a big bank website) that are often used to attract customers' attention from both within and outside the site itself.

Minimum Feature Set is another term used to describe *Minimum Viable Product*.

Minimum Viable Product (MVP) is the smallest group of features that will elicit customer feedback. Initially the MVP could be as simple as a PowerPoint slide, a video or demo. For web/mobile products it can be a *low- or high-fidelity MVP* that illustrates the "core" customer problem/need and demonstrates the product's solution.

Multi-sided Business Models may have several different customer segments. Each segment may have a different value proposition, revenue model and channel. For example, Google's search business has users who pay nothing to use its search site, and an advertiser or payer segment that uses its AdSense site and pays to reach the search users. Other business models, such as medical devices, may be even more complex and have four or more "sides" customer segments such as patients, doctors, insurers and hospitals.

Paid Media is media exposure that's purchased on TV, billboards, direct mail or the web. *See earned media.* Paid media are part of a company's *"Get customers"* programs.

Physical Channel is a sales and fulfillment channel with physical points of distribution and customer contact. Can include warehouses, retail stores, direct sales people. See *web/mobile channel.*

Physical Product is a product made out of atoms. Cars, planes, computers, and food are physical products, but social networks and search engines are not. See *web/mobile products.*

Pivot is a substantive change in one or more of the nine boxes of the business model canvas. (For example, a revenue model change from freemium to subscription model or a customer segment shift from boys 12-15 years old to women 45-60.) See *Iteration*.

Pricing describes the tactics a startup uses to determine how much it will charge in order to implement a profitable *revenue model*. (i.e. Freemium, Subscription, tiered or volume pricing, etc.)

Problem/Need (Customer) is why customers buy. In some markets customers rationally recognize they have a *problem* and search for a product that can solve it. (Think software, snow tires, catheters) In other markets products may be purchased for an emotionally perceived *need*. (Movies, fashion, video games, social networks.)

Product Development is the engineering group building the product. The *process* startup product development teams most often use to build the product is called *Agile Development*.

Reference Story is an introductory explanation used when first contacting a prospect via e-mail or phone. It emphasizes the problems you're trying to solve, why it's important to solve them, the solution you're building, and why it should be of interest to the prospect.

Revenue Model describes the *strategy* of how a company will make money. It answers the question, "Where will the revenue be coming from?" For example, eBay makes a small fee on every transaction on its site, while Netflix charges a monthly subscription. Also *see pricing*.

Sales Closer is the individual on the Customer Development Team responsible for "closing" (bringing in the order) initial earlyvangelist sales. They deal with the sales logistics founders may not have experience with (negotiating with purchasing agents, contract terms, etc.) They are not sales managers, and likely *not* going to become the company's VP of Sales.

Sales Funnel is a visual metaphor for tracking sales progress shaped like a dumb-bell. Consists of "Get/Keep/Grow" activities. Wide at the top with raw leads coming in, the "Get" stage of the sales funnel narrows at each stage as the leads get qualified and turn into suspects, then prospects, then probable closes, until finally an order comes out of the narrow neck of the funnel. The "Keep" portion is narrow like a pipe, and the "Grow" part of the funnel widens to represent ever increasing revenue from an existing customer base.

Sales Roadmap provides details of how to execute each step of the *sales funnel*: who at a company to call on, in what order, to make a sale.

"Search" for a Business Model is what startups do *before* they have found a repeatable and scalable *business model*. Searching uses the Customer Development process described in this book. See *execution*.

Sell-in is the first order a channel places for a new product. It can also be a seasonal order like the pre-Christmas sell-in.

Sell-through the volume of product sold by the channel to the ultimate consumer. When products are "sold through," they can seldom be returned to the company. See *channel stuffing*.

Splash page is an archaic term for landing or home page. *See home page.*

Split Testing *see A/B testing.*

Startup is a temporary organization built to *search* for the answers to what makes a repeatable and scalable *business model*.

Take rate is the percentage of customers accepting (or taking) an up-sell/next-sell offer.

Traffic is the measure of how many individuals visit a store or website. They can arrive from paid media (i.e. Google, TV, or Facebook ads) or earned media sources (public relations, referrals).

Up-Sell is a tactic used to grow existing customers. It tries to get customers to buy more units or upgrade to a higher priced product to increase the average order size. See *Cross-Sell*.

Value Proposition describes the job being done for the customer. It includes features that are solutions to customer problems or needs (productivity, status, simplicity, convenience, etc.) for the customer segment(s). A value proposition should match a startup's *customer segment*.

Viral Loop is the process of satisfied customers referring others to a business, whether web, mobile or physical. It produces exponential increases in customer/users/traffic. See *viral marketing*.

Viral Marketing are the marketing activities used to stimulate customers to refer others to the business.

Waterfall Development is the engineering process used to develop products (hardware, software or services) linearly, sequentially, with a stage-by-stage method. The entire product and all features are specified up-front. Each waterfall stage is assigned to a separate team to ensure greater project and deadline control. Waterfall is the antithesis of *Agile Development*.

Web/Mobile Channel is a sales and fulfillment channel using the Internet to deliver messages and products to desktop, laptop, and mobile devices. Can include websites, the cloud, phone app stores. See *physical channel*.

Web/Mobile Product is a product made out of bits: social networks, video games, mobile applications are examples. See *physical product*.

How to Build a Web Startup:
A Simple Overview

How To Build a Web Startup – Lean LaunchPad Edition

If you're an experienced coder and user interface designer you think nothing is easier than diving into Ruby on Rails, Node.js and Balsamiq and throwing together a website. (Heck, in Silicon Valley even the waiters can do it.)

But for the rest of us mortals whose eyes glaze over at the buzzwords, the questions are, "How do I get my great idea on the web? What are the steps in building a website?" And the most important question is, "How do I use the business model canvas and Customer Development to test whether this is a real business?"

My first attempt at helping students answer these questions was by putting together the Startup Tools Page at www.steveblank.com. It's a compilation of available tools for startups. While it was a handy reference, it still didn't help the novice.

So below, I offer my next attempt.

How To Build a Web Startup – The Lean LaunchPad Edition

Here's the step-by-step process we suggest our students use in our Lean LaunchPad classes. All these steps are covered in Chapters 4, 5 and 6.

1. Set up the logistics to manage your team
2. Craft company hypotheses
3. Write a value proposition statement that other people understand
4. Set up the Website Logistics
5. Build a "low fidelity" web site
6. Get customers to the site

7. Add the backend code to make the site work

8. Test the "problem" with customer data

9. Test the "solution" by building the "high-fidelity" website

10. Ask for money

(Use the Startup Tools page at www.steveblank.com as a resource for tool choices.)

> *The tools listed in these Steps are examples. They are not recommended or preferred, just representative of what's available. New tools appear daily. Do your homework. See www.steveblank.com for a list of the latest tools.*

Step 1: Set Up Team Logistics

- Read Chapter 2 – The Customer Development Model and The Customer Development Manifesto
- Set up a WordPress blog to document your Customer Development progress
- Use Skype or Google+ Hangouts for team conversations

Step 2. Craft Your Company Hypotheses

- Write down your 9-business model canvas hypothesis
- List key features/Minimal Viable product plan
- Size the market opportunity. Use Google Trends, Google Insights, and Facebook ads to evaluate the market growth potential. Use Crunchbase to look at competitors
- Calculate Total Available Market, and customer value
- Pick market type (existing, new, resegmented)
- Prepare weekly progress summary: business model canvas update + weekly Customer Development summary (described after Step 10)

Step 3: Write a Unique Selling Proposition statement that other people understand

- If you can't easily explain why you exist, none of the subsequent steps matter. A good format is "We help X do Y by doing Z"
- Once you have a statement in that format, find a few other people (doesn't matter if they're your target market) and ask them if it makes sense
- If not, give them a longer explanation and ask them to summarize that back to you. Other people are often better than you at crafting an understandable Unique Selling Proposition.

Step 4: Website Logistics

- Get a domain name for your company. To find an available domain quickly, try Domize or Domainr
- Then use godaddy or namecheap to register the name. (You may want to register many different domains (different possible brand names, or different misspellings and variations of a brand name)
- Once you have a domain, set up Google Apps on that domain (for free!) to host your company name, email, calendar, etc.

For coders: set up a web host

- Use virtual private servers (VPS) like Slicehost or Linode (cheapest plans ~$20/month, and you can run multiple apps and websites)
- You can install Apache or Nginx with virtual hosting, and run several sites plus other various tools of your choice (assuming you have the technical skills of course) like a MySQL database
- If you are actually coding a real app, use a "Platform As A Service" (PAAS) like Heroku, DotCloud or Amazon Web Services if your app development stack fits their offerings

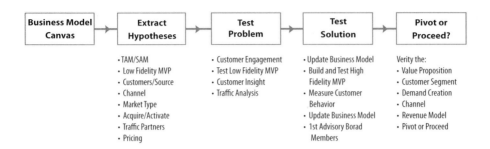

Customer Discovery for the Web

Step 5: Build a *Low Fidelity* Web Site

- Depending on your product, this may be as simple as a splash page with: your value proposition, benefits summary, and a call-to-action to learn more, answer a short survey, or pre-order)
- For surveys and pre-order forms, Wufoo and Google Forms can easily be embedded within your site with minimal coding

For non-coders:

- Make a quick prototype in PowerPoint, or
- Use Unbounce, Google Sites, Weebly, Godaddy, WordPress or Yola
- For surveys and pre-order forms, Wufoo and Google Forms can easily be embedded within your site with minimal coding

For coders: build the User Interface

- Pick a website wireframe prototyping tool, (i.e. JustinMind, Balsamiq)
- 99 Designs is great to get "good enough" graphic design and web design work for very cheap using a contest format. Themeforest has great designs
- Create wireframes and simulate your "Low Fidelity" website

- Create a fake sign up/order form to test customer commitment. Alternatively, create a "viral" landing page, with LaunchRock or KickoffLabs

- Embed a slideshow on your site with Slideshare or embed a video/tour using Youtube or Vimeo

- Do user interface testing with Usertesting or Userfy

Step 6: Customer Engagement (drive traffic to your preliminary website)

- Start showing the site to potential customers, testing customer segment and value proposition

- Use Ads, textlinks or Google AdWords, Facebook ads and natural search to drive people to your Minimally Viable web site

- Use your network to find target customers – ask your contacts, "Do you know someone with problem X? If so, can you forward this message on to them?" and provide a 2-3 sentence description

- For B2B products, Twitter, Quora, and industry mailing lists are a good place to find target customers. Don't spam these areas, but if you're already an active participant you can sprinkle in some references to your site or you can ask a contact who is already an active participant to do outreach for you

- Use Mailchimp, Postmark or Google Groups to send out emails and create groups

- Create online surveys with Wufoo or Zoomerang

- Get feedback on your Minimum Viable Product (MVP) features and User Interface

Step 7: Build a more complete solution (Connect the User Interface to code)

- Connect the UI to a web application framework (for example, Node.js, Rubyon Rails, Django, SproutCore, jQuery, Symfony, Sencha, etc.)

Step 8: Test the "Customer Problem" by collecting Customer Data

- Use Web Analytics to track hits, time on site, source. For your initial site, Google Analytics provides adequate information with the fastest setup. Once you've moved beyond your initial MVP, you'll want to consider a more advanced analytic platform (Kissmetrics, Mixpanel, Kontagent, etc.)

- Create an account to measure user satisfaction (GetSatisfaction, UserVoice, etc.) from your product and get feedback and suggestions on new features

- Specific questions, such as "Is there anything preventing you from signing up?" or "What else would you need to know to consider this solution?" tend to yield richer customer feedback than generic feedback requests

- If possible, collect email addresses so that you have a way to contact individuals for more in-depth conversations

Step 9: Test the "Customer Solution" by building a full featured High Fidelity version of your website

- Update the website with information learned in Steps 5-8

- Remember that "High Fidelity" still does not mean "complete product." You need to look professional and credible, while building the smallest possible product in order to continue to validate

- Keep collecting customer analytics

- Hearing "This is great, but when are you going to add X?" is your goal!

Step 10: Ask for money

- Put a "pre-order" form in place (collecting billing information) even before you're ready to collect money or have a full product

- When you're ready to start charging – which is probably earlier than you think – find a billing provider such as Recurly, Chargify, or PayPal to collect fees and subscriptions

For all Steps:

Give your team a weekly Lessons Learned progress report.

- Start by putting up your business model canvas
- Changes from the prior week should be highlighted in red
- Lessons Learned. This informs the group of what you learned and changed week by week – Slides should describe:
    1. Here's what we thought (going into the week)
    2. Here's what we found (Customer Discovery during the week)
    3. Here's what we're going to do (for next week)
    4. Emphasis should be on the discovery done for that weeks assigned canvas component (channel, customer, revenue model) but include other things you learned about the business model

Acknowledgements

I'VE LIVED THREE LIVES. MY FIRST CAREER STARTED in the Air Force during the Vietnam War. Next, I spent over two decades as a Silicon Valley technology entrepreneur. Now I'm into my second decade as an educator.

A few people changed my life at critical moments. In Thailand, John Scoggins, my first boss, took me off a flight line full of fighter planes and gunships and gave me part of the electronic warfare shop to run when I was 19. As an entrepreneur in my 20s and 30s, I was lucky to have four extraordinary mentors, each brilliant in his field: Ben Wegbreit, who taught me how to think; Gordon Bell, who taught me what to think about; Rob Van Naarden, who taught me how to think about customers; and Allen Michels, who taught me how to turn thinking into direct, immediate and outrageous action.

My eight technology startups had me working with, around and near some extraordinary people: Bill Perry, John Moussouris, John Hennessy, Skip Stritter, Jon Rubenstein, Glen Miranker, Cleve Moler, Tom McMurray, John Sanguinetti, Alvy Ray Smith, Chris Kryzan, Karen Dillon, Margaret Hughes, Peter Barrett, Jim Wickett, Karen Richardson, Greg Walsh, John McCaskey, and Roger Siboni. Some were active mentors, and others taught me by osmosis.

Sitting on startup boards, I watched world-class entrepreneurs at work: Steve Weinstein, Fred Amoroso, Fred Durham, Maheesh Jain, and Will Harvey. And I got to see how smart and thoughtful venture investors helped their companies solve problems: Kathryn Gould, Jon Feiber, Mike Maples, Bill Davidow and many more. At General Electric, I watched Prescott Logan use Customer Development to create a new Energy Storage division with the agility of a startup inside a 100-year old company.

As a board member of IMVU, Will Harvey and Eric Ries were the first corporate guinea pigs to implement the Customer Development process with me. As the best student I ever had, Eric Ries had the valuable insight that when Customer Development was combined with agile development, the sum of two made a powerful concept he called the Lean Startup. (He also named the feedback loop I drew between the customer validation and discovery steps, calling it the "Pivot.")

As one of Japan's most innovative VCs, Takashi Tsutsumi thought the Customer Development concepts so warranted adoption in Japan that he personally translated *The Four Steps* and evangelized the concepts. Other entrepreneurs followed with crowd-sourced translations into French, Russian, Korean and Chinese. Brant Cooper and Patrick Vlaskovits extended my ideas in their helpful book *The Entrepreneur's Guide to Customer Development*. Alexander Osterwalder's work about business model design and his book *Business Model Generation* are a conceptual breakthroughs that I've adopted as a way to "keep score" for the Customer Discovery process described in Chapter 3 of this book. A big thanks for his help. Dave McClure's insights about demand creation for web/mobile startup metrics inspired the web customer funnel discussions in several places.

Before anyone took my ideas seriously, Jerry Engel at U.C. Berkeley's Haas Business School gave me my first forum for teaching Customer Development. My first teaching partner, Rob Majteles, ensured that my enthusiasm was matched by a coherent syllabus. At Stanford University's School of Engineering, Tom Byers, Tina Seelig and Kathy Eisenhardt were gracious enough to invite me to teach with them in the Stanford Technology Venture Program. They offered additional insights, encouragement, and enough rope to hang myself when I created my Lean LaunchPad class, a new way to teach entrepreneurship. A big thanks to the National Science Foundation team including Errol Arkilic, Don Millard and Babu DasGupta, for adopting the Lean LaunchPad class and Customer Development for their Innovation Corps. And to Jon Feiber, Ann Miura Ko, John Burke, Jim Hornthal, Alexander Osterwalder and Oren Jacob for teaching it with me. Finally, Columbia Business School allowed me to offer the course to its students in its joint MBA program with the U.C. Berkeley Haas School of Business and invited me to teach in its short courses. I have learned immeasurably from the thousands of students who sat through my classes as unwitting victims of Customer Development while I experimented with new ways to teach entrepreneurship. None of these classes would have worked without the teaching assistants who kept the wheels on over the years, most notably Ann Miura-Ko, Thomas Haymore, Bhavik Joshi, Christina Cacioppo, and Eric Carr.

Besides the schools where I regularly lecture, other universities have invited me to teach, lecture and learn. Big thanks to: Professor Cristobal Garcia and the Pontificia Unversidad Catolica de Chile, in Santiago; Dave Munsen, dean of engineering, and Thomas Zurburchen, associate dean of entrepreneurship at the University of Michigan; Professor Nathan Furr of Brigham Young University, who turned my notion of business model competitions (instead of business plan competitions) into the first formal contest; at Aalto University in Helsinki, Finland, Tuula Teeri, president, Will Cardwell head of the Center for Entrepreneurship, and Kristo Ovaska and Linda Liukas, who all welcomed me; and Professor Tom Eisenmann of Harvard Business School's Entrepreneurial Management Unit, with whom I compare notes and teaching strategies in a semi-annual get-together.

Stephen Spinelli was at Babson when he was part of the team that taught me how to teach entrepreneurship, and when he became president of Philadelphia University, he gave me something I didn't deserve. Carl Schramm at the Kauffman Foundation turned into a friend in the pursuit of a new way to think about entrepreneurial education.

Numerous authors have written extensively (and more coherently) about each of the four steps of Customer Development I cover. A good many of the building blocks of Customer Development were first articulated by Eric Von Hippel (the Lead User), Rita Gunther McGrath and Ian MacMillan (Discovery-driven Growth), Mary Sonnack, Michael J. Lanning, Michael Bosworth (Solution Selling), and Thomas Freese, Neil Rackham, Mahan Khalsa, Stephen Heiman, and Charles O'Reilly. Technology Life Cycle Adoption was developed by Joe Bohlen, George Beal and Everett Rogers and popularized by Geoffrey Moore. Market Type is an extension of the brilliant work of Clayton Christensen. W. Chan Kim and Renee Mauborgne's work on Blue Ocean Strategy was a later influence on this edition of the book. A formal process of dealing with the chaos and uncertainty of a startup (and the company-building strategies) owes a tremendous amount to the theories of John Boyd and the OODA Loop. Frank Robinson independently came up with many of the concepts in the Customer Discovery and Validation long before I wrote about them. Frank coined the term minimum viable product. I liked it better than minimum feature set, which I used in the first book.

My partner and co-author, Bob Dorf, put up with more than any co-author could imagine. His contribution is matched only by his patience. A seasoned entrepreneur himself, Bob's success as a serial entrepreneur and his strengths in sales, marketing, and the Web have added immensely to our new joint work. I met Bob when he walked into my E.piphany office. My startup had five people aboard, and his had about a dozen. I bought his sales pitch, and he helped me launch E.piphany's customer development and promotion efforts. In 2010 he practically moved into my ranch and became my partner for the second time, helping to make *The Startup Owner's Manual* a work we're both proud of. The "get/keep/grow" sections and "metrics that matter" were his painful labor of love. Terri Vanech, our researcher/copyeditor, had to deal with both of our unreasonable demands.

Thanks to our intrepid reviewers: Entrepreneurs Jake Levine at News.me; Ross Gotler; Peter Leeds at Gabardine.com; Steve Weinstein of MovieLabs; Preston Bealle and Prescott Logan at GE's Energy Storage Technologies; venture capitalists Jon Feiber of MDV, Ann Miura-Ko at Floodgate, John Burke from True Ventures, Mike Barlow of Cumulus Partners, Takashi Tstusumi from Mitsui Sumitomo Ventures and Errol Arkilic at the National Science Foundation. Their comments made the book substantively better by imbuing it with their hundreds of years of collective wisdom.

Finally, my wife Alison Elliott who not only put up with my obsession with finding a methodology for early-stage startups and my passion for teaching entrepreneurship, but also supported me with her wise counsel and insight (along with numerous edits) which added clarity to my thinking. This book would not have happened without her.

About the Authors

Steve Blank

A RETIRED EIGHT-TIME SERIAL ENTREPRENEUR, Steve's insight that startups are not small versions of large companies is reshaping the way startups are built and how entrepreneurship is taught. His observation that large companies execute business models, but startups search for them, led him to realize that startups need their own tools, different than those used to manage existing companies.

Steve's first tool for startups, the Customer Development methodology, spawned the Lean Startup movement. The fundamentals of Customer Development are detailed in Blank's first book, *The Four Steps to the Epiphany* (2003), which together with his blog, www.steveblank.com, is considered required reading among entrepreneurs, investors and established companies throughout the world.

Blank teaches Customer Development and entrepreneurship at Stanford University, U.C. Berkeley Haas Business School and Columbia University, and his Customer Development process is taught at universities throughout the world. In 2011, he developed the Lean LaunchPad, a hands-on class that integrates Business Model design and Customer Development into practice through fast-paced, real-world customer interaction and business model iteration. In 2011, the National Science Foundation adopted Blank's class for its Innovation Corps (I-Corps), which trains teams of the nation's top scientists and engineers to take their ideas out of the university lab and into the commercial marketplace.

Steve is a prolific writer and speaker who enjoys teaching young entrepreneurs. In 2009, he earned the Stanford University Undergraduate Teaching Award in

Management Science and Engineering. In 2010, he earned the Earl F. Cheit Outstanding Teaching Award at U.C. Berkeley Haas School of Business. The *San Jose Mercury News* listed him as one of the 10 Influencers in Silicon Valley. Despite these accolades and many others, Steve says he might well have been voted "least likely to succeed" in his New York City high school class.

Eight Startups in 21 years

After repairing fighter plane electronics in Thailand during the Vietnam War, Steve arrived in Silicon Valley in 1978, and joined his first of eight startups. These included two semiconductor companies, Zilog and MIPS Computers; Convergent Technologies; a consulting stint for Pixar; a supercomputer firm, Ardent; peripheral supplier, SuperMac; a military intelligence systems supplier, ESL; Rocket Science Games. Steve co-founded startup number eight, E.piphany, in his living room in 1996. In sum: two significant implosions, one massive "dot-com bubble" home run, several "base hits," and immense learning that resulted in *The Four Steps to the Epiphany*.

An avid reader in history, technology, and entrepreneurship, Steve has followed his curiosity about why entrepreneurship blossomed in Silicon Valley while stillborn elsewhere. It has made him an unofficial expert and frequent speaker on "The Secret History of Silicon Valley."

In his spare time, Blank is a Commissioner of the California Coastal Commission, the public body which regulates land use and public access on the California coast. Steve served on the boards of Audubon California, the Peninsula Open Space Land Trust (POST), and was a trustee of U.C. Santa Cruz and a Director of the California League of Conservation Voters (CLCV). Steve's proudest startups are daughters Katie and Sarah, co-developed with wife Alison Elliott.

Bob Dorf

BOB DORF FOUNDED HIS FIRST SUCCESS AT AGE 22 and, since then, six more—"two homeruns, two base hits, and three great tax losses in all," as he puts it. He's advised and/or invested in at least a score more startups since. Dorf is often called the "midwife of Customer Development," having been among the first to help Steve Blank deploy it when Steve's eighth startup, E.piphany, opened its doors with five employees in 1996. Bob's sixth startup, Marketing 1to1, helped E.piphany engage its very first customers. He later critiqued the early versions of Steve's *Four Steps to the Epiphany* mercilessly along the way, and they've been friends and colleagues ever since.

When Bob and Steve aren't writing, Bob runs the K&S Ranch consultancy. Bob's deep experience consulting to *Fortune 500* companies and in online marketing balance Steve's VC and software-centric experience. Bob teaches a full-semester course at Columbia Business School, "Introduction to Venturing," on Customer Development and getting startups right.

Entrepreneurial from the age of 12, Bob received his last W-2 almost 40 years ago, when he quit his editor's job at New York's WINS Radio to launch his first startup. Dorf+Stanton Communications, founded in his living room, grew from a staff of two—Bob and a St. Bernard—to 150+, when Bob sold it in 1989. He's counseled dozens of nonprofits probono on "donor development," as well.

Bob co-founded Marketing 1to1 (later Peppers & Rogers Group), an early CRM strategy firm, and drove its growth to 400+ people worldwide. As founding CEO, Dorf spearheaded major strategic customer programs at a veritable "who's who" of companies including 3M, Bertelsmann, Ford, HP, Jaguar, NCR, Oracle, and Schwab. He's spoken before scores of U.S. and international audiences, and published dozens of articles including an indepth Harvard *Business Review* treatise.

Dorf lives in Stamford, Connecticut, with his wife Fran, a therapist and thrice-published novelist. His proudest startup by far is daughter Rachel, a psychologist who recently co-founded Bob's first grandchild, Maya Rose Gotler.

Index

It's not the beginning of the end,

but it is perhaps the end of the beginning